HOW TO WIN AT CHESS

HOW TO WIN AT CHESS

A Complete Course

I. A. HOROWITZ

Editor and Founder of *Chess Review*
Chess Editor of *The New York Times*

With 891 diagrams

DAVID McKAY COMPANY, INC.

New York

Library of Congress Catalog Card Number: 68-22889

MANUFACTURED IN THE UNITED STATES OF AMERICA

For EDNA

CONTENTS

FOREWORD

How to Win at Chess brings together four books previously written by the author under the titles: *How to Win in the Chess Openings, Modern Ideas in the Chess Openings, How to Win in the Middle Game of Chess,* and *How to Win in the Chess Endings.* Each was a complete book in itself, and the four constitute a fairly complete Short Course in Chess Play particularly adapted to the beginner who has learned how to make the moves and how to read chess notation but is groping for signposts in the vast range of chess knowledge and literature.

How to Win in the Chess Openings and *Modern Ideas in the Chess Openings* represent an effort to reduce to understandable level the utter confusion of the voluminous texts on openings which delve into variations, sub-variations, sub-sub-variations and, well, still more of sub-sub-subs! So here, first of all, we discuss the principles and concepts of opening play common to all openings. Then the most popular openings —attacks and defenses—are broken down into their individual moves and grand plans and are so explained as to show how the tactical strength of each move ties up with the strategic idea of the opening concerned. After the general idea of each opening has been explained, the individual moves are analyzed on a move-to-move basis with emphasis on their relation to the plan of the particular opening. To many readers it comes as a revelation that there is a general plan for each opening. Knowing those outlined here is a start to perceiving the plans of other openings and a practical help to playing better chess.

But to have a plan is not enough. You have to see how it works out in practical play. So each opening discussion is followed by a "Chess Movie" (a game so profusely illustrated with diagrams as to reveal clearly the effect of the plan of the opening). The reader can then see how a player benefits by following the plan of the opening, how another comes to grief by disregarding it. In addition, the illustrative games in the last chapter illustrate vital details of theory in the openings studied in these books. In many instances, the games are continuations of the main line of analysis in the preceding chapters, and the reader can by playing over these games arrive at a more precise judgment of the model variations. The general point is that understanding comes not from learning moves by rote, but from learning the ideas behind the moves. After understanding will come victories.

How to Win in the Middle Game of Chess likewise offers the reader an orderly insight into what may have impressed him hitherto as a hopeless welter of confusion and obscurity. Here are the guides to how to press home an opening advantage or lay the foundation for a winning ending. Here are the explanations of the middle-game complexities of thrust and riposte, sacrificial brilliancy, tactical surprise, masterly combination, attack against the King, grand over-all strategy, outlined and delineated from the wealth and complexity of a board full of pieces. No book, indeed, can hope to deal exhaustively with so vast a subject, but this section endeavors to furnish all the necessary information on how to handle practical problems. The most practical problem of all is the fellow who's been pushing you around because he knows a little more than you do. Now it will be his turn to feel the sting of your superior knowledge.

How to Win in the Chess Endings is especially valuable for the chess learner. There are some other books available on endings—notably Reuben Fine's very fine *Basic Chess Endings* —but not a single one caters to any extent to the learner, who must take one step at a time. This section on endgames, while not ambitious in scope, does offer readable signposts and lucid explanations.

All four of the books are, of course, interrelated, and each made its appearance in the above-mentioned sequence—opening, middle game, and ending. This order was warranted by the demand. For nearly every newcomer to chess wishes to be a general—to direct his forces and engage in strategy and tactics even before he has the faintest notion of what it is all about. A brief can be held for studying endings first, followed by the middle game next, and openings last; it is easier to study positions with fewer units. But, paradoxically, there is much to be said for a stagger system of study—a little of each book from time to time. Such a course will fulfill the psychological urge. In any case, each title is an independent and yet interrelated study. One thing is certain, understanding of the opening may lead to a happy ending.

Throughout the volume, moreover, the author has held to the thought that chess lessons should be a delight rather than a chore—or a bore. So he has sought to present chess instruction with due regard for the reader's pleasure in learning, to combine pedagogic with entertainment values and scrupulous accuracy with a light touch.

May this book make every reader a better player. More important, may it add a little to his joy.

I. A. HOROWITZ

HOW TO WIN AT CHESS

A PICTURE GUIDE FOR BEGINNERS

The chessboard

CHESS is a game of mental skill played by two adversaries on a board of 64 squares colored alternately light and dark and conventionally called white and black.

Slant line is a diagonal. Vertical line is a file. Lateral line is a rank.

The lines of squares running vertically up and down (from player to player on the board) are called files. The lines of squares running horizontally to right and left are called ranks. There are eight squares in each file and rank. There are also lines of squares which slant or run diagonally; these are called diagonals. Any one diagonal is composed of squares of the same color which run consecutively in one straight line.

The adversaries are known as "White" (player of the white or lighter-colored chessmen) and "Black." White and Black each use 16 chessmen, 8 pieces and 8 Pawns. The pieces are King, Queen, two Rooks (sometimes called Castles), two Bishops, and two Knights.

Here is how the pieces look in the conventional Staunton pattern.

Here is how the pieces look on the board before the start of a game. By convention, the board is so placed that each player has a light-colored square at his right-hand corner. And, by convention, White always moves first.

The pieces are placed on the two ranks at the opposite

Pieces before start of play

sides of the board, directly in front of the players. The four
Rooks occupy the four corner squares of the board. Next to
the Rooks are the Knights. Next to the Knights are the
Bishops. Between the Bishops are the Queen and the King,
with the Queen standing on a square of its own color. Thus,
each piece is directly opposite its opposing equivalent piece.

The Pawns stand on the squares of their respective second
ranks, White's 8 Pawns directly in front of his pieces and
Black's 8 before his pieces.

The King moves.

4

The object of the game is to "checkmate" the opponent's King. Mate (a shorter term commonly used) is achieved by so attacking the King that it cannot escape being captured.

Before one can think of mating, however, he must know how the pieces move and capture.

The King moves only one square at a time, but in any direction: that is, to any adjacent square along file, rank, or diagonal, forward, backward, sideways or slant-wise, at the player's option. But, like all the chessmen, the King cannot move onto a square occupied by a man of its own side. Uniquely, the King cannot legally move into the line of fire of any man of the opposing side. (The line of fire is a square

The White King can capture the Black Pawn by removing it from the board and occupying the square now taken by the Pawn. The White King cannot move directly or obliquely forward to the right or left, as it would step into the line of fire of the Black King. Nor can the White King step directly backward. Then it would be moving into the line of fire of the Black Pawn. But it can move obliquely backward to the right or left and sideways to the empty square.

Black is checkmated. His King is attacked and he has no way of getting out of attack.

or squares attacked by a chessman.) Thus, the King cannot move to a square adjacent to another King.

When a player attacks the enemy King, it is customary to say "check" in sociable games, though not necessary now under official tournament rules. In any such event, the King must get out of check on its player's next turn. There are three ways to do so: 1. capture the attacking man; 2. interpose a friendly man on the line of fire of the attacker; and 3. move the King out of that line of fire. If none of these resources works, the attacked King is *checkmated,* and the game is over.

Black is to move, and though he is behind a raft of material—a Bishop and Pawn—he has no legal turn. Hence he is stalemated, that is, the Black King is not attacked, but Black has no move. The game is drawn.

The Rook moves.

If the King of the player about to move (such player is known as the Player; the one not on the move as the Opponent) is not in check, that is, not subject to capture, and the said Player has no legal move available either by his King or other men, the position is termed a "Stalemate," and the game is a draw. In short, no King can walk into check and commit suicide.

The Rook moves along files and ranks, that is, vertically or horizontally, forward, backward, and sideways—but not diagonally. The Rook can move along its set line any number of squares which are unoccupied, in any one direction at a time.

The Rook, Bishop, and Queen, all of which move along lines of squares, cannot jump over men, friendly or enemy. They must stop when they come to the square in front of a "friend." As for an "enemy," see capturing below.

The Bishop moves.

The Bishop moves along diagonals, that is, slant-wise, in any one direction at a time, and so far as the squares are unoccupied (see capturing).

In this position, the Rook can capture the Bishop.

The Rook takes the Black Bishop. The Black Bishop is removed, and the Rook goes to the square where the Black Bishop was standing.

The Queen moves.

The Queen—most powerful of all pieces—combines the powers of both Rook and Bishop. It can move along a file, a rank or a diagonal, in any one direction at a time, so far as the squares in that line are unoccupied.

The Knight moves in the shape of an L or an inverted L, one square forward or backward and two squares to the left or right; or two squares forward or backward and one square

The Knight moves.

to the left or right. The Knight's move is actually a leap, to the nearest non-adjacent square of opposite color. Thus, it always moves from white to black, or vice versa. And also the Knight alone can leap over men, friendly or enemy. It cannot be obstructed on its line of movement by intervening men

The White Knight in this diagram can capture the Black Rook even though there are Black pieces intervening. The Knight can also move to the squares marked by a dot.

Here, it can capture the Black Knight though White pieces are intervening. It can also move to the squares marked by a dot.

and is the only piece which can move before Pawns at the start of a game.

The Pawn moves.

A Pawn moves in one direction only—forward along a file. It cannot move backward or to right or left along the ranks. It can move only one square at a time, except on its first move. On its first move, a Pawn can advance either one or two squares. (See capturing and queening, below.)

Capturing

All chessmen, except Pawns, capture much the same way as they move. Thus, Queen, Rook, and Bishop can capture an enemy man which stands at the end of their normal line of fire. The Player captures by removing the enemy man from the board and places his Queen (or Rook or Bishop) on the square formerly occupied by that man. Likewise, the Player captures with a Knight by removing an enemy man from a square onto which the Knight can leap and then placing his Knight there. And, similarly, the Player can remove an enemy man on any square adjacent to his King and place his King there, provided the King will not then be in check.

In this diagram, the White Pawn can capture the Black Knight. It cannot capture the Black Pawn or the White Bishop.

The Pawn alone captures differently than it moves. It can take an enemy man diagonally in front of it. The Player removes the enemy man from the board and places his Pawn there. Thus, in effect, the Pawn captures diagonally forward to the right or to the left. It does not capture directly forward.

En Passant

There is also a way of effecting a Pawn capture known as *en passant* or "in passing" (abbreviated e.p.). It concerns only

The White Pawn has just moved up two squares. It does not evade capture by having moved up two squares. The White Pawn may be taken in exactly the same way as if it had moved only one square. This is called *en passant*.

The *en passant* capture is effected. The White Pawn is removed. The Black Pawn does not take its place. It moves one square on the diagonal—as if the White Pawn had moved only one square and been captured.

Pawn against Pawn and occurs after an enemy Pawn makes its initial two-square move, by-passing on an adjacent file a Player's Pawn which had previously reached the fifth rank. Had the enemy Pawn moved only one square, it would have been subject to capture by the Player's Pawn, and the two-square move does not obviate the "subject to capture" condition. The Player can now capture the enemy Pawn just as if it had moved only one square. But he must exercise his *"en passant"* privilege on his present turn to play, or not at all. *En passant* capture cannot be postponed.

Queening

When a Pawn reaches its eighth rank, that is, the adversary's first rank, it must be promoted to a piece of its own color: a Queen, Rook, Bishop, or Knight (never to a second King). Usually, the promotion is to Queen—the strongest piece. For special reasons (such as to give mate or a forceful check), a different piece may be chosen. A player is allowed to have as many Queens (or other pieces) as he can promote, in addition to the original ones.

White's Pawn is now on his seventh rank. When it reaches the eighth rank, as in the next diagram, White must promote his Pawn to a piece of its own color.

The Pawn has reached the eighth rank and has been converted into a Queen. Generally, it is to the player's advantage to promote to a Queen—the most powerful piece on the board. Occasionally, for some special reason, a player prefers to underpromote to a Knight, Bishop, or Rook.

Castling

Kingside castling.

Once in a game, if at all, a player may safeguard his King and bring a Rook into action by "castling." This is a unique combined movement of King and Rook in which the King is moved two squares toward the Rook and the Rook is placed on the square jumped over by the King. The action must be simultaneous or, if need be, the King must be moved first. There are five restrictions to castling: 1. neither the King nor the Rook to be employed can have been moved previously; 2. the squares between King and Rook must be unoccupied by either

Castling Queenside.

friendly or enemy men; 3. the King must not be in check; 4. the King must not move into check; and 5. the King must not move over a square attacked by an enemy man. The Rook can, however, join in castling even if attacked or if it passes over a square under attack.

Comparative Values of the Chessmen

See page 17—How to Win in the Chess Openings

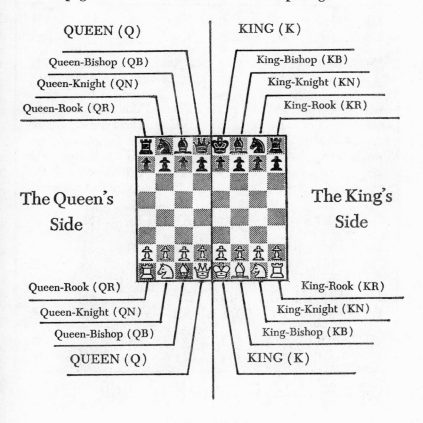

QUEEN (Q) KING (K)

Queen-Bishop (QB) King-Bishop (KB)

Queen-Knight (QN) King-Knight (KN)

Queen-Rook (QR) King-Rook (KR)

The Queen's
Side

The King's
Side

Queen-Rook (QR) King-Rook (KR)

Queen-Knight (QN) King-Knight (KN)

Queen-Bishop (QB) King-Bishop (KB)

QUEEN (Q) KING (K)

Naming the Files

For recording and reading notation

Drawn Games

A game ending without a decision, that is, with neither side winning, is drawn. Games may be drawn by stalemate (as described previously), by mutual agreement or by both sides being reduced to insufficient force to effect a mate.

BLACK

R8	N8	B8	Q8	K8	B8	N8	R8
R7	N7	B7	Q7	K7	B7	N7	R7
R6	N6	B6	Q6	K6	B6	N6	R6
R5	N5	B5	Q5	K5	B5	N5	R5
R4	N4	B4	Q4	K4	B4	N4	R4
R3	N3	B3	Q3	K3	B3	N3	R3
R2	N2	B2	Q2	K2	B2	N2	R2
R1	N1	B1	Q1	K1	B1	N1	R1

WHITE

Naming the Squares

For recording and reading notation; naming the squares.

Also, if the same position occurs three times in a game—not necessarily on successive turns—with the same player on the move, the player about to reply can claim the draw by repetition. Or the player about to make a move leading to such repetition can claim the draw before making that move. Once another move has been made, the right to claim a draw is abrogated until another repetition occurs or is about to occur.

Moreover, at any time that a player can prove that at least 50 moves have been made without a Pawn having been moved or a man captured, that player can claim a draw.

Reading and Recording a Chess Game

To read and record a chess game, a descriptive notation—a sort of chess shorthand—has been invented. Coded symbols appearing on the diagrams above in conjunction with the symbols below give the basis of that notation.

Symbols for the men and their movements:

K — King	O-O — castles King-side
Q — Queen	O-O-O — castles Queen-side
R — Rook	e.p. — captures en passant
B — Bishop	— — goes to (R-K1 means Rook
P — Pawn	goes to K1)
N — Knight *	x — captures (BxN means
ch — check	Bishop takes Knight)
dis ch — discovered check	(Q) — (Pawn) becomes Queen
dbl ch — double check	/KB4 — (man) on KB4

Here is an example of recording the shortest possible game of chess, known as the Fool's Mate.

	White	Black
1	P-KN4	P-K4
2	P-KB4	Q-R5 checkmate.

* Kt was traditional for Knight; N is phonetic and easier to read.

WHITE

Fools mate.

On White's first move, he advances the Pawn in front of his King Knight to the fourth rank, known as White's KN4 (see diagram). Thus, Pawn goes to King Knight four. Black replies on his first move P-K4, or Pawn goes to King four. Black moves the Pawn in front of his King, known as the King Pawn, to the fourth rank.

For his second move, White plays 2 P-KB4. This means that White moves his King Bishop Pawn—the Pawn in front of his King Bishop—to the fourth rank. And Black replies for his second move Queen goes to Rook five, checkmate.

Observe, incidentally, that White's King is attacked by Black's Queen. And, since there is no way to get out of the attack, White is checkmated.

How to Win in the **CHESS OPENINGS**

How to Win

IN THE

CHESS OPENINGS

BY

I. A. Horowitz

DAVID McKAY CO., INC.

NEW YORK

Contents

CONTENTS

How to Win in the **CHESS OPENINGS**

1

The original position from which the opening springs is the most difficult of the entire game. For here thirty-two potent units are animated and unleash a vast power.

Principles of Opening Play

THE game of chess is divided into three parts—the opening, the middle game and the endgame. The divisions are purely arbitrary, merely for the purpose of facilitating study. No dividing line separates the parts; the transition from the opening to the middle game and from the middle game to the endgame is indicated by the action and the number of men remaining on the board.

The opening covers approximately the first twelve moves of the game, with all or most of the pieces on the board. The middle game is characterized generally by the presence of

Queens; the endgame is greatly simplified, with few of the forces remaining.

The opening is a development of forces. It begins with the first move and ends with the mobilization of nearly all of the men. The Rooks, as a rule, are the last to enter the skirmish, and often do not participate in the play until well into the middle game.

TYPICAL OPENING POSITIONS

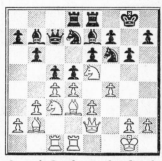 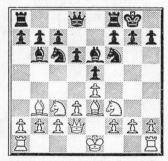

Queen's Gambit Declined with Rooks developed.

Giuoco Piano—White's Rooks not yet moved.

Ultimate Goal vs. Opening Goal

In order to understand the mechanics of the opening, it is necessary to know the opening goal. While checkmate is the principal goal of the game, it is subordinated in the opening, since the pieces are just beginning to get out. Of course, if the opponent plays very badly, or exposes his King critically or neglects his development glaringly, then checkmating ideas come to the forefront. With reasonably correct play by both contestants, lesser objectives are the goal. These all tie in with the prime purpose—checkmate of the opponent's King. Checkmate is the ultimate goal.

Try for Small Advantages

Opening play can contribute towards the checkmating goal in a minor way. Essentially, it can do so by laying a sound foundation for the middle and endgame; by gaining small po-

EXAMPLES OF RATIONAL AND IRRATIONAL DEVELOPMENT

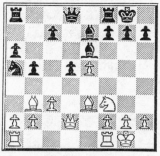

Ruy Lopez—Rational development on both sides. Checkmate is a consideration far in the future.

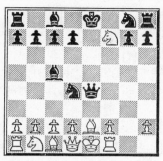

Ruy Lopez—. . . N-B6 mate. Violations of opening principles have brought a sudden end.

sitional and material advantages. Many small advantages add up to a large plus.

What is a sound foundation and what are the small advantages? The answers to these questions shed light on the function of opening moves.

A sound foundation is one which is free of structural weaknesses, weaknesses which require attention or which undermine anything built upon them. As the foundation pertains only to Pawns, the subject is better treated in a discussion of the endgame. Insofar as the foundation affects the opening, however, a limited discussion will appear later on.

More to the point is the question of small advantages. What are they?

There are two types of advantage in chess. One is positional; the other material.

Positional advantage is the plus which derives from the ability to control squares, vital for immediate or future action, as well as from the sounder Pawn structure. Superior mobility and command of greater terrain augment the advantage.

Control of the Center

While the opening is concerned with every conceivable advantage, emphasis is generally placed on the control of impor-

EXAMPLES OF POSITIONAL ADVANTAGE

Black's men are hemmed in behind his own lines. White enjoys operating space.

Black is a piece to the good. He lacks the time, however, to stave off mate.

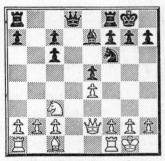

Black suffers from chronic structural weaknesses. His Queen-side Pawns are not self-supporting.

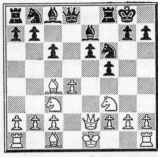

Black's backward King Pawn is a vulnerable target. Soon White will attack it again and again.

tant squares. In the absence of outright blunders ceding material, the initial goal is the gain of squares.

There are 64 squares on the chessboard. Half are white and half are black. Except for color distinction, to all appearances they are very much alike. Yet some squares are more valuable than others. Which are the more important squares and why?

As indicated on the diagram, the squares in the center of the board are the more important ones. The reason they are more important becomes apparent when the squares are considered in terms of a network of interlinked paths. It is clear that the player who controls the hub of the network can send his men from one side of the board, directly through the hub, to the other side of the board with ease. Whereas the player who does not control the hub must send his men from one side of the board to the other via devious routes, time-consuming

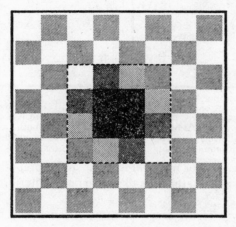

The most important squares are the very centermost (in black). Other squares taper off in importance as indicated on diagram above.

routes. As time is an important factor in chess—that is, as it is important to reach a goal in the least number of moves—it follows that it is important to control the central squares.

Control of the central squares is the primary positional advantage sought for in the opening. It enhances the player's mobility and operating space to the detriment of the opponent. Exploitation of structural weaknesses pertaining to Pawns is a subsidiary objective of the opening. These will be covered later on.

Gain of Material

The gain of squares is a gain of ground over which the chessmen may move. Even more important, however, is the

EXAMPLES OF CENTER CONTROL

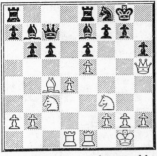

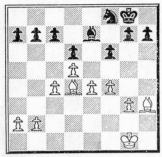

In this position, White is able to utilize his control of the center to institute an overwhelming attack. White plays R-K4, followed by R-N4—typical mid-game advantage.

Here the advantage of the center has been carried to the endgame. White can advance on either or both wings or in the center, while Black must bide his time.

gain of material. For material is force, and a preponderance of force, by its very nature, brooks little or no interference or resistance.

The power of the force of a lowly Pawn may be gleaned from the fact that, in a game between two chessmasters, the advantage of a Pawn is sufficient to win. Hence it is imperative at all times, in the absence of other consideration, to maintain an even or favorable balance of force. The sacrifice of material,

EXAMPLES OF PAWN MINUS

White has sacrificed a Pawn for position. Should his attack fail, White will lose.

This could be the windup of the previous position! The extra Pawn queens.

consequently, should be viewed with suspicion. "Always sacrifice your opponent's pieces" is a sound guiding principle.

In this connection, the table of the relative value of the chessmen is useful. Evaluating a Pawn as a unit of one, the Knight is the equivalent of three units, the Bishop three and a small fraction units, the Rook five and the Queen nine.

♞   ♟ ♟ ♟

♝   ♟ ♟ ♟   +

♜   ♟ ♟ ♟ ♟ ♟

♛   ♟ ♟ ♟ ♟ ♟ ♟ ♟ ♟

As it is not always possible or beneficial to exchange Pawn for Pawn or Knight for Knight, etc., it is well to calculate in an exchange the value of the units given for the units received. Two Rooks, for example, having a total value of ten units, may be considered better than a Queen, whose unit total is nine. A Rook, Bishop and Knight add up to eleven units plus and are clearly more valuable than a Queen.

In the absence of serious blunders, it is almost impossible to gain much material in the opening. Often, however, small profit may be gained by judicious exchanges, such as a Knight for the opponent's Bishop or a Rook for the opponent's Bishop and Knight. These small differences add up and their cumulative effect is a decisive factor in the outcome of the game.

The gain of material, no matter how little, is also the goal of the opening.

Changing Values

In any demonstration, the forces which join the fray may be momentarily more valuable than dormant forces of equal stature. This is particularly true when the King is the target. Thus an active Pawn or Knight, delivering checkmate to the opposing King, or compelling the surrender of material, cannot be given the wooden classification of one or three units. The worth of material at all times is related to the position. All things being equal, the preceding table of values applies.

EXAMPLES OF CHANGING VALUES

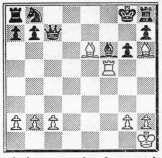

Black is a raft of material ahead. He cannot, however, prevent mate, after *1 . . . Q-B2; 2 RxB.*

Black is lost as he cannot save his Bishop Pawn or stop the advance of the White Bishop Pawn.

How to Try for Small Advantages

It is one thing to know the goal; it is another to reach it. The wide gap is bridged by the correct management of the forces.

Correct management requires the application of sound principles. As these, however, are founded on experience and logic, they are not difficult to master.

Technically, the principles fall into two classes—strategy and tactics. Strategy is the plan for obtaining advantages; tactics is the science of executing the plan by disposing of the forces.

As the major goal of the opening is to gain control of the central squares, that is the first strategic plan. As force is the only means of attempting to reach the goal, the principle evolves: *Bring out the forces so that a maximum of power is brought to bear on the central squares in the shortest time.*

Plan Your Development

To execute the plan properly, it is necessary to know in what order the forces should be brought out. Which should come first and which should follow? These are tactical considerations.

EXAMPLES OF PLANNED AND UNPLANNED DEVELOPMENT

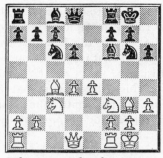
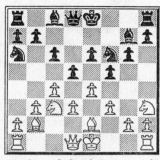

White controls the center; King Pawn and Queen Pawn, Knights and Bishops bear down on the vital squares.

Haphazard development with Knights on the wing. Position is far from ideal for either White or Black.

The advance of the King Pawn or Queen Pawn to the fourth rank generally initiates the opening. This is so because the advanced Pawn attacks the central squares and, at the same time, frees the Queen and a Bishop for future action.

Knights First

After the Pawn moves, the minor pieces—Bishops and Knights—follow. Knights should generally be developed before Bishops, and there are sound reasons for this.

At the beginning of the game, the Knight has a range of two squares—R3 and B3. As the King Pawn or Queen Pawn is advanced, the range increases by one square, including either K2 or Q2. Thus, in the first few moves, the Knight enjoys a choice of practically three squares. As the square R3 is almost out of the question—a Knight on R3 does not bear down on the center and controls only half as many squares as at B3—the choice is really of but two squares. Consequently, with only two moves from which to choose, it is easy to determine which of the squares the Knight ought to occupy. The Bishop, on the other hand, has a long range. After the King Pawn has moved, the Bishop could conceivably go to K2, Q3, B4, N5 or R6. R6, of course, is not a good choice, but it is within the realm of possibility. This adds up to four good squares. When it is possible to go to four squares, it is difficult to determine the correct one. When it is possible to go to two squares, it is comparatively easy to determine the correct one. Thus there is practically no guesswork in developing the Knight, while the Bishop moves are subject to doubt. That is one reason why the Knight usually precedes the Bishop.

Another important reason for this sequence is that the Knights on B3 are aggressively posted. They control the central squares, attack hostile Pawns in the center or prevent their advance to the fourth rank.

Then Bishops

All in all, it is clear that the development of the Bishop is best deferred until some such time as its most effective post is determined. When, however, the best square for the Bishop is already known, the Bishop may precede the Knight. In the absence of specific convictions, the Knight comes first.

Major Pieces Later

With the development of the minor pieces—Bishops and Knights—the first strategic plan is nearly complete. As it is necessary, however, to bring as much pressure as possible to bear on the central squares, the major pieces—Rooks and

EXAMPLES OF BISHOP AND KNIGHT DEVELOPMENT

What is the best square for White's King Bishop?

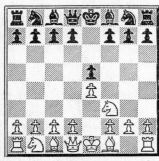

The Knight at KB3 attacks the center and a Pawn.

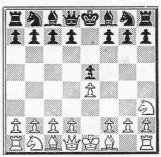

At K2, the Knight is less aggressive. Moreover, it blocks the King Bishop. Black can seize the initiative with . . . N-KB3, as he attacks a Pawn, controls the center.

A Knight at R3 commands half as many squares as a Knight at B3. Moreover, it does not attack the center. Again . . . N-KB3 gives Black the initiative.

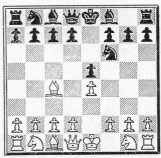

This is the Bishop's Opening. The attack on White's King Pawn gives Black a momentary initiative.

This is the Ruy Lopez. The early Bishop move attacks Black's support of the King Pawn in the center.

Queen—should also assist in the action. That is why, among other reasons, they should be developed.

As Rooks assert themselves best on open files, they should be placed on such files or on files which may reasonably be expected to open during the early course of the game. The King file or the Queen file or both are often most suitable. For these files have been half opened due to the advance of the King Pawn or Queen Pawn. On these files, moreover, the Rooks join the center action. Occasionally, the Bishop files serve as

EXAMPLES OF ROOK DEVELOPMENT

Here White's King Rook pins Black's Knight on the open King file in the early play. Black is already in trouble.

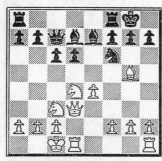

White's best move is to play his King Rook to K1, on a file which may reasonably be expected to open.

White's advanced King Bishop Pawn helps to open the King Bishop file for use by the King Rook.

By placing his Rook on the Queen Bishop file, White exerts pressure on Black's Queen Bishop Pawn.

excellent posts for the Rooks. For, in some openings, the Bishop Pawns advance and give free range to the Rooks.

The Rooks as a rule, get into play slowly and the Queen Rook is about the last to join the action. This sequence is justified by the necessity of contesting control of the center. Pawns and the minor pieces play a major role in this plan.

Function of Castling

In order to be able to bring the Rooks to the King file and also to enable the Rooks to cooperate, the King must get out of the way. As long as the King remains on King square, he not only pre-empts the square K1, but also prevents the Rooks from cooperating. Castling on either wing is the answer. Incidentally, also, castling *should* safeguard the King.

Develop the Queen with Care

The Queen generally assumes a positive role late in the opening. An early Queen sortie is apt to recoil: the Queen will serve as a target, be attacked and be compelled to retreat. The time expended in advancing and retreating will be used by the adversary to bolster his development. Moreover, since the Queen enjoys a wide variety of possibilities, it is difficult to determine its most suitable role. For the same reason that the development of the Bishop is deferred until its best post is known, the Queen should not join the fray until the position has crystallized. Then it is less of a "hit or miss" development.

Plan Soundly from the Start

From the first strategic plan, various propositions develop. It is obvious, for instance, that if a maximum power is to be brought to bear on the central squares in the shortest time, a haphazard development which fails to exert pressure on the center is a violation of principle. It is also clear that a unit

EXAMPLES OF LOSS OF TIME IN THE OPENING

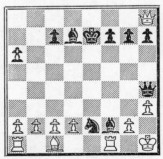
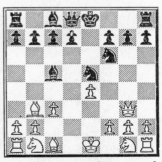

White's Queen has wandered over the board, picking up stray material. Black, however, mates in three, beginning with 1 . . . QxPch.

White's Queen has moved three times, while Black has brought out his pieces. Black now wins White's Queen with 1 . . . BxPch!

Black has moved his King Knight three times. Now Black must lose a piece, thus: *1* P-Q5, NxKP; *2* P-B5 and the Knight is trapped.

Black has lost time by Pawn-grabbing with *1* . . . BxQBP. He loses a piece after *2* Q-K2! for White threatens both *3* N-Q6 mate and *3* QxB.

should not be moved more than once in the opening, unless there is good reason for doing so. Two or more moves by the same unit, as a rule, are the equivalent of wasting opportunities to bring out more force. In fact, only special reasons will ever justify any deviation from the main plan—control of the center with a preponderance of quickly developed force.

When possible, the ideal placement for all units should be visualized before any one is moved. When that is not possible, then the choice and location of the unit to be moved should be judged on principle—in relation to the first strategic plan.

2

Exceptions to the First Principle

As was explained in the previous chapter, the first strategic principle points up the necessity for bringing maximum power to bear on the central squares in the shortest time. Likewise, it points out the fallacy of deviating from principle. Yet, while to toe the line with rigid obedience may be good discipline, it is wooden, unimaginative chess.

To Do or Not to Do?

Occasionally, during the opening stages of a game, an opportunity presents itself to pick off an opponent's Pawn or to go after his King. These pursuits are in violation of principle. For it is hardly possible to go Pawn-grabbing or checkmating and, at the same time, give the required attention to proper

EXAMPLES OF UNJUSTIFIED RISKS

Bringing his Queen out early, Black has violated one principle. Now he goes Pawn-grabbing and loses his Queen: *1 . . . QxP; 2 Q-N5ch, P-B3; 3 BxPch, KxB; 4 QxQ.*

White hopes that Black will miss the threat of mate. But Black now plays *1 . . . Q-K2* and soon follows with *. . . N-KB3* and gains time by attacking the White Queen.

EXAMPLES OF JUSTIFIED RISKS

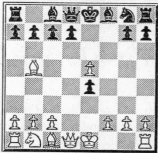

White has mismanaged his forces. That is why Black can afford to grab a Pawn: *1 . . . P-B3; 2 B-QB4, Q-R4ch; 3 N-B3, QxKP,* yet expect to escape with a whole skin.

White's Queen has moved early and moves again: *1 QxPch, KxQ; 2 B-R6ch, K-N1; 3 R-N6ch, RPxR; 4 N-B6 mate.* Black's early Queen moves justify White's.

development. Still a Pawn is a Pawn, and the King is the King. These are important considerations. Surely, if the target is the opposing monarch and if it can be ascertained with a reasonable degree of certainty that he will topple from his throne, then definitely it is correct to violate principle. Checkmate leaves no weaknesses in its wake. If, however, the target is a Pawn and even if its successful capture is assured, the consequences of the action should be further appraised in the light of its effect on the entire position. In the quest for immediate material gain, the strategic plan is bound to suffer. To appraise the gain of material against loss of position requires inordinate skill.

In the opening, Pawn-grabbing expeditions or premature mating attacks are apt to boomerang. Temptation in these directions should be resisted. One thing is certain, if the opponent has not violated any principles, any rash action is foredoomed. If he has violated principles, a calculated risk is justifiable.

OTHER PRINCIPLES

Besides the first strategic principle, there are other principles of chess common to all openings. Their application paves the way to opening goals.

Principle of Mobility

A piece which cannot move is a useless piece.

The potential force of a Queen is nine times as great as that of a Pawn. Its actual force depends on other considerations. Its ability to participate in the fray is the main one. If a Queen is bottled up and an opposing Pawn threatens mate which cannot be stopped, the Pawn—in this instance—is of greater actual value than the Queen. Similarly, the value of all the chessmen is modified by their ability to participate in the fray.

Force, of itself, is potential. Enclosed in a Queen or Bishop or Rook or Knight or Pawn, it is enclosed in just another piece of wood. To unleash its powers, avenues of action are essential. These avenues are technically called mobility.

To gain maximum utility of the chessmen, diagonals should be open for Bishops; files and ranks for the Rooks; files, ranks and diagonals for the Queen; and a choice of posts should exist for the Knights; Pawns should not be hindered in their forward

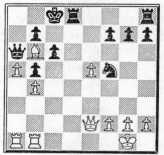

In this position, Black's Queen is practically worthless. Almost any White assault is apt to succeed.

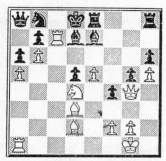

Because of the awkward position of the Black men, White mates in two moves: QxBch, NxQ; 2 N-K6 mate.

movement. Files, ranks, diagonals and open squares are the avenues of action for the chessmen.

Principle of Diversion

Forces decoyed are forces destroyed.

Often during the course of a game, a situation arises where a player threatens to gain a preponderance of force in a vital sector. To meet force equally with force in the selfsame sector is the most effective countermeasure. But this is not always possible. When it is not possible, some other means must be found to parry the threat.

The establishment of threats in another sector may be the answer. These counter threats may be of sufficient real or psychological importance to divert the enemy forces from their contemplated action, or they may defer the enemy action long enough to gain time in which to work out a permanent solution against it.

As attacks in chess occur in the center or on the wings, the principle of diversion as applied works as follows: an attack on the wing is met by a counter-attack in the center or on the other wing; an attack in the center is met by a counter-attack on the wing.

Diversion is necessary only when the attack cannot be met

EXAMPLES OF DIVERTING FORCES

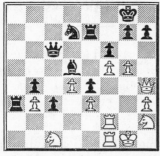
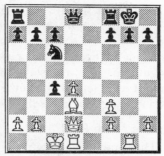

This position from an actual game is an example of diversion. White's King-side attack is gaining momentum and Black counters on the Queenside in hope of drawing off White's forces from his King.

White's center is weak and subject to further attack. So he diverts the play to the King-side: 1 RxP*ch*, KxR; 2 R-N1*ch*, K-B3; 3 Q-N5*ch*, K-K3; 4 R-K1*ch*, K-Q2; 5 Q-B5*ch*, K-Q3; 6 Q-B5*ch*, K-Q2; 7 B-B5 mate.

adequately by direct means, such as an attack in the center by a defense in the center, or a wing attack by a wing defense.

Principle of Give and Take

Better location is compensation.

Every move in chess gives up something and takes something in return. The move *1* P-K4, for instance, gives up control of the squares KB3 and Q3 by the King Pawn. In return, however, the move gains control of the squares KB5 and Q5 and

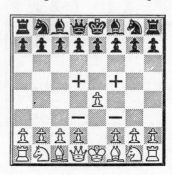

GIVE AND TAKE

The move *1* P-K4 adds a net plus to the position. For control of the central squares Q5 and KB5 is of greater value than loss of the control (by the King Pawn) of the squares Q3 and KB3. Every move in chess carries some minus as well as plus value.

also frees the Bishop and Queen for future action. As control of the central squares is of greater value than loss of control of the other squares, the move *1 P-K4* adds a net plus to the position.

Similarly, every move on the chessboard involves a sacrifice and a gain. It is a mistaken notion to think only in terms of gain. It is essential, however to weigh the gain against the loss in the light of immediate and future prospects.

The Move P-R3?

That practical nonentity of a move, P-R3, is not a principle; it is merely a move. It crops up, however, time and again in most games of chess and is therefore worthy of a note. Generally, it is of doubtful value; for it violates the principle of rapid development. A piece might be brought into action during the time it takes to play P-R3. Moreover, it does not bear down directly on the central squares and often even causes a slight but irreparable weakness in the Pawn structure.

Oddly enough, despite these drawbacks, there is purpose in the puny P-R3. It provides an exit for the King; it prevents an enemy pin or incursion; it is a prop for a Pawn advance; it is a clearance of the square R2 for a retreat or a maneuvering point—and, most wonderful of all, it is sometimes an attacking move.

White may play P-KR3 to prevent the pin . . . B-N5 and to restrict the movement of Black's Queen Bishop.

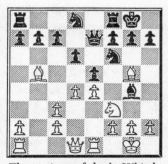

The actions of both White's and Black's King Knights at B3 are paralyzed because of the respective pins.

All of which confounds the issue. Is P-R3 good or bad? Unfortunately, there is no inflexible, ironclad rule, covering all cases. Adroit evasion is the answer. The move P-R3 is good when there is nothing better.

THE FOUNDATION

The Pawn skeleton forms the basic foundation of the chess opening. The original position presents a Pawn line in solid array. Each Pawn enjoys security and mobility.

As the Pawns advance towards the enemy, they are stronger because more threatening but also they are endangered and restricted. They form distinctive patterns around which the pieces rally to give character to the opening.

A — Pawn Weaknesses

IF A weakness develops in the Pawn structure, it may lead to serious difficulties. A weakness requires attention and places an added burden on the balance of the forces. It diverts force from the normal course and consequently lessens pressure in some sector. Weaknesses, therefore, should be avoided.

Which are the weaknesses pertinent to Pawns?

EXAMPLES OF DOUBLED PAWNS

 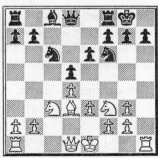

White's doubled Queen Bishop Pawn is unwieldy, hard to protect.

The opened King Rook file compensates for the doubled Pawn.

The Doubled Pawn

The doubled Pawn may be weak. It often suffers from lack of mobility. As a rule, it controls only half as many *vital* squares as two Pawns, lined up side by side. At times, however, the doubled Pawn offers a measure of compensation in the file which its displacement has opened.

The Backward Pawn

The backward Pawn is weak. It is a Pawn which hardly participates in the fray and shirks its normal assignment. Since it is more or less fixed, it becomes an easy, lasting target.

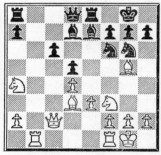
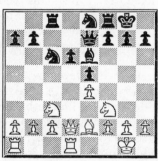

Black's Queen Bishop Pawn is backward.

Black's Queen Pawn is backward.

The Isolated Pawn

The isolated Pawn is weak. It is a Pawn which cannot be guarded by another Pawn. When attacked, it must be guarded by a minor or major piece. Hence it engenders a waste of force.

Over-extended Pawns

The foregoing is pertinent to single Pawns or, in the case of the doubled Pawn, to two Pawns. There are also weaknesses which are inherent in a group of Pawns. They stem mainly from the "one-way traffic" feature of a Pawn.

A Pawn can advance; it cannot retreat. Hence every Pawn move, to a certain extent, engenders two weaknesses. Its ad-

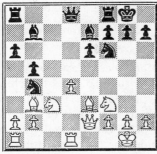

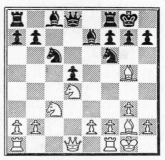

White's isolated Queen Pawn requires constant protection by forces, which otherwise might be used elsewhere.

The target is Black's isolated Queen Pawn. Its defense diverts Black men from more useful action.

vance brings it closer to the enemy, where it can be more readily attacked, and it is removed one step further away from its own men, where the natural protection which they afford is diminished. As the Pawn cannot retreat, any weakness in its wake requires reinforcement by the rest of the forces.

Occasionally, a group of Pawns will advance in an assault. The target is big game, often the opposing King. As long as the assault is successful, it matters little whether the Pawns are strong or weak or whether the Pawns are afforded or afford protection or not. If the assault fails, however, a day of reckoning is at hand. The group of Pawns becomes an over-extended

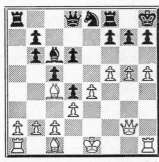

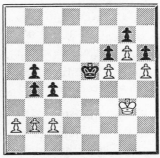

White enjoys a powerful Pawn storming assault. If it succeeds, all is well . . .

. . . If it fails, this may be the result. White's Pawns will be picked off one by one.

Pawn position. It is itself easy prey, and the men which it should shelter are at the mercy of enemy forces.

The Pawn "Hole"

As a result of unskilled Pawn advances, Pawn barriers are breached and Pawn weaknesses accrue. To a lesser extent, a single bad Pawn move affects the position. If a Pawn advances so that an enemy piece can lodge in front of it or in front of some other Pawn and the enemy piece cannot be driven away by a Pawn, then the Pawn position has been punctured. The puncture is technically called a "hole."

A "hole" is a weakness in the Pawn structure. It is a haven for an enemy piece—an outpost for an enemy attack.

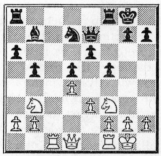

Black has holes at his K4, QB4 and QR4. White should exploit these.

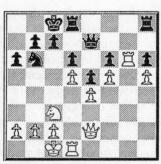

White occupies the hole at his KN6. This is a powerful post for the Rook.

B—Pawn Advantages

PAWNS have many weaknesses and many Pawn structures are faulty. What then may be sought to advantage in building up a Pawn structure?

Pawn Majority

At the beginning of the game, the opposing Pawn structures are perfectly matched. For every White Pawn, there is an equivalent Black Pawn. As the game progresses and exchanges take place, the Pawn position is apt to go out of balance. Pawn majorities may likely be established in different sectors. One side may obtain an extra Pawn in the center, while the other obtains an extra Pawn on the wing. Or one side may obtain an extra Pawn on the wing, while the other side obtains an extra Pawn on the other wing.

The unbalanced Pawn position often injects a new strategic plan into the game. The extra Pawn, whether it is on the wing or in the center, is a constant threat. It is a threat of a potential new Queen, which materializes when the Pawn reaches the eighth rank. While the actual Queening may take place in the endgame, opening play may account for the Pawn majority.

Technically, a Pawn majority exists when the Pawns on one side outnumber the Pawns on the other side. Actually, the majority is impotent if it can be held in check by the Pawn minority.

A mobile Pawn majority is another advantage which may be effected in the opening.

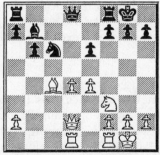

White has a center Pawn majority. Black has a Queen-side Pawn majority. Chances are about even.

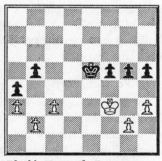

Black's King-side Pawn majority is mobile; White's majority on the other wing is fixed. Black should win.

The "Breaks"

Pawn chains perform various functions. They are the first line of fire. They attack and they defend.

In order to break through to the opposing forces, generally the opposing Pawn chain must be broken. Then pieces can

EXAMPLES OF THE "BREAK"

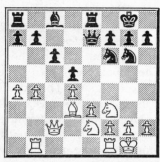

Black enjoys the "break" . . .
P-KB4, whenever he is ready.
In doing so, he may open the
King Bishop file.

White now can "break" with
P-QN5, forcing open the
Bishop file or weakening
Black's Pawn position.

penetrate on the newly opened line—file, rank or diagonal. As
a rule, a vulnerable point is selected for the break, and, after
due preparation, the break is effected. The ability to force
open lines in the opponent's Pawn chain is technically known
as the ability to "break." To enjoy the "breaks" is an advantage.
In building up opening patterns, it is wise to eye the possible
"breaks" in the position.

The Passed Pawn

The most dangerous Pawn on the chessboard is the one
which is not impeded in its advance by an opposing Pawn. It
is known technically as the "passed Pawn," meaning that it
has by-passed all the opposing Pawns. Ergo, it enjoys easy
access to the eighth rank, and, in turn, it will burden an opposing piece with the duty of preventing the Pawn from
Queening.

Often, in the opening melee, it is possible to obtain a passed
Pawn. Such a Pawn adds a definite plus value to the position.

THE INITIATIVE

According to the rules of chess, the first move is arbitrarily
bestowed upon White. This seemingly insignificant fact is

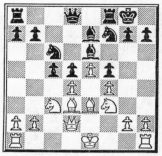

White's King Pawn is passed. It will bear constant watching all through the game.

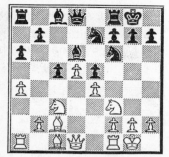

White's Queen Pawn is passed. It has by-passed all of Black's Pawns.

EXAMPLES OF THE INITIATIVE

Despite the symmetrical position, White's first move *1 NxNch* gives him a powerful attack. In a critical position (see next), it can even win.

Here the first move is good enough to win the Queen or give mate: *1* N-K7*ch*, K-R1; *2* BxP*ch*, KxB; *3* Q-N5*ch*, K-K1; *4* Q-B6 mate.

sufficient to give White the initiative. He is first to bring out his men; he is first to control the center. Black, on the other hand, is relegated to the role of defender.

The forces are so evenly balanced that White, with perfect play, can maintain the initiative far into the middle game. White's ambition is to translate the initiative into tangible gain. Black's aim is to reduce White's initiative to a minimum. The conflict is drawn along these lines.

IDEAL OPENING POSITIONS

The ideal position from a practical point of view is more or less of a pipe dream. It can be reached only if the opponent is oblivious of the principles of chess.

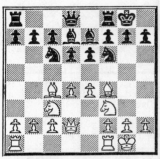

All of White's minor pieces and his King Pawn and Queen Pawn bear on the center. White's Rooks can move to the King and Queen files.

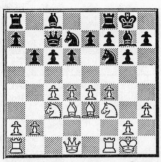

Here White's Pawns dominate the center with the assistance of the minor men. White's Bishops bolster any center action.

White's haphazard development gives Black control of the center, easy development, fine prospects—in short, an ideal formation.

There has been no contest in the center. White's Bishops participate in the center action from the wings, while his Pawns occupy the center.

PRACTICAL OPENING PATTERNS

During the last hundred years, patterns of play have evolved. They are called openings. Their names derive from the place or tournament in which they were first played or from the player who originated them or from the chessmaster who popularized them. The patterns are dissimilar even though their objectives are the same.

A discussion of the fundamental patterns, a knowledge of which is essential to the proper understanding of the game, will follow in succeeding chapters.

3

Giuoco Piano

THE Giuoco Piano is the first recorded opening. It is mentioned in the Göttingen Manuscript (1490) and by all the early authors. It dates from the time when Italy was the ruling power in chess.

Belying its name, which means quiet game, the Giuoco Piano currently is spirited and forceful. It grants White latitude for imagination, leading to exciting combinations, and it is full of pitfalls for the unwary. Its distinguishing feature is the development of White's King Bishop to QB4 on his third move. This characteristic move portends attack.

The opening arises as follows:

1 **P-K4** . . . .

The initial skirmish is to gain command of the central squares. *1* P-K4 is an attempt to control the central square Q5 and also the square KB5. While KB5 is not as valuable as Q5, it is within the domain of the central squares.

A secondary reason for the advance of the King Pawn is to release the King Bishop and the Queen for future action.

1 . . . . **P-K4**

Black's reasons for this move are basically the same as White's. Other moves, leading to other patterns, will be discussed in due time.

2 **N-KB3** . . . .

The primary purpose of this move is to put additional pressure on the central squares, in this case the squares K5 and Q4. Eventually, by concerted pressure, White hopes to reach the goal of gaining command of the central squares. Incidentally, the move attacks Black's King Pawn.

2 . . . . **N-QB3**

While the attack on the King Pawn is incidental to White, it is of prime importance to Black. The loss of even a puny Pawn, as a rule, is of greater value than control of the central squares. That is why Black defends the Pawn. His choice of defense, moreover, is good. For the text move does double duty: it defends the King Pawn and puts pressure on central squares — Black's K4 and Q5.

3 **B-B4** . . . .

Again, White eyes the center. The Bishop bears down on Q5. Also, the move does double duty. The most vulnerable square in Black's camp is KB2. That square is adjacent to the King and is defended only by the King. The newly developed Bishop, therefore, not only bears down on the center, but also on the vulnerable square.

The single attack on Black's weak spot, at this stage of the game, is almost insignificant. It may become potent, however, as the game progresses.

3 . . . .   B-B4

Black follows suit for the same reason.

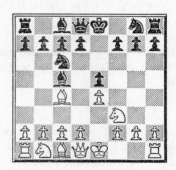

At this juncture, there are many ways of continuing—active and passive. For years, the passive way was in vogue. This consisted of emphasizing development, without any particular goal. White would bring out his Queen Knight to B3, play his Pawn to Q3 and castle; Black would do likewise. The resultant symmetrical position would tend towards a draw. Currently, White's treatment of the opening is different. He attempts to capture the center by force.

4 P-B3   . . . .

An effective way of dominating the center is by doing so with Pawns. The text move is preparatory to the advance of the Queen Pawn.

4 . . . .   N-B3

Black cannot afford to permit the execution of White's plan without adequate countermeasures. His choice is to attack White's King Pawn. This places obstacles in White's path. For the unguarded King Pawn requires attention.

Black's method of meeting White's threat to obtain control

of the center is technically known as the counter-attack. An alternative line is 4 . . . Q-K2. Then, if White continues with 5 P-Q4, Black does not capture, but retreats his Bishop to N3. Black's King Pawn is defended by Knight and Queen, and White cannot compel Black to exchange Pawns. In the event of the exchange, Black has no King Pawn, and White will remain with King and Queen Pawns. The extra center Pawn in White's favor will result in White's domination of the center.

The 4 . . . Q-K2 line of play may well be called the "hold the line" defense. In practice, however, it has been found deficient. For Black runs out of good moves, sooner or later, and must bide his time awaiting the moment when White will strike.

5 **P-Q4** . . . .

According to plan. White disregards the attack on his King Pawn as he is attacking Black's King Pawn with a preponderance of force.

5 . . . . **PxP**

More or less forced. If, for example, 5 . . . B-N3; 6 PxP, KNxP; 7 Q-Q5 and, since White threatens checkmate as well as the Black Knight, he must win a piece. Nor will 5 . . . B-Q3 do as it impedes Black's development. Black's Queen Bishop will be unable to get out for some time.

6 **PxP** . . . .

Again, according to plan. White wishes to dominate the central squares with Pawns. Observe that 6 NxP would be the complete negation of White's plan.

6 . . . . **B-N5**ch

This foreseen, tempo-gaining device is the saving clause. If the Bishop were to retreat to N3 or K2, White could completely rout the Black forces by advancing P-Q5, followed by P-K5.

7 **N-B3** . . . .

The text move has the earmarks of speculation, for it involves material sacrifice. One Pawn goes immediately, another will follow on the subsequent move, and in the main line there is a trap baited with a Rook. Experience, however, proves this to be the best plan at White's command. For he obtains excellent attacking chances.

Instead, White can play safe with 8 B-Q2. Then, after 8 . . . BxB*ch;* 9 QNxB, White's King Pawn is defended. Black, however, will continue with 9 . . . P-Q4, for, after 10 PxP, KNxP, White will remain with an isolated Queen Pawn. True, White commands more of the central squares than Black. But his isolated Pawn is a liability which does not add up to his asset.

7 . . . . NxKP

The capture of the King Pawn engenders a certain amount of risk for both sides! Black leaves himself open to attack, and White suffers from the material loss of the Pawn. Consequently, White will endeavor to capitalize his initiative, and Black will strive for consolidation.

Failure to capture the Pawn, on the other hand, would be an error of judgment. For then White would have achieved his goal—command of the center—at no cost.

Nor would it be wise for Black to cede the center in the hope of battering it down with 7 . . . P-Q4. This move has been tried and found wanting. (*See* CHESS MOVIE, *page 49.*) It is only by incisive play that White refutes 7 . . . P-Q4. This is traceable to the early opening of the King file for White's attack.

8 O-O   . . . .

In order to unpin the Queen Knight, secure the White King from molestation and mobilize the White King Rook for action, possibly on the open King file.

8 . . . . NxN

With a Pawn plus and the attacking chances favoring White, Black's best chance is to cut down the forces to reduce the impact of any brewing attack.

8 . . . BxN has been tried on the same grounds and found distasteful. This move leaves open the spectacular counter stroke 9 P-Q5, known as the Moeller Attack. The resultant position is perilous for both sides. (*See* CHESS MOVIE, *page 52.*)

9 PxN . . . .

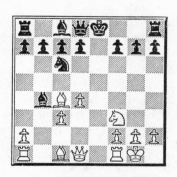

9 . . . . P-Q4!

An important interpolation. The counter-attack on White's Bishop gives Black the opportunity to open new lines for rapid development. Since Black's uncastled King will be in the crossfire of White's ready batteries, Black must utilize every available means to free his forces for defense.

Alternatives are dangerous for Black. For instance, if 9 . . . BxP, White obtains the better game as follows: 10 B-R3!, N-K2; 11 Q-N3, P-Q4; 12 QxB, PxB; 13 KR-K1, B-K3; 14 BxN, KxB; 15 P-Q5, QxP; 16 QR-Q1 with an overwhelming attack. E.g., 16 . . . Q-QB4; 17 R-K5, Q-N3; 18 RxBch!, QxR; 19 R-K1 and wins.

In this line, if—instead of 10 . . . N-K2—Black plays 10 . . . P-Q4, there follows: 11 B-N5, BxR; 12 R-K1ch, B-K3; 13 Q-R4, R-QN1; 14 N-K5, Q-B1; 15 BxNch, PxB; 16 QxPch, K-Q1; 17 NxPch, BxN; 18 B-K7 mate.

It is impossible within the scope of this work to cover the reasons behind the moves in the sub- and sub-sub-variations. Nonetheless, the learner can turn what seems like a fault into a virtue. By experimenting at each stumbling block, the learner will familiarize himself with the possibilities of the position. At the same time, he will obtain a firm grasp of what is involved.

For instance, in the above variation (see position after 9 PxN and play . . . BxP; *10* B-R3), what happens if Black plays *10* . . . BxR, instead of *10* . . . N-K2? After all, a Rook is more valuable than a Bishop. The answer comes rapidly. White will continue with *11* R-K1*ch*, compelling Black to interpose . . . N-K2. White will follow up *12* BxN, QxB; *13* RxQ*ch*, KxR; *14* QxB and should win.

Or, in the same variation, after *10* . . . N-K2; *11* Q-N3, if Black captures *11* . . . BxR, how shall White proceed? The answer here is less obvious. But it is not difficult. White plays *12* BxP*ch*, K-B1; *13* R-K1, P-Q3; *14* N-N5. In doing so, White threatens to retreat his Bishop to KN6 or KR5 and menace mate at B7. Black has no valid defense.

There is still another logical-looking move for Black at his 9th turn. (See position after 9 PxN.) It is 9 . . . B-K2. At first sight, this seems to consolidate Black's position and permits him to retain the extra Pawn — just what Black is seeking. Sharp play on the part of White, however, will make Black's task difficult. E.g., 9 . . . B-K2; *10* P-Q5, N-N1; *11* P-Q6, PxP; *12* BxP*ch*, KxB; *13* Q-Q5*ch*, K-B1; *14* N-N5, Q-K1; *15* R-K1, and White's positional superiority makes Black's material plus of no consequence.

Observe the lack of mobility of the Black forces. The entire Queen-side is hemmed in. Of course, the onus rests upon White to capitalize quickly on his plus, before Black develops. But it can be done. With correct play, the Black King should fall a target to White's trained guns. Or failing that, Black will be compelled to part with his ill-gotten gains and more.

10 **PxB**   . . . .

Now, if White moves his Bishop, Black is able to consolidate and retain the extra Pawn.

10 . . . .   **PxB**

11 **R-K1ch** . . . .

A Pawn behind, White has compensation in his pressure on the opposing King. He must utilize this to the full.

11 . . . .   **N-K2**

11 . . . B-K3; *12* P-Q5 wins a piece.

12 **P-N5!** . . . .

Threatening *13* B-R3.

Another way is *12* Q-K2, B-K3; *13* B-N5, Q-Q4; *14* BxN, KxB; *15* Q-B2. White's compensation for his Pawn minus is Black's awkward King position. While this line is also in the spirit of the opening, exacting play is required of both sides. The chances are about even.

12 . . . .   **O-O**

To release the annoying pin.

13 **B-R3**   **R-K1**

14 **Q-B2**   . . . .

White must recover his Pawn. *14 . . .* B-K3 is met by *15* N-N5, threatening mate and the exchange of the Bishop which guards the Pawn. White will be saddled with an isolated Queen Pawn as against which his superior development and greater command of terrain are compensation. With correct play, the outcome is likely a draw.

Conclusions

Since the Giuoco Piano is a wild and woolly game, with tactical threats and combinations predominating, it should appeal to the type of player whose imagination occasionally runs rampant.

Despite its age, the Giuoco still lends itself to current refinements. Black's 9th move, for instance, is a recent innovation, superseding another move which was long considered best and which now stands refuted.

The following two CHESS MOVIES are typical examples of lines in the *Giuoco Piano*.

Chess Movie
UNLUCKY SEVEN

RETRIBUTION in chess follows closely upon the heels of
omission. Below, however, von Bardeleben (Black) wears
seven-league boots; his imperceptible error on move seven
noticeably remains unpunished for many moves. Inevitable
fate and one-time world champion, W. Steinitz (White),
finally catch up with a classic refutation, for which Steinitz
obtained the brilliancy prize at Hastings, 1895.

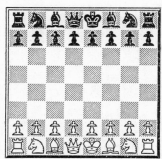

1 The coming scene is the
Giuoco Piano; the syn-
opsis: *1* P-K4, P-K4; *2*
N-KB3, N-QB3; *3* B-B4, B-B4;
4 P-B3, N-B3; *5* P-Q4, PxP;
6 PxP, B-N5*ch;* *7* N-B3, P-Q4.
By vigorous prosecution of
the initiative, and with a long
bead on the Black monarch,
Steinitz dooms Black's defense.

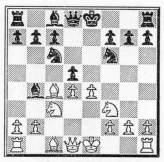

2 There follows *8* PxP,
KNxP; *9* O-O, B-K3, ar-
riving at the next posi-
tion. Superficially, Black is
well off. White's isolated
Queen Pawn is a handicap,
while Black's development is
sound and his Pawn chain is
solid. All is not what it seems.
A few deft strokes and Steinitz
is in command.

3 First comes *10* B-KN5, molesting the Queen. Bardeleben parries with *10 . . .* B-K2. Then follows a general exchange: *11* BxN, B/3xB; *12* NxB, QxN. The strategical plan is mysterious. If Steinitz wishes to attack, he must maintain his forces. But, instead, he is swapping down!

4 Violation upon violation: Steinitz continues to swap. There follows *13* BxB, NxB. In another move, Black will castle and hammer away at White's weak, isolated Pawn. But ho! the master has something up his sleeve. He plays *14* R-K1, pinning the Black Knight against its own King.

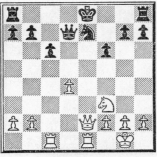

5 There are pins and pins. This pin appears to be a piddling pin. Bardeleben will snap it with ease. He plays *14 . . .* P-KB3, creating an exit for his King. By *15* Q-K2, however, Steinitz piles upon the pinned piece. Bardeleben defends with *. . .* Q-Q2, and there follows: *16* QR-B1, P-B3.

6 Bardeleben has built a barrier. Steinitz crashes through with *17* P-Q5. There follows *17 . . .* PxP; *18* N-Q4, K-B2; *19* N-K6. A Knight at K6 is like a bone in the throat, says Steinitz. Now he must prove it. He has already invested a Pawn in his principles! A Pawn from Steinitz is rarer than rubies!

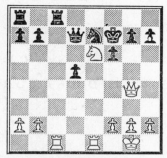

7 The threat is Rook to the seventh rank. A "pig on the seventh" can make life miserable. So Bardeleben parries with *19 . . . KR-QB1.* Now follows *20 Q-N4.* The threat is QxPch with mate to follow. White also focuses his attention on the Black Queen which is unguarded.

8 Bardeleben parries with *20 . . . P-KN3.* Steinitz withdraws *21 N-N5ch,* exposing Black's Queen to jeopardy. The King comes to the aid of the beleaguered lady with *. . . K-K1.* The moment is tense as Bardeleben awaits the next thrust. It is no thrust; it is a meat axe. *22 RxNch* is the move.

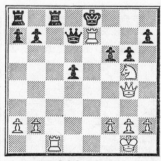

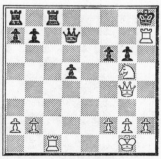

9 Bardeleben moves *22 . . . K-B1.* He can't play *. . . QxR* because of RxRch. A merry chase ensues: *23 R-B7ch, K-N1; 24 R-N7ch, K-R1; 25 RxPch.* All the time, Black's Queen is immune. For if ever RxQ, Black replies *. . . RxRch* with mate to follow. Bardeleben now bows out of the picture.

10 The finale would be *25 . . . K-N1; 26 R-N7ch, K-R1* when a mate in 9 ensues: *27 Q-R4ch, KxR; 28 Q-R7ch, K-B1; 29 Q-R8ch, K-K2; 30 Q-N7ch, K-K1; 31 Q-N8ch, K-K2; 32 Q-B7ch, K-Q1; 33 Q-B8ch, Q-K1; 34 N-B7ch, K-Q2; 35 Q-Q6 mate.* Small wonder Steinitz was world champion 27 years.

Chess Movie

SECOND FEATURE: MURDER AT K7

Position is everything on the chessboard. Forces entering the charmed circle of an engaging action are relatively more important at the moment than powerful pieces on the sidelines. Such is the course of the following game: The first engaging action is the last! The players? . . . merely White and Black. Their identity is lost in anonymity. The game opens with *1* P-K4, P-K4; *2* N-KB3, N-QB3; *3* B-B4, B-B4; *4* P-B3, N-B3. (*See diagram No. 1.*)

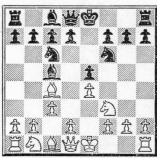

1 The game continues: *5* P-Q4, PxP; *6* PxP, B-N5*ch;* *7* N-B3, NxKP; *8* O-O, BxN; *9* P-Q5! This launches into a variation which is known as the Moeller Attack. From the beginning, it is clear this is a wild and woolly match between position and material.

2 Already a piece plus, Black is ready for punishment. Material salves abuse. He plays *9* . . . N-K4, counter-attacking the White Bishop. The game continues *10* PxB, NxB; *11* Q-Q4. White's Queen attacks in all directions—both Knights and the Knight Pawn are targets.

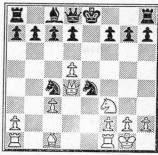

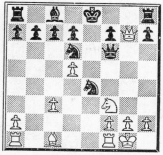

3 Safety first is not Black's code. He might as well be hanged for a Knight as well as for a Pawn. So he retreats *11 . . . N/B5-Q3.* White captures *12 QxNP,* attacking the Rook. And Black parries: *12 . . . Q-B3.* So far, so good. Black retains the loot.

4 Now White is accommodating. A piece behind, he swaps Queens: *13 QxQ, NxQ.* With Queens off the board and the mating attacks cut to a minimum, the extra piece looms large in the reckoning. But White is just beginning to fight. *14 R-K1ch* is the move.

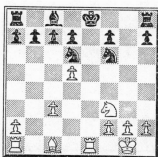

5 Black plays *14 . . . K-B1.* He holds on to everything. He does not wish to interpose and return a Knight. The onus of forcing the issue rests with White. He draws the mating net tight about the Black monarch, before Black's reserves come out. *15 B-R6ch, K-N1; 16 R-K5,* menacing mate.

6 Black staves off mate by *15 . . . N/B3-K5.* White continues *16 QR-K1,* meaning to capture the Knight. And Black defends with *. . . P-KB4.* Now White covers all the exits with *17 R-K7.* There follows: *17 . . . P-N3; 18 N-R4, B-N2; 19 P-B3.* The Knight must flee. But where?

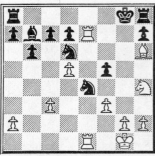

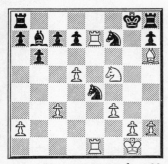

7 First Black counters with *19 . . . N-B2*. Attacking White's Bishop, he hopes to break up the intrusion. But White is adamant. The Bishop will not move. *20 NxP* is the move. All of White's men are in the fray. And Black dare not pare down. If he tries, he loses material but White keeps position.

8 Retreat is in order, *20 . . . N/5-Q3* follows. Still everything is intact. Maybe White's onslaught is spent. Maybe now the extra piece will tell . . . Maybe . . . But Black is day-dreaming. He is rudely awakened. The punishment will fit his crimes in overflowing measure.

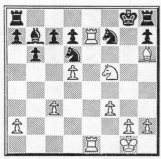

9 White crashes through with *21 R-K8ch*. Can such things be and overcome us? What of all the principles of chess? Can Rooks be flaunted defiantly in the face of overpowering material odds? . . . Well, all is well that ends well. For the right side, indeed, it is spectacularly so!

10 Now comes the denouement. *21 . . . RxR; 22 RxRch, NxR; 23 N-K7 mate!* What a picture! Black is a Rook and Knight ahead—a lot of useless wood strewn about the beheaded King. Moral: Material isn't everything in chess. Development is important—on the right squares.

4

Ruy Lopez

THE Ruy Lopez was named after a Spanish clergyman, Ruy Lopez of Safra, in Estramadura. About the middle of the sixteenth century, he edited a systematic work of one hundred and fifty pages, which presented the results of research into the openings.

First noticed by the writer of the Göttingen Ms. (1490) and later analyzed by other authors, including Lopez, the opening was seldom adopted in actual play until the middle of the last century. Credit for discovering its potency is due the Russian analyst, Jaenisch, who probed its possibilities during the years 1842–68.

White's third move, 3 B-N5, characterizes the Lopez. It is a move which attacks an adverse piece that is bearing on the center squares. Hence it exerts direct pressure on the center in an indirect manner.

The patterns which evolve from this opening are close and positional in the budding period. When in full bloom, however, there is a tendency towards wide-open play.

The opening arises as follows:

1 **P-K4**　**P-K4**　*2* **N-KB3 N-QB3**
　　　　3 **B-N5**　. . . .

White's last move is the signal for the opening strategical skirmish for control of the center. Pressure on Black's Knight, which defends its King Pawn, is the motivating reason.

The development of White's King Knight and King Bishop paves the way for early King-side castling. In turn, the King Rook may soon join the fray.

3 . . . . **P-QR3**

This move is the basis of Black's future defensive formation. Since he may not have the opportunity to do so later on, Black drives White's Bishop at once.

Alternatives are *3* . . . N-B3, *3* . . . B-B4 and *3* . . . N-Q5. These defenses are not in vogue today.

4 **B-R4**　. . . .

White retreats. If *4* BxN, QPxB; *5* NxP, Q-Q5! recovers the Pawn because of the simultaneous attack on Knight and Pawn.

Since White cannot win a Pawn by the exchange, there is no point to swapping a Bishop for a Knight.

It is to be noted that the reason White cannot win a Pawn is that his own King Pawn is unprotected. The retreat of the Bishop consequently is a marking-time maneuver, with a view to exchanging at a more propitious moment, when White's King Pawn is defended.

4 . . . . N-B3

Since White cannot win a Pawn by BxN, followed by NxP, Black has nothing to fear. He proceeds with his own development, attacking White's center Pawn.

5 O-O! . . . .

Usually, when a Pawn is attacked, it should be defended. Here, for example, White's King Pawn is attacked, and it might be defended by 5 P-Q3 or 5 N-B3. These moves, in fact, are alternatives to the text. Because of tactical reasons, however, which will soon become apparent, White need not defend the Pawn at this moment. And by this omission, White gains time to build up a strong formation which he has in mind.

The point becomes clearer when White's plan is revealed. He intends to establish a Pawn center by playing P-B3, followed by P-Q4. If he defends his King Pawn by playing 5 N-B3, he pre-empts the square QB3 for the Knight and consequently cannot use it for P-B3. If he defends the Pawn with

5 P-Q3, he must abandon the idea of playing P-Q4 later. Else, he loses time by advancing his Pawn to Q4 in two moves, instead of one. Any immediate defense of the King Pawn has certain drawbacks.

5 . . . .   **B-K2**

The text move and 5 . . . NxP are good alternatives at this point. 5 . . . NxP will be discussed in the next chapter. For the present, suffice it to say that, if 5 . . . NxP, White can recover the Pawn in various ways, the simplest being 6 R-K1.

From Black's point of view, it can be seen that the removal of White's King Pawn clears the path leading to the Black King. If the Pawn goes, a White Rook at K1 faces the opposing monarch. And this spells danger. It is with this in mind, that Black makes the text move.

The Bishop at K2 serves to shield the King from a subsequent attack on the King file. The move really is anticipatory. Since the danger is lessened, Black is in a better position to threaten to capture the King Pawn.

Incidentally, other moves with the Bishop will not do as well. For instance, 5 . . . B-Q3 is disadvantageous as the Bishop on Q3 blocks the advance of Black's Queen Pawn. The immobility of the Queen Pawn, in turn, ties up Black's entire Queen-side. 5 . . . B-B4 fails because White can play 6 NxP! Then, if . . . NxN; 7 P-Q4 and White recovers the piece and holds greater control of the central squares. 5 . . . B-N5 will not do, as White counters with the move he intends to make in any event—P-B3. Then the Bishop has to retreat and White gains his goal at Black's expense.

6 R-K1   . . . .

White defends the King Pawn. Now it is inadvisable to grant Black the option of capturing the Pawn.

6 . . . . P-QN4

Since White's King Pawn is defended, the threat of 7 BxN, QPxB; 8 NxP, gaining a Pawn, is real. Observe that 8 . . . Q-Q5 in this instance will not retrieve the Pawn. That is why Black destroys the threat by driving the Bishop.

7 B-N3   P-Q3

Black's last move has a threefold purpose: (1) it defends the King Pawn; (2) it permits the development of the Queen Bishop along its normal diagonal; (3) it institutes the minor threat of 8 . . . N-QR4, followed by 9 . . . NxB, gaining a Bishop for a Knight.

8 P-B3   . . . .

White's move has a twofold purpose: (1) it creates an exit for the Bishop, in the event it is attacked by the adverse Knight; (2) it prepares for the establishment of a Pawn center, with the Queen Bishop Pawn serving as a prop.

8 . . . . N-QR4

At first sight, this appears to be a purposeless move. The Knight moves out on a limb, merely to attack a Bishop, which will retreat. Closer examination will not reveal the purpose of the move. Only a knowledge of what Black has in mind will clarify the maneuver.

Black is following a preconceived plan. White's plan is to advance his Pawn to Q4, put pressure on Black's King Pawn and compel Black to exchange Pawns. Then White recaptures with the Bishop Pawn. The disappearance of Black's King Pawn, in effect, will be tantamount to the surrender of the center to White.

Black's plan is a parry to White's. He moves the Knight to clear the path of his Queen Bishop Pawn. He aims for a Pawn formation of his own in which the Queen Bishop Pawn plays an important part—in challenging or staying White's ambition to take over the center.

Since the opening has been played time and again, the best plans of both contestants are known to each other. Each side, therefore, is in position to anticipate and counter the other's ideas in the most effective manner.

9 B-B2   . . . .

The Bishop retreats, even at the expense of a move. For a Bishop is stronger than a Knight, and White wishes to avoid the exchange.

9 . . . .   P-B4

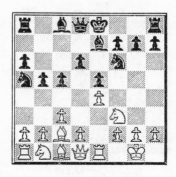

This is the reason for Black's 8th move. With Black's Knight at QB3, the Bishop Pawn was fixed.

Now, when, as and if White plays P-Q4, Black still exerts as much pressure on White's center as White on Black's. Moreover, Black's square QB2 is vacated and Black's Queen can occupy it to defend the King Pawn—again, when, as and if it is attacked.

Black's Queen-side Pawn structure is an effective one, known commonly as the Tchigorin formation.

All this delicate maneuvering is to balance the scale as far as the center is concerned.

10 P-Q4 . . . .

Actively striking at the center. The passive line, 10 P-Q3, also has much in its favor and will be discussed in another chapter.

10 . . . . Q-B2

Defending the King Pawn, which is doubly attacked. Note that this is possible only because of Black's 9th, which was preparatory to the text.

The exchange of Pawns: 10 . . . KPxP; 11 PxP, PxP; 12 NxP would be the surrender of the center to White. Moreover, Black would remain with an isolated and backward Queen Pawn.

Even the exchange of one Pawn in the center would benefit White. Thus, if 10 . . . BPxP; 11 PxP, the resulting open Queen Bishop file eventually would accrue to White. Or, if 10 . . . KPxP; 11 PxP leaves White in control of the center with good prospects for attack because of the added possibility of an eventual P-K5.

11 P-KR3 . . . .

The move P-KR3, as a general rule, does more harm than good. In this case, for example, it weakens White's King-side flank to a minor extent. The weakness, however, in this instance, is more than offset by the gain in other directions. Here,

the Pawn at R3 prevents Black from pinning White's King Knight with . . . B-N5. The pin would not be fatal for White, but it would mitigate the pressure which the White Knight exerts in the center.

In addition, the Pawn at R3 serves as a prop for an eventual P-KN4 and an all-out advance of the King-side Pawns against the opposing King — when the position calls for it.

11 . . . .   O-O

The skirmish to gain control of the center is a stand off; Black's defense has not yielded to White's pressure.

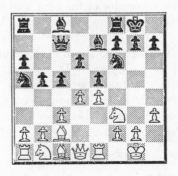

12 QN-Q2 . . . .

Such a Knight move is normally condemned by the layman. For the Knight at Q2 interferes with the development of the

Queen Bishop. The interference, however, is only temporary. In one move, the Knight can clear the path.

More important is its purpose. What does it portend? . . . It is the beginning of a maneuver to transfer the Knight to the King-side of the board. Why the King-side? . . . Because White is making plans to institute a King-side attack. In order to do this, he must bring forces within the range of the opposing King.

12 . . . . N-B3

So long as the tension exists in the center, it is difficult for either side to undertake a constructive plan on the wings. Since White is contemplating a King-side assault, Black piles on the pressure in the center — to keep White employed in that sector.

13 P-Q5 . . . .

As there is no way for White to put additional pressure on Black's center and compel Black to exchange Pawns, White ends the tension in the center by the advance of the Pawn. This relieves White of the need to guard the center and frees him for operating on the wing. In this instance, it is the King's wing in which White is interested.

Of course, with the end of the center tension, Black is also free to operate in other sectors.

13 . . . . N-Q1

A unique move which has all the superficial appearances of inanity. From Q1, the Knight cannot go the K3 or back to B3. Yet at QN2, it has little bearing on the position. Moreover, it interferes now with the communications between Black's other forces.

Despite appearances, *13 . . . N-Q1* is a good move. It is the first step in the plan to build up a defense against White's contemplated assault on the Black King. Follow the Knight meanderings to its final destination to observe what Black has in mind.

14 **N-B1**   . . . .

Primarily to maneuver the Knight to the King-side; secondarily to clear the path of the Bishop.

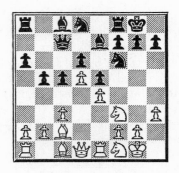

14 . . . .   **N-K1**

This is another unique move in Black's concealed plan of defense. Its immediate purpose is to threaten a break by the advance *15 . . . P-KB4*. Its long-term purpose will become clear when the final pattern of Black's defense is woven.

15 **P-KN4**   . . . .

This advance forestalls Black's intended break. That, however, is not the main purpose of the move. As a matter of strategy, it is important to provoke weaknesses in the enemy camp.

To do so by a Pawn advance is the least expensive way. In an assault which stands a fair chance of success, Pawns are expendable. Thus, the Pawns advance with a view to provoking weaknesses or opening gaps, and the major pieces will follow, intent upon exploitation.

True, White's Pawn advance is double-edged. Any Pawn advance is inherently weak. Here, the weakness is relatively unimportant at this stage of the game, while there is a respectable attack brewing. So long as the attack is significant, the weakness will not show up. Should the attack fail, however, there is danger that White's weaknesses will boomerang. But such a possibility, if it does arise, will turn up only at a much later stage of the game.

15 . . . . **P-N3**

With a dual purpose. The immediate reason for the move is to create a square at KN2 for the King Knight, where it will serve in a defensive capacity. The long-term purpose is to keep an eye on the possible break . . . P-B4, should the opportunity present itself.

16 **N-N3** . . . .

Attaining the object of the Knight maneuver, which was to bring the Knight into the vicinity of the adverse King.

16 . . . . **P-B3**

To vacate the square . . . KB2 so that the Knight on Q1 can move up for defense. The secret of Black's *13 . . .* N-Q1 is out.

17 **K-R2**   . . . .

To clear the King Knight file for future occupation by White's Rooks—all part and parcel of a grand attacking plan.

17 . . . .   **N-B2**

Building a defensive barrier, in anticipation of the attack.

18 **R-KN1** . . . .

Despite the presence of White and Black Pawns on the King Knight file, the Rook bears down, indirectly, upon the Black Monarch. White is looking ahead to the time when the Pawns may be cleared off the file.

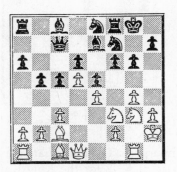

18 . . . . .   **K-R1**

To get out of the line of fire of the adverse Rook.

19 **B-K3**   . . . .

This assists in clearing the first rank so as to enable the Queen Rook to join the King-side assault.

19 . . . .   **N-N2**

Consolidating the defensive barrier. The final destinations of the Black Knights in the opening are achieved.

20 Q-Q2 . . . .

Completely clearing the way for the Queen Rook to join the fray. White also eyes B-R6 as a possibility.

20 . . . . B-Q2

To clear the last rank so as to enable both Black Rooks to cooperate.

21 R-KN2 . . . .

Vacating KN1 for the Queen Rook.

21 . . . . R-KN1

Neutralizing the indirect pressure on the King Knight file.

22 QR-KN1. . . .

Thereby joining the attack in full force. White's last is technically called "doubling the Rooks."

To all intents and appearance, White has the initiative. Black, however, is well poised for defense. With best play, a draw should result.

A cardinal wit summed up the position succinctly with "Black will probably win. White's attacking chances will undoubtedly drive him into a rash action."

Conclusions

Of all the openings beginning with *1* P-K4, the Ruy Lopez offers a longer-lasting initiative to White, with the least amount of speculation.

Current opinion concludes that the patterns evolving from this opening should result in a draw. The onus of best play, however, generally rests with Black, as he is the defender. One misstep in the defense is fatal.

♔ ♕ ⬭⬭⬭⬭⬭⬭⬭⬭⬭⬭⬭ ♕ ♚

Chess Movie

THE GREAT FALL

ALL the King's horses and all the King's men push Humpty Dumpty (the Black Monarch) right off the wall in this modern version of the great fall. Salo Flohr conducts the White forces with unusual vigor, sacrificing nearly more men than there are on the board! F. Lustig is the victim, and the game was played at Prague in 1928. It opens with *1* P-K4, P-K4; *2* N-KB3, N-QB3; *3* B-N5, P-QR3; *4* B-R4, N-B3 (*see diagram No. 1*).

1 The game continues: *5* Q-K2, B-K2; *6* P-B3, P-QN4; *7* B-N3, P-Q3; *8* P-KR3, N-QR4; *9* B-B2, P-B4; *10* P-Q4, Q-B2; *11* O-O, O-O. This makes an illustrative game for the analysis preceding, as the standard line has been reached. The Queen at K2 doesn't alter the *general* pattern.

2 Intent upon a King-side assault, Flohr relaxes the center tension with *12* P-Q5. Lustig counters with a Queen-side advance . . . P-B5, as he underestimates the power of the coming onslaught against his King. Both sides continue their development: *13* B-K3, B-Q2, readying for the next round.

3 Flohr retreats *14* N-K1. He intends to advance his King Bishop Pawn to open the King Bishop file for future operations. Lustig retires . . . N-N2. There follows *15* N-Q2, KR-K1. Lustig has ideas of his own concerning defense. Flohr spikes his Pawn: *16* P-KN4, and Lustig replies *16* . . . P-N3.

4 Now nearly all of the White forces are ready for the coming fracas. There is no reason why they should not all participate. So Flohr advances *17* P-B4, opening the Bishop file. Lustig captures . . . PxP, and Flohr recaptures *18* RxP. Black now returns . . . R-KB1 in order to guard his vital KB2.

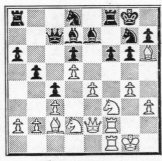

5 Flohr retires *19* R-B2, clearing the diagonal for his Queen Bishop, and Lustig replies . . . N-K1. Too late, he wishes to set up the typical Knight barrier. There follows: *20* N/1-B3, N-Q1; *21* QR-KB1, P-B3; *22* B-R6, N-KN2. The stage is neatly set for a penetrating incursion, in the brilliant style.

6 There are many ways of slowly building the attack. There is only one way of reaching the Sable monarch with full force, pronto. It involves the sacrifice of a Pawn for vague returns. As Flohr's good judgment commands, however, he now crashes through with the speculative *23* P-K5.

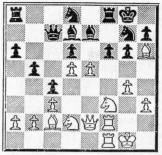

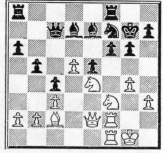

7 With one fell stroke, the White King Bishop aims at the Black monarch, and the White Queen Knight has gained a new base for operations at K4. Lustig takes 23 . . . QPxP, and Flohr moves in: 24 N-K4. Lustig covers with . . . N-B2, and there follows: 25 BxN, KxB. Can Black now survive?

8 Flohr plays 26 N-R4, and Lustig counters with . . . N-Q3. Now Flohr takes a do or die stand: 27 NxBP! and the Black barrier is breached. Lustig accepts the sacrifice by . . . BxN. Flohr hits hard with 28 P-N5. The fur is flying, and it is difficult to keep track of the fast-moving action.

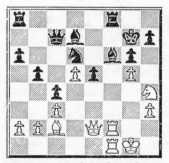

9 Lustig defends with 28 . . . N-K1, and Flohr rains another blow at the ill-fated King: 29 NxP!! Lustig takes . . . PxN, and the action waxes fast and furious: 30 BxP, KxB; 31 Q-K4ch. At long last and at the expense of all of three pieces, the Black monarch is nakedly exposed—to a fatal chill!

10 The King retreats, 31 . . . K-N2, seeking protection, and there follows a peaceful haymaker: 32 Q-R4. Now follows: 32 . . . K-N1; 33 PxB, NxP; 34 Q-N5ch, K-R1; 35 RxN and the well-known spite check . . . Q-B4ch. Flohr simply retires gracefully: 36 K-R2, and Lustig gives up the ghost.

5

Ruy Lopez

THE OPEN DEFENSE

IN THE main variation of the Ruy Lopez, White maintains the initiative clearly throughout the opening and well into the middle game. Although Black can achieve equality with best play, the onus of perfection rests on him. It is indeed unappetizing for a player to be confronted with a line which, at best and after taxing him to the utmost, grants mere equality. There is, nonetheless, no known method for Black to seize the initiative—bestowed upon White—without incurring certain risks.

There is, however, an active line for Black. This defense grants him a considerable measure of counterplay at the expense of security of position. For the player who prefers the

rough and tumble way, the active, or so-called open, defense is
the answer.

This defense arises as follows:

1	P-K4	P-K4	3	B-N5	P-QR3
2	N-KB3	N-QB3	4	B-R4	N-B3
	5	O-O	NxP		

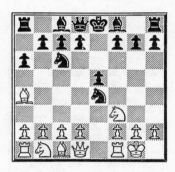

By capturing the King Pawn, Black exposes his King Knight
as a target and opens lines leading to his King. Since White
must devote his efforts to recovering the Pawn and maintaining
his initiative, Black enjoys some leeway.

6 P-Q4 . . . .

This move offers White the best chance of reaching both
his objectives—the recovery of the Pawn and the retention of
his initiative.

6 R-K1 also recovers the Pawn. For there is no good way for
Black to retain it. Thus, if 6 . . . P-Q4; 7 NxP. Or, if 6 . . .
N-B4; 7 NxP.

The text move, however, is superior to 6 R-K1; for, on
6 . . . N-B4; 7 NxP, B-K2, White is compelled to part with
one of his Bishops for a Knight, without getting any compensation in return.

6 . . . . P-QN4

Black wishes to play . . . P-Q4. He can not do so at once; for, after 6 . . . P-Q4; 7 NxP, Black is virtually forced to play 7 . . . B-Q2 or place his pieces on awkward posts. A rather subtle combination then follows: e.g., 6 . . . P-Q4; 7 NxP, B-Q2; 8 NxP! KxN; 9 Q-R5*ch*, K-K3; 10 N-B3, and White's on-slaught is overwhelming.*

Thus, by first driving the Bishop, Black is able to follow with . . . P-Q4 as his Queen Knight will not be pinned.

7 **B-N3**   **P-Q4**

As per plan.

8 **PxP**   . . . .

The text move is superior to 8 NxP on tactical and strate-gical grounds. If 8 NxP, for example, the continuation is 8 . . . NxN; 9 PxN, B-K3. Then the Black Queen Bishop Pawn is free to advance, and Black's Queen-side majority becomes danger-ous. Furthermore, since White is contemplating an eventual King-side assault, he should avoid any unprofitable exchanges. Attack is based on force, and consequently White should retain his forces.

8 . . . .   **B-K3**

Black defends the Queen Pawn. Now he threatens 9 . . . N-B4 to gain a Bishop for a Knight.

9 **P-B3**   . . . .

* Chernev, I., *Winning Chess Traps*, N. Y., *McKay*, p. 41.

White creates an exit for the Bishop in the event that it is attacked. 9 Q-K2 is an alternative but highly involved line of play. In it, White readily parts with his Bishop, if need be, in return for unmitigated pressure on the Black Queen Pawn. He follows up with R-Q1.

9 . . . . **B-K2**

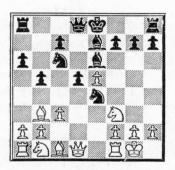

Black prepares to castle and to complete his development. 9 . . . B-QB4 is an inferior alternative.

10 **QN-Q2** . . . .

White aims to rid himself of Black's advanced Knight.

10 . . . . **O-O**

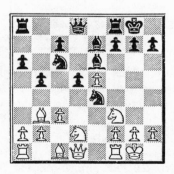

11 **B-B2** . . . .

White puts pressure on Black's well posted Knight. If instead *11* NxN, PxN; *12* BxB, PxB, White's King Knight must move, and his King Pawn goes by the wayside. Then White achieves mere equality, at best, when naturally he is seeking an advantage.

$$11 \ldots \ldots \quad \textbf{P-B4}$$

Black aims to maintain the Knight at K5. Inferior alternatives are: (*a*) *11* . . . NxN; *12* QxN, P-B3; *13* PxP, BxP; *14* N-N5, BxN; *15* QxB, QxQ; *16* BxQ after which the advantage of the two Bishops and the better Pawn structure rests with White; or (*b*) *11* . . . N-B4; *12* N-Q4 (intending P-KB4-5), NxP; *13* Q-R5, N-N3; *14* P-KB4, B-Q2; *15* P-B5, N-R1; *16* P-B6, with an irresistible attack for White. These alternatives arise from actual games.

Observe that, in order to maintain the Knight at K5, Black permits White to have a protected passed Pawn.

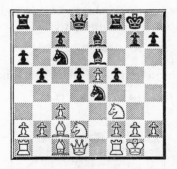

At this juncture, Black enjoys freedom of movement. His Pawn formation, however, is full of holes, which in turn jeopardize the security of his position. As yet, however, no sure way of exploiting these defects has been found.

$$12 \ \textbf{N-N3} \ \ldots \ldots$$

The alternative, *12* PxP *e.p.*, intending to undermine the support of the Knight, appears to favor Black. E.g., *12* PxP *e.p.,* NxP/3; *13* N-N3, B-KN5!; *14* Q-Q3, N-K5; *15* QN-Q4, NxN; *16* NxN, B-Q3, and Black enjoys attacking prospects: *17* N-B6, Q-R5; *18* QxP*ch,* K-R1; *19* P-KN3, NxNP; *20* RPxN, BxP, and it is difficult for White to ward off the onslaught.

12 . . . . Q-Q2

Black permits cooperation between the Rooks on the last rank. Black is resigned to parting with a Bishop for a Knight. For he expects quickly to utilize his Queen-side Pawn majority.

13 KN-Q4 . . . .

White attacks Black's Queen Bishop and aims to drive Black's well-posted Knight at K5, at the opportune moment.

13 . . . . NxN

If *13* . . . NxKP; *14* R-K1, the threat of *15* P-B3 or *15* NxB, followed by *16* P-B3, is difficult to handle.

14 NxN . . . .

If *14* PxN, in order to retard the advance of Black's Queen Bishop Pawn, the continuation might be *14* . . . P-QR4; *15* P-B3, P-R5, and Black emerges with a plus in position. For his forces are better posted.

14 . . . . P-B4

Black sets the Pawn majority immediately in motion.

15 N-K2 . . . .

15 NxB gives White the two Bishops. Since Black's Pawns are mobile, however, and White's King Pawn is fixed, the advantage of the two Bishops is dubious. For Knights show at their best in fixed Pawn positions.

The retreat of the Knight is mainly to retain resiliency in the position. The Knight can maneuver to a better post.

15 . . . . QR-Q1

Black reinforces the Queen Pawn, one of the weak spots in the position, and also prepares its advance.

16 N-B4 . . . .

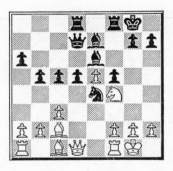

16 . . . . Q-B3

The impetuous advance of either the Queen Pawn or the Queen Bishop Pawn opens lines which White may utilize. For example, if 16 . . . P-B5, 17 B-K3 and Black's Queen Pawn remains backward. Or, if 16 . . . P-Q5; 17 PxP, PxP; 18 NxB, QxN; 19 B-N3 and White wins.

17 Q-R5 . . . .

White threatens to win a piece by 18 NxB, followed by 19 P-B3.

17 . . . . B-B1

Black avoids the threat.

> *18* **P-QR4** . . . .

White seeks to open the Rook file or to disrupt Black's Queen-side Pawn formation.

> *18* **P-N5**
>
> *19* **PxP** . . . .

White breaks up Black's chain of Pawns.

> *19* . . . . **PxP**

The position is about even. If any side is to be preferred, it is White's—his passed Pawn can be supported but Black's is isolated.

This variation is from the first game of the match, Bogolyubov vs. Euwe, 1928. The game with Euwe as Black continued:

20	Q-K2	N-B4	*27*	QR-Q1	P-R3
21	B-K3	P-QR4	*28*	P-R4	Q-K2
22	BxN	QxB	*29*	R-Q4	P-N4
23	B-N3	B-N4	*30*	PxP	PxP
24	Q-B3	BxN	*31*	Q-Q2	R-Q2
25	QxB	K-R1	*32*	R-Q1	P-B5
26	KR-K1	B-K3	*33*	Q-K2	P-B6
			34	Q-K3	Q-R2

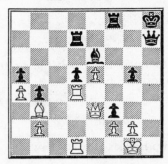

FINAL POSITION

After 35 BxP, BxB; 36 RxB, RxR; 37 RxR, Q-N8*ch;* 38 K-R2, Q-R2*ch* and Black gets a perpetual as 39 K-N3 is mere suicide.

Conclusions

In the Open Defense to the Ruy Lopez, the initiative which Black gains more than offsets his chronically weak Pawn structure. Up to the present, moreover, no sure way has been found of exploiting Black's weaknesses.

Chess Movie

ATTACK ON THE GUARD

THERE comes a time to strike in almost every game, and, having come, moves on. This fleeting moment may mean oblivion or immortality! At Vilna, in 1912, the mighty Akiba Rubinstein (Black) thus penetrated Alekhine's position by a deft sacrifice of the exchange. *1 P-K4, P-K4; 2 N-KB3, N-QB3; 3 B-N5, P-QR3; 4 B-R4, N-B3; 5 O-O, NxP (see diagram No. 1).*

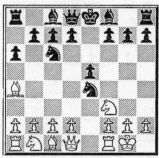

1 Then follow the usual moves of the Open Defense of the Ruy Lopez: *6 P-Q4, P-QN4; 7 B-N3, P-Q4; 8 PxP, B-K3; 9 P-B3, B-K2,* arriving at diagram 2. Alekhine versus Rubinstein! Their names will forever be inscribed on Caissa's banner. Both players are alert to exploit small advantages.

2 The game continues: *10 QN-Q2, N-B4,* reaching diagram 3. The great Akiba in fighting spirit has experience and reputation on his side. Twenty-one-year-old Alekhine has yet to prove himself, and the speculative text move takes him by surprise. His position, however, is solid, and a real fight ensues.

3 Alekhine retreats *11 B-B2* to preserve his Bishop. Rubinstein plays *11 . . . B-N5*, pinning White's King Knight and vacating his K3 square for occupation by his King Knight. Alekhine "puts the question" to the Bishop by *12 P-KR3*. The tempo of the game is rapid. The opening sparring is over.

4 Rubinstein retreats *12 . . . B-R4* and Alekhine answers *13 Q-K1*, breaking the annoying pin. Rubinstein follows with *13 . . . N-K3*, focusing on White's King position. Somehow the initiative has been transferred to Black. The slight weakness of his Pawn formation now assumes a minor role.

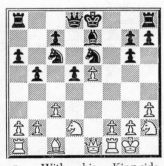

5 Alekhine withdraws *14 N-R2*, preparing the advance of his Kingside Pawn majority. Rubinstein parries *14 . . . B-N3*. Alekhine exchanges *15 BxB*. Capture towards the center is a good rule of thumb. Rubinstein, however, does not play with his thumbs. He plays *15 . . . BPxP* to open the Bishop file.

6 With his King-side Pawn roller stymied, Alekhine continues with *16 N-N3*. His opponent counters: *. . . P-KN4*. He checks any ideas of a White Pawn advance on the Kingside. Alekhine develops *17 B-K3*, and there follows: *17 . . . O-O; 18 N-KB3, Q-Q2; 19 Q-Q2*, and the critical story is told below.

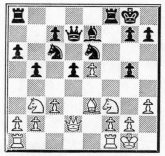

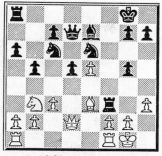

7 Strategically, Black has an uphill battle. White has a passed Pawn and Black's Pawn formation is disrupted. Tactically, there is another story. What does it matter if a Pawn is misplaced, so long as the opposing King is the target? Now *19 . . . RxN!* breaches the defense.

8 Alekhine captures *20 PxR* and then Rubinstein rejoins with *. . . NxP*, threatening a discombobulating check. Now Alekhine defends with *21 Q-K2*, and Rubinstein puts on the heat with *21 . . . R-KB1*. Again Alekhine defends: *22 N-Q2*. And Rubinstein maneuvers *22 . . . N-N3*, eyeing KB5.

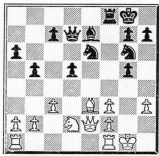

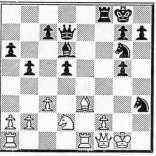

9 Alekhine plays *23 KR-K1*, vacating KB1 for defensive purposes. Rubinstein fires *23 . . . B-Q3*, aiming at White's King. White's ill-fated defenses are beyond repair. Feebly, he tries *24 P-KB4*. Now *24 . . . N/K3xP* penetrates. White retreats *25 Q-B1*, and Black slashes out with *25 . . . Nx Pch.*

10 Black is on the rampage. There follows: *26 K-R1, P-KN5; 27 Q-K2, Q-B4*. With the dire threat of *28 . . . Q-R4* staring him in the face, and with nothing to do about it, Alekhine resigns, without further play. Of such stuff is a reputation made.
Viva Akiba!

6

Ruy Lopez

THE STEINITZ SYSTEM

In THE main variation of the Ruy Lopez, White attempts to seize immediate control of the center, before undertaking action on the wing. Another line with equally good prospects for White begins in a more passive manner. White makes no effort to gain the center. Instead, he develops peacefully and soundly. The pacific development, however, is only a front for White's real intentions. All the while, White bides his time and appraises the opportunity to seize the center or to institute an attack against the opposing King.

This line arises as follows:

1 P-K4	P-K4	*3* B-N5	P-QR3
2 N-KB3	N-QB3	*4* B-R4	N-B3
	5 P-Q3	. . . .	

White directly defends the King Pawn. By not castling now, he reserves the option of castling later on either side, depending on which way the game turns. Or he may remain with his King in the center of the board in some contingencies.

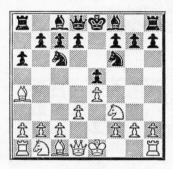

5 . . . . **P-Q3**

Black defends his King Pawn against the threat of *6* BxN, followed by NxP. In turn, Black now threatens *6* . . . P-QN4; *7* B-N3, N-QR4, followed by the exchange of a Bishop for a Knight.

6 P-B3 . . . .

White creates an exit for the Bishop in the event it is attacked by the adverse Knight. Also, the Queen Bishop Pawn may serve as support for the future advance P-Q4.

6 . . . . **B-K2**

Black develops the Bishop to permit castling.

7 QN-Q2 . . . .

The beginning of a Knight maneuver (QN-Q2-B1-N3) to the King-side of the board where the Black King will most likely reside. This same maneuver was employed in the earlier variation of the Lopez, discussed in Chapter 4.

7 . . . .   O-O

Whereas White can delay castling, Black finds it more difficult to do so; he cannot undertake a constructive plan so long as his King remains in the center to obstruct the communications between his forces. Moreover, Black believes he can thwart any undue aggression.

8 N-B1 . . . .

On the way to KN3.

8 . . . .   P-QN4

Not only to drive the Bishop, but also to make future prospects for the White King on the Queen-side of the board hazardous.

9 B-B2 . . . .

Temporarily the Bishop goes into hiding. It expects to emerge later on by the advance of P-Q4 or by returning to QN3. 9 B-N3 now is met by 9 . . . N-QR4; and, since the Bishop has a more promising future than the Knight, White has to retreat and lose time.

9 . . . .   P-Q4

Black forces the play in the center so as to take the sting out of any contemplated adverse attack on the wing.

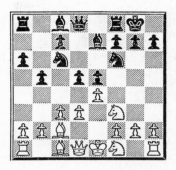

10 **Q-K2** . . . .

White avoids the exchange of Queens, in the event Black swaps Pawns. White wishes to retain his Queen for prospective attacking chances. Incidentally, *10 PxP* grants Black control of the center.

10 . . . . **R-K1**

Black creates a retreat for the King Bishop at KB1 and indirectly defends the King Pawn in the event White exchanges Pawns.

11 **P-KR3** . . . .

White aims to prevent the pin of his King Knight and also to set up a prop for a possible future King-side Pawn advance against the Black King.

11 . . . . **PxP**

Black opens the Queen file and an important diagonal on which his Queen Bishop can operate. Black is contemplating the maneuver . . . B-K3-B5.

12 **PxP** **B-K3**

In order to penetrate with *13* . . . B-B5 and drive the White Queen to what appears to be a less favorable post.

13 N-N5! . . . .

Practical Chess Openings * gives *13* B-Q2, instead of the text move. Black then obtains the superior game by . . . B-B5. For the White Queen is driven to an awkward position.

The text move vacates the square KB3 for occupation by the Queen, in the event it is attacked. At KB3, the Queen is well posted and does not interfere with the mobility of the other forces.

13 . . . . B-B5

As good as any. If the Bishop retreats, *14* B-N3 is good. If the Bishop remains, *14* NxB gives White the advantage of the two Bishops.

14 Q-B3   P-R3
15 P-KR4! . . . .

The point of White's 13th. Black dare not capture the Knight and open the King Rook file. Thus, if *15* . . . PxN?; *16* PxP, N-R2; *17* Q-R5, Black is unable to prevent an incursion of the White men.

* Fine, R., *Practical Chess Openings*, N. Y., McKay.

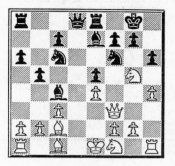

Now White's prospects are superior. He threatens *16* N-Q2, or *16* N-K3 to exchange Knight for Bishop and break up Black's Pawn formation. In addition, there is the possibility of a King-side Pawn advance which should expose the Black King as a target.

Conclusions

In this slow line of the Ruy Lopez, favored and exploited by one time world champion W. Steinitz, White invariably obtains a deferred initiative. This takes the form of an assault against the King or seizure of the center with all that it portends, or both. Moreover, since the pattern of this line is sounder than that of the main line, the risk of error is cut to a minimum.

Chess Movie

DEATH OF "THE BLACK DEATH"

E SSAYING the variation which he refined and popularized, Wilhelm Steinitz (White) subdues English grandmaster Joseph Henry Blackburne, alias "the Black Death." The overture is on a peaceful note and turns suddenly when Steinitz castles long. London, 1876, is the scene of the play. The game begins with *1 P-K4, P-K4; 2 N-KB3, N-QB3; 3 B-N5, P-QR3; 4 B-R4, N-B3; 5 P-Q3, P-Q3; 6 P-B3, B-K2 (see diagram No. 1).*

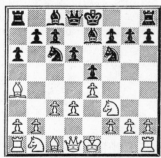

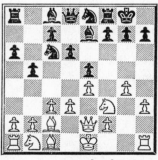

1 Now follows 7 P-KR3, O-O; 8 Q-K2, N-K1. Blackburne hopes to advance his King Bishop Pawn and gain a measure of counterplay. Steinitz checks this ambition with 9 P-KN4 and Blackburne feints on the other wing with 9 . . . P-QN4. Steinitz retreats 10 B-B2.

2 A wing development, 10 . . . B-N2 is Blackburne's choice. He hopes for the opening of the long diagonal. Steinitz plays 11 QN-Q2, heading for KB5 or Q5, via B1. Blackburne plays 11 . . . Q-Q2, and there follows 12 N-B1. Blackburne plays 12 . . . N-Q1, heading for KB5.

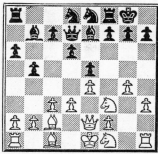

3 Both players advance their Knights on schedule: *13* N-K3, N-K3, and Steinitz enters the strategic square, *14* N-B5. There follows: . . . P-N3; *15* Nx B*ch.* To all appearances, White has wasted five moves to swap a Bishop. But he has provoked a weakness in Black's camp.

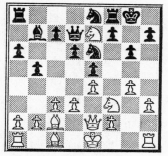

4 Blackburne recaptures *15* . . . QxN. Steinitz now sets out to exploit the weakness: *16* B-K3, N/1-N2; *17* O-O-O. This is the signal for action. With both monarchs on opposite sides of the board, it is a question of who gets there "first with the most!" White's attack, as we shall see, is much further advanced than Black's.

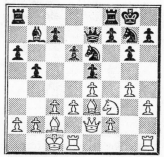

5 Blackburne plays *17* . . . P-QB4, preparing to open avenues of approach to the White King. Steinitz brazenly falls in line with *18* P-Q4. White enjoys the advantage of the Bishops. And Steinitz well knows that Bishops show up well in open positions.

6 Blackburne continues *18* . . . KPxP and Steinitz recaptures *19* PxP. Intent upon storming the White King position by a Pawn majority, Blackburne advances *19* . . . P-B5. Steinitz counters with *20* P-Q5, making room for his Bishop at Q4. Black retreats . . . N-B2.

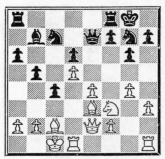

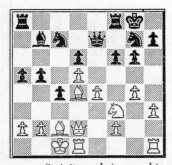

7 Steinitz plays *21* Q-Q2. When his Bishop goes to Q4, he will penetrate on the diagonal. There isn't much that Black can do to repair his own King position, so he tries to reach the White King. There follows: *21* . . . P-QR4; *22* B-Q4, P-B3. How can White open the position?

8 Steinitz brings his Queen into position: *23* Q-R6. Blackburne advances *23* . . . P-N5. Steinitz follows with *24* P-N5, clearing the diagonal of his Bishop. Blackburne parries: *24* . . . P-B4. Steinitz enters the breach with *25* B-B6. Who would think the game is nearly over?

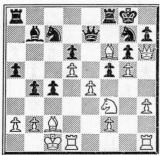

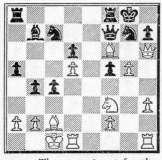

9 Blackburne plays *25* . . . Q-B2. Now follows *26* PxP, PxP. Black's King-side barrier is being loosed from its hinges. White's Bishops are in position to administer the last rites. The Black monarch must give up the ghost beyond all peradventure of a doubt.

10 The stage is set for the finale. *27* P-N6 is the move. There follows . . . QxNP. (If *27* . . . PxP; *28* N-N5 spells *finis.*) *28* BxN and Blackburne resigns. He dare not capture the Bishop on account of R-N1, pinning the Queen, and so he cannot regain the piece lost.

7

French Defense

CLASSICAL VARIATION

THE prerogative of the first move, if properly exploited, grants White a lasting initiative. It does not, however, determine the course of the game. Black has at least an equal say in this matter.

'For good and sufficient reasons, Black often directs the course of play. In doing so, he avoids lines unfamiliar to himself and arbitrarily compels his opponent to follow, rather than lead.

This does not mean that Black steals the initiative. The initiative is White's endowment. When Black originates the defense, however, he compels White to play to Black's tune. From the first move, therefore, White is burdened with the need to know all defenses which Black may use, and Black must know only one — the one which he will actually play. Ergo, to that extent, Black enjoys an edge.

Of the various defenses at Black's disposal, the prospects of the French are indeed promising; its pattern is firm, yet resilient; its snail-pace first move *1* . . . P-K3 is deceptive and often decoys an unsuspecting White into a false, impetuous attack, subject to recoil and boomerang.

The reply *1* . . . P-K3, designated at one time by the English players as "the King's Pawn One Game," was surnamed the French Defense, probably because the French writers have paid more attention to it than others. It was first mentioned, by Lucena in 1497.

It languished long, however, under what William Napier calls the "obsolete prejudice," that there was no good reason to shirk open, airy and pelting chess — and likely enough, also, under White's resentment that Black should direct the course of play. So, even after Morphy's day, his gifted and likeminded successor, Leonard, spoke of the French Defense as "the King's Pawn Sneaks One."

This defense arises as follows:

1 **P-K4   P-K3**

The advance of the King Pawn only one square, instead of two, momentarily cedes to White the greater control of the center. White's Pawn at K4 strikes the important squares, Q5

and KB5; the Black Pawn at K3 remains within Black's own half of the board. The Pawn at K3, moreover, hinders the natural mobility of Black's Queen Bishop. So, on the face of it, the defense appears foredoomed.

Such is not the case, however. These drawbacks are offset by advantages in other respects. For the Black Pawn pattern which evolves from the first move is structurally sound. White cannot pin on to a single target. Black's usual point of vulnerability, moreover, after *1* . . . P-K4, his KB2, is now safeguarded from direct attack. A White Bishop at QB4 would be biting on granite. In addition, the Pawn at K3 serves as a prop for the following move of . . . P-Q4, which is intended to challenge White's control of the center.

White's problem from the start is to capitalize on his infinitesimal center plus and free development. Black's problem is to check any undue aggression while catching up in development and locating his men in promising posts. Along these lines, the issue is drawn.

2 **P-Q4** . . . .

In nearly all cases in King Pawn openings, when an early P-Q4 can be played without incurring disadvantages, it is the proper move. As the Pawn pattern determines the character of the opening, correct strategy calls for the men to rally round the Pawns and not for the Pawns to cover haphazard development. That is why the King and Queen Pawns should take their places early, when possible.

(It should be noted that the move P-Q4 is not readily enforceable in King Pawn openings without disadvantage. For instance, after *1* P-K4, P-K4; *2* P-Q4, Black can play *2* . . . PxP and, after *3* QxP, N-QB3 gains Black a valuable tempo. In the French, the move has no drawbacks.)

2 . . . . **P-Q4**

In all King Pawn openings, the move P-Q4 for Black, is proper when it does not incur disadvantages.

3 **N-QB3** . . . .

The idea of the text move is to develop a piece and maintain pressure in the center. Various alternatives are:

(1) 3 PxP, PxP—the Exchange Variation. This line relieves the pressure in the center and leaves the Pawn structures so evenly matched that the remainder of the game is reduced to a tug of war. White still retains the minimal initiative of the first move. But, in practical play this is not sufficient to mean much.

It is important for Black to bear in mind, when playing the Exchange Variation, to avoid symmetry. Symmetrical positions are tricky. They have the earmarks of a dead draw and yet often lead to losing games for the defender. This is because the defender is unable to emulate the aggressor at some point, without risking immediate loss. A line offering good prospects for Black in the Exchange Variation runs as follows: 1 P-K4, P-K3; 2 P-Q4, P-Q4; 3 PxP, PxP; 4 N-KB3, B-Q3; 5 B-Q3, N-QB3; 6 P-B3, KN-K2; 7 O-O, B-KN5; 8 R-K1, Q-Q2; 9 QN-Q2, O-O-O; 10 P-N4, N-N3; 11 N-N3, QR-K1, with chances about even. (Maroczy vs. Spielmann, Bad Sliac, 1932.)

(2) 3 P-K5—a natural looking move, favored by Nimzóvich. Fundamentally, it is intended to usurp the terrain in the center, with White's Pawn at K5 serving as a bridgehead. Its advantages, however, are counterbalanced by disadvantages. To begin with, the time lost in moving the Pawn to K5 can be utilized to develop a piece. This, of course, is only of minor significance. More important is the fact that the bridgehead (the Pawn on K5) and its supporting props are subject to attack directly and from the wings, which will leave it in a precarious state.

On the other hand, if the Pawn at K5 can be successfully maintained, Black's position will be cramped and White may retain excellent attacking chances. The issue is drawn along these lines.

An example of this line runs as follows: 1 P-K4, P-K3; 2 P-Q4, P-Q4; 3 P-K5, P-QB4; 4 P-QB3, N-QB3; 5 N-KB3, Q-N3 (observe Black's pressure on White's Q4, which supports the bridgehead); 6 B-K2, PxP; 7 PxP, KN-K2; 8 P-QN3, N-B4; 9

B-N2, B-N5*ch;* *10* K-B1, P-KR4; *11* P-KR4, B-Q2; *12* N-B3, BxN; *13* BxB, R-QB1, with a better game for Black. In this instance, the bridgehead is still there. But White's King has been forced to move and White's general development is inferior to Black's.

The Nimzóvich Attack can also be played as a gambit, thus: *1* P-K4, P-K3; *2* P-Q4, P-Q4; *3* P-K5, P-QB4; *4* N-KB3, N-QB3; *5* B-Q3, PxP. In this line, White's plan is to maintain the Pawn at K5 at all costs, exploit the advantage of terrain to the full and attempt to recover the Pawn with the better position, as a last resort. With correct play, however, Black has little difficulty in maintaining equality.

(*3*) *3* N-Q2 — Tarrasch's favorite. This line will be discussed in Chapter 9.

3 . . . . **N-KB3**

This provocative move assists Black's development and puts pressure on White's King Pawn. *3* . . . B-N5, favored by Botvinnik, will be discussed in Chapter 8.

4 **B-N5** . . . .

White pins the Knight and threatens *5* BxN to disrupt Black's Pawn formation. For Black must guard his Queen Pawn with his Queen.

Here again, *4* P-K5 has been played with moderate success. Yet, after *4* P-K5, KN-Q2, White's pressure in the center is gone and Black undermines White's King Pawn with a ceaseless bombardment of White's Q4 via . . . P-QB4, . . . N-QB3 and . . . Q-N3. To boot, a direct clash with a properly timed . . . P-KB3 will wipe out White's entire center.

$$4 . . . .\quad \textbf{B-K2}$$

Black breaks the pin and once again threatens White's King Pawn.

A more adventurous line for Black is 4 . . . B-N5, known as the McCutcheon Variation. Oddly enough, this line is dangerous for both sides, and its intricacies require special study.

$$5\ \textbf{P-K5} . . . .$$

There is no good way for White to maintain tension in the center any longer. That is why he now advances his King Pawn. For instance, if 5 B-Q3, PxP; 6 NxP, NxN; 7 BxB, QxB; 8 BxN, Q-N5ch, followed by 9 . . . QxNP, Black gains a Pawn.

The end of the tension is the signal for White to exploit to the full his gain of terrain and whatever other minor pluses he can accumulate. For now Black intends to hammer away at White's Pawn chain, and White must engage in other compensating actions.

$$5 . . . .\quad \textbf{KN-Q2}$$

While, in effect, the text move is a retreat, it is by no means without prospects. At Q2, the Knight bears on White's King Pawn. While the Pawn is adequately protected, its support may be unhinged as the game progresses. When, as and if the support is unhinged, the Knight at Q2 will be exerting pressure on White's King Pawn.

The more aggressive 5 . . . N-K5 is met by 6 NxN. If then 6 . . . BxB; 7 NxB, QxN; 8 P-KN3, followed by P-KB4, White's position is superior. Or if 6 NxN, PxN; 7 BxB, QxB; 8 Q-K2, Black's Pawns are structurally weaker.

6 BxB   QxB

This exchange of Bishops weakens the black squares. Naturally, when Bishops which control black squares are removed from the board, the reinforcement of the squares by the absent Bishops is impossible.

Since, however, a White and Black Bishop are swapped, who stands to gain? In this instance, White stands to gain. During the future course of the game, Black's normal play calls for the demolishing of White's Pawn center. To accomplish this, Black must play . . . P-QB4. Just as soon as this move is made, there is a vulnerable square at Black's Q3 to which a White Knight may penetrate. Moreover, when White's Queen Pawn is exchanged, White can place a Knight at Q4—a black square—and dominate a good portion of the board.

Following this thought one step further, why should Black

play . . . P-QB4 when it involves him in disadvantages? The answer is that unless Black does so, he will be more or less compelled to mark time. Then White will continue with a King-side onslaught, which is apt to be successful. Strict passivity is likely to land Black in an unbearable squeeze, with no hope of counter play.

7 P-B4 . . . .

To bolster the center and begin an attack, after the pieces are brought out, with P-KN4 and P-KB5 and a breakthrough to the Black Monarch.

7 . . . . O-O

This is the most active continuation for Black. It is a prelude to a head-on clash of the center Pawns which will follow in due course.

The slower positional line is 7 . . . P-QR3, intending . . . P-QB4. Observe that 7 . . . P-QB4 will not do at once because of the reply, 8 N-N5, threatening 9 N-B7ch to win the exchange, and also 9 N-Q6ch, discombobulating the Black King position. Black squares!

The positional line also results in White's favor. E.g., 7 . . . P-QR3; 8 N-B3, P-QB4; 9 PxP, N-QB3; 10 N-K2! (heading for Q4—black square!), QxP; 11 Q-Q2, P-QN4; 12 QN-Q4, NxN; 13 NxN, N-N3; 14 P-QN3, B-Q2; 15 Q-K3! R-QB1; 16 B-Q3, with a plus for White. White's centralized Knight (on a black square) and the prospects of a successful Pawn storm of the King-side rule in his favor. Black's counterplay is limited. For should he attempt . . . P-B3, to break White's center, Black will be left with a weak King Pawn which will bear constant watching.

8 Q-Q2 . . . .

The purpose of this move is to clear the last rank so that White may castle on the Queen-side. With Kings on opposite sides of the board, White is in position to start an all-out attack against the Black Monarch on the other wing.

As a general rule, a King on the Queen-side is an easier target than one on the King-side. But experience shows this position to be the exception. Most likely because White controls the center and his men are better deployed.

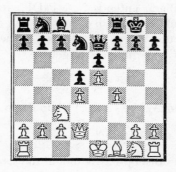

8 . . . . P-QB4

A good and necessary "break," with the intention of undermining White's strong hold on the center. Any delaying tactics would be met by simple development, such as N-B3, followed by B-Q3 and P-KN4, with a powerful attack in the offing.

9 N-B3 N-QB3

Putting more pressure on White's center.

10 O-O-O! . . . .

As per plan. Soon it may be a question of who gets to the adversary's King "fustest with the mostest."

10 . . . . P-B3

To demolish White's center Pawn phalanx in order to free the Black forces for a measure of counterplay. Another way is 10 . . . P-B5, followed by . . . R-QN1 and . . . P-QN4, and a Pawn-storming of the White King position. White can meet this with a demonstration of his own, beginning with P-B5 and followed up with P-KN4. Since White is in control of the center and since his men are better poised for attack, White's chances of success should be greater.

11 PxKBP . . . .

Otherwise, Black intends . . . PxQP, followed by . . . PxKP, after which White will wind up with an isolated King Pawn. After the text move, the opening of the King file leaves Black's King Pawn a permanent target.

11 . . . .   QxP

Black threatens White's King Bishop Pawn.

12 P-KN3 . . . .

Defending the Bishop Pawn and, at the same time, opening new avenues for White's Bishop at KN2 and KR3.

12 . . . .   PxP

In line with the plan to dissolve the opposing center.

13 KNxP   N-B4

Black's position is now free. He suffers, however, from a chronically weak, backward King Pawn.

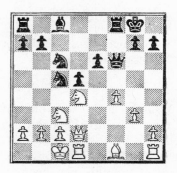

14 B-N2   . . . .

This move makes it difficult for Black to enforce . . . P-K4. It is interesting to note that *14* B-R3 equalizes the game, thus: *14* . . . NxN; *15* QxN, QxQ; *16* RxQ, P-K4; *17* RxP, BxB; *18* RxN, PxP, with an even game in sight.

14 . . . . **B-Q2**

Black clears his first rank so that his Rook can cooperate.

15 **KR-K1** . . . .

Pressure on the weak point.

15 . . . . **QR-B1**

The King Pawn requires no additional defense at present. Black tries therefore, to maintain the balance of position by preparing an attack against the White King.

16 **NxN**   **RxN**

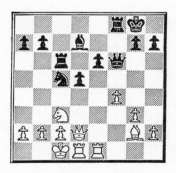

White has the better game, although adroit skill is required to prove a clear-cut advantage. A game, Stahlberg vs. Keres (Kemeri, 1937), continued from this point:

17 BxP, PxB; *18* NxP, Q-R3 (. . . Q-B2 loses to *19* R-K7, Q-B4; *20* R-K5, followed by N-K7*ch*, NxR and RxN); *19* N-K7*ch*, K-R1; *20* NxR, BxN; *21* Q-R5! White picks off another Pawn and the material remains with White having a Rook and three Pawns for two minor pieces. White won the game in 81 moves.

Conclusions

In the Classical Variation of the French Defense, White's immediate gain of the center gives him an edge which is difficult to blunt. With correct play, White should always come out on top, although the onus of finding the correct moves at each turn often proves too great in practical play.

The game in the following Chess Movie illustrates the solidity of White's game in the *Classical Variation* against the French Defense.

Chess Movie

KING PAWN ONE:
KING PAWN NONE!

Tactical thrills excite even the mighty into rash action. The "irresistible" Knight "sac" at Black's 16th in the following game is only a dud. The indomitable skill of the great Akiba Rubinstein shows it up for what it is worth. Levenfish is the victim. The game was played at Carlsbad, 1911. It opens with *1* P-K4, P-K3; *2* P-Q4, P-Q4; *3* N-QB3, N-KB3; *4* B-N5, B-K2; *5* P-K5, KN-Q2; *6* BxB, QxB, reaching diagram *No. 1.*

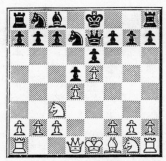

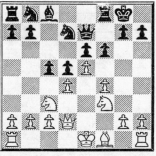

1 The game continues: *7* Q-Q2, O-O; *8* P-B4, P-QB4; *9* N-B3, P-B3. Each side conscientiously follows the prefabricated plan with confidence in his own pattern and a crocodile's concern for the opponent's. Only the grueling test of skill and skull in the arena will be the final judgment.

2 The center dissolves with *10* PxKBP, QxP. Then White defends his KBP with *11* P-KN3. Black develops his Knight, *11 . . .* N-QB3 and *12* O-O-O, P-QR3 follows. Black is preparing a Queen-side Pawn advance. Now comes *13* B-N2, N-N3. Black has more center Pawns. Are they strong or weak?

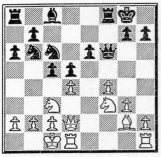

3 It appears that Black's wing demonstration is picking up momentum. This is deceptive. For White's grip on the center checks any undue advance. There follows *14 KR-K1, N-B5; 15 Q-B2, P-QN4.* What does it matter that Black remains with a weak King Pawn—if he checkmates the White King?

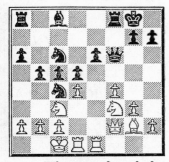

4 White cuts through the Pawn avalanche with *16 PxP.* Now Black follows with his "grand combination." *16 . . . NxP* is the move. White plays *17 KxN,* and there follows *17 . . . P-N5,* recovering the piece . . . Momentarily, it appears that Black is scoring. White's King position is now perforated.

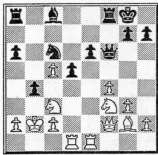

5 The atmosphere clears, however, after *18 N-Q4, PxNch; 19 K -R1.* Black's attack is running out of gas. Moreover, White's extra Bishop Pawn is no idle curiosity. It is a potential threat. And, in the background, Black's chronically weak King Pawn is the strategic target. It will figure in the denouement.

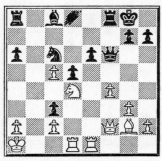

6 Black swaps Knights: *19 . . . NxN.* (What else? The threat was *20 NxP, BxN; 21 RxB, QxR; 22 BxP,* pinning the Queen.) There follows *20 QxN, R-N1; 21 R-K3, P-N4.* Black's Queen Bishop Pawn is doomed, and so Black breaks out in a new spot, to complicate and give White a chance to go wrong.

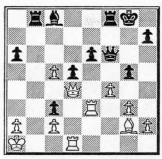

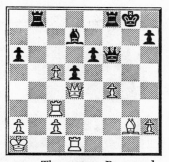

7 White continues simply with *22 RxBP*. There follows *22 . . . PxP; 23 PxP, B-Q2*. (White's KBP is poison. For, after *23 . . . QxP; 24 R-N3ch* is decisive.) Even the semblance of Black's attack has vanished. . . . Now is the time to take stock. White's passed QBP looms large in the reckoning. Now what?

8 The extra Pawn advances: *24 P-B6*. Black swaps Queens: *24 . . . QxQ; 25 RxQ* and retreats his Bishop *25 . . . B-K1*. Can the isolated Bishop Pawn be held? And at what expense? Black's survival depends on the answer to this question. Or is it too late to ask questions? The overt act is done.

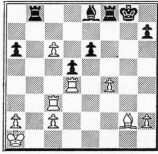

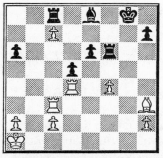

9 The answer is sad! First White molests the weak King Pawn. Observe that weakness will out! *26 B-R3* is the move. Black defends with *26 . . . R-B3*, and there follows *27 P-B7, R-QB1*. Black's defense is hanging by a thread. How much longer can he stand the strain of White's incursion?

10 The penetrating blow is at hand. *28 RxP* is *finis*. In a gesture of despair and hope, Black plays *28 . . . RxQBP*. (He hopes for *29 RxR, PxR*, after which he has a fighting chance.) But White continues *29 BxPch*. Black resigns. Curiously, the weak King Pawn falls at the very end. Poetic justice!

8

French Defense

WINAWER VARIATION

CURRENTLY in vogue is the variation of the French Defense known as the Winawer. It is an early foray of Black's King Bishop to the Queen-side of the board 3 . . . B-N5. Its popularity stems mainly from its use by world champion Botvinnik, whose constant and successful trials of it have attracted innumerable devotees.

By its very nature, the move is suspect. For Black assumes an aggressive post for his Bishop on the third move. Early aggression is part and parcel of White's stock in trade. For Black, it is almost always a violation of the precepts of good strategy.

This defense arises as follows:

$$
\begin{array}{lll}
1 & \text{P-K4} & \text{P-K3} \\
2 & \text{P-Q4} & \text{P-Q4} \\
3 & \text{N-QB3} & \text{B-N5}
\end{array}
$$

The Winawer Variation. By pinning the Knight, Black exerts pressure on the center and attempts to maintain equilibrium. Incidentally, Black threatens to capture White's King Pawn.

The one theoretical drawback of the move is that it practically commits Black to the eventual exchange of Bishop for Knight. Since a Bishop is minutely better than a Knight, this may wind up in White's favor.

4 P-K5 . . . .

The sharpest continuation. White establishes a salient in Black's territory, risking its collapse by counter-blows. Center tension is relaxed and, in turn, White emphasizes his gain in terrain. Note, for instance, the great sweep of both of White's Bishops and of White's Queen—how easily they can operate on the King-side of the board.

On the other hand, White's Pawn structure is now more vulnerable than Black's. Black enjoys a natural break with . . . P-QB4.

The issue is drawn along these lines.

Alternatives with the idea of maintaining the center tension are tricky. They run as follows:

(1) 4 N-K2. This involves the sacrifice of a Pawn. 4 . . . PxP; 5 P-QR3, B-K2; 6 NxP, N-QB3; 7 B-K3, N-B3; 8 KN-B3, O-O; 9 N-N3, P-QN3; 10 B-K2, B-N2; 11 O-O, Q-Q2; 12 Q-Q2, QR-Q1; 13 KR-Q1, Q-B1. White still retains a slight lead. This is from the fifth game of the match, Alekhine—Euwe, 1935.

(1a) 5 . . . BxNch; 6 NxB, P-KB4; 7 B-KB4, N-KB3; 8 Q-Q2, O-O; 9 O-O-O, N-R4; 10 B-B4, N-QB3; 11 P-B3, PxP; 12 PxP, NxB; 13 QxN. White's superior development and prospects of attack on the open King Knight file outweigh the Pawn minus.

(2) 4 P-QR3, BxNch; 5 PxB, PxP; 6 Q-N4, N-KB3; 7 QxNP, R-N1; 8 Q-R6, P-B4. Chances and counter-chances are rife. The position is wide open, and White still has the lead.

White can also play 4 PxP and convert the opening into one similar to the Exchange Variation of the French. Because of the balanced Pawn position, however, the prospects of inject-ing vitality are slim, and this method can not be termed an at-tempt at refutation.

4 . . . . P-QB4

The usual and essential counter-threat. Failure to attack White's center, either now or later, results in a one-sided game, with all the play on White's side. Pointless moves by Black will permit White to build up with, say, B-Q3, P-KB4, N-KB3, P-KN4 and P-KB5, resulting in a powerful attack. Hence, Black must engage White in the center action to forestall any such contingency.

The counter-thrust, however, may be deferred. Instead of the text move, Black may continue with 4 . . . N-K2, first. The point is that White is threatening Q-N4, aiming at Black's King Knight Pawn. It isn't easy for Black to defend the Pawn, with-out incurring a weakness or resorting to a counter-combination.

Consequently, 4 . . . N-K2 anticipates Q-N4. For Q-N4 would be meaningless, if Black could reply to it simply by castling. Q-N4 may be good if, in order to defend the King Knight Pawn, Black must move his King and so forfeit the privilege of castling, or if he must advance the King Knight Pawn and so perforate his King-side Pawn position.

But 4 . . . N-K2 does not engage White in the center soon enough and consequently has other disadvantages. Against 4 . . . N-K2, the game might continue: 5 P-QR3, B-R4; 6 P-QN4, B-N3; 7 N-R4, B-Q2; 8 P-QB3, with a better game for White.

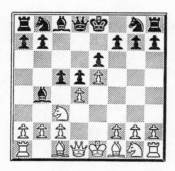

5 **P-QR3** . . . .

It is important to "put the question" to the Bishop at the earliest convenient opportunity.

5 . . . . **PxP**

5 . . . BxN*ch* is also tenable, although, after 6 PxB, White's strong center and two Bishops should leave him with the advantage.

6 **PxB**   **PxN**

7 Q-N4! . . . .

In effect, White is now playing a gambit, with a Pawn minus. Evidently, however, his prospects are superior. For White manages to win most of the games where Black tries to pin on to the Pawn, with 7 . . . PxP.

On the other hand, 7 PxP is the game Em. Lasker — Maroczy, New York, 1924, which favored Black (and which White won!). This game continued: 7 . . . Q-B2; 8 N-B3, N-K2; 9 B-Q3, N-N3; 10 O-O, N-Q2; 11 R-K1, QxBP.

7 . . . . P-KN3

7 . . . K-B1, forfeiting the privilege of castling, is hardly better. The text move leaves holes in Black's King-side Pawn structure.

8 N-B3 . . . .

Protecting the King Pawn and now threatening to recapture the Pawn minus.

8 . . . . Q-B2

White's superior development, plus his two Bishops, makes it imperative for Black to eye material advantages, even though he can hardly afford the time to acquire more material. A sorry state!

9 B-Q3 . . . .

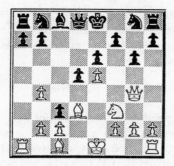

Protecting the Queen Bishop Pawn, so that, if Black captures . . . PxP, the Queen Bishop Pawn will be defended. Moreover, the Bishop is pointing in the direction of Black's King-side for future reference.

9 . . . . N-QB3

Black must continue his development. If he stops for, say, 9 . . . PxP, then 10 BxP leaves Black's development lagging to a point where he will be unable to prevent some serious penetrations. White can open the position wide with P-QB4. Then the absence of Black's Bishop controlling the black squares will stick out like a sore thumb. Observe, particularly, that White can continue with P-N5, followed by B-R3, after which the Bishop enjoys a terrific sweep of the diagonal.

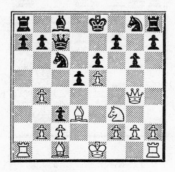

10 O-O . . . .

White can defend the King Pawn, if he so desires, by *10 Q-KB4*. He prefers not to, for he rightly feels that Black will not have the time to go Pawn-grabbing. Therefore, he continues his development.

10 . . . . KN-K2

You might inquire, however, why not *10 . . . NxKP?* Black might as well be hanged for a sheep as for a lamb. If *10 . . . NxKP; 11 NxN, QxN; 12 B-KB4*, observe that both of White's Bishops are operating, that White's Queen is well posted, that White is castled and that Black hasn't a single piece out, other than his Queen. Given such a position, you know that White must have something, that it is up to you to find it. You will not necessarily be able to win on the following move, but you can continue to make it uncomfortable for Black to the point where he will be unable to put up resistance. One thing, however, you must bear in mind. The basis of your advantage is the possibility of an attack. Hence, you must not swap Queens, unless, of course, you can win a piece in doing so. For your Queen is the most important piece in any brewing attack. Experiment with this position for some time and you will convince yourself how easy it is to bring matters to a head.

11 R-K1   . . . .

White defends the King Pawn. By the same reasoning as before, you might inquire, why defend the King Pawn, why not let it go? To begin with, your Rook defends the King Pawn not only for the sake of the Pawn but also because it operates well on the open King file. Moreover, as Black catches up in his development, the sacrifice of additional material is apt to be unsound.

11 . . . . **B-Q2**

Black is still intent on catching up his laggard development. Yes, he can toy with the tainted *11 . . .* PxP; but after *12* QBxP, his defensive chores are more difficult and his means possibly inadequate under any circumstances.

12 **PxP**   *. . . .*

Now White retrieves his Pawn in order to free his Queen Bishop for action.

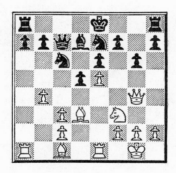

White is for choice.

There is no safety for the Black Monarch on either wing. For instance, if *12 . . .* O-O, White infiltrates with *13* Q-N5, followed by *14* Q-R6, *15* N-N5 or *15* B-N5-B6. Black has no adequate defense.

A game Bogolyubov–Danielsson, Zoppot, 1935, continued as follows: *12 . . .* O-O-O; *13* P-N5, N-QN1; *14* Q-N4, B-K1;

15 B-N5, R-Q2; *16* RxP, Q-N3; *17* R-R8, Q-Q1; *18* N-Q4, P-R3; *19* B-B6, R-N1; *20* P-N6, *Resigns.*

Conclusions

The Winawer Variation of the French Defense has enjoyed a measure of success in tournament practice. This is based not so much on its theoretical accuracy, but rather on its practical exponent, Mikhail Botvinnik, chess champion of the world.

This much can be said in its favor. The patterns which evolve are different and call for sharp play on White's part.

Chess Movie

THE SQUIRM WILL TURN

Sᴛᴏᴜᴛ heart does not a chessplayer make. But it saves many a game! Many a Black would throw in the towel with Ragozin's position at move 22. But not Ragozin! Out of nothing, he fabricates a mating net, and poor Lilienthal is enmeshed. The game was played in Moscow in 1944. It opens with: *1* P-K4, P-K3; *2* P-Q4, P-Q4; *3* N-QB3, B-N5; *4* P-K5, P-QB4 (*see diagram No. 1*).

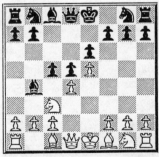

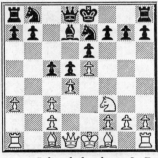

1 There follows 5 P-QR3, BxN*ch;* 6 PxB, N-K2; 7 N-B3, B-Q2. Lilienthal will try to capitalize his stronger center, his two Bishops and the greater terrain. Ragozin will pin on to the superior Pawn position. Each player will have his day in court, and judgment will be rendered under due process.

2 Lilienthal plays 8 P-QR4. He hopes to decoy Black forces to the mangy Pawn. The game continues . . . Q-R4; 9 B-Q2, P-B5. The board has been rent in two. The King-side belongs to White; the Queen-side is Black's. And Black is ready to collect Pawnence! The isolated Pawn is doomed.

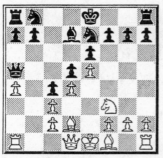

3   White prepares the entry of his King Bishop with *10* P-N3, and Black fortifies himself with . . . B-B3. Then follows *11* B-R3, N-Q2; *12* O-O, N-QN3. Black is making assurance triply sure; the Queen Rook Pawn will not escape. That, however, is old stuff. What goes on the other side?

4   White continues with *13* N-R4, and Black plays . . . NxP. Now White plays *14* P-B4, planning a break-through on that wing, which Black checks with . . . P-KN3. Or does he? White follows through with *15* P-B5. He must make progress at all cost. Yet can this sacrifice be progress?

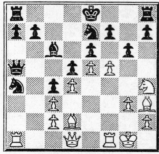

5   Black captures *15* . . . KPxP, and now comes the point. White plays *16* P-N4! There is no way for Black to prevent the opening of a file and a diagonal. Black hies himself to the other side of the board with *16* . . . O-O-O, and there follows *17* PxP, PxP. One Pawn is coming home. Then what?

6   There follows *18* NxP, NxN; *19* BxNch, K-N1; *20* B-R3, QR-KB1. The atmosphere has cleared somewhat. Black is a Pawn plus. Black's King Bishop Pawn, however, is an easy target, and White has all the play. If Black's King Bishop Pawn falls, White's King Pawn will assume a stellar role.

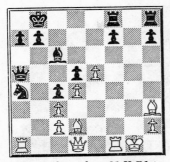

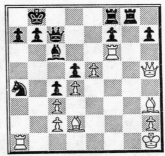

7 White plays *21 K-R1* to get out of any counter checks. Black plays . . . KR-N1. Then follows *22 Q-R5, Q-B2; 23 R-B6??* (after *23 B-B4*, Black could hardly survive). To all intents and appearances, White is progressing rapidly. Is he not hammering away at Black's weaknesses?

8 Now comes a surreptitious surprise. Black replies *23 . . . N-B4!* White captures *24 PxN*, and then continues . . . *P-Q5ch*. White interposes *25 R-B3*, and there follows: *25 . . . P-B3; 26 P-K6*. Even now, White appears reasonably happy. But he reckons without his host. He is soon rudely awakened.

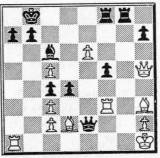

9 *26 . . . Q-K4* is the sockdolager. White cannot afford to swap Queens, nor can he afford not to! He plays *27 B-N4*, and the game continues . . . *P-B4; 28 B-R3, Q-K7*. How the picture has changed in a few short moves. A moment ago, Black was on the run. Now White barely manages to keep going.

10 White continues with *29 B-B4ch*, and Black replies . . . K-R1. Then White plays *30 R-KB1*. Again, it seems that White is coming out on top. But Black puts an end to all conjecture with *30 . . . R-N5*, cutting the communication between the Queen and Rook. Nought is to be done. White resigns.

9

French Defense

TARRASCH VARIATION

THERE is another way of treating the French Defense. It is to play N-Q2 on White's third move. This method may well be labeled Tarrasch's line, after its leading exponent of several decades ago. Even today, however, the line is in vogue.

While the Classical and Winawer Variations lead to academic pluses for White, they are beset with practical problems. In the Classical, for instance, White is compelled to lock the center comparatively early and absorb pummeling blows in his own mid-section. In the Winawer, White must submit to an annoying, even though innocuous pin. By maintaining a fluid center and avoiding the pin, the Tarrasch aims to retain the good features of the other variations and discard the bad ones.

This line arises as follows:

1	**P-K4**	**P-K3**
2	**P-Q4**	**P-Q4**
3	**N-Q2**	. . . .

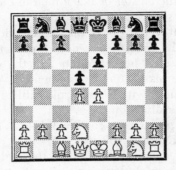

The Tarrasch. White protects his King Pawn via N-Q2, instead of N-QB3, averts the annoying pin *3* . . . B-N5 and keeps open the fortifying move of P-QB3, in the event it is necessary.

Its main drawback is that the Knight at Q2 fails to exert pressure on Black's Queen Pawn, which, in turn, gives Black more leeway than in the other variations. The temporary blockade of White's Queen Bishop is of minor significance. In many variations the Queen Bishop does not take an active part in the early play; in others, the Knight clears the path when necessary.

3 . . . . **P-QB4**

Because White's Queen Knight is not bearing down on Black's Queen Pawn and because White's Queen is also obstructed in its view of the Queen file, Black can afford to intensify the center tension with the text move. If White's Queen Knight were at B3, Black's Queen Pawn would become a comparatively easy target.

Another way for Black is *3* . . . N-KB3, as in the Classical. This line might pursue the following course, taken from a game Alekhine—Capablanca, AVRO, 1938: *4* P-K5, KN-Q2; *5* B-Q3, P-QB4; *6* P-QB3, N-QB3; *7* N-K2, Q-N3; *8* N-B3, PxP; *9* PxP, B-N5*ch;* *10* K-B1, B-K2; *11* P-QR3, N-B1; *12* P-QN4, B-Q2; *13* B-K3, N-Q1; *14* N-B3, P-QR4; *15* N-R4, Q-R2; *16* P-N5, P-N3; *17* P-N3, P-B4; *18* K-N2, with a far superior game for White. Observe the cluster of Black men in the center and the disunity of Black's forces.

Note also that White locks the center with *4* P-K5, as in the Classical. The main difference, however, between this line and the Classical is that White has the move P-QB3 in reserve to fortify his center. Consequently, White is able to maintain the center with Pawns and utilize his pieces for advantage in other directions.

A somewhat irregular try for Black is *3* . . . N-QB3. Then might follow *4* KN-B3, N-B3; *5* P-K5, N-Q2, with advantage for White. Here again, White takes the rigid center, since Black is unable to crack down upon it with the usual . . . P-QB4, at least until he makes adequate preparations.

4 KPxP   . . . .

The point of this move is to leave Black a comparative choice of evils. *4* KN-B3 is also good, but more complicated.

4 . . . .   KPxP

This results in an isolated Pawn for Black. After *4* . . . QxP, however, White continues in gambit fashion with KN-B3

and gains the lead in development. If then, for example, 5 . . .
PxP; 6 B-B4, followed by 7 O-O; 8 Q-K2; 9 N-N3; and, if
necessary, 10 R-Q1 and the recovery of the Pawn with a
powerful position. Should Black attempt to hold the Pawn
with . . . P-K4, he will fail. For his King Pawn as well as
his King will become exposed.

Black, of course, need not accept the gambit Pawn. The
game might be played as follows: 4 . . . QxP; 5 KN-B3, N-
QB3; 6 B-B4, Q-Q1; 7 N-N3. But it is clear that White gains
a substantial lead in development.

5 B-N5ch . . . .

Usually a check of this nature is to be discounted. For
White's Bishop is better deployed in some attack, rather than
a positional pin.

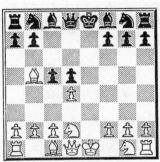

Here there is a point to the check. Since Black is going
to be left with an isolated Queen Pawn, White has already
established his advantage. Now he does not mind swapping:
the more he swaps, the less opportunity will there be for Black
of gaining compensation for the defect in his Pawn structure.

White has no intention, of course, of an immediate swap
which reinforces the isolani. Nor does he intend to trade
Bishop for Knight, without some gain in return.

5 . . . . N-B3
6 Q-K2ch . . . .

Pursuing the plan of leading to an endgame in which Black suffers from an isolated Queen Pawn.

6 . . . .   Q-K2

Practically forced. If 6 . . . B-K2; 7 PxP and White can maintain the Pawn plus. If 6 . . . B-K3; 7 KN-B3, and White threatens 8 PxP, followed by 9 N-N3 and 10 QN-Q4, with terrific pressure against Black's Queen Knight and Queen Bishop. Black will experience difficulty warding this off.

7 PxP   QxQch

Otherwise, White will defend and retain the extra Pawn.

8 NxQ   BxP

Now White enjoys a handsome lead in development. This, plus Black's isolated Pawn rules in White's favor. The only thing that might be said for Black is that he experiences more freedom than is usual for Black.

9 N-QN3   B-N3

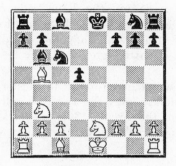

10 QN-Q4 . . . .

A game Euwe—Botvinnik, World's Championship, The Hague, 1948, continued with *10* B-Q2 and resulted in a draw, after particularly alert defense on the part of Botvinnik.

The text move is consonant with the theme of White's opening play, which is pressure, direct or otherwise, against Black's Queen Pawn. Euwe's *10* B-Q2 appears to be too labored.

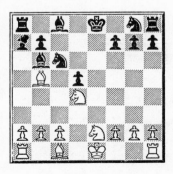

White is for choice. He might continue with *11 B-KB4*, followed by *12 O-O-O*, and then pile up on Black's Queen Pawn. This he can do by doubling Rooks on the Queen file and/or swinging his King Bishop to QN3.

Conclusions

In the main variation, the Black side of the Tarrasch leaves much to be desired by Black. Saddled with an isolated Pawn in what is virtually an endgame, the prospects are decidely uninviting even though Black may be able to eke out a draw.

Unless some way can be found to bolster Black's play in the main or subsidiary lines, the Tarrasch will compel masters to shy away from the French. The spectacle of the isolani, however, should not instill fear in others than masters.

Chess Movie

CAPA COMES A CROPPER

WEAKNESS will out. It will assert itself in the remotest corners of the board, far removed from the intrinsic defect. Thus Capablanca's weak Queen Bishop Pawn makes him fall prey to Keres' King-side assault on the other wing at the fabulous AVRO Tournament of 1938. The game begins with: *1 P-K4, P-K3; 2 P-Q4, P-Q4; 3 N-Q2, P-QB4; 4 KPxP, KPxP* (*see diagram No. 1*).

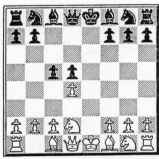 

1 There follows *5 KN-B3, N-QB3; 6 B-N5, Q-K2ch*. Capablanca (Black) wishes to swap Queens. Even he has a healthy respect for Keres' flamboyant nature. But the wily Keres will not swap. *7 B-K2* is the move. True, the Queen Pawn is inadequately defended. That doesn't matter. Capa plays *7 . . . PxP*.

2 Keres plays *8 O-O*, and Capa replies . . . Q-B2. He will not leave his Queen in the crossfire of a White Rook at King square. The game continues *9 N-N3, B-Q3; 10 QNxP*, and White has retrieved his Pawn. The threat is now N-N5. Capa parries: *10 . . . P-QR3*. Then comes *11 P-QN3, KN-K2*.

3 Keres now usurps the long diagonal with *12 B-N2*, and the game continues . . . O-O; *13* NxN. Keres consolidates Black's Pawns, only to create a target in the new cluster. There follows . . . PxN; *14* P-B4, B-K3; *15* Q-B2, PxP; *16* BxBP, BxB; *17* QxB. The QP has become an isolated BP.

4 Capa seeks scope for his men and plays *17* . . . KR-N1. There follows *18* P-KR3, R-N4; *19* QR-B1, R-QB1. Capa believes in over-protection of weak spots. Now comes *20* KR-Q1, N-N3; *21* N-Q4. The target is under fire and requires additional support. A good Pawn is at stake.

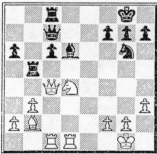

5 Capa defends with *21* . . . R-N3, and then comes a bombastic surprise with *22* N-K6. The Knight is immune, and it is headed for the Black King. Capa replies . . . Q-N1, and there follows *23* N-N5, R-N2; *24* Q-KN4. The scene of combat has changed. Keres is focusing his attention on the King.

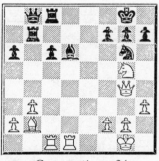

6 Capa continues *24* . . . B-B5, and Keres replies *25* R-B4. Capa's Rook again pops up with . . . R-N4. In the background is the isolated Pawn, for future reference if need be. At hand is a concealed sockdolager, *26* NxBP! Now the barrier to the monarch is broken down. Soon the men will penetrate.

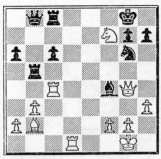

7 Capa plays *26* . . . R-K1, and Keres follows with *27* P-N3. Capa continues . . . Q-B1, and a general exchange ensues: *28* RxB, QxQ; *29* RxQ, KxN. Oddly enough, the isolated Pawn is to blame for Black's loss on the other wing. And it still remains to be attacked. But first, Keres can pick up another Pawn.

8 Keres plays *30* R-Q7*ch*, and Capa interposes . . . R-K2. Keres swaps Rooks: *31* RxR*ch*, KxR, and then he swipes the second Pawn: *32* BxP. The rest is the law of inertia. Capa in motion cannot stop; otherwise he might resign. For two Pawns minus is not a death warrant. It is death.

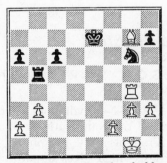

9 Now come the feeble gestures. Capa plays *32* . . . R-QR4, and Keres defends with *33* P-QR4. Capa replies with . . . R-QB4, and Keres with *34* R-N4. Capa continues: *34* . . . K-K3. To the bitter end, the spectators expect a miracle from the former world champion. It is not to be.

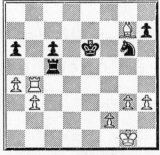

10 Keres gets down to business. The mopping-up operation was a success. Now for the finishing touches. *35* K-N2 is the move. Capa replies . . . P-KR4. There follows *36* R-QB4, RxR; *37* PxR, K-Q3; *38* P-B4, and the invincible Cuban resigns. And the isolated Pawn is still there!

10

Sicilian Defense

THE MODERN DRAGON VARIATION

The Sicilian Defense, *1* P-K4, P-QB4—a half hold on the center—is the most aggressive of all the comparatively sound defenses at Black's command. From its very beginning, an unbalanced Pawn formation arises, which gives opportunity to both contestants to explore advantages in different directions. The result is unabated action.

The favored line of the Sicilian is known as the "Dragon" Variation. Its name cannot be traced with certainty but is most likely derived from Black's Pawn pattern in the early stages of play—as seen here, it most definitely forms a serpentine outline.

The Sicilian dates from Polerio, 1590. Receiving scant attention in its incipience, its popularity rose with the celebrated MacDonnell—Labourdonnais match of 1834 and the Staunton—St. Amant match of 1843. The great London tournament of 1851 marked the occasion of its first practical test, after which it was relegated to limbo. Since then, it has been revived on and off with intermittent success, and its present rating is on the ascent.

The "Dragon" arises as follows:

1 P-K4   P-QB4

The Sicilian Defense. The move 1 . . . P-QB4 incorporates a number of ideas. To begin with, it avoids symmetry in the Pawn pattern. Thus, instead of the tedious attempt to neutralize White's initiative, it is an independent action and calls for original planning on the part of the aggressor.

Theoretically, as between White's first move and Black's, White enjoys the edge. White's Pawn at K4 strikes at Q5 and KB5—a center and a near-center square—and Black's Pawn at QB4 strikes at Q5 and QN5—a center and a non-center square. So White's move is more dominating. Yet Black's has its point. To all intents and purposes, it divides the board in two: White commands the King's wing and Black, the Queen's. As the Kings abide on the King-side, Black's plan is to check any undue aggression there and expand on the far side, where he often gains an endgame advantage. For the same reason, however, White dominates the more vital terrain.

2 N-KB3 . . . .

A good developing move with an eye to supporting the following move of P-Q4. The immediate 2 P-Q4 will not do because of . . . PxP; 3 QxP, N-QB3, gaining a valuable tempo for Black.

The ancient alternative, 2 P-QB3, with a view to establishing a Pawn center, is of doubtful merit. For, after 2 P-QB3, Black can reply . . . P-Q4 and obtain a free and easy game. As a rule, Black cannot play . . . P-Q4 in the early stages of play for then White captures PxP and, on . . . QxP, gains time by attacking the Queen with N-QB3. Once White plays P-QB3, however, and preempts the square QB3, Black can safely play . . . P-Q4. For he no longer need fear N-QB3 and the loss of the tempo.

Another way of continuing is 2 N-QB3. This, however, is not a sharp attempt to obtain minute advantages out of the opening. It is the prelude to a slow, positional, planned development which can be met by an equally good counter-development. The resulting position leads to an even game, thus: 2 N-QB3, N-QB3; 3 P-KN3, P-KN3; 4 B-N2, B-N2; 5 P-Q3, P-K3; 6 B-K3, Q-R4; 7 N-K2, N-Q5; 8 O-O, N-K2; 9 K-R1, O-O; 10 P-QR3, KN-B3; 11 R-QN1, P-Q3; 12 P-QN4, Q-Q1; 13 Q-Q2, R-N1; 14 B-N5, Q-K1.

2 . . . . P-Q3

At this point, Black has a choice of moves, among which are the usual 2 . . . N-QB3 and the less usual 2 . . . N-KB3. These moves, however, may involve Black as the butt of a particularly critical attack, for example, the Richter Attack after 2 . . . N-QB3. Hence the modern text move, which enables Black to reach a comparatively sound and promising development, without much ado.

3 P-Q4 . . . .

White's plan is to nullify any hold which Black exercises on White's Q4 and, at the same time, maintain and build up his own grip on the center. In doing this, however, he makes a somewhat uneven exchange. He swaps his Queen Pawn—a good center Pawn—for Black's Bishop Pawn—not a center Pawn. Insofar as White's hold on the center is enhanced, the move is good. Over the long term, Black's extra center Pawn should stand him in good stead. Consequently, White's plan is to capitalize his advantage—greater control of the center and terrain—in the near future. Whereas Black attempts to neutralize White's advantage and remain with the extra center Pawn. These considerations are germane to the text move.

Again, White cannot very well build up a Pawn center with 3 P-QB3, to be followed by P-Q4. For, if 3 P-QB3, N-KB3, White's unguarded King Pawn requires an awkward defense—if his Queen Pawn is slated for Q4.

3 . . . .   PxP

White threatens 4 PxP, PxP; 5 QxQch, denying Black the privilege of castling. Since there is no other good way of preventing this, Black exchanges.

Certain advantages, however, accrue to Black from the exchange. First, he swaps an inferior Pawn for a superior one. Also, he opens his Queen Bishop file for future use.

4 NxP . . . .

Not *4* QxP, as . . . N-QB3 gains a tempo.

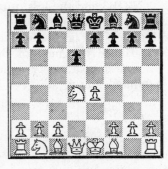

4 . . . . N-KB3!

An important interpolation. The text move is not just a developing move. It is *the* developing move. Any other may involve Black in serious positional difficulties. It is necessary to understand the reason for this.

White's mainstay in the center is his King Pawn. If this falls or is exchanged or if Black establishes a strong Pawn of his own in the center, then White's control vanishes—while Black remains with an extra center Pawn. So Black eyes the possibility of . . . P-Q4, constantly. Technically, however, *4* . . . P-Q4 is impossible. If *4* . . . P-Q4, then *5* PxP, QxP; *6* N-QB3, and White is too far ahead in development. But Black must keep the possibility open. If he continues with any move, say *4* . . . P-KN3, White replies with *5* P-QB4 and closes the chance of . . . P-Q4 forever more. If White succeeds, moreover, in playing P-QB4, he nullifies all the pressure which Black hopes to exert on his own, open Queen Bishop file. The text move precludes the possibility of P-QB4 for White, under favorable circumstances, and keeps White constantly on guard against a Black . . . P-Q4.

5 N-QB3 . . . .

This blocks the move P-QB4. Black need no longer concern himself over that possibility.

There are, indeed, other ways for White to protect his King Pawn and still retain the option of playing P-QB4. But they leave much to be desired. For instance, if 5 P-KB3, P-K4; 6 N-N5, P-QR3; 7 N/5-B3, B-K3, and there is no good way of preventing 8 . . . P-Q4. Thus, if 8 N-Q5, NxN; 9 PxN, B-Q2, Black's Pawn pattern is better.

Note that 6 . . . P-Q4 will not do: 7 PxP, NxP; 8 QxN, QxQ; 9 N-B7*ch*, and a full piece accrues to White.

5 . . . .   P-KN3

The Dragon Variation. Black intends to fianchetto his King Bishop and so dominate the long diagonal throughout the center of the board.

Observe here that Black cannot play 5 . . . P-Q4. For, after 6 PxP, NxP; 7 B-N5*ch,* Black has no good move.

6 B-K2   . . . .

A good post for the Bishop. For it clears the path for cas-tling and prevents Black from playing . . . N-N5 later on. Of course, 6 . . . N-N5 is meaningless. But, in some contin-gencies, say when White develops his Queen Bishop at K3, the move may be purposeful.

6 P-KN3, followed by 7 B-N2 is also good for White, inas-much as it practically prevents . . . P-Q4 for all time.

Another possibility is 6 P-B4 in attempt to refute Black's

formation by storm. In that case, Black must play carefully, for a misstep will be fatal. Thus, if *6 P-B4*, best is *6 . . . N-B3*. Then, if *7 NxN, PxN; 8 P-K5, N-Q2*, Black's position is tenable. The following gamelet is indicative of what can happen when Black goes astray; *6 P-B4, B-N2?; 7 P-K5, PxP; 8 PxP, N-Q4; 9 B-N5ch, K-B1; 10 O-O, BxP; 11 B-R6ch, K-N1; 12 NxN, QxN; 13 N-B5! Q-B4ch; 14 K-R1, Q-B2; 15 B-QB4, BxN; 16 RxB, B-B3*, and White mates in five! —*17 Q-Q5, P-K3; 18 QxKP, PxQ; 19 BxPch, Q-B2; 20 RxB* and mate next move (Horowitz — Carrigan, simultaneous exhibition).

6	**B-N2**
7 **O-O**	**O-O**

Development goes on apace. Black now threatens to get the better game with *8 . . . P-Q4*.

8 **N-N3**	. . . .

To clear the Queen file so Black is unable to play . . . P-Q4.

8	**N-B3**

Developing—so as not to interfere with the mobility of the other men.

9 **P-B4**	. . . .

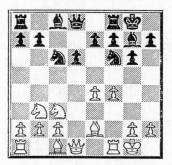

Preparing for a King-side Pawn assault and also making way for *10* B-B3 to prevent . . . P-Q4. In this way, White sews up control of the center.

9 . . . . P-QR3

So that Black's Queen can establish a haven at Black's QB2 without fear of being molested by a White Knight at its QN5. Also, Black is preparing a Queen-side Pawn advance for the future.

It is possible for Black to play 9 . . . P-QN4 without losing a Pawn. This, however, is a somewhat involved combination. Thus, if *9* . . . P-QN4; *10* BxP, NxP! whatever piece White captures, Black is able to recover with *11* . . . Q-N3*ch*. White, however, retains the better game simply with *10* B-B3.

10 B-B3   Q-B2

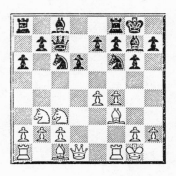

White is for choice because of his control of the center, though play is extremely difficult for both sides.

White's further plan may consist of a King-side Pawn assault, beginning with P-N4. This is perilous, however, in the event that it miscarries. White may occupy Q5 or the open Queen file or try to utilize all the different advantages in conjunction with each other.

Black has prospects on the open Queen Bishop file, after developing his Queen Bishop either at Q2 or K3. He may maneuver a Knight to QB5, where it exerts a bind on the Queen-side, and follow with a Queen-side Pawn advance.

Conclusions

The Modern Dragon Variation of the Sicilian Defense offers Black about as good prespects as Black can expect in any line. While, theoretically White is for choice, practically, the onus of proving the advantage rests on White, and a misstep can be fatal—to White.

Chess Movie
CLASH OF CHAMPIONS!

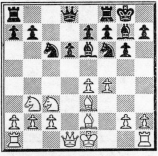

W HEN the irresistible Alekhine meets the immovable Botvinnik, what happens? Chaos? . . . No, just a rollicking jamboree, with chessmen being blown to the four winds. This game between world champion Alekhine and the future world champion Botvinnik was played at Nottingham, 1936. It opens with *1* P-K4, P-QB4; *2* N-KB3, P-Q3; *3* P-Q4, PxP; *4* NxP, N-KB3; *5* N-QB3, P-KN3; *6* B-K2, B-N2 (*see diagram No. 1*).

1 There follows 7 B-K3, N-B3; 8 N-N3. Alekhine prevents the freeing move of . . . P-Q4. Botvinnik, however, continues with 8 . . . B-K3, preparing the Pawn advance and eyeing Black's strategic QB5 for future reference. Alekhine plays 9 P-B4, and Botvinnik follows with 9 . . . O-O.

2 The usual move here is the safe and sane *10* O-O. But usual moves are foreign to world champion Alekhine. He will make the move that will hurl his opponent from the *Sessel*—something original that will teach this pretender a lesson. *10* P-N4 is the move. It signals an attack.

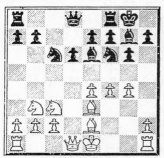

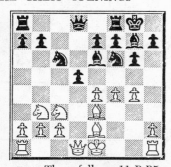

3 Botvinnik hurls defiance at his noted adversary. He will not be scared into abject retreat. Despite the vise-like grip which White maintains on his Q5, Botvinnik assails the mid-section. *10 . . . P-Q4* is his adventurous reply. The ensuing complications baffle even the giants of chessdom.

4 There follows *11 P-B5, B-B1; 12 KPxP, N-N5*. Botvinnik has sacrificed a Pawn but now threatens to recover it. If Alekhine relinquishes his material plus, his position will remain in tatters. What devilish continuation can infuse new life into what is becoming a mere matter of technique?

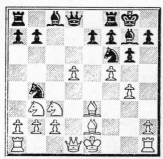

5 *13 P-Q6* is the problem-like rejoinder. To *13 . . . QxP*, Alekhine replies *14 B-B5*, forking Queen and Knight. Again, Botvinnik has to escape from a predicament. It is important to keep track of material. For the day of reckoning may not be far off, and material still has its relative value.

6 Botvinnik defends his Knight with *14 . . . Q-B5*. Alekhine chases the Queen by *15 R-KB1*. A Black "critter" is doomed. Still Alekhine's King Rook Pawn is *en prise*, and Botvinnik stoops to pick this up with *15 . . . QxRP*. No equivalent for a Knight. But open lines to the White King promise action.

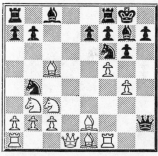

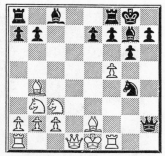

7 There follows *16* BxN, NxP. Another "critter" is immolated on Caissa's altar to pacify the White monarch. This method of making peace is no olive branch variety; it is the meat cleaver! The throne of the White King is demanded, and Black will not abide a sultry "no" by way of an answer.

8 Alekhine plays *17* BxN, out of compulsion, and *17* . . . Q-N6*ch* is the reply. Now Alekhine has two pieces for a few paltry Pawns. But what can he do? Not K-K2, Botvinnik would take a Bishop with a check and one without. Nor K-Q2 either, because of . . . B-R3*ch* with even more dire consequences.

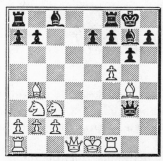

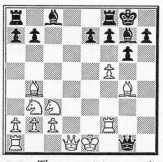

9 Alekhine plays *18* R-B2, Botvinnik follows with . . . Q-N8*ch*. Again, what is Alekhine to do? Not K-K2. For it still loses both his Bishops. Nor yet K-Q2. For it would cost all his material gain, and, to boot, his King would fall. Still he has a preponderance of material. He may find something.

10 The spectators wait with bated breath. Surely, the world champion will pick something out of the thin air. . . . Alekhine, however, retires gracefully with *19* R-B1. The move signifies his intention to draw, and a draw is agreed upon by the contestants. What a pretty finish. Perpetual check!

11

Queen's Gambit Declined

Tʜᴇ unostentatious move *1* P-Q4 is nowadays considered the most effective way of beginning a game of chess. This is evinced by a preponderance of Queen Pawn games in modern master tournaments.

Odd, indeed, is the apparent reappraisal of this debut. It was first mentioned in the Göttingen Manuscript of 1490. And not until the Vienna Tournament of 1873—nearly four hundred years later—did it receive any legitimate recognition.

There is, of course, room for argument over the relative merits of *1* P-Q4 as against other opening moves. This much, however, can be said in its favor. It leads to structurally sound patterns of play, with few intrinsic defects; it averts surprise mating attacks—for the White King is generously protected; it restricts the adversaries' defenses to the sparser branches of the Queen Pawn and, consequently, permits White to concentrate on only a few lines; and it affords excellent prospects for slow but sure progress.

Preliminary move in the Queen's Gambit Declined is usually *1* P-Q4. Often, however, the same patterns are reached by a transposition of moves.

The opening arises as follows:

1 **P-Q4**   . . . .

The advance of the Pawn to Q4 embodies many purposes.

(*1*) *Control of the center.* The Pawn at Q4 strikes at the important central square K5 and the square on the rim of the center, QB5.

(*2*) *Freedom of action.* The advance of the Queen Pawn releases White's Queen and Queen Bishop for future action.

(*3*) *Safety of the King.* When White plays *1* P-K4, Black often effectively posts a Bishop at Black's QB4, pointing at the White King's field. *1* P-Q4 averts even this latent threat.

1 . . . .   **P-Q4**

Black follows suit for the same reasons. Alternative lines of play such as *1* . . . N-KB3 or *1* . . . P-K3 may lead to the same opening by transposition of moves. Or they may lead to independent defenses, not within the scope of the Queen's Gambit Declined.

2 **P-QB4** . . . .

The Queen's Gambit. White offers a Pawn in order to decoy Black's center Pawn from its control of vital squares.

2 . . . .   **P-K3**

The most popular defense, since it has been extensively analyzed. According to the results of the analysis, Black is able to hold his own, with precision defense.

The paramount drawback of the move is that it locks in Black's Queen Bishop. From here on, Black is saddled with the problem of developing this Bishop, which is often referred to as the "problem Bishop."

The question arises: why lock in the Bishop? Why not continue with 2 . . . P-QB3 and bring out the Bishop later on? The fact is that 2 . . . P-QB3 is quite playable. But not for the reason that Black will be able to bring out the Bishop.

Black's Queen Bishop is tied to the defense of Black's Queen Knight Pawn. As soon as the Bishop moves, White continues with Q-N3 and attacks the Knight Pawn. Black must then defend the Pawn. He can do so by playing . . . Q-B1. Then, however, his Queen is relegated to the menial task of defending a Pawn—a sorry job for the Queen. Or he can do so by advancing his Queen Knight Pawn to QN3. The advance of this Pawn leaves a marked weakness on the white squares in Black's Queen-side Pawn structure. Such a weakness can be exploited profitably by the expert. Hence Black reconciles himself to retaining the Queen Bishop on its original square until some such time in the future that he is able to bring it out, without damaging his position. And he willingly locks in the Bishop for the present by the text move as being the wisest of unhappy choices.

The alternative 2 . . . P-QB3, however, is good. In fact, it is the theoretical rejoinder. For should White capture 3 PxP,

Black can recapture with the Bishop Pawn and keep the Pawn formation in symmetrical balance. On the contrary, after 2 . . . P-K3; 3 PxP, PxP, White remains with two center Pawns —the King Pawn and the Queen Pawn—as against Black's one Pawn—the Queen Pawn.

Despite these considerations, the text move is more often employed. Black has a difficult position, in any event; and it is merely a question of which defense Black prefers to suffer through before he can reach equality.

2 . . . PxP is the Queen's Gambit Accepted, which, in a sense, is not a valid gambit insofar as White can recover the Pawn at will.

After 2 . . . PxP, the continuation runs as follows: 3 N-KB3, N-KB3; 4 P-K3, and Black makes no effort to defend his extra Bishop Pawn, which is attacked by White's King Bishop. A defense will be of no avail, thus: 4 . . . P-QN4; 5 P-QR4, P-B3; 6 PxP, PxP; 7 P-QN3; Now, if 7 . . . PxP; 8 BxPch, followed by 9 QxP, recovers the Pawn with the better position.

It is to be noted that after 1 P-Q4, P-Q4; 2 P-QB4, Black must either accept the gambit, resort to a speculative counter-gambit, or protect his Queen Pawn with a Pawn. Should Black make any old developing move at this stage, White will gain an advantage. For example, if 2 . . . N-KB3; 3 PxP. Now, if 3 . . . QxP; 4 N-QB3, and White's development has been enhanced at Black's expense. Or, if 3 . . . NxP; 4 P-K4, and White's has established a superior center at Black's expense.

3 N-QB3 . . . .

A good developing move, exerting pressure on the center.

3 PxP, known as the Exchange Variation, also offers excellent prospects. In making the exchange, White expects to profit from his extra center Pawn and the newly-opened Queen Bishop file on which he can exercise permanent pressure during the future course of the game. On the other hand, the exchange ends the tension in the center and frees Black's

problem Bishop. The sum total of pluses and minuses, in the opinion of the experts, seems to favor the text move.

3 . . . . N-KB3

A good developing move, defending the center and clearing Black's first rank in order to make early castling possible.

If 3 . . . PxP, the game reverts to the Queen's Gambit Accepted.

4 B-N5 . . . .

Putting additional pressure on the center, White threatens to continue with 5 BxN. For, if . . . QxB; 6 PxP, PxP; 7 NxP gains a Pawn. Or, if 5 . . . PxB, Black's King-side Pawn position is shattered.

4 . . . . QN-Q2!

An indirect defense of the Queen Pawn, involving a pretty trap.

Again, if 4 . . . PxP, White has no difficulty in retrieving the Pawn by 5 P-K3.

5 P-K3 . . . .

White now defends the gambit Pawn, so that he need no longer concern himself with whether or not he will be able to recover it, in the event it is captured.

White must not attempt to win a Pawn with 5 PxP, PxP; 6 NxP. For Black continues with 6 . . . NxN and wins a piece! 7 BxQ, B-N5*ch;* 8 Q-Q2, BxQ*ch;* 9 KxB, KxB.

5 . . . .   B-K2

The best post for the Bishop, since it relieves the pin on Black's King Knight. On Q3, the Bishop is aggressively disposed but in a somewhat incongruous position. For Black's role is to defend successfully and break loose only after he has achieved equality and freedom of action. Black must first solve the problem of the "problem Bishop."

6 N-B3   . . . .

Since Black's King Knight is no longer pinned, there is no point to swapping the Queen Pawn, except to revert to the Exchange Variation. As already mentioned, the Exchange Variation frees Black's problem Bishop. It does not matter, in this instance, that Black's Knight is posted at Q2 and blocks the problem Bishop. This block is only temporary.

The text move is in line with the plan of development, to put pressure on the center.

6 . . . .   O-O

Black completes his King-side development, establishing a new haven for his King.

7 R-B1   . . . .

White elects to put the Rook on a file which will be opened, sooner or later. This is what is technically called a positional move.

7 . . . .   P-B3

Black reinforces the Queen Pawn so that Black's King Knight will be able to move, when necessary.

8 B-Q3 . . . .

White brings out his last minor piece and puts it on a square which bears in the general direction of the Black Monarch, for future reference.

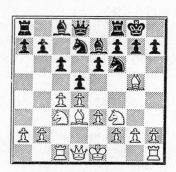

A résumé of the position at this point discloses the following advantages in White's favor. (*1*) White has a better grip on the center. (*2*) White enjoys greater freedom of action. (*3*) Black must solve the problem of the "problem Bishop."

8 . . . . PxP

The first step in Black's over-all plan to solve all of his difficulties. The exchange vacates Black's Q4 and enables Black to use that square to relieve pressure and simplify the forces by exchanges.

9 BxP   N-Q4

Black virtually forces the exchange of White's Queen Bishop; the second step in the plan.

10 BxB   QxB
11 O-O   . . . .

White's development goes on apace.

11 . . . . **NxN**

The third step in the plan. Soon the idea of how Black expects to free his problem Bishop will become clear.

12 **RxN** . . . .

To exercise pressure on the Queen Bishop file and also, in some contingencies, to swing the Rook over to the King-side of the board, after P-K4.

12 . . . . **P-K4**

The fourth step. Now the original diagonal of Black's Queen Bishop — closed on Black's second move — is open once again.

From here on, Black should be able to ward off any on-slaught against his King, with exacting defense.

Two suggested continuations are:

(*1*) *13* PxP, NxP; *14* NxN, QxN; *15* P-B4!, Q-K5!; *16* B-N3, B-B4; *17* Q-R5, P-KN3; *18* Q-R6, QR-Q1; *19* B-B2, Q-Q4; *20* P-K4, BxP, with about even chances.

White has a strong continuation in *21* R-KR3.

(*2*) *13* Q-B2, P-K5; *14* N-Q2, N-B3; *15* R-B1, B-B4; *16* P-B4, QR-Q1; *17* P-QR3, P-KR4; *18* P-QN4, P-KN3; *19* Q-N3, R-Q2, with even chances.

Conclusions

Of all the openings at White's command, those beginning with the move *1* P-Q4 grant White the longest-lasting pressure. True, Black is able to hold his own with correct defense. But the onus of exactitude rests with the defender.

Chess Movie

MOVE CLIMACTERIC

THE Orthodox Defense to the Queen Gambit Declined is a low-geared starter. About midway during hostilities, it shifts to second gear and then quickly to high. At a whirlwind pace, Dr. Max Euwe defeats Sir George Thomas in the memorable contest of Hastings, 1934–5. The game begins with: *1 P-QB4, P-K3; 2 N-QB3, P-Q4; 3 P-Q4, N-KB3 (see diagram No. 1).*

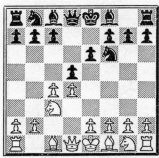 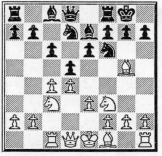

1 There follows: *4 B-N5, B-K2; 5 P-K3, O-O; 6 N-B3, QN-Q2; 7 R-B1, P-B3.* Each player sticks to the accredited line, reaching the book position by slight transpositions in sequence. The moves are more or less automatic, with years of logic and reason engraved into every turn.

2 Still the players keep to the tried and true. So there follows: *8 B-Q3, PxP; 9 BxP, N-Q4; 10 BxB, QxB; 11 O-O, NxN; 12 RxN, P-K4.* Sir George at last solves the problem of his "problem Bishop." He has not yet, however, resolved the bigger problem—the further course of the game.

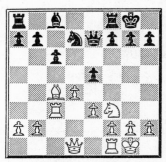

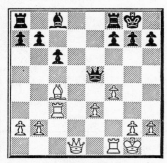

3 Euwe continues with 13 NxP, and a general exchange ensues: 13 . . . NxN; 14 PxN, QxP. Then Euwe signals an attack with 15 P-B4. The King Bishop Pawn is full of portent. It reaches out in the direction of the Black King. How shall Sir George stave off the impending onslaught?

4 Sir George retreats his Queen, with 15 . . . Q-K2, and he errs in not preventing the further advance of the King Bishop Pawn. Now 16 P-B5 is the move, Black's natural development is subdued. His Bishop, once more, must find a way out. To boot, Black's King-side Pawn structure is menaced.

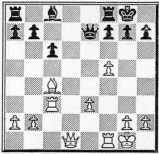

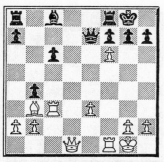

5 Sir George counters with 16 . . . P-QN4— a wing demonstration. He now hopes to divert his noted adversary's attention from his own King. At the same time, he creates an exit for his Bishop. Euwe retreats: 17 B-N3, and 17 . . . P-N5 follows. Now comes the initial break-through. 18 P-B6 is the move.

6 Sir George captures: 18 . . . PxP, and Euwe follows up with 19 QRxP. A Pawn or so, when the King is exposed, does not add up. Sir George plays 19 . . QxPch, and Euwe retreats, with 20 K-R1. At long last, the problem Bishop enters the fray, with 20 . . . B-N2. Both sides are now alerted.

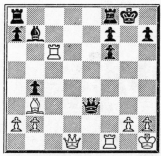

7 There follows: *21 QRxP, Q-K5.* Black focuses his attention on the White King. Euwe defends, with *22 Q-Q2* and, at the same time, prepares to swing his Queen into action against the opposing King. There follows: *22 . . . K-R1,* and each side appraises the open King Knight file enviously.

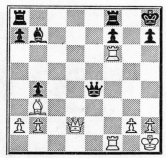

8 Euwe continues with *23 BxP.* No enemy Rook will occupy the King Knight file if he can prevent it. And Sir George counters with *23 . . . QR-B1.* Now Euwe defends with *24 R/6-B2.* Attack and defend— that is the order of play. Now the question is: who is going to break out next—and where?

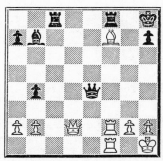

9 Sir George temporizes by *24 . . . QR-Q1,* and Euwe penetrates, with *25 Q-N5.* For a moment all is calm. Sir George seizes the opportunity to utilize his Rook for what appears double duty —attack and defense. *25 . . . R-Q3* is the move. Little does he realize that the climax is at hand.

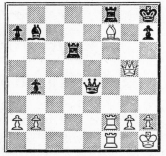

10 This is the calm before the storm. With one fell move, the game is about to end. *26 B-Q5* is the move. It spells *finis.* Everything is under fire at once. The Queen, the Rook, the Bishop and the hapless monarch. No mortal could withstand such a blow. Sir George is but mortal after all. He resigns.

12

Réti Opening

A HYPERMODERN OPENING

Dᴜʀɪɴɢ the past few decades, brand new ideas have developed in opening play. The fight for control of the center —the paramount issue in modern openings—has been given a new twist. A new school of thought has been born. Whereas, in the modern school, the skirmish waxes openly and merrily for domination of the mid-section of the playing field from the very first move, in the new school—the hypermodern school—the contest for center control takes the form of long distance, sniping, wing attacks on the opposing center.

The modernist will not give ground in the center. The hypermodernist, on the other hand, will permit, induce or even provoke his opponent into taking early control of the center. This seems rather strange. For, if it is important to control the center—and the modernist and the hypermodernist agree that it is—why should the *ne plus ultra* school of thought deliberately present to the adversary what is so valuable? The reasons for this, even though apparently obscure, are really pointed. What the hypermodernist really grants to the opponent is the occupation of the center. The occupied field then sets up as a ready target. And the hypermodernist shoots. His long-term plan is to demolish the occupied enemy field and take over the vital terrain, while he is still strong and the opposing center is in shambles.

This is the new idea. And Réti's opening is part and parcel of it.

The opening begins with *1* N-KB3, attributed to Zukertort for popularizing it. *1* N-KB3 is recorded in Lopez, 1561, and the first known game wherein it was essayed was dated 1845.

The Réti arises as follows:

1 **N-KB3** . . . .

The first move, of itself, does not have any exemplary significance; it is purely noncommittal and may transpose into the regular lines of the Queen's Pawn Game. White's second move, in conjunction with the first, gives the opening the hypermodern turn. This is called the Réti, after the late grandmaster, Richard Réti, one of the disciples of the hyper-modern school.

The hypermodern idea, like all ideas, is excellent—when it succeeds. When it fails because the opponent has been presented with the center and all it portends, the hypermodern-ist is left in a sorry state.

The development of the Knight on the first move does not, of itself, indicate what course White will pursue. It might be a prelude to the Queen's Pawn Opening or even a King's Pawn game, in some contingencies. Insofar as White's intention is momentarily concealed, the move is meritorious. On purely theoretical grounds, the move is also good. The Knight strikes at two important central squares, Q4 and K5.

1 . . . . P-Q4

At this point and later on, the order of moves lends itself to transpositions. For instance, Black might also play 1 . . . N-KB3. Or he might begin with 1 . . . P-K3 or 1 . . . P-QB4. In the latter cases, White may choose to convert the opening into the French Defense or the Sicilian Defense by playing 2 P-K4. Insofar as Black's Pawn at Q4 strikes at two important squares, K5 and QB5, the move is good.

2 P-B4   . . . .

The move which characterizes the Réti. It is a direct assault against Black's staunch Queen Pawn.

2 . . . . P-QB3

Defending the Queen Pawn and maintaining Pawn symmetry, if White should exchange. At this point, Black again has a choice of replies:

(1) 2 . . . PxP. For an effective counter-pattern. The line might run as follows: 2 . . . PxP; 3 N-R3, P-QB4; 4 NxP, N-QB3; 5 P-KN3, P-B3; 6 B-N2, P-K4; 7 P-Q3, B-K3; 8 O-O,

KN-K2; 9 KN-Q2, N-Q4. Black maintains a strong grip on
the center with excellent prospects.

Observe that Black does not capture the Pawn with a
view to retaining it. With correct play, it is not possible to
hold the Pawn. Moreover, an attempt to hold it weakens the
Black position.

After 2 . . . PxP, however, White may continue with 3
P-K3 and lead into the Queen's Gambit Accepted, thus: 3 . . .
N-KB3; 4 BxP, P-K3; 5 O-O, P-B4; 6 P-Q4. In this line, opinion
favors White.

(2) 2 . . . P-Q5. To establish a bridgehead in enemy
territory. This variation is in line with White's plan of inducing occupation of the center so that the occupied field will
set up as a target. It is double-edged, however. For, if Black
can successfully maintain the advanced Pawn, White will
be cramped. If the bridgehead and its props can be battered
down, however, White will gain the advantage. The line
might run as follows: 2 . . . P-Q5; 3 P-K3, P-QB4; 4 PxP,
PxP; 5 P-KN3, N-QB3; 6 B-N2, P-KN3; 7 P-Q3, B-N2; 8 O-O,
P-K4; 9 R-K1, P-B3. Although White enjoys a Queen-side
Pawn majority, Black's position is freer, and Black can maintain the bridgehead.

(3) 2 . . . P-K3. The routine, neutral development. The
line might run as follows: 3 P-KN3, N-KB3; 4 B-N2, B-Q3; 5
P-N3, O-O; 6 O-O, QN-Q2; 7 B-N2, P-B3; 8 P-Q4, N-K5; 9
QN-Q2, P-KB4; 10 NxN, BPxN; 11 N-K1, N-B3; 12 P-B3,
B-Q2; 13 PxKP, NxP, with about even chances.

3 **P-QN3** . . . .

To defend the unguarded Bishop Pawn, which is now in
danger of being captured. At the same time, the move makes
way for the fianchetto of the Queen Bishop—the hypermodern
idea of eyeing the center from the wings.

3 . . . . **N-B3**

A good developing move which strikes at the center.

4 P-N3   . . . .

Making ready for the fianchetto of the King Bishop—also in line with the hypermodern idea of bearing down on the center from a distance. The pressure which the White Bishops will exercise on the bias is the highlight of the over-all plan.

4 . . . .   **B-B4**

In the Queen Pawn openings, Black, as a rule, is saddled with the "problem Bishop." For the Queen Bishop is tied down to guarding Black's Queen Knight Pawn. So long as White does not have ready access to Black's Queen Knight Pawn—the usual method is Q-N3 for White—there is no reason not to develop the Queen Bishop. Hence it is brought out before Black locks the diagonal with . . . P-K3. Now the Bishop will participate in the play, actively.

5 B-KN2 QN-Q2

Bringing out additional force and intending *6* . . . P-K4.

6 B-N2   . . . .

Preventing the opposing . . . P-K4 and dominating White's K5 via long distance.

6 . . . . **P-K3**

Black must content himself with moving the King Pawn one square for the present. Should he play 6 . . . Q-B2, with the idea of playing the Pawn up two squares, he will find that his Queen is misplaced, after a few moves. White will soon place his Queen Rook with telling effect on QB1 and this will be the equivalent of an indirect frontal assault on the Queen. White is also at liberty to play his Queen Pawn to Q4 and prevent Black from playing . . . P-K4. This, however, is out of the spirit of the hypermodern opening. Moreover, it cedes Black's K5 to Black.

7 **O-O** . . . .

Continuing the development.

7 . . . . **B-Q3**

To prepare for . . . P-K4 and also to allow for a good square for Black's Queen at K2. That is why the text move is superior to . . . B-K2. At K2, Black's Queen cannot be molested.

8 **P-Q3** . . . .

White also prepares for P-K4. The text move is the first step.

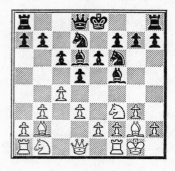

8 . . . .   O-O!

Because of technical reasons, 8 . . . P-K4 would expedite White's reply of P-K4. Thus, if 8 . . . P-K4; 9 P-K4, and Black dare not win a Pawn with 9 . . . PxKP; 10 PxP, NxP, for 11 N-R4 will win a piece for White.

9 QN-Q2 . . . .

Continuing the development and reinforcing the K4 square for the eventual P-K4.

9 . . . .   P-K4

Now Black has occupied the center. Black's center Pawns are supposed to set up as a target—according to hypermodern theory. Unfortunately, however, they do not. For it is difficult for White to put additional force against the opposing center.

10 PxP   . . . .

In order to open the Queen Bishop file for use by White's Queen Rook.

10 . . . .   PxP
11 R-B1   Q-K2

Black's development seems to be sound.

A game Réti—Emanuel Lasker, New York, 1924, continued as follows: *12* R-B2, P-QR4; *13* P-QR4, P-R3; *14* Q-R1, KR-K1; *15* KR-B1, B-R2; *16* N-B1, N-B4.

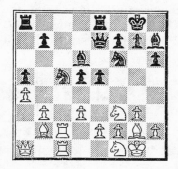

Réti then sacrificed the exchange with *17* RxN but did not obtain sufficient compensation.

Conclusions

The Réti system has infused new life into opening play. When first introduced, it met with remarkable success, mainly because adequate parrying, defensive formations were unknown. At present, there is no known way which leads to an advantage for White. Moreover, Black enjoys more latitude in this system than against the usual Queen Pawn Game.

Chess Movie

READY FOR THE RETI?

W HEN pure ideas clash, only a fine line separates success from failure. Here grandmaster Kashdan is the hypermodernist against the modernist Horowitz, in the USCF Open of Philadelphia, 1936. The game begins with *1* N-KB3, P-Q4; *2* P-B4, P-Q5; *3* P-KN3, P-QB4; *4* B-N2, N-QB3; *5* O-O, P-K4 (*see diagram No. 1*).

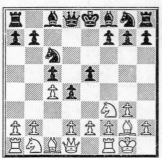

1 Black has usurped the center, with White's knowledge and consent. The question arises, is the center field a ready target? There follows 6 P-K4, B-N5; 7 P-KR3, B-K3; 8 P-Q3, P-B3. To all appearances, Black's wedge-shaped Pawn formation is secure. But White has his own ideas.

2 Kashdan plays 9 N-R3. He intends to swing the Knight to B2 and concentrate on a break at his QN4—The first step in undermining the Pawn array. Then comes 9 . . . Q-Q2; *10* K-R2, P-KN4; *11* N-B2, P-KR4. Black's target is White's King. A bit of speculation is involved.

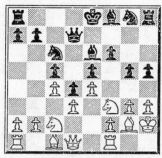

3 White retreats *12 N-N1*, and Black follows with *12 . . . KN-K2*. The Knight is headed for the vicinity of the White King. There follows *13 B-Q2*, lining up on QN4. Black replies *13 . . . N-N3*. Now comes *14 P-R3, B-N5*. Black wishes to force open a file leading to the opposing monarch.

4 White captures *15 PxB*, and Black recaptures *15 . . . PxPch*. Now White closes the file by returning a piece with *16 N-R3*. White prefers a slow, peaceful game, where he can demolish the opposing center in good time. Black has other ideas. *16 . . . N-B5* is the move, and it poses difficult problems.

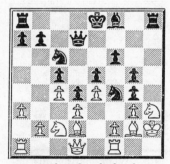

5 White has little choice. He captures the Knight with *17 PxN*, and then comes *17 . . . KPxP; 18 P-B3, PxN; 19 B-R1, N-K4; 20 Q-K2, B-Q3; 21 R-KN1, O-O*. The battle waxes furious. Black is a piece behind, but with two Pawns to the good and a powerful attack. Can White survive?

6 White attempts a diversion with *22 P-N4*. Black parries with *22 . . . P-N3*, and White continues with *23 P-R4*. There follows *23 . . . QR-N1; 24 P-R5, P-N5*. Each player is racing to get in heavy blows against the hostile King. And right now it looks like a toss-up. It is White's turn.

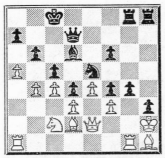

7 The fast-moving action places both players on the alert. White plays 25 BxP, and the game continues 25 . . . NxP*ch;* 26 BxN, BxB*ch;* 27 K-R1, P-N6; 28 RxP, RxR. Now Black is the exchange to the good. But he must reckon with White's assault; his own seems stymied. Can he contain the counterattack?

8 White opens the line of his own Rook's battery with 29 RP*x*P, and Black ignores the apparent danger by playing 29 . . . KR-N1. Now White captures 30 P*x*RP. For a moment it appears that all is over. A new Queen is the menace. Black captures, however, 30 . . . Q*x*P, and the scene changes.

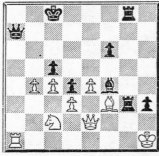

9 The Queen is immune from capture on account of mate! Now White combines to simplify the position. He plays 31 B-N4*ch,* and there follows 31 . . . R/6xB; 32 QxR*ch,* RxQ; 33 RxQ. After all, material is even. But White is in a mating net. Black plays 33 . . . R-N7 and draws the net tighter.

10 White retreats his unguarded Knight: 34 N-K1, and there follows 34 . . . R-KB7, closing in. White plays 35 K-N1 and Black counters with 35 . . . P-R7*ch,* pinning down the monarch. White captures 36 KxR, and Black plays 36 . . . P-R8(Q). The game is over. The Queen decides.

English Opening

ANOTHER HYPERMODERN OPENING

T HE English Opening—once known as the Queen's Bishop's Pawn Game—is so called after Staunton who adopted it in the match between England and France, 1843.

With *1* P-QB4, the English Opening is a Sicilian Defense in reverse, with White having a move in hand. If the Sicilian is tenable for Black, it should definitely be good for White, with a tempo to spare. At least, that is the underlying theory of the opening. As Réti says, however, in *Masters of the Chess-*

*board,** such a policy may be too passive for White's best chances.

As commonly played, the English is a product of the hypermodern school. So White makes no attempt to build up a Pawn center in the early stages of play. Instead, he concentrates on speedy development, encouraging Black to set up a Pawn center which may become fixed as a target. When Black does not fall in line, White's plan is to set up a Pawn center of his own, after he is fully developed, which will be difficult for Black to challenge. In that case, White uses his square Q5, as a focal point around which to rally his men or establish a bridgehead in enemy territory.

The English lends itself to easy transpositions. A player whose repertoire is large may easily steer the English into a favorable variation of some other opening.

The English arises as follows:

1 P-QB4 . . . .

This move constitutes the English Opening. The Pawn at QB4 strikes at the central square, Q5, and the less important one, QN5. The advance of the Bishop Pawn also releases White's Queen for future action.

The eventual pattern which evolves from the initial move depends, in a large measure, on Black's choice of defense.

1 . . . .   P-K4

* Réti, R., MASTERS OF THE CHESSBOARD, N. Y., *McGraw-Hill.*

As a general rule, and this is a case in point, it is good for Black to play . . . P-K4 at the first convenient opportunity. Black's King Pawn now strikes at Black's Q5, an important central square, and Black's KB5, a near central square. The advance of the King Pawn, moreover, releases Black's Queen and his King Bishop for future action.

Momentarily, Black appears to have the more dominating position. This appearance is somewhat of an illusion, since White has the first move and is able, at will, to swap off Black's King Pawn.

For players versed in the intricacies of the defense to the Queen Pawn, 1 . . . P-K3 is apt to transpose into that opening. In such case, White can avoid the Queen Pawn only by continuing with 2 P-K4. Then, by playing 2 . . . P-Q4, Black obtains a favorable position, thus: 3 KPxP, KPxP; 4 PxP, N-KB3. With correct play, Black recovers the Queen Pawn, and White remains with an isolated Queen Pawn. Of course, Black can play 4 . . . QxP, in this line, and avoid any speculation as to the recovery of the Pawn. Then, however, White gains an important tempo by 5 N-QB3, attacking the Black Queen.

2 N-QB3 . . . .

A good developing move, bearing on the center and particularly on Q5.

2 . . . . N-KB3

A good developing move, bearing on the center and neutralizing the effect of White's Queen Knight.

3 N-B3 . . . .

Again, a good developing move, bearing on the center and particularly on Black's King Pawn.

3 . . . . N-B3

Defending the King Pawn and maintaining the delicate balance in the center.

Observe that the natural 3 . . . P-K5 loses a Pawn: 4 N-

KN5, Q-K2; 5 Q-B2, and Black has no way of reinforcing the King Pawn.

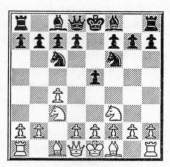

The Four Knights' Game of the English.

4 P-Q4 . . . .

The most logical line. In the actual Sicilian Defense, Black has a difficult time enforcing . . . P-Q4. When he does, however, he achieves at least certain equality. With the move in hand, White has no trouble battering down Black's King Pawn. After White's Queen Pawn and Black's King Pawn are swapped off, Black must still equalize the pressure on the center, exerted by the White Bishop Pawn.

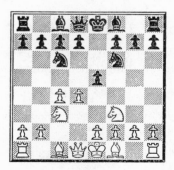

The slower, positional continuation leads to no advantage for White. For example, *4* P-KN3, P-Q4; *5* PxP, NxP; *6* B-N2, N-N3; *7* O-O, B-K2; *8* P-Q3, O-O; *9* P-QR3, P-B4; *10* P-QN4,

B-B3; *11* B-N2, Q-K2; *12* N-Q2, R-Q1; *13* P-N5, N-R4; *14* Q-B2, P-B4; *15* N-R4, B-K3; *16* B-B3, N-N6 with the better game for Black (Santasiere—Horowitz, New York, 1939).

4 . . . .   **PxP**

Black can attempt to maintain the King Pawn by *4 . . .* P-K5. With best play, however, White obtains a positional advantage, although the line is beset with traps. Thus, if *4 . . .* P-K5; *5* N-Q2, NxP; *6* KNxP, N-K3; *7* P-KN3, NxN; *8* NxN, B-N5*ch;* *9* B-Q2, BxB*ch;* *10* QxB, O-O; *11* B-N2, P-Q3; *12* O-O, B-Q2; *13* N-B3, B-B3; *14* N-Q5, and White enjoys command of the center and greater freedom for his forces.

The trappy line runs as follows: *4 . . .* P-K5; *5* N-KN5, P-KR3!; *6* KNxKP, NxN; *7* NxN, Q-R5; *8* Q-Q3, P-Q4; *9* PxP, N-N5; *10* Q-N1, B-KB4; *11* N-Q6*ch,* PxN!; *12* QxB, P-KN3; *13* Q-N1, R-B1, and there is nought to be done about . . . N-B7.

5 **NxP**   **B-N5**

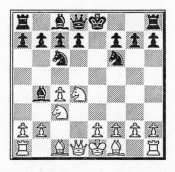

Black pins White's Queen Knight in order to lessen the pressure on White's Q5. This move practically commits Black to the exchange of Bishop for Knight. Black obtains compensation, however, in doubling and isolating White's Pawns.

6 **B-N5**   *. . . .*

By the same token, White pins Black's King Knight in order to increase the pressure on Q5. At the same time, the pin is an-

noying and restricts the freedom of Black's King Knight and
Queen.

6 . . . . P-KR3

"Putting the question" to the Bishop. The point of the move
is to break the pin.

7 B-R4 . . . .

Maintaining the pin. Clearly, any other Bishop moves are
pointless.

7 . . . . BxN*ch*

Since Black is more or less committed to this exchange, he
might as well make it while he is certain that White's Pawn position will suffer. Otherwise White defends his Queen Knight
by R-B1, after which . . . BxN is less efficacious.

8 PxB   N-K4

Black follows up his 6th move, in conformity with the idea
of breaking the pin on his King Knight.

9 P-K3 . . . .

To defend the unguarded Pawn.

9 . . . . P-Q3

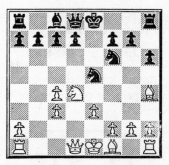

A necessary interpolation, sooner or later, in order to prevent White from playing P-B5. That move would give freer range to White's King Bishop and, at the same time, assist White in getting rid of his doubled Pawn.

10 B-K2   N-N3

Breaking the pin, at last. Observe the three steps involved in this process: . . . P-KR3, . . . N-K4 and . . . N-N3.

11 B-N3   N-K5

Black aims to rid White of his two Bishops before he can consolidate his position with P-B3 and P-K4.

12 Q-B2   . . . .

Defending the unguarded Bishop Pawn and, in turn, attacking the aggressively posted Black Knight.

12 . . . .   Q-K2

Since White cannot avoid the exchange of Bishop for Knight, Black has no present need to pare off and give up the centrally posted Knight.

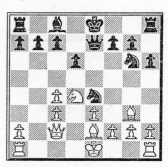

13 B-Q3   . . . .

This move was played by the late world champion, Dr. Emanuel Lasker. After *13* O-O, there is an element of danger in the following continuation: *13* . . . P-KR4; *14* B-Q3, NxB; *15* RPxN, N-K4; *16* B-K2, P-R5.

13 . . . .   NxB
14 RPxN   N-K4

The position is considered even. The weak White Queen-side structure rules in favor of Black, and White's centrally located forces favor him.

Conclusions

In most of the book lines of the English Opening, White enjoys the advantage. Only by accurate play is Black able to equalize. The onus of accuracy is with the defender, and this is not a burden lightly to be discounted. There is every reason, moreover, to believe that White's play can be refined and improved, in which case Black's burden will be even greater.

Chess Movie

THREATS IN ALL DIRECTIONS

Paradoxically, a weakened Queen-side can incur a loss on the opposite wing, as is masterfully demonstrated in the following Fine game. In the U. S. Championship, New York, 1936, Reuben Fine opens hostilities with Weaver Adams (Black): *1 P-QB4, P-K4; 2 N-KB3, N-QB3; 3 N-B3; N-B3; 4 P-K4 (see diagram No. 1).*

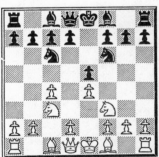

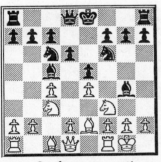

1 Fine chooses a Nimzo-vich idea, departing from the more usual *4 P-Q4.* Adams replies *4 . . . B-B4* (since *5 NxP, NxN; 6 P-Q4, B-N5; 7 PxN, NxP* leaves White's Pawns weak). There follows: *5 B-K2, P-Q3; 6 O-O,* and Black now makes the excellent move, *6 . . . B-KN5!* (preventing *7 P-Q4*).

2 So the game continues with *7 P-Q3, O-O;* after which White pins Black's King Knight, *8 B-N5,* and Black reacts with *8 . . . P-KR3* (hoping for *9 B-R4, P-KN4; 10 B-N3, N-KR4* to gain the two Bishops). White rejoins *9 B-K3.* (Now Black misses the equalizer: *9 . . . BxN; 10 BxB, N-Q5!*)

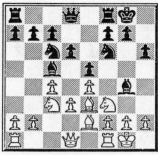

3 Instead, he plays 9 . . . B-N3? and White prepares for an eventual P-KB4, by 10 K-R1. Black still ignores the equalizer and decides to get in the "break" first. There follows: 10 . . . N-KR4; 11 N-Q5, P-B4; 12 PxP, and Black's maneuver has left him with the inferior game.

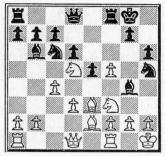

4 Adams now sees he must permit P-Q4 (as 12 . . . RxP?; 13 BxB, RPxB; 14 N-K3 loses for him). Hence 12 . . . BxP and a general exchange follows: 13 P-Q4, PxP; 14 Nx QP, NxN; 15 QBxN, BxB; 16 QxB. Adams then returns his Knight, 16 . . . N-B3, and seemingly he has simplified the game safely.

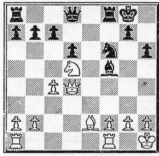

5 Actually, Black's Queenside is weak, and White now builds his game to a win on that account. There follows: 17 B-B3, K-R1; 18 N-K3, B-B1; 19 QR-Q1, Q-K2; 20 KR-K1, Q-B2; 21 N-Q5. And Black is constrained to exchange: 21 . . . NxN; 22 BxN (as 21 . . . B-K3? loses to 22 NxP!).

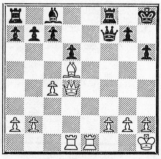

6 Black dare not capture 22 . . . QxP because of 23 R-K8! So there follows: 22 . . . Q-N3; 23 R-K7, P-B3; 24 B-B3 (White could win a Pawn by 24 B-K4, B-B4; 25 BxB, RxB; 26 RxP, but the position then is drawish). Now Black sees 24 . . . B-R6 loses to 25 QxQP, R-B3; 26 Q-N3.

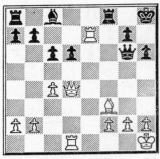

7 So there follows: *24 . . . R-B3; 25 R/1-K1, K-R2?* (Now *25 . . . B-R6* is Black's sole hope: *26 B-K4, B-B4;* and *27 P-B3,* and White must win a Pawn but faces a very difficult ending with Queens and two Rooks on each side.) As is, White now scores: *26 B-R5!* is the move which upsets the apple cart.

8 Pressure on Black's weak Queen-side Pawns has restrained Black; but now the action switches drastically to the King-side. (*26 . . . QxB? 27 QxR* will not do.) Hence *26 . . . Q-N4; 27 P-KR4, Q-B5* follows. (Danger lies in *27 . . . Q-B4; 28 B-K2, Q-N3; 29 P-R5, Q-N4; 30 R-K8* and *31 B-Q3ch* next!)

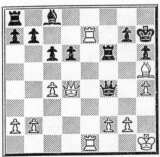

9 But White now makes his point: *28 QxQ, RxQ; 29 P-KN3!* He'll double Rooks on the 7th if Black retreats. Black takes: *29 . . . RxQBP* (as *29 . . . RxKBP* leads to a mating net: *30 R-K8, P-QN3; 31 K-N1!* R-B3; *32 R/1-K7* and B-K2-Q3ch). There follows: *30 R-K8, P-QN3; 31 B-B7!*

10 White threatens P-R5 and B-N6 mate! Black covers: *31 . . . R-KN5,* vainly, as then comes: *32 P-R5, B-N2; 33 RxR, BxR; 34 R-K8,* with threats in all directions. (On *34 . . . B-N2,* White wins by *35 B-N8ch, K-R1; 36 B-K6ch.*) Black resigns. Even at the end, his Queen-side ruins his King-side.

14

Alekhine's Defense

HYPERMODERNISM IN DEFENSE

The last word in hypermodernism is Alekhine's Defense. In this weird ripost to 1 P-K4, Black brings out his Knight to KB3 on the very first move, where it can be mauled and pummeled and driven clear across the board to what appears to be innocuous desuetude. Yet Black's play is not buffoonery; it is purposeful. It is a designed attempt to lure an onrush of enemy Pawns and set them up as fixed targets. In doing so, Black completely cedes the center. This is, however, the essence of hypermodernism.

Alekhine's Defense is named after late world champion Alexander Alekhine, who introduced it to master play at Budapest, 1921. Long before this time, it made an occasional appearance, and its debut can be traced to the International Handicap Tournament of London, 1862. In the game, Anderssen–Pearson, at odds of a Knight, play proceeded *1* P-K4, N-KB3. This provoked two question marks from annotator von Gotschall, who went on to say that *1* . . . N-KB3 must lose quickly, even at Knight odds. Schallopp's seventh edition of Bilguer's *Handbuch* ° had a kindlier word for Black's enigmatic first move. "If you are playing an inferior player," it reads, "you can try *1* P-K4, N-KB3; *2* P-K5, N-N1, as your opponent will often not be in position to prevent the break-up of his advanced center."

So it goes. Ideas, frowned upon one hundred years ago, enjoy the limelight today. Others that were significantly prominent have fallen from grace and are looked upon askance. *Chess marches on!*

The defense arises as follows:

1 P-K4   N-KB3

Black's move is forcefully provocative. The Knight attacks the King Pawn. Hence White must defend or advance.

The defense of the Pawn with *2* N-QB3 or *2* P-Q3 is hardly within the spirit of rebuttal. In a game of chess, nevertheless, the spirit is to be counted lightly. If the move produces a plus, it is to be played; if it leads to equality or a minus, it is to be discarded.

° Schallopp, E., *Handbuch des Schachspiels*, Leipzig, *Veit & Comp.*

2 N-QB3 fails mainly because Black is able to continue with
. . . P-Q4, without loss of time. This move is usually barred to
Black. For, after *1* P-K4, P-Q4; *2* PxP, Black must recapture
with the Queen. Then *3* N-QB3 gains a vital tempo for White.
Here, if *1* P-K4, N-KB3; *2* N-QB3, P-Q4; *3* PxP, NxP and Black
has nothing to fear.

The line beginning with *2* N-QB3 might run as follows:
2 . . . P-Q4; *3* PxP, NxP; *4* B-B4, P-K3; *5* N-B3, P-QB4; *6* O-O,
B-K2; *7* P-Q4, NxN; *8* PxN, O-O; *9* N-K5, Q-B2, with about
even chances.

In this line, if *3* P-K5, Black can equalize with *3* . . . P-Q5
or *3* . . . KN-Q2.

The passive *2* P-Q3, however, conceals tricky tactical plays
which must be parried exactly. A game, Nimzóvich—Alekhine,
New York, 1927, went as follows: *2* P-Q3, P-K4; *3* P-KB4,
N-B3; *4* PxP, QNxP; *5* N-KB3, NxN*ch;* *6* QxN, P-Q4; *7* P-K5,
Q-K2; *8* P-Q4, N-K5; *9* B-Q3, Q-R5*ch;* *10* P-N3, Q-N5; *11*
N-Q2, QxQ; *12* NxQ, with equality.

2 **P-K5** . . . .

In view of the above, White advances his Pawn and attacks
the Knight out of compulsion and choice. Since the Pawn cannot be defended to advantage, it must advance. Since White
gains time in the advance, he is satisfied.

2 . . . . **N-Q4**

All part of the grand hypermodern plan. The Knight goes where it may be directly attacked again in order to lure onwards White's center Pawns.

3 P-QB4 . . . .

White accepts the challenge. He is willing to be lured on.

From here on, the issue is whether the time gained by advancing the Pawns at Black's expense is equal to the minimal inherent weakness in the center Pawn structure. So fine is the line drawn.

Observe that it is important to drive Black's Knight from the center field. This can be done in another way: *3* N-QB3, NxN; *4* NPxN, P-Q3; *5* P-KB4, P-KN3; *6* N-B3, B-N2; *7* P-Q4, P-QB4; *8* B-Q3, O-O; *9* O-O, Q-B2; *10* Q-K1, BPxP; *11* BPxP, N-B3; *12* P-B3, N-R4. The position is equal.

3 . . . .   N-N3

4 P-Q4 . . . .

White enjoys what appears to be an imposing center. Black has other ideas about the strength of the center.

An interesting alternative here is 4 P-B5, N-Q4; 5 N-QB3. After 5 . . . NxN; 6 NPxN, P-Q3, Black can equalize. Also in this line, 5 B-QB4 develops into a lively gambit.

4 . . . . **P-Q3**

The first thrust at the opposing center. Curiously, 4 . . . N-B3 loses a piece! 5 P-Q5, NxKP; 6 P-B5, N/3-B5; 7 Q-Q4, threatening P-KB4 and P-QN3, each of which forces the abandonment of one of the Knights.

5 **PxP** . . . .

The all-out acceptance of Black's plan is 5 P-B4. In that case, White obtains a commanding array of center Pawns.

Whether they are strong or weak, however, is the question. In any event, after 5 P-B4, Black enjoys quite a lot of counterplay, and White must continue accurately. This line might go as follows: 5 P-B4, PxP; 6 BPxP, N-B3; 7 B-K3, B-B4; 8 N-QB3, P-K3; 9 N-B3, N-N5; 10 R-B1, P-B4; 11 B-K2, PxP; 12 NxP, B-N3; 13 P-QR3, N-B3; 14 NxN, PxN; 15 QxQch, KxQ. Despite Black's weak Queen-side Pawn structure, the chances are level. White has no easy way of exploiting the weaknesses and Black enjoys a free and easy development for all his forces.

Of course, Black can also go wrong. For instance, if 9 . . . B-K2 (instead of 9 . . . N-N5), White gets a terrific onslaught by 10 P-Q5, PxP; 11 PxP, N-N5; 12 N-Q4, B-N3; 13 B-N5ch, K-B1; 14 O-O. The threat of 15 N-K6ch gains more time, and Black's position is extremely critical.

The text move consolidates White's position and maintains the advantage of a stable center.

5 . . . .   KPxP

5 . . . BPxP is an alternative which keeps the Pawn position unbalanced and consequently creates greater winning and losing chances for both sides. White, however, can obtain an excellent bind on the position with correct play, thus: 6 N-KB3, P-N3; 7 B-K2, B-N2; 8 N-R3! N-B3; 9 P-Q5, N-K4; 10 N-Q4. The advance of P-KB4 compels a retreat and cramps Black. Moreover, Black cannot free his game easily by . . . P-K3, as, after PxP, PxP, his center is weak.

Observe the unique move of 8 N-R3. The immediate purpose of the move is to defend the Queen Bishop Pawn, so that when Black plays 8 . . . N-QB3, White can immediately play 9 P-Q5, N-K4; 10 N-Q4, and not worry about exchanging his King Knight. He might have to—if the QBP were not defended.

6	**N-KB3**	**B-K2**
7	**B-K2**	**O-O**
8	**O-O**	**B-N5**

9 N-R3

All the foregoing moves are good developing moves. White's last, however, is unusual. Oddly enough, it is not made with the intention of defending the Queen Bishop Pawn. For Black does not threaten 9 . . . BxN; 10 BxB, NxP. In such an instance, White could reply BxP and win the exchange. The reason for 9 N-R3 becomes clear later.

9 . . . . B-B3
10 P-QN3 N-B3

11 N-B2 . . . .

Observe the maneuver of White's Queen Knight.

$$11 \ldots \ldots \quad \text{R-K1}$$
$$12 \text{ B-N2} \quad \text{Q-Q2}$$
$$13 \text{ N-K3!} \ldots \ldots$$

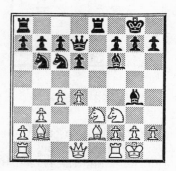

The final destination of the Knight.

White is for choice. On the surface, Black appears to have an adequate development. The fact is, Black has just about reached his maximum development and can hardly improve his position. White, on the other hand, has a flexible position. His future plan may be to play 14 Q-Q2, followed by P-Q5 and N-Q4. Then, he will be in command of greater terrain, which he should be able to exploit and capitalize.

Conclusions

Alekhine's Defense, which has all the earmarks of arrogant nonsense, is really a comparatively sound weapon in the hands of those looking for a lively encounter. While White's prospects are brighter, with sound play, the chance for error is greater than in most other defenses.

Chess Movie

OLD WHAM IN NEW BATTLES

Slow, plodding, positional Hypermodernism tussles with old Modernism. A long, drawn-out contest is in store. Tactics makes an entry. The scene changes and the play is over. U. S. Championship Tournament, New York, 1942, produced this contest between Horowitz and Seidman. Follow the game "movie style." *1 P-K4, N-KB3; 2 P-K5, N-Q4; 3 P-QB4, N-N3; 4 P-Q4, P-Q3.* (*See diagram No. 1.*)

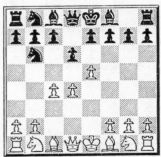

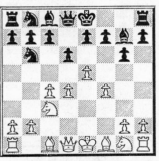

1 White plays the Four Pawn game. There follows *5 P-B4.* Black counters with the infrequent *5 . . . P-N3.* His King Bishop is destined for a wing development, from which point of vantage it will bear directly on the opposing center. *6 N-QB3, B-N2* are next in order, reaching diagram No. 2.

2 *7 N-B3, PxP; 8 BPxP, B-N5* is the sequence. White's impressively expanded, though also somewhat shaky, center is under fire. How is White to capitalize his advantage in terrain, before his midsection crumbles? This is the perpetual problem of the obstreperously hypermodern opening.

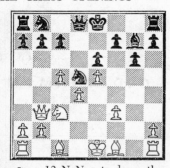

3 9 P-B5 sets the men in motion. Black is prodded from his complacency and the picture changes. Immediate, tactical plays overrule the strategic concept. There follows 9 . . . N-Q4; 10 Q-N3, BxN; 11 PxB, P-K3. Black wishes to cash in on the weakness in White's King's camp.

4 12 NxN cuts down the wood and takes the sting out of any brewing counter-attack. Because the ending is unfavorable, Black does not swap Queens. He gambles on molesting the White King. There follows 12 . . . Q-R5ch; 13 K-K2, PxN. White's Kingdom for a Rook is the tempting (?) offer.

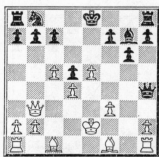

5 White accepts a Pawn with 14 QxNP and Black plays 14 . . . Qx QP. Then White goes after the Black King. 15 Q-B8ch, K-K2; 16 B-N5ch, P-B3; 17 QxPch, N-Q2 are the moves. Both Kings are insecure, and it is a question of who brings out his attacking forces more rapidly. It is White's turn.

6 18 PxPch opens new lines, and Black plays 18 . . . BxP. Then follows 19 Q-Q6ch. Black is compelled to retreat and cut the communication of his Rooks—a decisive factor here and now. 19 . . . K-K1 is Black's move. Both Kings eye each other reproachfully on the open King file.

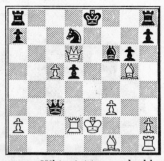

7 White brings up reinforcements, as 20 R-Q1 drives the opposing Queen with tempo. Black replies 20 . . . QxPch, and White interposes 21 R-Q2. Again, the Queen must move. Now it is 21 . . . Q-B6. White's last two moves have enabled him to swing the favorable balance of power.

8 White initiates a double threat with 22 QxP. It is too late to parry everything. Black goes in for a mad scramble. 22 . . . BxB is the move. White plays 23 QxRch and Black replies 23 . . . K-K2. Now it is necessary to consolidate, if it is at all possible to consolidate.

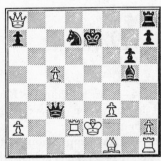

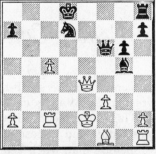

9 24 Q-K4ch is the right move in that direction. Black holds on to everything with 24 . . . K-Q1. Comes a positional move: 25 R-B2, reinforcing the dangerous passed Queen Bishop Pawn. Black retreats 25 . . . Q-B3. With an active majority of men, White overwhelms his adversary.

10 26 P-B6 does the trick. Suddenly the passed Pawn has assumed major significance. Vainly, Black pins the opposing Queen with 26 . . . R-K1. Who would dream that the game would be over with one fell blow? White replies 27 P-B7ch. The mite is now mighty. Black resigns.

15

Center Counter Defense

THE Center Counter—*1* P-K4, P-Q4—is an attempt by Black to wrest away White's endowed initiative on the very first move. This is in direct conflict with theory.

Axiomatic—and almost comical—is the proposition in the chess opening that, when White plays *1* P-Q4, he sets his sights for P-K4, and, when he plays *1* P-K4, then P-Q4 is his militant goal. The moves P-K4 and P-Q4 (or *vice versa*) cannot be successfully enforced in consecutive order, when both players immediately fight for control of the center. For the scales of opening play are so delicately balanced that the sequence would cost as little as a tempo or as much as a Pawn. By the same token, Black may not respond to *1* P-Q4 with . . . P-K4 or to *1* P-K4 with . . . P-Q4. Material or time will be his price.

On this ground, the Center Counter, which violates that tenet, is doomed from the beginning. For, on the second move, Black presents White with a valuable tempo. Yet, since there is no known way for the elected defender to seize the lead without some kind of investment, the offer of a tempo is his calculated risk.

The Center Counter was first recommended by Lucena (1497). Since then it has cropped up time and again in serious play, with intermittent success. A favorite with Mieses, it has enabled him to chalk up innumerable and brilliant victories. Because new ways to capitalize the extra tempo have come to light, however, the popularity of the defense is on the wane.

The defense arises as follows:

1 P-K4   P-Q4

The Center Counter. Black's Queen Pawn strikes White's King Pawn, suggesting an exchange of Pawns. The idea behind Black's move is the opening of the Queen file, the release of the Queen Bishop for immediate action and the relocation of the Queen to a dominating position, bearing on the center of the board.

The idea is good insofar as its attainment leads to a free and easy game. Its execution, however, is impossible to achieve with proper play on White's part.

2 PxP   . . . .

The only way to attempt a refutation of Black's move. 2 P-K5 sets no problems, for Black is able to develop all his forces with facility. 2 N-QB3 is a poor alternative since it grants Black the option of advancing . . . P-Q5 or capturing . . . PxP. He obtains an easy game in either case. 2 P-Q4 is a needless gambit which compels White to pursue the recovery of a Pawn.

2 . . . .   QxP

This is the main variation. Black's Queen momentarily enjoys a dominant role.

Alternatives here are 2 . . . N-KB3 and the gambit, 2 . . . P-QB3. In both instances, White obtains the superior position. For example, if 2 . . . N-KB3; 3 P-QB4, P-B3; 4 P-Q4, PxP; 5 N-QB3, N-B3; 6 B-N5, P-K3; 7 P-B5. With proper procedure, White nurses his Queen-side Pawn majority into a real threat. Or, if 2 . . . P-QB3; 3 PxP, NxP, Black's minimal lead in development is insufficient for the Pawn minus.

3 N-QB3

The Knight develops and attacks the adverse Queen, thereby gaining a move. Thus, instead of the usual initiative which is White's lot, White picks up an extra tempo.

3 . . . .   Q-QR4

Black's idea is to exercise pressure on his diagonal, QR4-K8, as well as on the open Queen file later on. The issue is whether the pressure will offset the effect of White's superior development.

The unappetizing alternative is 3 . . . Q-Q1. On the face of it, this move is ruled out, because the time in bringing out and retreating the Queen is spent to no avail. The opening of the Queen file, of itself, is insufficient compensation for White's superior development.

4 P-Q4   . . . .

White may venture on the gambit 4 P-QN4 at this point. In that case, White promotes his development at a rapid pace at the expense of a Pawn. While the gambit may be sound, there is no need to speculate so long as the normal moves produce an excellent position.

The text move controls the important central squares.

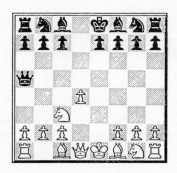

4 . . . . N-KB3

A temporizing, developing move, bearing on the center. Black hopes to bring out all his men soon and crack down on White's Queen Pawn.

An interesting alternative is 4 . . . P-K4. With correct play, however, this falls short because the game opens wide, while White is still ahead in development. On the other hand, it is best for White to familiarize himself with its possibilities. The line might run as follows: *4* . . . P-K4; *5* N-B3 (accent on development), B-QN5; *6* B-Q2, B-N5; *7* B-K2, PxP; *8* NxP, Q-K4; *9* QN-N5! QBxB; *10* QxB, BxB*ch;* *11* KxB, QxQ*ch;* *12* KxQ, N-QR3; *13* KR-K1, O-O-O; *14* NxP*ch,* K-N1; *15* N/7-B6*ch.* This is from a game Tarrasch—Mieses, Gothenburg, 1920. White won the endgame.

After *4* . . . P-K4; *5* PxP, Black is able to equalize as follows: . . . B-QN5, *6* N-B3, B-N5; *7* B-K2, N-QB3; *8* O-O, KN-K2. Black must recover the Pawn.

5 N-B3 . . . .

Normal development, bearing on the center.

6 . . . . **B-N5**

Neutralizing the Knight's effect on the center and clearing the path for an eventual Queen-side castling, with pressure on White's Queen Pawn.

6 **P-KR3!** . . . .

Putting the question to the Bishop.

6 . . . . **B-R4**

The Bishop retreats to maintain the pin on the Knight. If *6* . . . BxN; *7* QxB, White not only maintains control of the center but also has the advantage of two Bishops.

7 **P-KN4!** . . . .

This wing demonstration liberates the King Knight at the expense of White's King-side Pawn structure. Since White is ahead in development, however, he wishes to capitalize this plus before Black can consolidate. By doing so, he hopes that the weakness of the Pawn structure will play little part in the future proceedings.

7 . . . . **B-N3**

8 **N-K5** . . . .

The Knight is now in a dominant post and threatens to molest the Black Queen, by retreating to QB4. The Queen is shy a good escape square.

$$8 \ldots \quad \textbf{P-B3}$$

Creating an exit for the Queen.

$$9 \ \textbf{N-B4} \ \ldots$$

Compelling the Queen to retreat and to relinquish the pin on the Queen Knight.

$$9 \ldots \quad \textbf{Q-B2}$$

The Queen's haven. 9 . . . Q-Q1 is an admission that the entire Queen Maneuver—Q-Q4-QR4—is pointless.

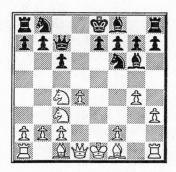

$$10 \ \textbf{Q-B3!} \ \ldots$$

The star move in White's play. The objectives of the sacrifice are:

(*a*) to support the Queen Bishop at KB4. This, in turn, will promote White's development at Black's expense;

(*b*) to clear the first rank in readiness for Queen-side castling;

(*c*) to bolster and make more potent White's contemplated King-side Pawn advance by nullifying Black's K5. Thus, this square will not be available to the Knight or Bishop in the event one or the other is attacked.

10 . . . .   **BxP**

On other moves, *11* B-B4, followed by *12* O-O-O, leaves White with an overwhelming position.

The text move is definitely faulty and Black's play may be considered to be refuted.

11 **B-B4** . . . .

11 . . . . **Q-Q1**

Because Black's last move loses immediately, the less appetizing *11* . . . Q-Q2 is worthy of consideration. Even that, however, leaves Black in dire straits: *11* . . . Q-Q2; *12* R-B1, B-N3; *13* N-K5, Q-Q1; *14* P-Q5. If now *14* . . . PxP; *15* B-N5*ch*, QN-Q2; *16* NxQP, White wins at least a piece by the threat of *17* NxN*ch* and *18* BxN*ch*. On *16* . . . Q-R4*ch*, there follows *17* P-N4! In this line, if *13* . . . QxQP; *14* N-N5 is a crushing rejoinder: . . . Q-K5*ch*; *15* QxQ, BxQ; *16* N-B7*ch*, K-Q1; *17* NxR, BxR; *18* NxP*ch* and *19* NxR—also *16* P-B3, N-R3; *17* PxB, PxN; *18* BxP*ch*, N-Q2 (forced) *19* BxN*ch*.

12 **Q-K2!!** . . . .

Even though the movement of the Queen twice in the opening is contrary to principle, it is, in this case, the sockdolager. And the apparent violation is based on Black's complete misconception of the strategy of the opening.

12 . . . . B-N3

If *12* . . . QxP; *13* B-K5 wins the unguarded Bishop.

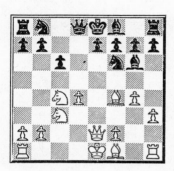

13 N-Q6ch. . . .

The point of White's 12th. Black's King Pawn is pinned and his King is prodded into insecurity.

13 . . . . K-Q2
14 NxNP . . . .

Black is lost. White has recovered the Pawn.

The entire line is based on the game Horowitz–Kibberman, Warsaw, 1935, which ended as follows:

14 . . . Q-N3; *15* N-B5*ch*, K-B1; *16* B-N2, P-K3; *17* O-O, N-Q4; *18* NxN, BPxN; *19* QR-B1, K-Q1; *20* B-N5*ch!* B-K2; *21* BxB*ch*, KxB; *22* BxP, N-Q2; *23* BxR, RxB; *24* NxN, KxN; *25* KR-Q1, Q-N2; *26* P-Q5, PxP; *27* Q-K5, Resigns.

Conclusions

While the strategic concept of the Center Counter Defense is laudable, its tactical execution is impossible of fulfillment. In the line where Black plays *4* . . . P-K4 (see note to Black's fourth move), Black succeeds in obtaining a free game and a comparatively easy development for all his men. His position bogs down, however, because he is two tempi behind in development. If some way can be found to bolster this plan, the defense may yet be tenable.

Chess Movie

COUNTER COUNTERED

A COURSE in winning chess tactics is the fare of this classic brevity. Knight forks, pins, double attacks are rampant. To boot, the strategic concept of simultaneous attack and defense is exemplified. Duras, White, finally belays his pugnacious opponent, Spielmann, by a well-directed grenade. Vienna, 1907, is the scene of play. Follow the game "movie style." *1* P-K4, P-Q4; *2* PxP, QxP; *3* N-QB3, Q-QR4; *4* P-Q4, N-KB3. (*See diagram No. 1.*)

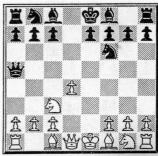 

1 There follows 5 N-B3, B-N5. White omits any King-side Pawn demonstration. The slow, positional 6 B-K2 is his move. This gives Black the opportunity to show his stuff. With 6 . . . N-B3, Black readies for Queen-side castling and powerful pressure against the Queen Pawn.

2 Anticipating the attack on the Pawn, Duras plays the prophylactic 7 B-K3 and Spielmann counters with 7 . . . O-O-O. A Knight maneuver further wards off the pressure: 8 N-Q2. There follows 8 . . . BxB; 9 QxB, Q-KB4. Observe that a Knight fork had immunized the weakling Queen Pawn.

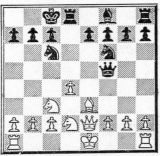

3 Duras swings his Knight to the long side of the board with *10 N-N3*, and Spielmann furthers his development with *10 . . . P-K3*. Now follows: *11 P-QR3, . . . B-Q3*. In order to contain the battle on one side, White castles long: *12 O-O-O*. Black responds *12 . . . N-Q4*. *13 . . . NxN* is his threat.

4 *13 N-R4* is the follow-up. White's men begin to close in on the Black monarch. Black counters with *13 . . . P-K4* and there follows the exchange *14 PxP, BxKP*. White pre-empts a strategic square with *15 N/4-B5* and Black consolidates his position with *15 . . . N-N3*.

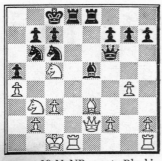

5 Duras attempts to force a weakening on the flank with *16 P-QR4*, and Spielmann parries with *16 . . . P-QR4*. Now Duras drives the Black Queen with *17 P-N4*, and the Queen retreats: *17 . . . Q-B3*. There follows *18 P-QB3, KR-K1*. As yet, no perceptible incursion is under way. But wait.

6 *19 NxNP* upsets Black's equanimity. A free-for-all ensues: *19 . . . Rx Rch; 20 RxR, BxBP*, and both Kings are in jeopardy. The complications are thick and the action fast. Who will come out on top of this perplexing maze? Whose attack will hit home hardest?—that is the vital question.

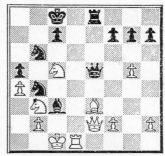

7 Duras retreats *21 N/7-B5* and opens a direct avenue to the Black monarch. Spielmann counters with *21 . . . N-N5*. There follows *22 P-N5, Q-K4*. Both sides are on tenterhooks. To attack and defend simultaneously is a difficult feat. One slip, and the game falls by the wayside.

8 Now comes the prelude to one of the finest combinations of the sixty-four squares. White plays *23 NxP*, heading for the general direction of the opposing King. Offhand, it has the earmarks of a trap. (Black dare not play *23 . . . QxN* on account of *24 Q-N4ch.*) Black plays *23 . . . P-R4.*

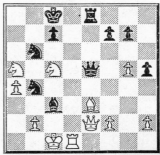

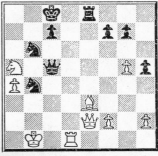

9 Now, however, White can capture the loose Bishop and he does with *24 PxB*. Black continues with *24 . . . QxPch* and perforce White plays *25 K-N1*. There evidently is no reason why Black cannot take the Knight at this moment. So Black plays *25 . . . QxN*, satisfied that the game is in the bag.

10 Maybe it is and maybe it isn't. One thing is certain, White's King is just as exposed to flailing blows as Black's. Who would dream that in one fell move the game is over? *26 R-Q8ch* is the move!! and Black topples from the *Sessel*. He cannot capture the Rook safely. Black resigns.

MODERN IDEAS IN THE
CHESS OPENINGS

Modern Ideas

IN THE

CHESS OPENINGS

BY

I. A. Horowitz

With 205 diagrams

DAVID McKAY COMPANY, INC.

NEW YORK

Contents

MODERN IDEAS IN THE
CHESS OPENINGS

1

A Review of the Principles of Opening Play

IN THE good old days, map makers used to fill in the space devoted to Central Africa with the legend: "Here be monsters." This is the feeling that most chessplayers have when they consult an opening manual with a thousand tabular columns of opening play, with innumerable side lines, variations, and references to thousands of master games.

Aside from the forbidding look of such compilations, they omit what the student needs above all: a survey of the *principles* of good opening play. Not knowing what to look for, he is only confused and exasperated by the richness of the material. Hence, before we proceed to study individual openings, we shall want to familiarize ourselves with some of the grand principles that rule all opening play.*

* These principles are explained in great detail, with many examples, in *How to Win in the Chess Openings.*

The opening stage is usually limited to the first twelve or so moves. It is that part of the game in which we develop our forces, or prepare to develop them. We do not aim for ultimate goals at the very start—we do not try for checkmate right off the reel.

Generally, it is small advantages that we seek at the start. We try to avoid Pawn weaknesses; we try to avoid loss of material. We strive to control the important center squares—particularly K4 and Q4 in each camp. We try to develop our pieces so that they are placed in the center or bearing down on the center. If they are so placed, they can reach any part of the board rapidly and with great effect.

To win material is important at any time—in the opening as well as later on. Why? Because a Pawn has the ability to become a Queen if it reaches the eighth rank unharmed, giving its possessor a decisive material advantage.

If we can win greater material than a Pawn, so much the better. That is why it is important to know the relative value of the forces.

Thus, a Knight is worth about three Pawns. The Bishop has a *slightly* greater value in most cases. The Rook is worth five Pawns—more than a Bishop or Knight. The Queen, the strongest of the forces, is worth nine Pawns. That is to say, more than a Rook and Bishop or Rook and Knight, but somewhat less than two Rooks.

It is vital to be familiar with these relative values, for there are innumerable cases of possible exchange or capture where we have to be guided by the relative values of the pieces involved. This is our main guide in answering the questions: Do I capture? Do I exchange? Do I let him capture? Do I let him exchange? Do I retreat? Do I force him to retreat?

Though these problems often arise in the opening stage, you are not likely to win large material in the opening unless your opponent blunders crassly. Also, you must remember that these values are modified by extraordinary circumstances. A Pawn that administers checkmate is worth a million dollars!

An undeveloped Knight or a Queen far off from the scene of action may be worth far less than its academic value. So, it is not only relative value that matters; you must realize that particular forces that are especially active are thereby more valuable, while inactive forces depreciate in value.

Development, we know, is important in the opening. Generally you want to bring out your Knights first, because their best squares are easy to hit on. The King Knight goes almost invariably to KB3, from where it hits at the important center squares Q4 or K5. (Playing this piece to KR3 will deprive it of practically all influence on the center.)

The Bishops generally come out after the Knights, as it is not always clear at the very beginning which square is best for a Bishop.

The development of the Queen can be deferred still more, because she is only likely to be harried by hostile pieces of lesser value. As a rule, the Queen will be developed only when the battle lines are already drawn. Sometimes the Queen will be played to K2 or Q2 or QB2 to make room for a Rook move to a center square. But this is unlikely to happen before the eighth move or thereabouts. The Rooks take quite a while to be brought into play—generally after castling. It takes time until the pieces are developed (moved from their original squares on the back row). Until the pieces are played out, the Rooks are unable to move along the back row.

To what squares should the Rooks be played? That will be determined by the existence of open files. As we know, open files are created by Pawn captures or recaptures, so that gives us the key to placing the Rooks. To post a Rook on a file that is closed and is likely to be closed means that we are not getting the full value of the Rook's power and possibilities. Like the other pieces, the Rook belongs on lines where it has mobility.

Castling (the combined move of Rook and King) is almost always a valuable contribution to development. The Rook is brought nearer to the center, and at the same time the King is removed from the center so that its presence will not hamper the action of the other pieces. (Castling is also a help by making the King safer. This eases the defensive burden imposed on our forces.)

Try to be economical in developing. Inexperienced players often make the mistake of moving one piece several times without appreciably increasing its effectiveness—and at the same time they neglect their other pieces.

One of the great problems of economical developing is deciding whether a Pawn capture in the opening costs too much time. It takes practice and experience to be able to appraise such situations accurately. Be guided, also, by your own temperament. If you chafe under the need for being on the defensive, avoid spending time on Pawn-grabbing if it means yielding the initiative to your opponent.

Be wary of weakening your Pawns; try to weaken your opponent's Pawns. What does this mean in concrete language?

There are various kinds of weak Pawns. An isolated Pawn, for example, is one which has no Pawns of its own color on neighboring files, and therefore cannot be protected by Pawns. It has to be protected by pieces. Obviously it is good policy to train your guns on your opponent's isolated Pawn, if he has one.

A doubled Pawn is also a weakness to some extent, because two Pawns on the same file cannot give each other protection. A doubled, isolated Pawn is an even worse weakness. Of course, doubled Pawns offer a certain amount of compensation: their very existence guarantees an open file—sometimes two open files—on which your Rooks can be active.

One of the most flagrant weaknesses in Pawn structure comes about when a Pawn has been advanced into enemy territory. Such overextended Pawns make easy targets and at the same time cost their defender much time and effort to keep them safeguarded.

Pawn "holes" are another type of weakness frequently encountered. A "hole" is a square that cannot be guarded by

Pawns because the Pawns on the neighboring files have already advanced. Thus, on page 129, Black's K4 square is a hole because his King Bishop Pawn and Queen Pawn can no longer protect that square (both ... P-KB3 and ... P-Q3 are impossible).

To complete the roster of Pawn weaknesses, we must mention the backward Pawn. This type of Pawn has neighbors, but they have already advanced and are thus unable to guard the backward Pawn. On page 129, Black's King Pawn is a backward Pawn.

But Pawns are not always weaknesses. Sometimes they can be remarkably powerful. The center Pawn, for example, which controls a vital square by depriving hostile pieces of access to that square, is playing a role of the greatest value.

Even more valuable are passed Pawns—those whose advance is not impeded by hostile Pawns on neighboring files. A passed Pawn is a potential Queen, and has already surmounted one of the greatest obstacles to queening.

It is this factor that gives Pawn majorities their great importance. If you have three Pawns to your opponent's two on the Queen-side, you are said to have the Queen-side majority of Pawns. By judicious advance and exchange, your three-to-two majority should eventually result in a passed Pawn. You should therefore view a Pawn majority as a potential passed Pawn.

Finally, Pawns are of enormous value in opening lines by capture or recapture. This is a point that cannot be stressed too highly. If you keep your eye on Pawn play in games that you study, you will observe again and again that the opening of lines is made possible in most cases by well-timed Pawn moves. In master play a Pawn—occasionally more than one Pawn—is sacrificed to open up a line for a decisive attack. We admire the incisive play that winds up the game, but if anything, we ought to admire even more the elegant Pawn move that makes it all possible.

From this point it is logical to proceed to the idea that the

Pawn position gives us a great many priceless pointers on how to plan. The pattern of the Pawns after the tenth move or so usually tells us how Bishops are placed most effectively, where the Knights should head, what the Rooks can accomplish, what targets to aim for, what lines to open.

If this notion strikes you as a novel one, turn to the following chapters, and see how the nature of the Pawn position influences the plan of the game. In one opening after another, you will observe that the Pawn position sets the "tone" of the remaining play.

For example: in the Center Game, White's Pawn move 2 P-Q4 opens up the game too soon. In the Danish, the Pawn sacrifices set off a heated controversy of development versus material. In the King's Gambit, the opening struggle centers about White's attempt to pre-empt the center with the Pawn thrust 2 P-KB4. In Philidor's Defense, Black remains with a permanently constricted position after the Pawn move 2 ... P-Q3.

And so it goes. Test this idea on the openings treated in this book, and on all openings in general. The Pawn pattern will teach you a great deal and sharpen your eye for the possibilities inherent in any given position.

2

The typical position in the Center Game

Center Game

Perfect symmetry and nearly perfect balance mark the original position of the chess game. With the exception of the first move, which is endowed to White and from which springs a minimal initiative, all is equal. From that first move, however, unlike and variable factors—time, space, and force—come into play. And immediately the equilibrium is upset.

When a Pawn is paired off against an opposing Pawn, or a Knight for a Knight, etc., it is easy to see that, as far as material goes, an even relationship exists. When an open line, however, is measured against a tempo or a strategic square against some other complement—that is, intangibles against in-

9

tangibles—real skill is required for appraising the net plus or minus.

So it is with the Center Game proper. After the moves 1 P-K4, P-K4; White plays 2 P-Q4 in order to open lines quickly—the Queen file and the diagonal for the Queen Bishop. Moreover, he collapses Black's strong point, his K4, in one fell move. On the face of it, consequently, the move is good; but there is one drawback. In recapturing the Pawn, *White brings his Queen out early.* The White Queen is vulnerable, and thus Black is able to gain one move. One tiny tempo, and that is all that is necessary to weight the scale in favor of the defender. So delicately are the scales balanced.

Favorable opinion is on the side of the defender. In modern times the opening has been championed by such masters as Mieses, Spielmann, and Tartakover, but without success.

The Center Game dates from Polerio, 1590, although White's third move 3 QxP was first noticed in Stamma, 1737.

The Center Game arises as follows:

1	P-K4	P-K4
2	P-Q4	....

The Center Game. The advance of the Queen Pawn serves three purposes: (1) it opens the Queen file for White; (2) it releases White's Queen Bishop for immediate action; (3) it suggests an exchange of center Pawns, after which White's King Pawn will remain in a dominating position, striking the enemy squares Q5 and KB5, while its counterpart, Black's Queen Pawn, will be backward, touching squares only within its own half of the board.

To capture is best. The alternatives leave much to be desired. For instance, if Black defends with 2 ... P-Q3, then 3 PxP, PxP; 4 QxQch, KxQ; and Black has forfeited the privilege of castling. If 2 ... N-QB3; 3 PxP, NxP; 4 P-KB4, White usurps the center. This line, incidentally, has the earmarks of hypermodernism insofar as Black's Knight provokes the advance of White's Pawns with a view to leaving them weak and as fixed targets.

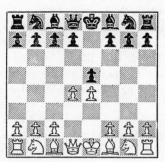

2 .... **PxP**

The counterattack by 2 ... N-KB3 leaves White with the superior game after 3 PxP, NxP 4 Q-Q5, N-B4, 5 B-B4. Then 5 ... N-K3 grants White a more flourishing development while 5 ... Q-K2 causes obstruction in Black's ranks.

3 **QxP** ....

The Center Game proper. Other moves, such as 3 N-KB3 or 3 B-QB4, although branches of the Center Game, are openings in their own right.

3 .... **N-QB3**

Developing with gain of tempo by attacking the Queen. This one move is Black's compensation for the advantages that have accrued to White thus far.

The recommended book line. The strategic idea involved here is for White to swing his Queen eventually to KN3 (toward where he hopes the Black Monarch will be), castle Queen-side, and exert pressure on the open Queen file.

Black's problem is to find suitable counterplay with a plan of his own.

Alternatives for White are 4 Q-B4, 4 Q-R4, and 4 Q-Q1.

4 Q-B4 gives Black a free and easy game after the moves 4 . . . N-B3; 5 N-QB3, P-Q4! This tricky, temporary sacrifice of a Pawn solves all of Black's problems of development. For example, after 5 PxP, N-QN5 (simultaneously attacking the Queen Pawn and the Queen Bishop Pawn); Black must recover the Pawn. Or, in this line, if 5 NxP, NxN; 6 PxN, N-N5; again Black must recover the Pawn.

4 Q-K3 . . . .

4 Q-R4 is the most desirable of the alternatives, although, up to the present, White has not been able to demonstrate any advantage from it. A line of play might follow this order: 4 Q-R4, B-B4; 5 N-KB3, P-Q3; 6 N-B3, KN-K2; 7 B-KN5, B-Q2. Black appears to have sufficient resources, mainly because of the threat of discovering an attack on White's Queen.

This writer holds a deep conviction that somewhere along the line, White might improve his technique, although he is not prepared at the moment to present any satisfactory suggestion.

4 Q-Q1 fails inasmuch as the tempo presented to Black counterbalances the advantages gained by White's second move.

4 . . . . N-B3!

This star move dates back to an analysis by Berger in 1884. Any other move permits White to further his grand plan without much opposition.

The move invites tricky play.

5 **N-QB3** . . . .

5 P-K5 puts Black to the test. It can be refuted, however, with correct play, thus: 5 P-K5, N-KN5; 6 Q-K2, P-Q3; 7 P-KB3, N-R3; 8 PxPch, B-K3; 9 BxN, Q-R5ch; with an attack worth the Pawn.

In this line, Black can sacrifice a piece on his seventh move with 7 . . . KNxKP, but White should come out on top. The play might go as follows: 7 . . . KNxKP; 8 P-KB4, N-Q5; 9 Q-K4, P-QB4; 10 N-QR3, B-B4; 11 Q-K3, Q-R4ch; 12 K-B2!, O-O-O; 13 PxN, PxP; 14 P-B3, N-B3; 15 N-B4.

5 . . . . **B-K2**

Good also is 5 . . . B-N5; 6 B-Q2, O-O; 7 O-O-O, R-K1; 8 Q-N3, NxP!; 9 NxN, RxN; 10 B-KB4, Q-B3!; 11 N-R3, P-Q3; 12 B-Q3, N-Q5!; 13 B-K3, R-N5; 14 BxN, RxB; 15 P-QB3, BxP; 16 PxB; R-KN5; 17 Q-K3, QxQBPch; 18 B-B2, QxQch; 19 PxQ, RxP.

It is to be observed that the onus of precision play, however, rests with Black in this variation. One misstep could be fatal.

6 **B-Q2** . . . .

Developing apace and making ready for Queen-side castling, which is part of the grand strategic plan.

6 ....   **P-Q4!**

The correct procedure. If Black submits to ... P-Q3 out of choice or circumstance, White's plan will shape up effectively; whereas after his last move, Black should experience no development problems.

7 **PxP**	**NxP**
8 **NxN**	**QxN**

Observe that Black enjoys the lead in development, traceable to White's early Queen moves.

9 **N-K2**   ....

White still eyes the prospects of castling Queen-side and intends to fortify his Queen Rook Pawn and drive Black's Queen by continuing with N-B3.

9 ....   **B-KN5**

But this move restrains the execution of White's plan. Now, if *10* N-B3, White will be unable to castle as his King cannot pass the line of Black's Queen Bishop.

> *10* **N-B4** . . . .

White accommodates himself to the change.

> *10* **Q-Q2**
>
> *11* **P-KB3** . . . .

White drives the Bishop so as to make Queen-side castling possible.

> *11* . . . .   **O-O-O!**

Oddly enough, it is Black who castles first on the long side. The move, however, offers a piece. Just as good is *11* ... B-KB4, although the text sets a trap.

> *12* **O-O-O** . . . .

Capturing the piece will get White into trouble, thus: *12* PxB, B-R5ch; *13* K-Q1 (*13* P-KN3 loses), KR-K1; *14* Q-Q3, QxPch; *15* B-K2, RxB; *16* QxR, QxN; *17* K-B1, N-Q5; with a powerful attack.

> *12* **B-KB4**
>
> *13* **B-Q3** . . . .

Since White's plan has gone awry, he is content to draw and offers a friendly exchange of material.

13 ....   **B-B3**

But it is Black who enjoys the initiative and plays for whatever the position offers.

14 **BxB**   **QxB**
15 **KR-K1**   **N-Q5**

Black has the better game.

Conclusions and recommendations

While the Center Game proper theoretically places no great obstacles in the way of the defender, it does burden him with the necessity of finding innumerably difficult and treacherous moves.

The line beginning with *1* P-K4, P-K4; *2* P-Q4, PxP; *3* QxP, N-QB3; *4* Q-R4 has met with tournament reverses, up to the present. Sometime, somewhere, this line will be bolstered, and White will enjoy the benefit of a new opening weapon.

Chess Movie

O-O-O OH! OH!

THE EVOLUTION of an opening depicts any number of plausible ideas, which have come and gone, and left their imprint in the golden treasury of chess. Here Russian grandmaster Tchigorin (White) refutes Mackenzie's rational defense to the Center Game. The scene is Vienna, 1882. The game begins with the moves: *1* P-K4, P-K4; *2* P-Q4, PxP; *3* QxP, N-QB3; *4* Q-K3. (Continue from Diagram 1.)

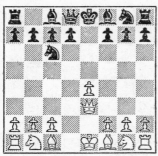 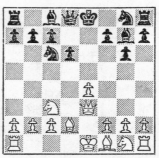

1 Mackenzie adopts an old-fashioned defense. 4 ... P-KN3 is the move. Tchigorin continues with the grand plan. There follows 5 B-Q2, B-N2; 6 N-QB3, P-Q3. White is to castle long and attack on the other wing, where he hopes the opposing monarch will be. Black develops systematically.

2 7 P-B4 signals White's plan, and Black continues his development apace with 7 ... KN-K2. There follows 8 O-O-O, B-K3; 9 N-B3, Q-Q2. Black is developing and jockeying at the same time. He has not determined to castle on the King-side; the Queen-side may do too.

17

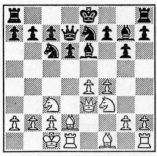

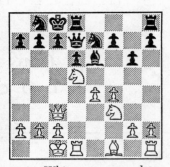

3 *10* N-Q5 is White's move, and Black follows with *10* ... O-O-O. And why not? Is White not ready for him on the other wing? There follows *11* B-B3, BxB; *12* QxB, N-QN1. Just in time, Black manages to avoid the menacing checkmate to his Queen! Still Black suffers from a backward game.

4 White accommodates himself to the new conditions. Black's King is on the Queen-side, and he heads for that direction. *13* Q-R3 is the move. Black plays *13* ... BxN, and *14* PxB, Q-B4 follows. Two Pawns are attacked. White defends one with *15* P-KN3, and Black takes one with *15* ... NxP.

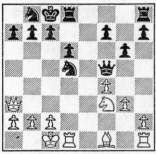

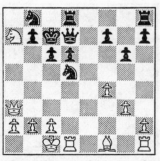

5 White inches in with *16* N-Q4, and Black retires with *16* ... Q-Q2. White comes closer with *17* N-N5, and Black defends with *17* ... P-QB3. Then follows *18* NxRPch, and the Black monarch is budged from his haven with *18* ... K-B2. Material is even, but White is gaining ground.

6 The time has come for a quickening pace. *19* RxN! shatters Black's defensive barrier. Black replies *19* ... PxR; and there follows *20* B-N5 driving the enemy Queen. Black plays *20* ... Q-K3 and then comes *21* Q-B3ch, K-N3. White draws a long bead on the Black King. The end is in sight.

7 But first the Black Queen must be removed from the vital scene. *22 R-K1* is the move. Black takes two Rooks for the Queen by playing *22 ... KxN.* There follows *23 RxQ, PxR.* Then White aims at the King with *24 Q-K3ch*, and Black retreats with *24 ... K-R1.* The King is cornered.

8 Now comes the fatal incursion. The sequel is *25 Q-R3ch, N-R3; 26 BxN, PxB; 27 QxPch, K-N1.* The monarch is at White's mercy. A perpetual check is the least of his troubles. Is that, however, enough compensation for White's valor? The answer is written on the next panel.

9 *28 Q-N6ch* puts the opposing monarch in position. *28 ... K-B1* is the move. Then *29 P-QN4* is the follow-up. A Queen and two passed Pawns against a lone King ought to be more than sufficient to decide the fate of the game, if no reinforcements are available. Is there any defense?

10 Quickly, Black plays *29 ... KR-K1.* He feints a threat with his King Pawn and builds a psychological defense. White plays *30 Q-R7*, and Black advances *30 ... P-K4.* White follows with *31 P-N5*, and there is no defense to the further advance of this mighty Pawn. Black resigns.

3

A typical position in the Danish

Danish Gambit

ONCE UPON A time it was considered ungentlemanly to decline a gambit. Then it was that the King's Gambit, the Max Lange, the Evans, and the Danish, among others, saw their heyday.

In those blissfully romantic days, chess technique was not fully developed. Not yet mastered was the art of sound defense. Advantages in time and space—the goal of the gambit—were given top rating. Material was looked upon askance. During this profligate era, the Danish was born. For the true

20

Danish, extended to its thematic finale, involves the sacrifice of two Pawns, in return for rapid development.

This enterprising opening, according to historian H. J. R. Murray, was played by a Danish jurist in Jutland in the 1830's. It was well known in Scandinavian countries before Von der Lasa, the Prussian Ambassador at Copenhagen, introduced it generally in 1867. And it was first noted in the game Lindehn versus Swanberg, 1859.

Today it is considered foolhardy to decline a real gambit. "Take first and look later" is the guiding principle. For accent is on material! Hard-boiled cynicism has brought about the pragmatic transition. For the gambiteer, self-handicapped and under constant pressure to convert intangible assets into something real, often fails of his mark. Lack of force and even lack of *sitzfleisch* undo him.

Despite these qualms, gambiteers will not be suppressed. Control of the center and two powerful Bishops, exercising full sway on commanding diagonals are inducements for the Danish, in particular. And, in general for gambits in over-the-board play, there is an actual, though intangible, advantage in pressuring a queasy opponent.

The Danish arises as follows:

1	P-K4	P-K4
2	P-Q4	PxP
3	P-QB3	. . . .

3 QxP is the Center Game proper. (See the previous chapter.)

The text move is the first step in the Danish Gambit. It is the offer of a Pawn in return for development.

$$3 \ldots \quad \text{PxP}$$

This is in line with the guiding principle: "Take first and look later." As a matter of fact, however, no other Black move is apt to produce an advantage. Black, moreover, must do something about White's threat to play 4 PxP and regain his Pawn and remain with a powerful Pawn center.

An alternative for Black is 3 ... P-Q4; after which the game also becomes lively. Then 4 KPxP, QxP; 5 PxP, N-QB3; 6 N-KB3, B-N5; 7 B-K2, N-B3; 8 N-B3, Q-QR4; White's minimal lead in development overshadows the disadvantage of his isolated Pawn.

4 B-QB4   ....

This move aims primarily at the most vulnerable square in Black's camp—Black's KB2. One of White's ideas is to concentrate enough pressure on that square, during the future course of the game, so as to make it embarrassing for the defender.

In this position, however, Alekhine warmly recommends 4 NxP. The line might run as follows: 4 ... P-Q3; 5 B-QB4, N-QB3; 6 N-B3, B-K3!; 7 B-Q5, N-B3; 8 O-O, B-K2; with a good game for Black. For example, if 9 BxB, PxB; 10 Q-N3, Q-B1; and Black stands well. The spirit of the gambit, moreover, dictates the text move—the sacrifice of a second Pawn—whose object is the gain of time and space in return for material.

Black need not go all out in accepting the gambit. He can pull in his horns with 4 ... P-Q3 and lead to the variation given in the preceding note. Or he might continue with 4 ... N-QB3; 5 N-B3, B-B4; 6 NxP, P-Q3; 7 Q-N3, Q-Q2; 8 N-Q5, KN-K2; 9 Q-B3, O-O; 10 O-O, NxN; 11 PxN, N-K4; 12 NxN, PxN; 13 QxP, B-Q3; with about equal chances.

4 ....   PxP

The text move gives Black a plus of two Pawns for the inferior position. It is, however, the only clear-cut way of refuting the gambit.

5 BxP   ....

(See Photo)

The Danish proper. Observe the commanding sweep of both of White's Bishops. Observe also that White maintains control of the center—but that he is two Pawns behind.

The question is: Can White exploit his advantages before Black is able to consolidate?

5 ....   P-QB3

The first move of a deep defensive plan. The move is sharp and flexible. The Pawn at QB3 serves as a barrier, eliminates a White threat of entering at White's Q5, and also serves as a prop for a later move of ... P-Q4 or ... P-QN4.

The recommended book line at this point runs as follows: 5 ... P-Q4; 6 KBxP, N-KB3; 7 BxPch, KxB; 8 QxQ, B-N5ch, 9 Q-Q2, BxQch; 10 NxB, P-B4.

At one time, authorities agreed that Black enjoyed the better chances on account of his Queen-side Pawn majority, which can be mobilized rapidly. It was thought that White's King-side majority could be checked with the assistance of the Black King. The books concur in this belief. A number of un-

official games, however, challenges this conclusion. For, after
11 N-KB3, Black's King is somewhat of a target, and, instead of hindering the adverse Pawns, actually promotes their
advance.

6 **N-QB3**   . . . .

A good developing move, although White has the option
of a number of good developing moves at this stage. In each
case, however, Black resorts to the same kind of defense that
he sets up here and manages to come out on top.

Some of White's possibilities are crafty and must be handled with care. For instance, if 6 P-K5, Black must batter down
White's restraining hold on the Black Pawns. This is done in
the following manner: 6 . . . Q-K2, threatening . . . P-Q4 as
well as . . . Q-N5ch, each of which routs the White men. White
then has no better than 7 K-B1. Then, if Black persists with
7 . . . P-Q4; 8 PxP e.p., QxP; 9 QxQ, BxQ; 10 BxNP wins the
Rook. Therefore, if 6 P-K5, Q-K2; 7 K-B1, P-B3. Now, whatever White does, Black must enforce . . . P-Q4 and consolidate
his forces and obtain a free and easy development.

Incidentally, if 6 Q-N3, Q-K2; Black's threat of . . . P-Q4 as
well as . . . Q-N5ch bogs down White's assault.

It should be borne in mind that Black is two Pawns ahead.
If necessary, he is willing to part with one of them (or even
both) in order to emerge with the better position.

6 . . . .   **P-Q3**

This move is played not merely to free Black's Queen Bishop. It is part and parcel of a system of defense. The Pawn at Q3 is part of the barrier to enemy incursion.

Black's over-all plan is to prevent any breach in his Pawn position and then slowly bring out his forces and remain with material plus.

7 N-B3 . . . .

There is no crushing or even impetuous rejoinder. Consequently, White must develop apace. His hope is that after all his men are brought out, he will be able to find or provoke a weakness in Black's camp.

7 . . . . N-Q2

This is the third step in the defensive plan. Watch the maneuver of the Queen Knight to its final destination.

8 O-O . . . .

Again, development goes on steadily. If 8 Q-N3, Black defends with . . . Q-K2 and later drives the Queen with . . . N-B4.

8 . . . . N-B4

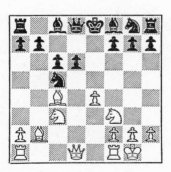

Black is for choice. There are a number of good continuations at his disposal. He can play . . . B-K3 and compel the retreat or exchange of White's mighty King Bishop. Then he can continue with his King-side development, until it is complete. In the interim, White has no penetrating moves or such as will increase the pressure before Black is able to develop and consolidate. In the long run, the extra two Pawns will make themselves felt.

Conclusions and recommendations

Like most gambits, the Danish leads to exciting play. The attacker always enjoys the game, at least during the early stages. Against accurate defense, however, the attack peters out, and then the defender reaps his material reward.

Unless some way can be found to breach the barrier set up by Black, beginning with his third move, the Danish will be relegated to use by the dilettante, who cares little about book plays or exactitude.

At present, it appears that the Danish proper is refuted.

Chess Movie

THE DANISH DOES IT

WHEN IS A Pawn not a Pawn? When it is dished up in a Danish, of course. Then it is only a decoy to lure enemy men away from their King. Janowski and Soldatenkoff (White) offer two Pawns to ambush the mighty Lasker and Taubenhaus in this brilliant miniature, played at Paris, 1909. It opens with *1* P-K4, P-K4; *2* P-Q4, PxP; *3* P-QB3, PxP; *4* B-QB4, PxP; *5* BxP, reaching the position in Diagram 1.

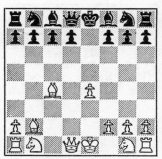

1 The Black team treats the position the same as any other. Development is accented: *5* ... N-KB3 is the move. This provokes the reply, *6* P-K5, driving the Knight from its post. Then follows *6* ... B-N5ch. Black's plan is to cut down material or compel White's King to move.

2 White interposes *7* N-B3, and Black pins the adverse King Pawn with *7* ... Q-K2. White breaks the pin with *8* N-K2, and Black enters *8* ... N-K5. Both sides are happy—White, because his development is supreme—Black, because he is managing to swap forces. What now?

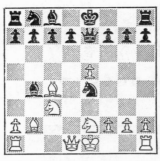

3 More men to battle is White's plan as he plays *9 O-O.* Less men is Black's idea as he swaps: *9 ... NxN; 10 BxN, BxB.* White recaptures *11 NxB,* and off to safety goes the Black monarch with *11 ... O-O.* (Safety is only relative. The King must yet rebuff a few enemy forces.)

4 White penetrates with *12 N-Q5!* offering, as it were, even another Pawn. And Black captures *12 ... QxP.* He'll be hanged for a sheep rather than a lamb. With three Pawns to the good, Black's prospects are promising. It is White's turn, however, and the game is young.

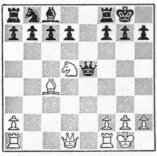

5 First comes *13 R-K1,* gaining another valuable tempo. Black retreats *13 ... Q-Q3.* Then follows *14 Q-R5,* fixing the sights on the enemy King. Already the threats are mounting, and there is little to be done about them. Black's entire Queen's wing is bottled up, pathetically.

6 Black is sadly lacking the time, which he so readily gave up in the beginning. He continues with *14 ... P-QB3,* attacking White's critter. White replies startlingly with *15 N-B7!* He must clear the path of the King Bishop. Material gain is only a secondary consideration.

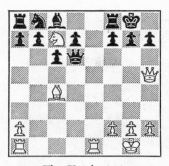

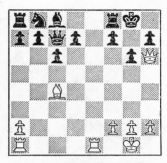

7 The Knight is immune. (If *14* ... QxN; Black is checkmated in two!) Black tries to make the most of a bad position and continues with *15* ... P-KN3. White replies *16* Q-R6, and now a piece goes with *16* ... QxN. White can hardly give up more material. He needs a mating force.

8 Yet White does give up more. *17* BxPch! is the move. Black has no choice; he plays *17* ... KxB. Then follows *18* QxRPch!, and the Black King advances, *18* ... K-B3. The monarch is due for a walk—one of those compulsory walks, with a bayonet at his midriff. All is gloom in the Black camp.

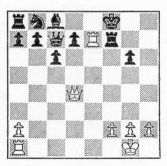

9 *19* Q-R4ch forces the retreat *19* ... K-N2. Then follows *20* R-K7ch. Black interposes *20* ... R-B2. For a moment, it appears that Black is squirming out. But ho! *21* Q-Q4ch places the King in target range. The King retreats *21* ... K-B1. He is to be forced into the open for the last time.

10 A combination winds up the game in magnificent style. *22* Q-R8ch! is the first move. Black plays *22* ... KxR. Now follows *23* R-K1ch. Black plays *22* ... K-Q3. *24* Q-K5ch is checkmate. All the King's horses and all the King's men are quite unable to save the King.

4

The typical position in the King's Gambit

King's Gambit

Long before basic principles of chess were expressed in so many words, competent players essayed correct stratagems. The importance of controlling the center while promoting development—the paramount tenet for openings today—for example, was recognized as far back as 1561, when Lopez inaugurated the King's Gambit.

After the moves, *1* P-K4, P-K4; White offers a Pawn with *2* P-KB4. This simple move embodies a dual purpose, which strikes at the heart of opening theory. It aims to decoy the staunch enemy King Pawn from its occupation of the center proper and, at the same time, it opens the King Bishop file for future use. Whether these gains offset the value of a Pawn, however, is the moot question.

In 1842, the King's Gambit was analyzed at length by Jaenisch, who enthusiastically designated it "an imperishable monument of human wisdom," for it had evolved during the course of centuries and was far from obsolete. A while later, it languished under a niggardly fashion for closed games that became prevalent and then made its reappearance at the Gambit Tournaments of Abbazia, 1912, and Baden, 1914. There it was shown that Black could obtain equality by returning the extra Pawn. Sporadic attempts to revive the popularity of the King's Gambit have just about fallen short of their mark. The present trend, however, is toward a revival of the gambit.

The King's Gambit arises as follows:

1 P-K4   **P-K4**
2 P-KB4   . . . .

The King's Gambit—so called because White proffers a Pawn on the King's side of the board.

The immediate purpose of the sacrifice is to sidetrack Black's King Pawn from the central zone and enable White to gain a preponderance in that sector. The long-term purpose is to open the King Bishop file for future use. Since the most vulnerable point in Black's camp is his KB2, it is clear that an open line leading directly to that square enhances White's prospects of assault.

Unlike the Queen's Gambit, the offer of the gambit Pawn here is firm; the Pawn cannot be retrieved at will. Under the circumstances, White is prepared to give up material for compensating gain in space and mobility. Whether one offsets the other is the issue.

2 . . . .   **PxP**

As a general principle, it is always best to accept a gambit, with a view to returning the material at an auspicious moment, when the material plus can be converted to gain in other directions. Opinion on the acceptance of the King's Gambit, however, is divided. There are those who prefer the prospects of the gambit declined or the countergambit.

Now Black is a Pawn to the good and it is up to White to capitalize on his advantages—the control of the center, the open King Bishop file, and the usual minimal initiative—by exploiting them to the full.

The King's Gambit Declined—2 . . . B-B4—and the Falkbeer Counter Gambit—2 . . . P-Q4—will be discussed in the next chapter.

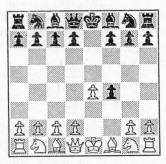

3 **N-KB3**　　　　. . . .

After the text move, the opening is technically known as the King Knight's Gambit as distinguished from 3 B-B4, which is the Bishop's Gambit.

Whereas the latter was in vogue for many years, it is now believed that the former is the sounder of the two and sets up greater problems for the defender.

If 3 B-B4, however, the game might continue as follows: 3 . . . N-KB3; 4 N-QB3, P-B3!; 5 Q-B3, P-Q4; 6 PxP, B-Q3; 7 P-Q3, B-KN5; 8 Q-B2, O-O; 9 BxP, R-K1ch; 10 K-B1, P-QN4; 11 B-QN3, P-N5; 12 QN-K2, NxP; with the better game for Black.

It is to be observed in the above line that after 3 . . . N-KB3; if White thrusts forward with 4 P-K5, Black parries with 4 . . . P-Q4!; and if then 5 PxN, PxB; Black's prospects are superior.

In this connection, it ought to be noted for future reference that this tactical parry (... P-Q4!) applies as well to similar situations in other openings, as well as the King's Gambit.

The text, a good developing move, bears on the center.

3 .... **B-K2**

At the present moment in the evolution of the defense, the text move supersedes the perennial 3 ... N-KB3 and 3 ... P-Q4. These moves have been temporarily shelved, because of some refinements in White's play, which seem to give the first player the upper hand.

For example, 3 ... N-KB3; 4 P-K5, N-R4; 5 P-Q4, P-Q4; 6 N-B3, P-KN4; 7 B-K2, P-N5; 8 O-O!, R-N1!; 9 N-K1, B-R3; 10 B-Q3, B-K3; 11 N-K2!, Q-R5; 12 BxBP. Black's Pawn structure is inferior and his offensive is spent.

Or 3 ... P-Q4; 4 PxP, N-KB3; 5 B-N5ch, P-B3; 6 PxP, PxP; 7 B-B4, B-Q3; 8 Q-K2ch, Q-K2; 9 QxQch, KxQ; 10 P-Q4, B-KB4; 11 N-K5, BxN; 12 PxB, N-Q4; 13 BxN, with advantage for White.

Of course, any new move or idea could easily rehabilitate either of the above lines. They are, however, still to be discovered.

The traditional defense of the gambit Pawn—3 ... P-KN4— has long since been relegated to limbo. This move might be a prelude to the following course: 3 ... P-KN4; 4 P-KR4!, P-N5; 5 N-K5, N-KB3; 6 P-Q4, P-Q3; 7 N-Q3, NxP; 8 BxP, Q-K2;

9 Q-K2, B-N2; *10* P-B3, P-KR4; *11* N-Q2, NxN; *12* KxN with superiority for White. The defect in this defense is that White can exploit Black's weakened King-side Pawn structure and then make penetrating inroads into the Black King's camp.

Oddly enough, the move that offers Black the best chance, according to the "book," is the puny *3 . . .* P-KR3, known as Becker's Defense. This move, however, is so much anathema to the principles of good chess (at least in the mind of this scribe), that it can hardly be recommended, even if good! Its point is that it is preparatory to defending the gambit Pawn with . . . P-KN4. At the same time, it exercises a temporizing effect, waiting for White's next move. Clearly, White can hardly afford, after *3 . . .* P-KR3, to continue with *4* P-KR4 to prevent Black from playing . . . P-KN4. For, in that case, White disrupts his own King-side Pawn formation, without breaching Black's. Accordingly, White must continue his development, with some such move as *4* B-B4. Then Black can essay *4 . . .* P-KN4; and the sting is taken out of White's stroke of *5* P-KR4. This line might run as follows: *3 . . .* P-KR3; *4* B-B4, P-KN4; *5* O-O, B-N2; *6* P-Q4, P-Q3. The position is approximately even, since Black's Pawn plus is offset by White's control of the center.

That Black can afford to neglect his development by playing so many Pawn moves in a row, such as *2 . . .* PxP, *3 . . .* P-KB3, *4 . . .* P-KN4, is questionable. This idea is bound to fall from grace, just as soon as the masters seriously apply themselves to discover its refutation.

A point in favor of the text move, *3 . . .* B-K2, as against *3 . . .* N-KB3, is that White cannot advance his Pawn to K5 and drive the opposing Knight to KR4, where it is more or less on a limb.

4 B-B4   . . . .

White continues his development apace, controls the center, and bears down on the vulnerable point in Black's camp, his KB2 square.

4 .... **N-KB3!**

A suggestion credited to Schlechter. 4 ... B-R5ch, known as the Cunningham Gambit, is too risky. On the face of it, it is doomed. Black can hardly afford to neglect his development, even for the sake of forcing the adverse King to move. This line might run as follows: 4 ... B-R5ch; 5 K-B1, P-Q4; 6 BxP, N-KB3; 7 N-B3, O-O; 8 P-Q4, P-B3; 9 B-N3, B-N5; 10 QBxP, N-R4; 11 Q-Q2, BxN; 12 PxB, with the better game for White.

5 **P-K5** ....

In order to drive the Knight from the center and prevent the usual counterstroke ... P-Q4. The defense of the King Pawn by 5 N-B3 ought to give Black the upper hand by the reply 5 ... NxP. Then, if 6 NxN, P-Q4. Or if 6 BxPch, KxB; followed by ... P-Q4.

5 .... **N-N5!**

Black cannot employ the usual parry 5 ... P-Q4, as his Bishop rests at K2. Therefore he loses a piece: 5 ... P-Q4?; 6 PxN, PxB; 7 PxB.

The text move is better than 5 ... N-R4 insofar as the Knight bears down on White's King Pawn and is a direct challenge to its existence.

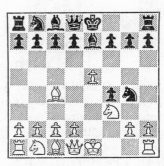

6 **O-O** ....

The plausible 6 P-KR3 will not do: 6 P-KR3, B-R5ch; 7 K-B1, N-B7; and Black will be able to capture the Rook and to exit via the loophole at his KN6 square.

The text move seems to promote White's development in as good a way as any. It has been suggested that after 6 N-B3 (instead of 6 O-O), P-Q3; 7 P-Q4, PxP, 8 PxP, QxQch; 9 NxQ, the end game rather favors White, because of his better development.

We take exception to this opinion. After 9 ... B-K3, Black should have no trouble in equalizing. If, for example, 10 BxB, PxB; 11 BxP, O-O, followed by 12 ... N-QB3, Black's development is as good as White's. White's King Pawn, moreover, is at least as much of a target as Black's King Pawn. If, in this line, White interpolates by 11 N-Q4 (instead of 11 BxP), with the idea of picking off Black's King Pawn, Black can defend in different ways. 11 ... B-R5ch, followed by 12 ... K-K2 is one way. 11 ... O-O; 12 NxP, R-B1; 13 BxP,

N-QB3, recovering the Pawn with an easy game, is still another way.

6 . . . .   P-Q3

This move successfully collapses White's bridgehead in the center.

7 PxP   . . . .

Otherwise, Black threatens to exchange and simplify. Since he enjoys a free and easy development, he ought then to have no problems.

7 . . . .   QxP

Black keeps his Bishop at K2 to support a possible . . . P-KN4. White will experience difficulty recovering the Pawn.

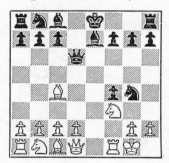

Black is for choice.

Conclusions and recommendations

The King's Gambit ought to be part of the repertoire of every chessplayer. It does not, however, lead to a forced win for White. It does lead to a stimulating, combinative game, which is the essence of chess, as far as most players are concerned.

Theoretically, Black can equalize or do even better. Practically, the pitfalls for the defender are many—and one of them can be enough!

Chess Movie

TWO PAWNS VERSUS A "PERP"

W<small>HEN</small> English grand master Yates was in a game—win, lose, or draw—his opponent knew that he was going through the wringers. Even Akiba Rubinstein, master of masters, as White, knew it in the following contest, played at Hastings, 1922. The opening: the King's Gambit. It begins *1* P-K4, P-K4; *2* P-KB4, PxP; *3* N-KB3, N-KB3; leading to Diagram 1.

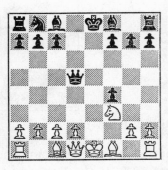

1 The mighty Akiba plays *4* N-B3, and Yates parries with *4 ...* P-Q4. White swaps: *5* PxP, NxP; *6* NxN, QxN. The features of the position indicate action. It is unbalanced; White has the extra center Pawn and Black has a free and easy development, his Queen dominantly posted, and a Pawn up.

2 The game continues with *7* P-Q4, B-K2; *8* B-Q3, P-KN4. Rubinstein occupies the center, and Yates defends his material gain. There follows *9* Q-K2, B-KB4; *10* BxB, QxB. Black's strategy is to pare down. For a Pawn plus in the end game is no minor matter, especially in master play.

38

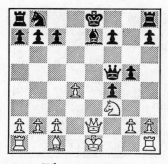

3 White contrives an ingenious tactic. *11 P-KN4!* is the move. The Pawn is poison, and Black retreats *11 ... Q-Q2.* White continues his development with *12 B-Q2,* and Black keeps pace with *12 ... N-B3.* Both sides castle long: *13 O-O-O, O-O-O.* All is in readiness. The action begins!

4 Rubinstein attempts to shatter Black's Kingside Pawn chain with *14 P-KR4!?* Yates calmly keeps it intact with *14 ... P-B3.* Rubinstein shifts to the center with *15 P-B4,* and Yates bows to his predatory instincts with *15 ... QxNP.* There now follows *16 PxP, PxP.*

5 *17 P-Q5!* unhinges the Black men from their moorings. Black plays *17 ... N-N5.* And White picks off the Bishop with *18 QxB.* Now Yates comes up with *18 ... N-Q6ch* and will soon recover his piece. There follows *19 K-B2, QxN.* The extra Pawns loom large momentarily.

6 But ho! The master knows what he is doing! There follows *20 Q-K6ch, K-N1; 21 R-R3!* Black must lose a piece after all. Wily Yates fights gamely back. *21 ... QxQRch!* is his answer, and the game continues *22 KxQ, N-B7ch;* forking King and Rook. Has Yates enough in recompense?

7 White plays 23 K-K1, and now Black follows through with 23 ... NxR. White replies 24 QxN, and Black gets his Pawns in motion with 24 ... P-KR4. Then comes 25 B-B3, P-N5; 26 Q-R4, KR-N1. One Pawn must fall. But the others are much closer to the goal. Can they be held?

8 "Take first and look later" is the guiding principle as Rubinstein plays 27 QxRP. Then follows 27 ... P-N6; 28 B-Q4, QR-K1ch; 29 K-Q2, QR-KB1. The situation is uncomfortably warm. Rubinstein attempts a diversion with 30 P-Q6! The scene shifts again. 30 ... PxP is the move.

9 31 Q-R6 follows, looking in the direction of the Black monarch. Yates seeks a haven with 31 ... K-R1. Rubinstein plays 32 QxQP, and Yates checks the immediate danger with 32 ... R-Q1. 33 Q-B5 threatens mate, and Yates continues with RxBch! The denouement is at hand.

10 There follows 34 QxR, P-N7; 35 Q-N1, R-N6. The White King shall not cross the Rubicon. White plays 36 P-N4, and Black makes a loophole with 36 ... P-R3. Then comes 37 K-K2, P-B6ch; and a draw is agreed, for if 38 K-B2, R-R6; 39 Q-Q1, R-R8; 40 Q-Q8ch with perpetual check!

5

A typical King's Gambit Declined position

King's Gambit Declined

CONFLICTING MAXIMS rule the chessboard. "Take first and look later" is one guiding principle, blatantly contradicted by the dictum, "Beware of gifts—Grecian or otherwise." Clearly, chess by maxim leads to quiet confusion.

When material is at stake, instinct favors its appropriation. And with good reason. For *material* is *force*. And a preponderance of force brooks little or no interference or opposition. In theory, the idea behind a capture, even a predatory one, is to build superior reserves in order, if need be, to dole out the booty and maintain the advantage as your opponent loses time in recapturing. In practice, instinct is tempered with judgment. All the factors—time, space, and force—are pitted

41

against each other, and only then is a decision rendered. You have seen this struggle in many a game.

So it is with gambits. Even the simplest of them involves the deepest complexities. It is impossible to determine with certainty that a gain or loss will be offset by some other plus or minus. Consequently, there are those who avoid speculation and decline gambits.

Particularly is this true of the King's Gambit. For White's second move 2 P-KB4, which characterizes the gambit, is double-edged. It aims for pertinent gain but leaves a perceptible weakness in White's Kingside Pawn structure. It is with a view to exploiting that weakness that Black declines the gambit.

Schemes for evading the numerous attacks arising from the King's Gambit were proposed by Lopez as far back as 1561. All in all, about ten lines of play have been tried, most of which have been found wanting. Today, one or two lines are considered good enough to give Black at least equality.

This is the King's Gambit Declined:

| 1 | **P-K4** | **P-K4** |
| 2 | *P-KB4* | **B-B4** |

Since Black wishes to maintain the center instead of giving it up by sidetracking his King Pawn, he declines the gambit Pawn. At the same time, he hopes to exploit the weakness created on White's diagonal, KN1-QR7. Now Black's King

Bishop bears on the most vulnerable square in White's King's camp, White's KB2.

Before continuing with the line that develops from Black's second move, it is worth while to digress briefly upon another likely alternative.

There are many other ways for Black to decline the Gambit. Nearly all of them, however, are beset with drawbacks. 2 ... P-Q3, for instance, leaves Black with a backward development, after 3 N-KB3, N-QB3; 4 P-Q4.

The most aggressive parry to the King's Gambit is 2 ... P-Q4; known as the Falkbeer Counter Gambit. The main variation of this line runs as follows: 1 P-K4, P-K4; 2 P-KB4, P-Q4; 3 KPxP, P-K5; 4 P-Q3, N-KB3; 5 Q-K2, QxP; 6 N-QB3, B-QN5; 7 B-Q2, BxN; 8 BxB, B-N5; 9 PxP, QxKP; 10 QxQch, NxQ; 11 BxP, R-N1; 12 B-K5, N-QB3; 13 B-Q3, with a better game for White (see diagram below).

DIAGRAM FOR VARIATION

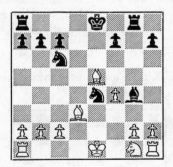

The idea behind the Falkbeer is for Black to ruin White's chances of establishing a strong center and of opening the King Bishop file and the normal diagonal of the Queen Bishop. Black actually succeeds in these aims. For White's King Bishop Pawn stands out like a sore thumb, when it is by-passed by ... P-K5. But Black's plan costs him a Pawn. Up to the present, Black has been unable to show adequate compensation for the Pawn minus.

The Falkbeer, moreover, is rife with tactical motifs. The simplest one, for instance, occurs on the third move. Thus, after *1* P-K4, P-K4; *2* P-KB4, P-Q4; *3* BPxP, White is a dead cock in the pit: *3* ... Q-R5ch; *4* K-K2, QxKPch; *5* K-B2, B-QB4ch; *6* K-N3, Q-N3ch; etc. If *4* P-N3 (after *3* ... Q-R5ch), QxKPch; and White loses a Rook.

When, as, and if the Falkbeer is bolstered, it will write finis to the King's Gambit.

To resume with the main line (from the first diagram):

3 N-KB3 ....

This is probably White's best developing move, since it puts pressure on Black's center. Any other move might raise the argument as to whether ... BxN is good or bad for White —an argument that could not be settled lightly.

It is to be noted that White cannot afford to play *3* PxP?? on account of the reply ... Q-R5ch, which wins at once: thus, *4* P-N3, QxKPch, followed by ... QxR, or *4* K-K2, QxKP mate.

3 .... P-Q3

Defending the King Pawn and making ready for the development of the Queen Bishop.

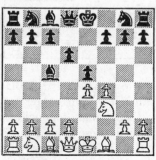

4 N-B3 ....

A good developing move, bearing on the center.

Alternative lines are no better. For instance, if *4* B-B4, N-KB3; *5* P-Q3, B-K3!; *6* BxB, PxB; *7* PxP, PxP; *8* N-B3, N-B3; *9* B-N5, P-KR3; *10* B-R4, Q-Q3; *11* Q-Q2, O-O-O; *12* O-O-O, P-KN4; *13* B-B2, B-N5; with better attacking prospects for Black.

Or *4* P-B3, N-KB3; *5* PxP, PxP; *6* P-Q4, PxP; *7* PxP, B-N3; *8* P-K5, N-Q4; *9* B-QB4, B-K3; *10* Q-N3, O-O; *11* N-B3, P-QB3; *12* O-O, N-B2; *13* B-K3, N-Q2; with about even chances. White's development is superior; his Pawns are weaker.

4 . . . .   **N-KB3**

Black's development goes on apace. The issue is whether White's pressure on the center and the King Bishop file, which will eventually open and accrue to White, will offset Black's command of the long diagonal by his King Bishop and the consequent insecurity to the White monarch.

5 **B-B4**   . . . .

White develops according to general principles—first Knights then Bishops.

5 . . . .   **N-B3**

6 **P-Q3**   . . . .

Development of both sides is nearly completed and the opening assumes a distinctive pattern.

6 . . . .   **B-KN5**

Now the threat is ... N-Q5, followed by the capture of White's King Knight and the ensuing breach in White's King-side Pawn position.

7 P-KR3! ....

Putting the question to the Bishop, before Black has the opportunity of executing his tactical plan.

An alternative but complicated line arises by 7 N-QR4, with a view to getting rid of Black's King Bishop. In that case, Black continues 7 ... N-Q5, and White's position becomes precarious.

7 .... BxN

There is no point to retreating. 7 ... B-KR4? loses a piece after 8 P-KN4, and the retreat in the other direction is clearly a waste of time. White now enjoys a minute material advantage—a Bishop for a Knight.

8 QxB N-Q5

But Black has established an annoying bridgehead in White's camp. Black threatens the Queen and the Queen Bishop Pawn.

9 Q-N3! ....

The retreat, 9 Q-Q1, grants Black a definite superiority in position. In that case, Black continues with ... P-B3, followed

by either ... P-Q4 or ... P-QN4 and ... P-QR4. Perforce
Black gains the upper hand as the position opens up, while
White's King is still in the middle of the board.

By a pointed counterthreat, the text move maintains an
even balance of the position.

9 ....   **Q-K2**

9 ... NxPch leads to a powerful attack for White: e.g.,
10 K-Q1, NxR; *11* QxP, R-KB1; *12* PxP, PxP; *13* R-B1, B-K2;
14 B-KN5, etc.

Playable, however, is 9 ... PxP and, if *10* QxNP, R-KB1;
11 K-Q1, Q-K2; *12* R-B1, R-KN1; *13* Q-R6, RxP, with a plus
for Black.

10 **PxP**   ....

White opens the King Bishop file and the normal diagonal
of his Queen Bishop and, at the same time, cancels the option
that Black exercises of capturing in Black's good time.

10 ....   **PxP**
11 **K-Q1**   ....

White protects the Queen Bishop Pawn. In doing so, White
forfeits the privilege of castling. *11* B-N3 would mean that
White must part with his Bishop, and he prefers to give up
castling rather than the powerful King Bishop.

11 ....   **P-B3**

With a dual purpose. Now White is denied the use of his
Q5 square, and, at the same time, Black readies for a Queen-
side Pawn demonstration, with the Queen Bishop Pawn serving
as a prop for ... P-QN4.

12 **P-QR4**   ....

To prevent the Queen-side Pawn advance, which could
prove embarrassing.

12 ....   **O-O-O**

Black castles long in order to avoid a head-on clash with the opposing forces, waiting for him on the other wing.

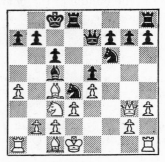

13 **R-B1**   . . . .

Not *13* QxNP, KR-N1; *14* QxBP, QxQ; *15* BxQ, RxP, as Black is for choice. White's King position has been penetrated.

The position is about even after *13* R-B1. White's men are better poised for action, with the exception of White's Queen Rook, which cannot join the fray until the White monarch makes way. On the other hand, the slightly unfavorable position of the White King is in Black's favor.

Conclusions and recommendations

The King's Gambit Declined is an excellent psychological weapon against a King's Gambit player. Whereas the player is poised for aggression, he suddenly finds himself in the role of defender—a role that may not suit his style.

As to the actual merits of the Gambit Accepted and the Gambit Declined, they are about on a par.

Chess Movie

ACTIONS SPEAK LOUDER THAN CHECKS

U NABATED ACTION from the first move on is the theme of this brilliant King's Gambit Declined. Swedish master Gosta Stoltz (White) picks off a Rook in the opening—with a prayer! —and, by devious defensive plays, manages to contain Rudolph Spielmann's onslaught. Stockholm, 1933, is the scene of play. The game begins: *1* P-K4, P-K4; *2* P-KB4, B-B4; *3* N-KB3, P-Q3; *4* P-B3, P-B4; reaching Diagram No. 1.

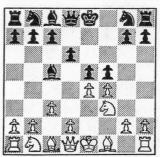

1 There follows: 5 BPxP, QPxP; *6* P-Q4, PxQP; *7* B-QB4, PxKP. Each side has indicated a willingness to mix it. Tension reigns supreme as the vulnerable positions of the White and the Black monarchs beckon for enemy incursion. And each opponent is ready to oblige—in a real combat.

2 Stoltz begins the invasion with 8 N-K5, and Spielmann calmly develops *8* . . . N-KB3. *9* N-B7 forks Queen and Rook. And Spielmann is unperturbed. *9* . . . Q-K2 is his move. There follows *10* NxR, P-Q6. One whole Rook is Spielmann's investment for the position that Black now has.

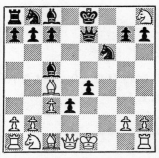

3 Stoltz pins back the ears of Black's King Knight by *11 B-KN5*. Naturally, with a Rook to the good, safety is the first rule, and to swap is the second. Spielmann, however, will die fighting: *11 ... B-B7ch* jolts the White King into insecurity. The game then continues: *12 KxB, Q-B4ch.*

4 Double attack must recover one piece; and, in the meantime, Spielmann has scored the initial check. White retreats: *13 B-K3*, and *13 ... QxKB* follows. Now for precaution and development with *14 P-KR3, B-K3; 15 N-Q2, Q-Q4.* The question is: can White withstand the coming onslaught?

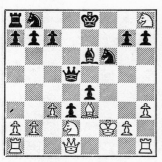

5 White seems unaware, however, that he is being attacked. He thrusts forward: *16 P-KN4*, aiming to dislodge one of the props of Black's King Pawn. Then comes *16 ... N-B3; 17 P-B4, Q-Q2; 18 P-N5, B-N5.* Black's last is intended to restrain the counterdemonstration.

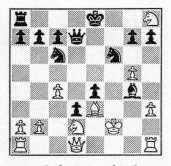

6 Stoltz swings his Queen to a new focal point. *19 Q-KB1* is the move. Spielmann plays *19 ... B-K7*. Stoltz parries with *20 Q-N2*, training his sights on the King Pawn. Then comes *20 ... Q-B4ch; 21 K-N1, N-Q2.* At last, Black's King Pawn is unguarded. And his attack is now on the wane. '

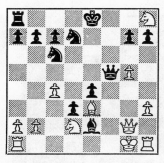

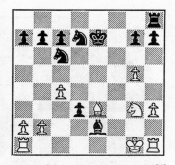

7 *22 QxPch is now consequent. There follows 22 ... QxQ; 23 NxQ, K-K2; 24 N-N3, RxN. Black is an exchange behind for a Pawn. But the sting has been removed from his attack. And his Queen Pawn is doomed. The position appears forlorn, and it looks like merely a matter of mopping up.*

8 *Mopping up it is. 25 NxB begins the operation. Black plays 25 ... PxN, and his isolated King Pawn is the next target. 26 R-R2 practically ends its career. Now follows 26 ... K-B2; 27 RxP, R-K1. Technically, it is all over. Spielmann, however, will not give up the ghost.*

9 *28 R-Q1 is the move. There is still plenty of resistance in 28 ... N-B1, followed by ... N-K3. But Spielmann plays the natural 28 ... N/Q2-K4. This permits more exchanges. 29 B-B4, R-K3 follow, and Stoltz averts any annoying Knight checks by 30 K-B1. Black continues 30 ... K-N3.*

10 *31 R-Q5 applies more pressure. Spielmann defends with 31 ... K-B4. Now follows 32 B-N3, and Spielmann stalls with 32 ... R-K2. 33 P-N4 is the finishing touch. The threat is P-N5 to unhinge the support of the King Knight. As this cannot be met, Spielmann resigns.*

6

The typical position in Petroff's Defense

Petroff's Defense

Jockeying for control of the center is the sum and substance of the opening goal. Different strategic concepts, however, govern the opening maneuvers: attack and defense, attack and counterattack in the same sector, and attack and counterattack in different fields. The Ruy Lopez, for example, illustrates attack and defense. Black's King Pawn is the fixed target under fire, and a good many of the Black forces are tied to its protection during the early skirmish. The Sicilian, on the other hand, exemplifies independent invasions by both players. There White dominates certain central squares, and Black appropriates other terrain. Petroff's Defense falls in the second category above—attack and counterattack in the same sector.

Perfect symmetry marks Petroff's Defense. After the moves, 1 P-K4, P-K4; 2 N-KB3, Black maintains the balance with 2 . . . N-KB3. Yet, strangely enough, symmetry does not grant practical equality. Since White moves first, as a rule, White "gets there first." Almost always a position is certain to occur in which Black cannot afford or is not able to emulate White's move. This is the inherent danger of the Petroff.

Despite the theoretical overtones, the Petroff has survived the rigors of the tournament arena for a good many years. One of the oldest defenses to the King Knight Game, it is mentioned in the Gottingen manuscript of 1490. Under the caption, "Two Kings' Knights' Opening," Jaenisch gave it special attention in 1842, and Petroff introduced it into actual play about the same time. Pillsbury, Marshall, and Kashdan have been its champions in more recent times.

The Petroff arises as follows:

1	P-K4	P-K4
2	N-KB3	N-KB3

Tit for tat. Attack and counterattack on the invaluable center Pawns.

The prospective exchange of Pawn for Pawn favors the

defender inasmuch as White's King Pawn is the keystone in a mass for aggression as well as a bulwark of defense. The delay involved in effecting the exchange, on the other hand, leaves Black laggard in time, which is translated into superior development for White.

3 NxP . . . .

Usual. 3 N-B3 transposes into the Four Knights' Game. An indifferent defense, such as 3 P-Q3, has no merit at all as it leads to a cramped position.

A tenable alternative is 3 P-Q4, after which the following line of play might ensue: 3 . . . PxP; 4 P-K5, N-K5; 5 QxP, P-Q4; 6 PxP e.p. NxQP; 7 B-KN5, N-B3!; 8 Q-B3, P-B3; 9 B-KB4, Q-K2ch; 10 B-K2, B-K3; 11 QN-Q2, O-O-O; 12 O-O, Q-B2; with approximately even chances. White's play against the Black monarch on the long side of the board is counterbalanced by Black's possible Pawn demonstration on the other wing.

In this line, special consideration ought to be given to Black's fourth move: . . . N-K5. The tendency of the amateur is to retreat 4 . . . N-N1, or to play 4 . . . N-Q4, where the Knight is not particularly well posted. When projecting a Knight to K5, a vague fear that it may be attacked overcomes the learner.

The alternative line may also follow this course: 3 P-Q4, PxP; 4 P-K5, N-K5; 5 QxP, P-Q4; 6 PxP e.p., NxQP; 7 N-B3, N-B3; 8 Q-KB4, P-KN3!; 9 B-Q2, B-N2; 10 O-O-O, O-O; 11 B-Q3, B-K3; 12 P-KR4, Q-B3—again with equality. Here, oddly enough, White castles long and Black short.

After the text move, White is a Pawn to the good and Black must make every effort to recover it.

Fatal for Black is 3 . . . NxP?; e.g., 4 Q-K2, N-KB3; 5 N-B6 dis ch wins the Queen. Or 3 . . . NxP?; 4 Q-K2, Q-K2; 5 QxN, P-Q3; 6 P-Q4, and White maintains the powerful Pawn plus.

3 ....   **P-Q3**

By first compelling the adverse Knight to move, Black establishes the position to recover the Pawn.

4 N-KB3   ....

There is no better post for the Knight. *4* N-B4, for instance, interferes with the later development of White's King Bishop. On QB4, the Knight is also vulnerable to future attack.

4 ....   **NxP**

Now Black can and must recover the Pawn. Otherwise, he is out a Pawn.

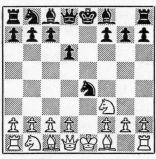

5 P-Q4   ....

White can maintain symmetry by 5 P-Q3, N-KB3, when he enjoys an infinitesimal plus of the first move. He seeks more, however. His plan is to leave the Black Knight in the advanced post, where it is subject to further attack. In this way, White intends to enhance his development at his opponent's expense.

An alternative frequently encountered at this point is 5 Q-K2. This move attempts to gain development, but involves the exchange of Queens. The line may follow this course: 5 Q-K2, Q-K2; 6 P-Q3, N-KB3; 7 B-N5, QxQch; 8 BxQ, B-K2. White's development is superior, but the absence of Queens cuts down the attacking chances. In the long run, with accurate play, Black equalizes. For White soon reaches his maximum potential and cannot make progress. The onus of accuracy, however, rests with the defender.

5 ....   **P-Q4**

Also playable is 5 ... B-K2 at once. Black prefers, however, to expand the diagonal of his King Bishop. The omission of ... P-Q4 can conceivably lead to a cramped game as it grants White the opportunity to play P-Q5 and usurp a large chunk of terrain.

6 **B-Q3**   ....

While the attack on the projected Knight seems meaningless at the present, it is a prelude to a future plan to unhinge its support by an eventual P-QB4.

6 ....   **B-Q3**

Black follows suit. Note that the position is symmetrical, except that Black's Knight at K5 is a theoretical target. Contrariwise, if the Knight can be maintained on its present square, it may serve as a base for incursion into White's domain.

Black may avoid symmetry and lead to interesting play by 6 ... B-K2. Then the game may take the following course: 6 ... B-K2; 7 O-O, N-QB3!; 8 P-B4, N-QN5; 9 PxP, NxB; 10 QxN, QxP; 11 R-K1, B-KB4; 12 N-B3, NxN; 13 QxN, P-QB3; 14 R-K5, Q-Q2; 15 P-Q5!, O-O; 16 PxP, PxP; with equality.

This line, however, is extremely tricky and places a premium on accuracy.

$$7 \textbf{ O-O} \qquad \textbf{O-O}$$

Development goes on apace.

$$8 \textbf{ P-B4} \qquad \text{....}$$

First step in the plan to unhinge the Knight.

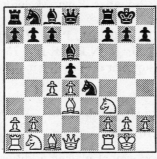

$$8 \text{ ....} \qquad \textbf{P-QB3}$$

Supplying a prop.

Marshall's favored line was 8 ... B-KN5. But it involves the sacrifice of two Pawns for a dangerous attack. When played by Marshall, the whole idea was little explored, and the U.S. champion scored many notable successes with it. Current analysis, however, has shorn the line of its terror. The line may pursue the following course: 8 ... B-KN5; 9 PxP, P-KB4;

10 N-B3, (or A), N-Q2; *11* P-KR3, B-R4; *12* NxN, PxN; *13* BxP, N-B3; *14* B-B5, K-R1; *15* P-KN4, NxQP; *16* B-K6, and Black has insufficient compensation for his material minus. The excellent squares K5 and N5 beckon the White Knight, and this more than makes up for White's shaky King-side position.

(A) Not *10* R-K1?, BxPch; *11* KxB, NxP; *12* Q-K2, NxB; *13* QxN, BxN; *14* QxB, Q-R5ch; followed by *15* ... QxR. (This is Marshall's trap, in which this writer had the unfortunate experience to fall.)

9 R-K1 . . . .

With the idea of continuing pressure on the target Knight, while gaining development.

Alternative lines lead to no advantage. If *9* N-B3, for instance, *9* ... NxN; *10* PxN, B-KN5; *11* P-KR3, B-R4; *12* PxP, PxP; *13* Q-N3, BxN; *14* QxNP, N-Q2; *15* PxB, N-N3; *16* R-N1, Q-B3; and Black's sounder Pawn skeleton compensates for his material minus.

Or *9* Q-B2, N-R3!; *10* BxN, PxB; *11* QxP, R-K1; *12* Q-R4, QxQ; *13* NxQ, N-N5; *14* N-R3, R-K5; *15* N-B3, B-N5; and Black's position is superior despite the momentary Pawn minus.

9 . . . . **R-K1**

Maintaining the advanced post.

10 N-B3 . . . .

There is no good way of placing additional pressure on the Knight. Consequently, White must permit simplification.

10 . . . . **NxN**

To maintain the Knight on its advanced post by *10* ... P-KB4 is perilous. Then White continues with *11* PxP and attempts to exploit the weakness created on Black's long diagonal (KN1-QR7) by Q-N3.

11 RxRch . . . .

If *11* PxN, RxRch; *12* QxR. White is somewhat better off with his Queen on Queen square than on King square.

11	**QxR**
12 **PxN**	**B-KN5**

Black's men are a bit more aggressively posted, though White still leads in development and enjoys a better Pawn position.

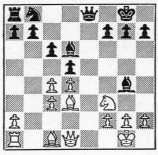

13 **B-Q2**   . . . .

Now White threatens *14* BxPch, KxB; *15* N-N5ch, followed by the recovery of the piece—not possible on the previous move on account of Black's mate at K8.

13 . . . .   **Q-Q1**

To prevent the threat, while gaining future access for the Queen to KB3 or QB2 or N3 or R4. Any Pawn move, such as *13* . . . P-KR3, weakens the King-side Pawn structure.

14 **R-N1**   . . . .

Seizing the open file with a view to exploiting the lead in development.

14 . . . .   **PxP**

A necessary interpolation. After the following move, Black

can defend himself by ... Q-B2, without allowing White to execute his earlier threat of BxPch.

15 **BxP**   **Q-B2**

White's position is slightly preferable.

Conclusions and recommendations

Since most lines of the Petroff lead to a somewhat symmetrical position, with White having a move in hand, the prospects for Black are none too inviting. In any one of the alternative variations at White's disposal, moreover, the onus of accuracy falls upon Black. This, coupled with the fact that Marshall's line has been shorn of its sting, rates the Petroff below par—unless, of course, Marshall's variation can be bolstered.

Chess Movie

GIVEAWAY CHESS

W HEN TWO disciples of the art of sacrifice in chess meet over the chessboard, the result ought to be "giveaway" chess. It is. First Marshall gives up a couple of Pawns, then Spielmann gives up three. Then Marshall gives up the exchange and keeps giving until mate. The scene: Hamburg, 1910. The game begins with *1* P-K4, P-K4; *2* N-KB3, N-KB3; *3* NxP, P-Q3; *4* N-KB3, NxP (see first diagram). Marshall is Black.

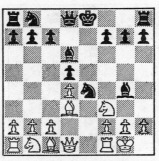

1 The game continues with the usual *5* P-Q4, P-Q4; *6* B-Q3, B-Q3. Marshall more or less duplicates his opponent's moves. Here, however, the players get off on a new tack. Spielmann plays *7* O-O, and Marshall follows with *7* ... B-KN5. Both Black Bishops are directed against White's King.

2 Spielmann attempts to unhinge the advanced Knight with *8* P-B4, and Marshall "sacs" a Pawn with *8* ... O-O. Then comes *9* PxP, P-KB4; *10* N-B3, N-Q2. A second Pawn is proffered. What are a couple of Pawns, when the enemy King is at stake? That is the idea, and only time can test it.

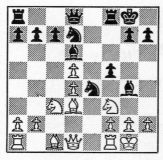

3 First Spielmann plays 11 P-KR3, now driving the opposing Bishop. After 11 ... B-R4, he continues with 12 NxN, PxN; 13 BxP, picking off the second Pawn. Marshall goes on nonchalantly with 13 ... N-B3, and the picture clarifies. White's Bishop will move, and so his Pawn structure weakens.

4 Spielmann plays 14 B-B5, indirectly defending his Queen Pawn, and Marshall gets out of the line of check by 14 ... K-R1. Now follows 15 P-KN4, NxQP. White has been compelled to overexpand his King-side Pawns. But then he has a Pawn plus to salve the pain of any coming abuse.

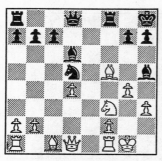

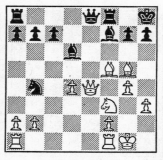

5 Spielmann falters. 16 Q-Q3 is his move. Now Marshall lets fly a sockdolager. 16 ... N-N5 puts the White Queen to rout. Spielmann follows with 17 Q-K4, and the game continues: 17 ... B-B2; 18 B-N5, Q-K1. Marshall offers a friendly exchange of Queens. That is, if you want to call it friendly!

6 Spielmann disdains the offer with 19 N-K5. He will rue the day. Marshall lets go another humdinger, with 19 ... B-Q4, compelling a retreat. There follows 20 Q-K2, N-B3. One Pawn has already come home, and now the powerful pin brings glad tidings of the other. Is more to come besides?

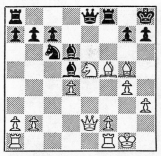

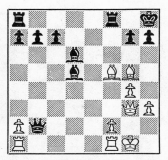

7 *21* Q-Q3 is Spielmann's move. He wishes to salvage whatever he can out of the coming melee. The game continues: *21* . . . NxN; *22* PxN, QxP, threatening mate. Spielmann tosses this off easily with *23* Q-KN3, and Marshall picks off another Pawn, with *23* . . . QxP for a Pawn to the good.

8 Spielmann replies with *24* Q-R4. Now he's threatening a little mate, too. Marshall won't waste time retreating or advancing his Pawns. *24* . . . RxB is the move! When Marshall gives, he gives full measure. Spielmann then captures with *25* PxR, and Marshall's inevitable sequel is *25* . . . Q-K4.

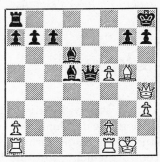

9 This mate isn't so easy to thwart. Spielmann tries *26* Q-N3, and so Marshall now plucks off yet another Pawn, *26* . . . QxP. Spielmann pleads for an exchange with *27* Q-N4, but Marshall is adamant. He returns: *27* . . . Q-K4. There follows *28* KR-K1, Q-R7ch. White's King must march.

10 *29* K-B1 is Spielmann's move, and Marshall plays *29* . . . R-KB1, again menacing mate. This time it isn't easy to parry either. White runs for the open with *30* K-K2. He is cut down in his tracks with *30* . . . QxPch; *31* K-Q3, P-N4. Facing threats from all directions, Spielmann resigns.

7

The typical position at the outset of Philidor's Defense

Philidor's Defense

THE SIMPLE WAY is not always the best way. Ready riposte
is its goal, while long-term considerations are discounted lightly.

So it is with the Philidor. In the delicate thrusts and
parries revolving about center control, which constitute the
opening skirmish, Black employs an easy expedient. After the
moves *1* P-K4, P-K4; *2* N-KB3, he defends his King Pawn with
the simple *2 ... P-Q3.* His plan is to hold the strong point at
his K4 square not by devious, tortuous maneuvers, but by
straightforward defense. This is all well and good—as far as it
goes. It does not, however, go far enough. For one thing,
it frees White instantly to play P-Q4—whereas the usual course

compels the first player to resort to intricate stratagems before he can successfully enforce this move. In turn, this means that the pressure on Black's center mounts rapidly, and Black is reduced to a doubly defensive cramped position. Black's second move, moreover, obstructs the development of his King Bishop. This fault is negligible since Black often posts his King Bishop on the second rank. By no stretch of the imagination, however, can it be considered a virtue.

Philidor's Defense was first noticed in the Gottingen manuscript (1490). It gains its name from the celebrated French player, François André Danican Philidor, who remodeled and popularized it.*

Today, it is occasionally adopted to steer the play away from routinized channels. Late world champion Alekhine sometimes gave it a fling—using the modernized Hanham Variation. In the main, its prospects may be summarized as expressed in the first line of a poem: "The Philidor is a horrible bore."

It may, however, win games!

The Philidor arises as follows:

1	P-K4	P-K4
2	N-KB3	P-Q3

As a rule, when 1 P-K4 is met by 1 . . . P-K4, White's plan is to put mounting pressure on Black's King Pawn, until it is dislodged. When and if it gives way, White intends to usurp the center.

Black, on the other hand, places as many obstacles—tactical and strategical—in White's way as he can. With perfect defense, the struggle for the center is a standoff, and the players then direct their efforts to other fields.

Perfect defense for Black calls for counterthreats sufficient to prevent White from successfully enforcing an early P-Q4.

---

* According to Chernev and Reinfeld in *The Fireside Book of Chess,* Philidor never played the defense named after him. For one thing, he practically always gave odds! But he did present and recommend a line in that defense in his famous book, *Analyze du Jeu des Échecs.*

For, when White's Queen Pawn engages Black's King Pawn, the pressure rises to such an extent that Black is soon compelled to swap. Then White remains with a dominating King Pawn as against a backward Queen Pawn for Black, and White virtually controls the center.

Black's efforts, therefore, are bent upon preventing an adverse P-Q4. In the Philidor, this is not the case, and, consequently, Black practically concedes the center. In turn, this means that his development will be retarded and backward.

In order not to confuse the issue, it should be noted that in many openings, such as the Scotch and Center Game, White can and does play an early P-Q4. The situation, however, is not analogous. For, in these openings, Black always gets some compensation for White's impetuosity. The compensation may be no more than a tempo. But it is compensation.

The text move permits, even provokes, the adverse P-Q4 and gains nothing in return. On this account, it is deficient.

It is also deficient, to a lesser extent, in that it limits the mobility of the King Bishop.

3 **P-Q4** . . . .

The natural continuation. The idea is to force Black to play ... PxP. In that case, White's King Pawn dominates a good portion of the center by commanding vital squares on the fifth rank, while its counterpart, Black's Queen Pawn, ineffectually touches only the fourth rank.

3 . . . . **N-Q2**

Black must maintain his King Pawn at all cost. *3* ... N-QB3 will not do; for after *4* PxP, PxP; *5* QxQch, Black either loses a Pawn or forfeits the privilege of castling. The Knight on Q2, moreover, allows for the construction of an interesting Pawn array, which is to serve as a barrier against invasion as well as a prop for a possible counterattack later on.

4 **B-QB4** . . . .

The Bishop aims at the most vulnerable point in Black's camp—his KB2 square.

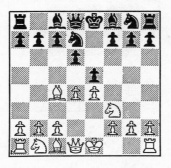

4 ....   **P-QB3**

The purpose of this move is threefold: To begin with, it clears the square QB2, so that it may be occupied by Black's Queen, whence it must protect Black's King Pawn. Then the move foreshadows a future Queen-side demonstration based on . . . P-QN4–P-QR4 and a general expansion on the Queen's wing. Lastly, the move guards Black's Q4 square so that no opposing man can penetrate with facility.

Note that *4 . . .* B-K2? loses a Pawn at once: e.g., *5* PxP, NxP; *6* NxN, PxN; *7* Q-R5, threatening simultaneously the King Pawn and the King Bishop Pawn. After *4 . . .* B-K2?; *5* PxP, PxP; then *6* Q-Q5 wins.

The maneuver . . . P-QB3 and . . . Q-B2 is part and parcel of a system worked out and introduced into tournament practice by Major Hanham. The variation under discussion is therefore referred to as the Hanham Variation.

White's next move is a good way to continue development, although alternative moves, such as *5* N-B3 are also tenable. An interesting idea here is *5* PxP, PxP; *6* BxPch, KxB; *7* NxPch. White gets a powerful attack, but it can be rebuffed by proper defense.

5 **O-O**   . . . .

Another try is 5 N-N5. Then the line might run as follows:
5 . . . N-R3; *6* O-O, N-N3!; 7 B-N3, B-K2; *8* Q-R5, O-O; and
Black is able to hold the position with precision defense.

One misstep in the above line can be fatal. For example, if
5 N-N5, N-R3; *6* O-O, B-K2?; 7 N-K6!, PxN; *8* BxN, N-N3;
9 BxNP, and White wins because of the uncomfortable position
of the Black monarch. In this line, *8* . . . PxB?; *9* Q-R5ch,
and White soon mates.

Finally, Alekhine recommended 5 P-QR4, after . . . P-QB3
(as in his game against Marco) to prevent . . . P-QN4 once
and for all.

5 . . . .   **B-K2**

Here again, Black can falter: 5 . . . KN-B3?; *6* PxP, KNxP;
7 PxP, QN-B3; *8* R-K1, and Black is in trouble. There are even
pitfalls within the pitfalls. For example, if 5 . . . KN-B3?;
6 PxP, QNxP; 7 NxN, PxN; *8* BxPch, and Black is out a Pawn.
Or 5 . . . KN-B3?; *6* PxP, PxP; 7 N-N5, and Black cannot hold
the King Bishop Pawn.

It is quite possible White's strongest line is now *6* PxP, PxP;
7 N-N5!, BxN; *8* Q-R5, P-KN3; *9* QxB, QxQ; *10* BxQ, and White
has the advantage of the two Bishops.

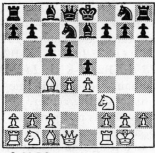

6 N-B3 . . . .

The text move, however, maintains the character of the
game, insofar as it does not drive for an immediate end game,
even a favorable one.

6 . . . . **KN-B3**

At last, after avoiding the traps and stratagems, Black is
able to bring out all his King-side men.

7 P-QR4 . . . .

This move is unusual, but pointed. Eventually, White con-
templates action on the other wing. For the moment he therefore stifles any counterplay on the Queen-side. This would be
possible if Black got in . . P-QN4-5. For the Pawn advance
would dispossess White's Queen Knight and leave White's King
Pawn unguarded.

7 . . . . **P-KR3**

Usual here is 7 ... O-O. Then White gets the better game by perfectly routine moves. The following is an example from the game Alekhine–Marco, Stockholm, 1912: 7 ... O-O; 8 Q-K2, P-KR3; 9 B-N3, Q-B2; 10 P-R3, K-R2; 11 B-K3, P-KN3; 12 QR-Q1, K-N2; 13 N-KR2, N-KN1; 14 P-B4.

Observe the Hanham idea in this line—Black's Queen at the QB2 square to maintain the center.

The text move conceals its real purpose. It is not to prevent the adverse B-KN5, as appears at first sight. Instead, it is intended as a prelude to a King-side assault, with the Rook Pawn serving as a prop for the later advance ... P-KN4. This plan, in conjunction with the maneuver ... N-B1-N3 has the makings of a formidable assault in view.

8 **P-QN3!**   . . . .

The idea here is to fianchetto the Queen Bishop, which then exerts indirect pressure on Black's King Pawn.

Against normal developing moves, Black is able to obtain equal chances. A game Alexander–Fine continued as follows: 8 B-R2, P-KN4; 9 PxP, PxP; 10 Q-K2, B-Q3; 11 R-Q1, Q-K2; 12 B-K3, N-B4; 13 N-Q2, N-K3. Black's prospects are good.

8 . . . .   **Q-B2**

Indirectly protecting the King Pawn, which will be under attack in the immediate future. On general principles, when a Queen is relegated to defending a Pawn, something is chronically wrong!

9 **B-N2**   . . . .

Nimzovich–Marco, Gothenburg, 1920, continued as follows: 9 ... N-B1?; 10 PxP, PxP; 11 NxP!, QxN; 12 N-Q5!, Q-Q3; 13 B-R3, PxN (13 ... P-B4 14 P-K5!); 14 BxQ—in favor of White.

9 ... N-B1?, however, is a blunder. Better is 9 ... O-O. Even then White's position is superior.

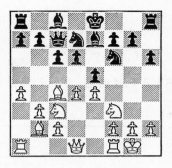

Conclusions and recommendations

The one variation of the Philidor that has enjoyed even slight favor in tournament practice is the Hanham. Practically, it is self-condemned, per se, since it relegates a Queen to the menial task of guarding a Pawn, which *may* be attacked.

Despite the numerous pitfalls and dour prospects that exist for the defender, the Philidor is worth an occasional fling against a player who is oblivious of its proper course. The execution of Black's plan, unmolested, leaves him, strangely enough, with the upper hand.

Chess Movie

A FLAILING PHILIDOR

Simultaneous attack and defense is the order of the following sparkling classic. Both Kings are exposed to flailing blows from all directions. Finally, Hungarian master Breyer sets up a series of irresistible checks, and the immovable White King of Havasi is moved to resignation. Budapest, 1917, is the scene of play. The game begins with *1* P-K4, P-K4; *2* N-KB3, P-Q3; *3* P-Q4, N-Q2; *4* B-QB4, P-QB3.

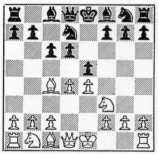 

1 There follows 5 O-O, B-K2; *6* N-B3, Q-B2; *7* B-K3, P-KR3. White is making the usual routine moves, and Black is contemplating an assault against the opposing monarch. His intentions, however, are well concealed. For who would suspect the puny ... P-KR3 as packing a wallop?

2 White prepares the advance of his King Bishop Pawn by 8 N-Q2, and Black signals the attack with 8 ... P-KN4. Immediately, White swings his other Knight to the King-side with *9* N-K2, and Black follows suit. *9* ... N-B1 is his move. Now follows *10* N-KN3, N-N3. All is yet serene.

72

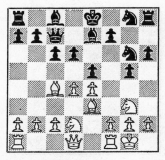

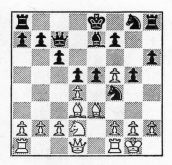

3 White is first to enter with *11* N-B5. Black parries with *11* ... P-Q4. White retreats *12* B-Q3, and Black swaps *12* ... BxN. White recaptures *13* PxB, and Black now enters *13* ... N-B5. The opposing maneuvers are along the same line, except that Black knows where the White King lives!

4 There follows *14* BxN, KPxB; *15* R-K1, O-O-O. Black's abode is on the other side. White now readies for an onslaught against the Black King and prepares with *16* P-QB3. Black brings out the rest of his forces with *16* ... N-B3. This is the proverbial calm before the storm.

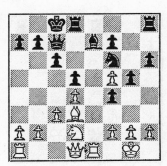

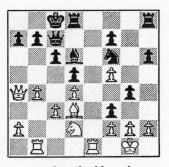

5 *17* P-QN4 is White's way of instituting the attack. The race is on. Black plays *17* ... P-N5. There follows *18* R-N1, B-Q3; *19* Q-R4, P-B6. Each side is poised for action against the enemy King. The same old question obtains: "Who will get there first with the most?" Only time will tell.

6 White builds a barrier with *20* P-N3, which Black immediately sets out to breach with *20* ... P-KR4. White counters with *21* P-N5, and it appears that he has arrived. Black plays *21* ... P-R5. It all seems so slow. Now comes *22* PxBP, PxNP. With one fell move, all fury is loosened!

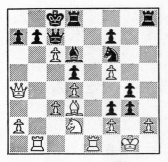

7 White attempts to consolidate with 23 RPxP. His attack can wait for a move. *But it can't.* Black replies *23 ... BxP!*; and White's King position is deftly penetrated. *24 RxP* is White's move, and *24 ... BxPch* is Black's bombastic reply. Checks must be respected, and so Black has the lead.

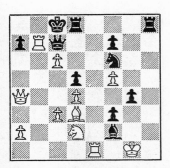

8 White captures *25 KxB,* and Black closes in with *25 ... Q-R7ch.* White attempts to exit with *26 K-K3,* and black keeps the King in place with *26 ... Q-R3ch.* Black dare not let up. If he fails to give check, he will be on the receiving end. And not for long. For White's checks can be deadly.

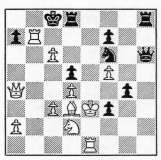

9 White retreats with *27 K-B2,* and Black captures *27 ... QxNch.* Always with check! White plays *28 R-K2.* Perhaps this will compel a respite. But no, Black pitches everything at his command into the fray. *28 ... N-K5ch* is the move. There is no letup, for Black can't afford one.

10 *29 BxN* is forced, and Black answers with *29 ... QxRch.* The material gain is only incidental. The King is the target. White plays *30 K-N3,* and Black continues with *30 ... Q-R7ch.* More checks. It is impossible to avoid the checks. In fact, it is impossible to avoid mate. White resigns.

8

The typical position in the Caro-Kann Defense

Caro-Kann Defense

Every chess opening revolves about the play in the center. This ties up with the ultimate goal of the debut, which is to usurp the vital terrain so that the opponent, limited as it were to marginal squares, will be at a disadvantage. By virtue of his first move, White is first to drive a stake into the center. And Black is faced with a problem. Shall he follow suit on adjacent squares or shall he attempt to undermine his adversary's claim?

The problem is clear cut. But its solution leads to multifarious byways, each, in turn, with many ramifications ending in a plus or minus.

Out of this maze comes the Caro-Kann, another way of challenging White's birthright—the initial move. It is nothing more than a solid attempt by the defender to set up a well-fortified stake of his own in the center—or, failing that, to yield Pawn control of the center in return for a free and easy development.

The Caro-Kann is an ancient defense, mentioned by Polerio in 1590. Originally, however, Black's play was so badly manhandled that the defense was snugly tucked away for many years. Later, it was introduced into modern play by Kann of Pesth and practiced by Caro of Berlin. Hence the name.

Though not played too frequently, the Caro-Kann does crop up regularly today; so any 1 P-K4 player must know it.

It is generally considered a safe though dull defense. Some of its disciples, however, may be noted as in the top fringe of the chess fraternity, among them Capablanca, Nimzovich, and Flohr.

The Caro-Kann arises as follows:

1 P-K4   P-QB3
(See photo)

Black's first move characterizes the Caro-Kann. Of the two moves, however, White's is clearly the better. For his Pawn strikes at the vital central terrain, whereas Black's is merely a prop for what is to follow. But this is not the true criterion of values. Future prospects must also be weighed. After Black's next play, a fairer comparison can be made.

Black's move inaugurates a series of patterns—depending upon White's replies. Each of these patterns has something in Black's favor. In general, the move is a forerunner to a direct challenge in the center. Noteworthy is the fact that Black is able to develop his Queen Bishop—contrasting favorably with the French Defense in which that critter is locked in.

2 P-Q4   . . . .

This is probably White's best move, though by no means his only one. 2 N-QB3 leads to interesting and trappy lines. For example, 2 N-QB3, P-Q4; 3 N-B3, PxP; 4 NxP, B-B4; 5 N-N3, B-N3; 6 P-KR4, P-KR3; 7 N-K5, B-R2; 8 Q-R5, P-KN3; 9 B-B4!, and White is definitely for choice.

Black may play 4 . . . B-N5, however, instead of 4 . . . B-B4. In that event, White gains a minimal advantage with 5 P-KR3, BxN; 6 QxB. He has the two Bishops.

2 . . . .   **P-Q4**

To challenge the center.

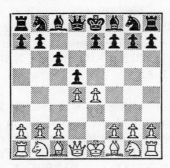

3 **N-QB3**   . . . .

Here White concentrates on bringing out his forces rapidly, while bearing on the center. Other lines are also tenable.

One line in particular, known as the Panov-Botvinnik Attack, has enjoyed considerable popularity. It runs as follows: 3 PxP, PxP; 4 P-QB4, N-KB3; 5 N-QB3, N-B3; 6 B-N5, PxP; 7 P-Q5, N-K4; 8 Q-Q4, N-Q6ch; 9 BxN, PxB; 10 N-B3, and White leads in development and prospects.

In playing the Panov-Botvinnik, however, White must be prepared to accept an isolated Queen Pawn. Thus, if 6 . . . P-K3 (instead of 6 . . . PxP); the game may take the following course: 7 N-B3, PxP; 8 BxP. Here, too, the advantage in space overshadows the chronic weakness of the isolated Pawn. But the onus of capitalizing on that extra space falls upon White. Should he fail to make that good, his ending will, indeed, be difficult.

Another continuation is 3 PxP, PxP; 4 B-Q3. This simplifying plan is based on aggressive considerations. White hopes to poise his men for attack against the Black King, while he checks Black's aspirations on the other side of the board. Note that White will control the half-opened King file, while Black possesses the half-opened Queen Bishop file.

In practice, however, White's assault in this line can be contained, and Black's demonstration on the other wing can become a real menace. The game may go as follows: 4 . . . N-QB3; 5 P-QB3, N-B3; 6 B-KB4, B-N5; 7 N-B3, P-K3; 8 Q-N3, Q-B1; 9 QN-Q2, B-K2.

Still another interesting try is 3 P-KB3. It is an effort to maintain Pawn control of the center—or, in the event of an exchange of Pawns, to open lines for a fierce attack. For example, 3 . . . PxP; 4 PxP, P-K4; 5 N-KB3, PxP; 6 B-QB4, B-K2; 7 O-O, N-B3; 8 N-N5, O-O; 9 NxBP, RxN; 10 BxRch, KxB; 11 P-K5, K-N1; 12 PxN, BxP; 13 N-Q2, B-K3; 14 N-K4, and White has the better game (Teichman–Mieses, 1913).

On the other hand, Black need not fall in line with White's plan. He may continue quietly with 3 . . . P-K3 and attempt to exploit the weakness inherent in White's advance of the King Bishop Pawn: 3 . . . P-K3; 4 B-K3, Q-N3; 5 N-Q2, N-Q2; 6 B-Q3, P-QB4; 7 P-B3, P-B5; 8 B-QB2, QxNP; 9 N-K2, Q-R6; 10 O-O, N-N3; 11 PxP, PxP; 12 R-K1, B-Q2.

Black decides to yield the center, for he is at a loss for any good temporizing move. By ridding himself of White's King Pawn, however, he has created a square for his Queen Bishop at his KB4.

Position after 3 N-QB3

3 . . . .   **PxP**

Any other move, such as *3 . . . N-B3;* invites perilous complications: on *3 . . . N-B3; 4 P-K5, N-Q2; 5 P-K6,* for example, the sacrifice of the Pawn opens lines leading directly to the Black monarch. The defense is difficult, if not hopeless.

4 NxP   . . . .

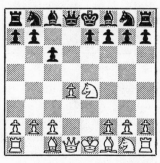

4 . . . .   **B-B4**

An alternative, difficult for both sides, is *4 . . . N-B3.* After *5 NxNch,* Black suffers from a poorer Pawn position: e.g., *5 . . . KPxN; 6 B-QB4, B-K2; 7 Q-R5!, O-O; 8 N-K2, P-KN3; 9 Q-B3, R-K1; 10 B-KR6, B-KB4; 11 O-O-O, B-K5; 12 Q-QN3,* and White's prospects for both middle game and end game are superior. The extra Pawn on the Queen-side is a determining factor in the end game.

After *4 . . .* N-B3; *5* NxNch, NPxN, Black has the inferior game. See the Chess Movie on page 84.

4 . . . P-K3 does not commend itself as it shuts in Black's Queen Bishop. And *4 . . .* N-Q2—to prepare . . . KN-B3 without risk of doubled Pawns—may be met by *5* N-KB3, KN-B3; *6* N-N3. In this line, White retains his edge in terrain and favorable disposition of forces and can aim, as a last resort, at utilizing his Queen-side Pawn majority in the end game.

The text is part and parcel of the Caro-Kann in that the Queen Bishop obtains a satisfactory development.

5 **N-N3** . . . .

This move gains a vital tempo—unless Black wishes to concede "the two Bishops."

Instead, White could essay a gambit with *5* B-Q3, and, after *5 . . .* QxP; *6* N-KB3, have a tremendous lead in development. That this is sufficient for the Pawn, however, is another story—even though many of the giants of chessdom have experimented successfully with the idea.

5 . . . . **B-N3**

Black remains on the strong diagonal.

6 **N-B3** . . . .

This veers from *Practical Chess Openings* in which 6 P-KR4 is given. The sequence above is slightly better insofar as Black is now compelled to play accurately—on his own! Otherwise he may oblige by meeting White's plan (see next note) half-way.

6 . . . .   **N-Q2**

On the natural 6 . . . N-B3, White's plan leaps to life with 7 P-KR4, P-KR3; 8 N-K5 (gaining a tempo by threatening to capture the Bishop and so disrupt Black's Pawn structure), B-R2; 9 B-QB4, P-K3; 10 Q-K2 (threatening *11* NxBP with a crushing assault).

The text move forestalls N-K5.

7 **B-QB4**   . . . .

Practical Chess Openings may now be reached by transposition with 7 P-KR4, P-KR3; 8 P-R5, B-R2; 9 B-Q3, BxB; 10 QxB, P-K3; 11 B-Q2, KN-B3; 12 O-O-O, B-Q3; 13 QR-K1, BxN; 14 PxB, O-O; 15 R-R4, and White is for choice.

The text move is played on the theory that since White is the aggressor, he ought to maintain his forces for the attack rather than submit to exchange (as by 7 B-Q3). If he can post his pieces to bear in the direction of the opposing monarch, so much the better.

An alternative is 7 N-R4, gaining the minimal advantage of Bishop for Knight.

7 ....   **P-K3**

To limit the scope of White's King Bishop.

8 **Q-K2**   ....

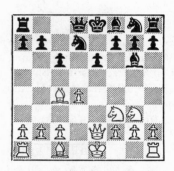

White is for choice. A good plan for future action is O-O, followed by the development of the Queen Bishop, posting a Rook on the Queen file and then the retreat of the King Bishop to QN3, making way for P-QB4. It is not easy for Black to meet this proposed action.

Conclusions and recommendations

The Caro-Kann is inherently deficient since Black must sacrifice his foothold in the center in order to gain a facile development. With correct play, all lines lead to a plus for White. Despite this, White's edge is of such a minimal nature, a misstep may easily throw the advantage the other way. On this ground, and also for the sake of variety, the Caro-Kann can be recommended.

Chess Movie

CRIME FAILS AGAIN

CLASSICAL punishment for violations of long-tested principles is the motif in this Caro-Kann. When Salo Flohr (Black) neglects his strategic ABC's, I. A. Horowitz launches a punitive expedition. The result is an impressive triumph for sound, imaginative chess. The game (U.S.A.–U.S.S.R. Radio Match, 1945) opens: *1* P-K4, P-QB3; *2* P-Q4, P-Q4; *3* N-QB3, PxP; *4* NxP, N-B3; *5* NxNch, NPxN (see Diagram 1).

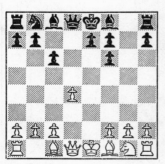 

1 White now signals aggressive intentions by *6* N-K2. Flohr will not be permitted to relax with a humdrum variation! The game continues: *6* ... B-B4; *7* N-N3, B-N3; *8* P-KR4, P-KR3; *9* P-R5, B-R2; *10* P-QB3, Q-N3; *11* B-QB4, N-Q2; *12* P-R4! Now castling on *either* side is risky for Black!

2 Alarmed by the threat of a crippling advance of the White Queen Rook Pawn, Flohr blocks that with *12* ... P-R4. There follows: *13* Q-B3, P-K3; *14* O-O. Horowitz has an ideal setup, while Flohr's pieces lack coordination. Black switches his Queen Bishop to a better diagonal by *14* ... B-B7.

3 White continues developing with *15* B-B4, and Black pursues his plan, replying *15* ... B-N6. The next moves are: *16* B-Q3, P-K4; *17* B-K3, B-Q4; *18* B-K4, Q-N6. Black is getting nowhere fast. He has lost time; his King is insecure; and his men are still awkwardly deployed.

4 And matters are rapidly coming to a head: *19* PxP, PxP; *20* QR-Q1, BxB; *21* QxB, Q-K3; *22* R-Q2. Every move by Horowitz underscores the defects of Flohr's game. Soon the Russian will be left without plausible ideas. Flohr tries *22* N-B3, and Horowitz plays *23* Q-B3.

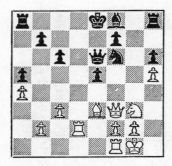

5 Unable to unite his Rooks, Black at least takes a file: *23* ... KR-N1. White's *24* KR-Q1 now trains heavy siege guns on the Black King. The threat is *25* N-B5. Black seeks to stop it with *24* ... R-N5? *25* N-B5!! anyway. But how will White meet the next move?—*25* ... P-K5.

6 White's threat was *26* N-Q6ch or *26* R-Q6. With his Queen attacked, however, White has no time for this. Apparently, he must lose a piece. But his next move reveals the brilliancy in the position. He lunges *26* B-N6! He threatens mate at Q8—and Black is left without any sound resource.

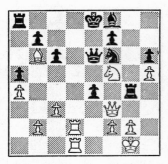

7 Flohr makes the best of a bad business: 26 ... RxPch. What follows is easily understandable: 27 QxR, QxN; 28 R-Q8ch, RxR; 29 RxRch, K-K2. Now precision chess—30 Q-N3!—deprives Black of any last-minute chance for a swindle. Mate is again threatened, and Black's reply is virtually forced.

8 For a split second, 30 ... N-Q2 holds White at bay. But the kill is not far off. White presses on with 31 B-B7, renewing the mating threat. Note the futility of Black's Bishop In effect, White may almost be said to be a Rook ahead! The game now continues with 31 ... Q-Q4; 32 P-QB4, Q-KN4.

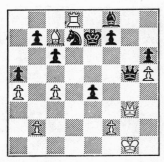

9 With a won ending, Horowitz cheerfully exchanges Queens. There's not much left: 33 QxQch, PxQ; 34 R-R8, K-K3; 35 BxP, P-KB4; 36 B-B3, P-B5. The Black Pawn moves represent the final twitches of a moribund position. Elementary care is all that is needed now to deliver the quietus.

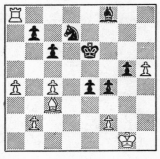

10 There follows: 37 P-R5, P-N5; 38 P-N4, P-B6; 39 B-Q2, and White's King Rook Pawn is primed to race on for a touchdown. Black therefore plays 39 ... K-B2. The lethal blow, 40 R-R7, promptly follows; and, when 40 ... P-N6 is answered by 41 RxP, Flohr resigns. A fine didactic game.

9

The typical position in the Nimzo-Indian

Nimzo-Indian Defense

S TRANGE as it may seem, this defense which is rooted in a theoretical fallacy, enjoys a large share of success and, in fact, is the current leaning post of the majority of masters. After the moves, *1* P-Q4, N-KB3; *2* P-QB4, P-K3; *3* N-QB3, Black resorts to an early sortie with his King Bishop by playing *3 . . .* B-N5, setting up a pin.

Such a speedy pin of the Knight, as a general rule, is justifiable only insofar as it exerts indirect pressure on the center. By nullifying the scope of the beleaguered "critter," the pin in turn cuts off its command of the mid-section of the playing field.

So far, so good. The Bishop move achieves its main purpose. There is, however, another consideration. What is to become of the Bishop during the future course of the game, particularly when it is under attack? Will it retreat or will it capture the Knight?

When a *King* Knight is thus pinned, a Pawn assault on the Bishop weakens the position of the King. When a Queen Knight is pinned, the consequence of a Pawn assault is not the same. The King does not enter into the reckoning, and the advanced Pawns dominate important terrain, which fact overshadows the weakness innate in the advance. *Ergo*, in the Nimzo-Indian, when, as, and if Black's King Bishop is attacked, say, by P-QR3, it is committed to the swap ... BxN. Since a Bishop is definitely, though minutely, more valuable than a Knight—Q. E. D.—Black's policy is inept.

On the surface then, the Nimzo-Indian ought to be a losing game. In its favor, however, is one modifying clause. White often winds up with an awkward Pawn cluster on his left wing. That this is sufficient compensation for the exchange of Bishop for Knight is dubious. Yet up to the present the success of the Nimzo-Indian remains unchallenged. And nothing succeeds like success.

The Nimzo-Indian is a product of the Queen's Indian Defense, patterned by the late grand master Aron Nimzovich. Under the rules that prevailed in India years ago, a Pawn could move only one square at a time—never two squares. Hence fianchetto developments were popular, and these later became known as Indian defenses. Strictly speaking, the Nimzo-Indian need not contain a fianchetto—and often does not as it is played today. Still there is always a possibility that a fianchetto will pop up; and, in Nimzovich's day, a deferred Queen-side fianchetto was generally pertinent against White patterns which that bold hypermodern encountered.

The Nimzo-Indian arises as follows:

1	P-Q4	N-KB3
2	P-QB4	P-K3
3	N-QB3	B-N5

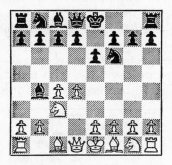

With these three moves, a critical pattern has been set up, and the game has assumed its distinctive character.

Black's last move embraces a number of points:

1. The Bishop pins the Knight and neutralizes any effect the Knight may have on the center.

2. In some contingencies, the Bishop captures the Knight and leaves White with an awkward Pawn cluster.

3. A measure of aggression accrues to Black in the opening. Even a minimal initiative is generally denied the defender in nearly all openings.

4. No clear-cut system, leading to a plus for White, has yet been perfected.

As against these nebulous advantages, Black practically commits himself to parting with a Bishop for a Knight. While the difference between these two minor pieces is microscopic, it is nevertheless tangible.

4 Q-B2 . . . .

This move, too, embraces a number of ideas:

1. Should Black play 4 . . . BxN, White is in position to recapture with his Queen and avoid doubled Pawns.

2. White clears the Queen file for occupation by his Queen Rook. This assures him a lead on the file, which may be of importance during the future course of the game.

3. Indirectly, White's Queen bears along the entire Bishop file. Often this action is pertinent to the later play.

Instead of the text move, there are any number of alternatives, each of which has been tried without leading to any pointed plus. Among them are 4 Q-N3, 4 N-B3, 4 P-QR3, and 4 P-K3. In some respects, these moves are sharper than others; they are, however, deficient, too. The text move and 4 P-K3 have been in vogue in master play since the thirties.

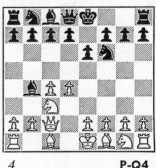

4 . . . .   **P-Q4**

Immediately challenging for direct Pawn control of the center. Other lines begin with 4 . . . P-B4, 4 . . . N-B3, 4 . . . O-O, 4 . . . P-Q3, and 4 . . . BxNch. Each of these alternatives leads to quite a different pattern.

After 4 . . . P-B4, for example, the game may continue as follows: 5 PxP, N-B3; 6 N-B3, BxP; 7 B-N5, N-Q5; 8 NxN, BxN; 9 P-K3, Q-R4; 10 PxB, QxB; 11 B-Q3, O-O; 12 O-O, P-Q4; 13 P-B4. White's prospects are better. For one thing, Black's Queen is clumsily posted.

After 4 . . . P-Q3, Black reserves the option of playing either . . . P-Q4 or . . . P-K4 later on. In each instance, however, with perfect play, White's chances are superior. For example, 4 . . . P-Q3; 5 N-B3, QN-Q2; 6 B-Q2, O-O; 7 P-QR3, BxN;

8 BxB, Q-K2; *9* P-K3, P-K4; *10* B-K2, P-K5; *11* N-Q2, R-K1; *12* P-KN4, N-B1; *13* P-N5, with a plus for White. Black's King Pawn is under fire, White enjoys the advantage of the Bishop, and, to boot, there is a formidable King-side assault in the offing.

It does not follow from the foregoing examples that Black's play is perfect. Unquestionably, somewhere down the line a better plan may evolve.

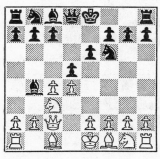

5 **PxP** . . . .

5 P-K3 defends White's Queen Bishop Pawn but shuts in White's Queen Bishop; whereas, after 5 N-B3, Black may make a serious effort to capture and hold the Queen Bishop Pawn by . . . PxP. That is the basis for the exchange.

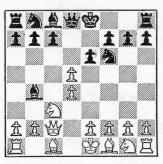

5 . . . . **QxP**

Centralizing the Queen, which is a good policy so long as the Queen cannot be molested. After 5 ... PxP, White may continue with N-B3, B-N5, and straightforward development. Then Black will have nothing better to do with his Queen Bishop than the retreat to K2, at the cost of losing a move, or exchanging it off for the Knight at the cost of giving up the minor exchange (a Bishop for a Knight).

6 N-B3 ....

White maintains his lead in development. 6 P-K3 is an alternative, though less appealing, since it shuts in White's Queen Bishop, even if only temporarily.

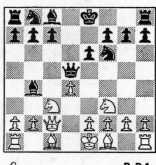

6 .... P-B4

Black must demolish White's Pawn control of the center, while he is able. Any temporizing will result in an overwhelming position for the first player.

7 B-Q2 ....

Compelling Black to part with his Bishop for the Knight. If Black moves his Queen now, his development will become extremely laggard.

7 .... BxN
8 BxB ....

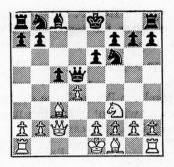

8 PxB is a sound reply, too. While the text move keeps the Queen Bishop file open, the Queen Bishop is transferred to another effective diagonal. Now, it points directly into the vicinity of the Black monarch.

8 ....   **N-B3**

Developing apace. Not 8 ... N-K5; 9 PxP, and Black may not play 9 ... NxB because of 10 QxN, defending the extra Pawn.

9 **R-Q1!**   ....

Quickly to capitalize on the open Queen file.

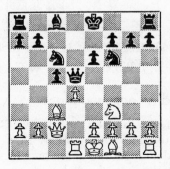

9 ....   **O-O**

If now 9 ... QxRP; *10* PxP, O-O; *11* P-K4, White has a favorable position. After the text move, Black threatens to take off the Rook Pawn.

| *10* **P-QR3** | .... |

Merely to defend the Pawn. There ought to be some way to defend the Pawn, without losing the move to advance it. Unfortunately, such is not the case.

| *10* .... | **PxP** |

Black simplifies by exchanging.

11 **NxP**	**NxN**
12 **RxN**	**Q-B3**
13 **P-K4**	**P-K4**
14 **R-B4**	....

White is for choice, mainly because of his two Bishops. The edge is indeed minimal.

Conclusions and recommendations

Of all the defenses to the Queen Pawn Game, the Nimzo-Indian is currently the most popular. It is popular because Black has succeeded in getting more than his share of victories. This writer inclines to the belief that an opening which commits one side to parting with a Bishop for a Knight is theoretically unsound, and that in time, some way will be found to bolster White's play to grant him more than the usual initiative that is his due.

So far that way has not been found.

Chess Movie

THE TWO BISHOPS

THE WORLD TITLE is at stake in the following masterpiece from the Alekhine–Euwe world championship bout, played in Holland in 1937. Alekhine's Bishops rake the diagonals and enmesh Euwe's poor Black monarch. The game begins with *1* P-Q4, N-KB3; *2* P-QB4, P-K3; *3* N-QB3, B-N5; *4* Q-B2, P-Q4. Continue from Diagram 1.

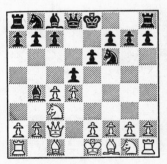

1 Alekhine continues with 5 PxP, and there follows 5 ... QxP; *6* P-K3, P-B4. A minimal initiative has accrued to Black, but he is committed to part with a Bishop for a Knight to hold his Queen in its dominant position. The line is drawn extremely fine, and the issue is clear cut.

2 7 P-QR3 compels the exchange. There follows 7 ... BxNch; *8* PxB. Now White has a preponderant Pawn center, while Black has a temporary lead in the development of his Knights. 8 ... QN-Q2 is Euwe's move. How will Alekhine proceed to utilize his forte—the powerful Pawn center?

96

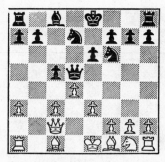

3 By playing *9 P-B3* and menacing *P-K4*, he undermines Black's security. This is a game of give and take. There follows *9 ... PxP; 10 BPxP, N-N3*. Momentarily, White's central demonstration is contained. It requires a bit of bolstering before Alekhine can push it through.

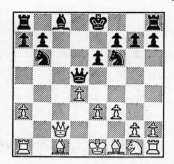

4 *11 N-K2* is Alekhine's move. The enemy Queen will be driven from its dominating post. Euwe continues to bring out his forces with *11 ... B-Q2*. There follows *12 N-B4, Q-Q3*. White's progress is slow but sure. Now Alekhine's aim is to assure an active role for his two Bishops.

5 *13 B-Q2* initiates their action. Black in turn develops his Rook with *13 ... R-QB1*. The Queen sidesteps the Rook with *14 Q-N2*, and Black attempts to penetrate or swap with *14 ... KN-Q4*. A few favorable exchanges will take all the zoom out of White's setup. Or so it seems, at least.

6 There follows *15 NxN, PxN*. Now White's center advance seems to be checked. The advance, *P-K4*, will leave the White Pawns in a tenuous state. But the Bishops must not yet be discounted. *16 B-N4* ties the Black King to the center of the board after *16 ... Q-K3*.

98

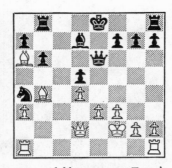

7 17 K-B2 safeguards the King Pawn and, incidentally, makes way for a Rook at King square. There follows 17 ... N-R5; 18 Q-Q2, P-QN3. To maintain his Bishop at QN4, White continues with 19 B-R6, and Black replies 19 ... R-QN1. He now threatens to confine White's King Bishop.

8 Alekhine ignores Euwe's threat. The time has come to strike. 20 P-K4 opens the game, high, wide, and handsome. Euwe parries with 20 ... P-QN4. White's Bishop *is* trapped. But wait! Alekhine has a counter: 21 Q-B4, to which Euwe replies: 21 ... R-N3. For the moment, all is well.

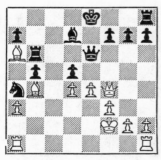

9 Now 22 PxP opens the vital King file. White'll infiltrate with all his forces. Black plays 22 ... QxP, and there follows 23 KR-K1ch, B-K3. The King Bishop is still *en prise*, but tactical counterthreats have made it immune from capture, so far. What then is the next resource for White?

10 24 QR-B1 is in fact the beginning of the end. The threat is R-B8ch. Black plays 23 ... P-B3, and Alekhine continues with 25 R-B7. The King will not escape. Euwe's last gasp is 25 ... K-Q1. There follows 26 RxRP, resigns. The power of the two Bishops has proved decisive.

10

The typical position in the Gruenfeld Defense

Gruenfeld Defense

THE WORLD of chess has witnessed a great search for new ways to cut down White's long-lasting initiative. Hypermodernism has introduced one whole and totally novel vista for the defense. The introduction of Alekhine's Defense, for example, taught that White may be lured into occupying the center—only *perhaps* to find that he has set up that center as a fixed and ready target for a Black counterstroke. The parallel idea, however, of an early sacrifice of the center against the Queen Pawn did not materialize so quickly. Not until 1922 did the Austrian master, Ernst Gruenfeld, evolve such a conscious and plausible system of defense.

The series of moves: *1 P-Q4, N-KB3; 2 P-QB4, P-KN3;*

3 N-QB3, known as the King's Indian Defense, offered the opportunity. Gruenfeld veered from "the book" and audaciously essayed 3 ... P-Q4. His move enabled White to capture (4 PxP) and follow up immediately, after the recapture, with 5 P-K4, usurping all the dominant terrain in the middle of the board. Such a plan would have been frowned upon even less than half a century ago. And now—suddenly—it was good! What brought about the change of attitude? Was not the ceding of all the valuable, central squares tantamount to slow death?

The answers to these questions lie in the hypermodern approach. Black can afford to cede the center, if later he can make an appreciable dent there. That is the issue.

The Gruenfeld arises as follows:

_1_ P-Q4   N-KB3

From a purely theoretical standpoint, Black's move is good inasmuch as the Knight controls very important central squares. Since the Knight move is also a prelude to any number of Black defenses and, consequently, conceals the defender's specific plan, its "keep your opponent guessing" feature rates an additional plus.

_2_ P-QB4   . . . .

White builds a pattern that will mesh with any defense Black decides on. The advance of the Queen Bishop Pawn paves the way for White to continue quickly with N-QB3 and P-K4—obtaining a powerful lead in the center—unless Black proscribes this action.

_2_ P-KN3

The King's Indian Defense. Black intends to fianchetto his King Bishop (B-N2), where it will bear down directly through the center of the board.

The fianchetto development has its good and bad points. While the Bishop at N2 strikes at the vital center, its effectiveness depends on what auxiliary support it will command from the rest of the Black forces. In other words, the Bishop at N2 will most likely bear down on a well-defended White Queen Pawn. Alone, the force of the Bishop will be meaningless. In conjunction with other forces bearing on the same sector, the fianchettoed Bishop may play an important role.

The Bishop at N2 exercises its influence on a commanding diagonal. On K2 or Q3 or some other square, the Bishop may be posted on a less valuable line, but its influence may go farther in other directions.

From a defensive point of view, also, the fianchetto is meritorious. The Bishop at N2 generally shields the position of its King at KN1, where it is apt to be. And the Pawn at KN3 limits the action of an enemy Bishop, bearing in the direction of Black's KR2.

On the other hand, Black's projected King Knight Pawn also is the source of possible weakness in that White may eventually institute a Pawn assault, which gains in momentum when, say, White's King Rook Pawn engages Black's King Knight Pawn.

All these considerations are involved in the simple fianchetto.

Instead of the text move, Black has a wide range of alternative replies. He may transpose into the Queen's Gambit by 2 ... P-K3 or 2 ... P-QB3, followed by ... P-Q4. Or he might even venture on the tricky Budapest Defense, 2 ... P-K4. This defense will be covered in a future chapter. Or he might try any number of other tenable, orthodox and unorthodox defenses.

3 **N-QB3**   . . . .

The sharpest developing move, controlling the center and preparing to follow up with P-K4.

3 . . . .   **P-Q4!**

[chess diagram]

The Gruenfeld, most important branch of the King's Indian Defense and, in fact, most popular.

At first sight, the text move appears to be a tactical violation of principle. For Black presents White with the opportunity to play 4 PxP, NxP; 5 P-K4, gaining full Pawn control of the central squares. There is, however, more to the move than the superficial appraisal discloses.

While Black cedes the center, he aims to open lines—files and diagonals—leading to White's center Pawns, which Black hopes will set up as a fixed target. The text move, for example, opens the Queen file so that later on, a Black Rook, posted on his Q1 square will press on White's Queen Pawn. With a Bishop at KN2, bearing on the same target, and most likely a Pawn at Black's QB4 square, White's Queen Pawn is apt to give. If that is the case, White's strong center becomes weak. And Black assumes the upper hand.

All this is based on "iffy" ideas. Nevertheless, the issue is drawn along these lines.

4 **PxP**   . . . .

At this juncture, there is a great difference of opinion, even among the masters, as to what continuation offers White the best prospects. Of the alternative possibilities, the text move leads to a clearly defined pattern, wherein White is able to maintain the center.

4 Q-N3 held sway for a while and is still favored by some players. The point of this move is to avoid the exchange of Black's King Knight, which now only obstructs the diagonal intended for Black's King Bishop. In playing 4 Q-N3, however, White cannot build up a strong Pawn center quickly. Yet Black enjoys less counterplay. This line might go as follows: *4* Q-N3, P-B3; *5* N-B3, B-N2; *6* PxP, NxP; *7* P-K4, N-N3.

The straightforward 4 B-B4 is also a good alternative and leads to an infinitesimal plus in position for White. This line might go as follows: *4* B-B4, B-N2; *5* P-K3, O-O; *6* Q-N3, PxP; *7* KBxP, QN-Q2; *8* N-B3, N-N3; *9* B-K2, B-K3; *10* Q-B2, KN-Q4; *11* B-K5, R-B1; *12* NxN, QxN; *13* BxB, Q-R4ch; *14* Q-Q2, QxQch.

The moves Q-N3 and B-B4 can be interpolated by White by transposition in various lines of the Gruenfeld.

4 . . . . **NxP**

Of course, Black must recapture; otherwise he is out a Pawn.

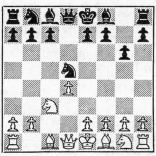

5 **P-K4** . . . .

Here again, there are any number of patterns that might suit White's fancy: for instance, 5 P-KN3, followed by B-N2, or 5 P-K3 and 6 B-B4.

With the text move, White takes a stand in the center and feels that he will be able to meet Black's contemplated blows. In that event, White will come out on top.

5 ....   **NxN**

This and the next move are part and parcel of Black's grand plan. Should Black retreat his Knight to N3 or B3, he will not only have permitted White to build up a strong center, but he will also have lost time in development.

6 **PxN**   ....

Is the center weak or strong? At present the answer depends largely from which side the board is viewed!

6 ....   **P-QB4!**

The first blow at the enemy center. It involves the temporary sacrifice of a Pawn.

7 **B-QB4**   ....

To capture the Pawn is unwise. Thus, if 7 PxP, QxQch, and White forfeits the privilege of castling. Moreover, Black will sooner or later recover the Pawn by lining up against it on the open Queen Bishop file. When the Pawn is retrieved, White will then be left with a weaker Pawn structure.

7 P-Q5 is also an inferior alternative. In advancing the Pawn, White, of his own volition, breaks the solid front of his Pawn line and extends the scope of Black's King Bishop (when at KN2) to an attack on White's Queen Bishop Pawn.

The text move involves tactical considerations. White is looking ahead to the future. He wishes to support his Queen Pawn with his King Knight. But he has found, from previous experience, that the Knight is better posted on K2 than at B3. For at B3 it is subject to a pin by Black's Queen Bishop. Hence, in order not to cause interference in the ranks, White brings out his King Bishop and clears the path for a later N-K2. And at QB4, White's King Bishop bears down on the most vulnerable point in Black's camp—Black's KB2 square.

7 .... **B-N2**

Developing as per plan. The Bishop strikes clearly throughout the center of the board, augmented in effect by Black's Pawn at his QB4.

8 **N-K2** ....

Developing and defending the center. 8 N-B3 is less favorable, since Black can weaken White's center by 8 ... B-N5, pinning the Knight. Now 8 ... B-N5 is useless, as the Bishop can be driven by P-B3.

8 .... **O-O**

Continuing his development and making ready for the pieces on the first rank to co-operate with each other. 8 ...

N-B3 is an alternative that can be met by 9 B-K3. By omitting to bring out his Knight to QB3 now, Black reserves the right to bring it out to Q2 later on.

9 **O-O**   . . . .

White also completes his development and gains the co-operation of his forces on his first rank.

An interesting thought here is 9 P-Q5. While this move definitely breaches White's solid Pawn front, it offers the possibility of establishing a Pawn majority in the center (White's King Pawn and Queen Pawn versus Black's King Pawn), which then tends to restrict Black's movements. On the other hand, the weakness inherent in the advance might offset the gain. It is a moot question.

9 . . . .   **N-Q2**

After the more natural 9 ... N-B3, there might follow
10 B-K3, Q-B2; *11* R-B1, R-Q1; *12* P-KR3, P-K4; *13* P-Q5. Then
White's passed Queen Pawn and Black's cramped position
would rule in White's favor.

The temporary obstruction of Black's Queen Bishop by
Black's Knight is of no real concern, since the Bishop will most
likely be developed on the flank at Black's QN2 square. From
that point of vantage, it also bears on White's center Pawns.

10 **B-KN5** . . . .

Up to recently, *10* B-K3 was the usual move. The text move
is somewhat more precise, since the Bishop bears down on
Black's King Pawn and ties a Black man to its defense.

10 . . . . **P-KR3**

To drive the Bishop. In doing so, however, Black weakens
his King-side Pawn structure to some extent.

11 **B-K3** . . . .

Having provoked a slight weakness in Black's King-side
structure, the Bishop retreats. Its sights are now trained on
both wings.

11 . . . . **Q-B2**

Clearing the path for ... R-Q1, to exert additional pressure on White's Queen Pawn. The move also threatens to win a piece by 12 ... PxP, simultaneously attacking two minor men.

12 **R-B1**   ....

So that if 12 ... PxP, 13 PxP, and White's Bishop is defended by the Rook.

12 ....   **P-R3**

Since White's center holds firmly, Black must create a diversion on the wing. The text move is the prelude to the advance of Black's Queen-side Pawns. Black aims to establish a Pawn majority on that side.

13 **Q-Q2**   ....

Developing and attacking Black's King Rook Pawn, thanks to White's tenth move.

13 ....   **K-R2**

White is for choice. Black has been unable to dent White's Pawn center.

White can now undertake action on the King-side by P-KB4-5, or he may inch in with N-B4-Q5.

Conclusions and recommendations

The Gruenfeld Defense, popular since its inception, has definitely added to the repertoire of those seeking to get away from the drab defenses to the Queen Pawn, which is the unhappy lot of the player of the Black men. From a theoretical point of view, it has had its ups and downs. Currently, opinion favors White, as Black is unable to make an appreciable dent in White's strong Pawn center.

 ◊ ◊ ♌♌♌♌♌♌♌♌♌♌♌♌♌♌♌♌♌ ◊ ◊

Chess Movie

THE PATHS OF GLORY

Struggle for supremacy invokes the gamut of all strategical and tactical concepts. Here hypermodernism tallies a telling success under the expert guidance of grand master, Dr. Feodor Bohatyrchuk (Black) against Savonov (White). The scene is Moscow, 1940. The game begins with *1* P-Q4, N-KB3; *2* P-QB4, P-KN3, *3* N-QB3, P-Q4 (and now continue from Diagram 1).

1 White adopts straightforward development: *4* B-B4. There follows *4 ...* B-N2; *5* P-K3, O-O; *6* PxP, NxP. This is all a prelude to a predatory grab of a Pawn. In the interim, Black's development is promoted, and his men usurp the central squares. Is White's policy sound?

2 There follows *7* NxN, QxN; *8* BxP. White is now material plus. But Black assumes the initiative. Bohatyrchuk plays *8 ...* N-B3, continuing his development, and the game goes on with *9* N-K2, B-N5. (White hopes to bring his men out before Black can make an impression.)

110

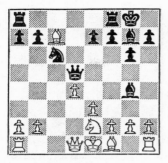

3 First, however, White drives the advanced, enemy Bishop with *10 P-B3*. This innocent rejoinder provokes the immediate assault. Black now counters with a piece sacrifice. *10 ... QBxP* is the move! Can such things be and overcome us? Has Black lost track of values?

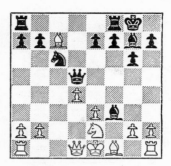

4 Of course, Savonov takes the Bishop. He plays *11 PxB*, and Bohatyrchuk follows with *11 ... QxBP*; attacking White's Rook. White moves his Rook: *12 R-KN1*, and Black plays *12 ... QxP*. Now he has two Pawns and a creditable onslaught for the piece. The scales are delicately balanced.

5 Because his King is somewhat exposed, White attempts to consolidate. The game continues *13 B-B4, Q-K5; 14 B-N2, Q-B4; 15 Q-Q2*. Now White readies for Queen-side castling, when all will be well. Then the extra man will more than make up for the absence of the Pawns—White hopes.

6 There is, however, no rest for the wicked. *15 ... P-K4* places new obstacles in White's path and at the same time opens new lines. White plays *16 BxN*, and there follows *16 KPxB; 17 B B3, KR-K1*. (Black has fouled up White's plan. If White now castles, *... RxN!* is the sockdolager.)

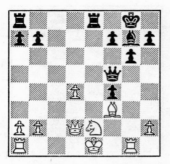

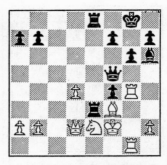

7 White accommodates himself to the new conditions. He plays *18* K-B2, and Black penetrates with *18 ... R-K6*. White feints a counterdemonstration with *19 R-N4*, which Black ignores with *19 ... QR-K1*. There follows *20 QR-KN1*, B-R3. White still has his piece, but not his peace!

8 White stalls with *21 R-R4*, and Black routs the defense with *21 ... R-Q6*. The White lady flees with *22 Q-N4*, and Black tears through with *22 ... RxBch*. Black has scored the first check and now there is no letup. The mating net is set. Only a few loopholes must be closed.

9 Savonov feebly gestures a retreat with *23 K-K1.* This is tantamount to an admission of defeat. And now comes the incisive *23 ... RxNch*, which must be respected. And it is. White plays *24 KxR*, and Black follows relentlessly with *24 ... Q-Q6ch*. The rest should be silence.

10 *25 K-K1* is the move. Black follows up with *25 ... R-K6ch*. All the avenues of escape lead to mate. The White monarch is cornered. Savonov plays *26 K-B2*, and Bohatyrchuk follows with *26 ... Q-K7 mate*. Hypermodernism has wound up in a crowning blaze of glory.

11

The typical position in the Budapest

Budapest Defense

Be it good, bad, or indifferent, every debut embraces a strong point. There is hardly an opening in Caissa's repertoire —whether the Corkscrew or the Ghulim Kassim—which does not rate a potent wallop. Intensify the forte and subdue the weakness is the governing strategy of inferior openings.

So it is with the Budapest, a precarious defense. On his second move, Black sacrifices a whole Pawn! The magnitude of this gesture can be appraised in the light of comparison. When White gives up a Pawn in the opening, its soundness rests, so to speak, on a hair. When Black does so with a move behind, the odds are overwhelmingly against its validity. Yet, despite this exceedingly slim factor of safety, many a defender plays the Budapest. Why?

To begin with, there is always the psychological reason. A player taken by surprise and not conversant with the theoretical details of an idea is apt to go wrong. White may go wrong. And then there is the inherent, although insignificant, forte of the defense, which grows to great proportions, if not properly conquered. Add these two factors together, and there is reason enough for the adventuresome chess-player to play any opening.

The Budapest is one of the later-day openings. It made its advent about 1915, and its popularity rose for quite a while. It has been used especially by American masters: Kevitz, Simonson, and Bisguier, for example. Thorough analysis, however, has revealed its weak points, and today it crops up only occasionally in the tournament arena.

The Budapest arises as follows:

1	P-Q4	N-KB3
2	P-QB4	. . . .

White's first two moves are characteristic of the Queen Pawn Game. Their purpose is to maintain pressure on the central squares, K5 and Q5.

2 . . . .   P-K4!?

Black's move is a most unusual Pawn sacrifice. At first sight, it appears pointless; it neither promotes development nor opens lines. Despite these apparent drawbacks, it is not completely without merit. White is beset at once with a problem of refutation.

3 PxP   . . . .

Other moves, such as 3 N-KB3 or 3 P-K3, lead to tenable variations, but with no perceptible advantage. On the contrary, the declination of the gambit can be considered as a moral victory for the defender, inasmuch as he has steered the play into a line not contemplated by White. General principles, moreover, dictate that a Pawn should be captured when offered, unless its acceptance interferes with a necessary defense or greater gain in some other direction.

The reason for Black's Pawn sacrifice, as yet, is not clear; but it will become evident as the game progresses.

3 . . . .   **N-N5**

The text move is the one generally employed by Black. It aims to recover the Pawn or to provoke fundamental weaknesses in White's Pawn structure.

An alternative, recently popularized but still found wanting is 3 . . . N-K5, known as the Fajarowicz Variation. The line may run as follows: 3 . . . N-K5; 4 Q-B2, P-Q4; 5 PxP e.p., B-B4; 6 N-QB3!, NxQP; 7 P-K4, NxKP (otherwise Black has nothing for the Pawn minus); 8 B-Q3, NxP; 9 BxB, NxR; 10 N-B3, B-B4; 11 N-K4, Q-K2; 12 B-N5 with a plus for White. The above is from the match game, Kottnauer–Martin, Czecho-

Slovakia—France, 1946. The game continued *12* ... P-KB3;
13 O-O-O!, N-R3; *14* R-Q7 with an overwhelming position.
If, in this line, *12* ... B-N5ch; *13* K-K2, P-KB3; *14* B-K3, White
still maintains the lead.

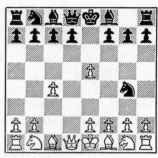

4 B-B4   . . . .

This is one of a number of alternative possibilities. The
text move is the beginning of a concerted effort to maintain
the extra Pawn in a positional way.

If White favors an attack, he may venture upon the following line: *4* P-K4, NxKP; *5* P-B4, N-N3; *6* N-KB3, N-B3; *7*
P-QR3 (to drive Black's Bishop from Black's QB4, when it
goes there), P-QR4; *8* B-K3, P-QN3; *9* N-B3, B-B4. Despite
White's superior command of the central terrain, his advantage is questionable because his Pawns are advanced and have
a weak quality about them. It may well be, in fact, that Black's
prospects are better.

The sequence of the text move is of paramount importance. If White plays *4* N-KB3, for example, his extra Pawn is
doomed, thus: *4* ... B-B4; *5* P-K3, N-QB3; followed by
... Q-K2.

     4 . . . .   **N-QB3**

Black piles up on the extra Pawn with a view to recovering it.

     5 N-KB3   . . . .

White protects the Pawn and develops at the same time.

5 ....   **B-N5ch**

This check is one of the tactical moves in the defense. It limits White's replies, which will be examined later.

Another way is 5 ... P-B3; 6 PxP, QxP; 7 Q-Q2, B-N5; 8 N-B3, BxN; 9 PxB, P-Q3; 10 P-K3, P-QN3; 11 B-K2, B-N2; 12 O-O, N-K2; 13 N-Q4, N-K4; 14 B-N3, O-O-O; 15 P-B4, with a plus for White. White's King is comparatively safe and Black's King can be smoked out sooner or later. Note particularly that White has an extra center Pawn, which will require consideration. This line is from the match game, Eliskases–Bogolyubov, 1939.

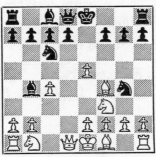

6 **N-B3**   ....

6 QN-Q2 leaves White with a trifling positional advantage, thus: 6 ... Q-K2; 7 P-QR3, KNxKP (threatening 8 ... N-Q6 mate!); 8 NxN, NxN; 9 P-K3, BxNch; 10 QxB, P-Q3; 11 O-O.

White enjoys the advantage of the two Bishops. This, however, may be insufficient for a decision.

	6	Q-K2

Still piling onto the Pawn.

	7 Q-Q5	. . . .

Still defending.

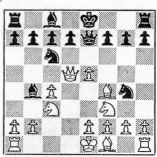

	7	BxNch

The point. White's Queen-side Pawn structure is left in shambles, and Black reckons this as compensation for his Pawn minus. That this is sufficient, however, is a moot question.

	8 PxB	Q-R6

An immediate attempt to exploit the weak Pawns.

	9 R-B1	. . . .

Practically forced. But good enough. If 9 Q-Q2, Q-B4 recovers the Pawn by virtue of the triple attack on various assorted Pawns.

9 . . . .   **P-B3**

Black hardly has time to pick off the White Rook Pawn, since White threatens to drive the King Knight by P-KR3 to an awkward post.

With the text move, Black resigns himself to the permanent loss of the Pawn, but hopes that his better Pawn position will serve as compensation.

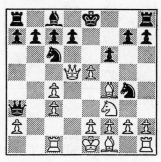

10 **PxP**   . . . .

White must capture. Otherwise Black recovers the Pawn and maintains the superior position. And not *10* P-K6, PxP; *11* Q-R5ch, P-N3; *12* QxN, P-K4; with a plus for Black.

10 . . . .   **NxP/3**

After which all of Black's men are fairly well disposed. But the Pawn minus still lurks in the background.

11 **Q-Q2**   **P-Q3**

Black guards the unprotected Queen Bishop Pawn and prepares the development of the Queen-side men.

12 **N-Q4**   . . . .

Centralizing the Knight, which is more or less immune, since Black cannot afford to capture and straighten out White's Pawns.

12 ....   O-O

Continuing the natural development.

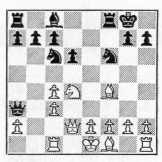

13 P-B3   ....

Preparing for P-K4 and the annexation of the center, while, at the same time, avoiding a pitfall: *13* P-K3??, NxN; *14* BPxN, N-K5; *15* Q-B2, Q-R4ch; *16* K-K2, RxB; *17* PxR, B-B4; *18* Q-N2, R-K1; with a powerful attack—Rubinstein–Vidmar, Berlin, 1918.

White is for choice. His extra Pawn is the deciding factor.

Conclusions and recommendations

Every theoretical and practical conclusion on the Budapest grants White a decided advantage. This writer, nevertheless, harbors a feeling that somehow the Budapest will eventually be vindicated. In any case, those who enjoy unbalanced positions and flights of fancy will find the Budapest a happy medium.

Chess Movie

WHO KILLED COCK ROBIN?

Victory in a chess game indicates one or more blunders
on the part of the vanquished. A piece *en prise*, an inadvertent,
overlooked mate, something awry—all spell disaster. In the
1936 U.S. Championship, Hanauer (White) follows the pre-
scribed technique and loses to Horowitz. Where did he err?
The game begins: *1* P-Q4, N-KB3; *2* P-QB4, P-K4; *3* PxP,
N-N5; *4* N-KB3, B-B4; *5* P-K3, N-QB3 (see first diagram).

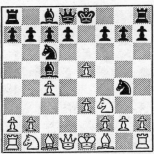

1 White follows a system
recommended by Alek-
hine. His long-term idea
is to dominate his Q5 square.
There follows: *6* P-QR3, P-
QR4; *7* N-B3, KNxP/4; *8*
B-K2, O-O. Black has suc-
ceeded in restraining White's
aspirations to expand on the
Queen-side. White's position
and Black's are both structurally sound.

2 The game continues
with *9* O-O, P-Q3; *10*
P-QN3, readying for the
development of the Queen
Bishops. There follows: *10* …
NxNch; *11* BxN, N-K4. Since
Black's Bishops are pointed
in the general direction of
the enemy King, Black plans
to launch an incursion on
that wing. What is his
method?

121

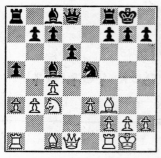

3 Out comes White's Queen Bishop with *12 B-N2*, and Black replies *12 ... Q-R5*. One by one, his forces approach the target. White rejoins *13 N-Q5*, and Black drives the Knight with *13 ... P-QB3*. His Queen Pawn becomes backward, but he gains time in order to bring up reinforcements.

4 There follows: *14 N-B3, B-B4; 15 B-K2, QR-K1*. Somehow, White has let his initiative slip. The game continues: *16 Q-Q2, R-K3*. Oddly enough, White is now doomed. In only a move or two, all the heavy artillery will be bearing on White's King. And what is White to do about it?

5 Hastily White musters a defense. *17 N-Q1* is the move. There follows: *17 ... R-R3*, and White is embarrassed. The Rook Pawn is a "goner." White cuts down the potential onslaught by *18 BxN*, and then Black recaptures with *18 ... PxB*. The backward Pawn is gone; but the attack remains.

6 *19 P-R3* is White's move. Black pursues his course with *19 ... QBxP*. The Bishop is immune from capture on account of the exposed position of White's King. The multifarious threats leave White without resource. He counters with *20 P-N3*, and Black replies with *20 ... Q-K5* with grim effect.

7 Mate is threatened, and White can safely resign. But who gives up the ghost when he is so materially rich. Feebly, White continues with *21 P-B3*, and Black follows up with *21 ... Q-N3*. Now again, mate is in the offing. White defends with *22 K-B2*, and Black captures with *22 ... BxR*.

8 White recaptures with *23 BxB*, and Black plays *23 ... P-K5*. The hardest game to win is a won game; so Black continues sharply. There follows: *24 P-B4, Q-N5*. Black infiltrates the punctured position. The threat now extant at KB3 requires prompt attention, likewise that at his KR2.

9 There follows: *25 B-N2, R-N3*. Now the King Knight Pawn falls, and with it also White's whole King-side structure. White plays *26 K-B1*, and Black captures: *26 ... QxNP*. White offers a friendly exchange of Queens, with *27 Q-KB2*. And, after all, why should Black refuse? He plays *27 ... QxQch*.

10 White, of course, recaptures. *28 KxQ* is his move. Black follows with *28 ... P-B4*, and then the sequel is *29 R-R2, R-Q3; 30 N-B3, R-Q6*. After that, White faces a current deficit of an exchange and two Pawns—with yet another Pawn going. White has had enough. White resigns.

The typical position in the Dutch Defense

Dutch Defense

ORTHODOX DEFENSES to the Queen's Pawn Game encounter a gantlet of trying problems. Black's Queen Bishop, for example, is the perennial offender in most usual variations. Its development leaves the Queen Knight Pawn unguarded, and this, in turn, is subject to peremptory exploitation. Symmetrical lines give White a lasting initiative; other lines, emanating from these defenses, grant White spacious domain and sound structures, while Black is cramped and often crippled. Orthodox defenses leave much to be desired.

Irregular and independent defenses also suffer from certain drawbacks. In short, Black's lot is not a happy one.

With the points to be solved in proper focus, however, the pursuit has been for a defense which yields a measure of *Lebensraum* and counterplay, without risking too many structural defects. Such is the Dutch Defense.

After the moves, *1* P-Q4, P-K3; *2* P-QB4, Black essays *2* ... P-KB4. Immediately, the pattern of the position is unbalanced. White presses on his Q5, while Black bears down on his K5. Point and counterpoint. By the very nature of his defense, Black enjoys a fighting formation. Add to this the desirability of determining the opening and that of employing a not too well-analyzed sequence of moves, and there is reason enough to justify the Dutch.

The Dutch, sometimes called the Hollandish Defense, dates from 1775, when it was first noted in *Traité des Amateurs*. In 1779, it was elaborated upon in Stein's *Nouvel Essai sur les Échecs*. Today, it is included in the repertoire of leading masters, with World Champion Botvinnik among its stalwart disciples.

The Dutch arises as follows:

1 **P-Q4**   **P-K3**

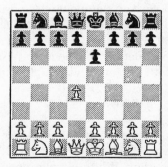

The original Hollandish Defense arose after *1* P-Q4, P-KB4. While the interpolation, *1* ... P-K3, leaves Black open to a French Defense*, it is a "risk" that he must assume. Otherwise,

* After *2* P-K4.

he must chance the perilous Staunton Gambit: *1* P-Q4, P-KB4; *2* P-K4!, in which each side treads on thin ice. While it is possible that the gambit may be contained, practical odds favor the aggressor. A model game, Denker–Dake, Syracuse, 1934, runs as follows: *2* ... PxP; *3* P-KB3, P-K3; *4* N-Q2, PxP; *5* KNxP, N-KB3; *6* B-Q3, P-B4; *7* O-O, PxP; *8* N-N5, P-Q4; *9* NxRP, with a powerful attack.

2 P-QB4   P-KB4
(See photo)

The Dutch Defense as it is generally played today. From the point of view of dominating the central squares, the formation favors White. Observe that his Pawns strike at K5, Q5, QB5, and QN5—squares in or near the center—while Black's Pawns strike at K5, KN5, and Q4. Those squares of immediate moment, however, are White's Q5 and Black's K5. Though important for the long term, the other squares are of subsidiary significance.

One other consideration is worthy of note. The advance of Black's King Bishop Pawn—a Pawn in Black's King's sector—has a tendency to weaken the monarch's position. It is for this reason, in fact, that the Staunton Gambit (mentioned previously) is tenable.

The unbalanced nature of the text position indicates a fighting game, with threats and counterthreats in different fields.

3 P-KN3   . . . .

Preparatory to the fianchetto of the King Bishop, which is a direct challenge to Black's control of his K5 square.

Alternate lines grant White equally good prospects. Even the simple development of each Knight at B3, followed by B-KB4, P-K3 and B-Q3 is fair enough. The text line is in favor today, possibly because it is meeting with success.

3 . . . .   N-KB3

Developing apace and bearing down on K5.

    4 **B-N2** . . . .

As per plan.

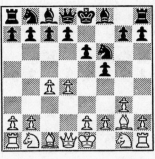

    4 . . . .   **B-K2**

4 . . . B-N5ch has been tried and found wanting. White can play 5 B-Q2 or 5 N-Q2, in each case with the better prospects. The latter may be preferred since the Bishop at N5 is practically committed to the exchange of Bishop for Knight—a welcome exchange for White.

    5 **N-KB3** . . . .

This move, as is well known, commands vital center squares. Alternatives are 5 N-Q2 and 5 N-KR3. The former practically forces Black to adopt the Stonewall formation with 5 . . . P-Q4, since it threatens 6 P-K4, opening lines that will eventually lead to the Black King. True enough, the Stonewall is playable. With Black's laggard development, however, he must be wary of creating holes in his position. (Note the hole at Black's K4 square, after the move . . . P-Q4.) The maneuver 5 N-KR3-B4 has also been tried with fair success.

It is difficult to say which of the alternatives grants White the best prospects. White stands well in each line.

    5 . . . .   **O-O**

Before defining his plan for bringing out the rest of his forces, Black gets his King into comparative safety.

$\quad$ 6 **O-O** $\quad\quad$ . . . .

White follows suit. White still controls the greater portion of the central squares and maintains the minimal initiative vested in him with the first move.

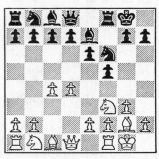

$\quad$ 6 . . . . $\quad\quad\quad\quad$ **P-Q4**

The text is the Stonewall formation. Black's Pawns are posted as a powerful barrier against enemy incursion. To boot, Black fortifies his hold on the square K5. Despite these salient features, the move has inherent defects. For one thing, White now gains unchallenged command of his K5 square. Again, Black's position is backward and with a serious hole at his K4 square. Nevertheless, it is difficult for White to exploit the defects, and if he is slightly remiss, Black can work up a creditable onslaught against the White King by transferring his men to that side of the board.

The alternative line is 6 . . . P-Q3. The game might then pursue the following course: 7 N-B3, Q-K1; 8 R-K1, Q-R4; 9 P-K4, PxP; 10 NxP, NxN; 11 RxN, N-B3; 12 B-B4, B-B3; 13 P-KR4, P-KR3; 14 R-B1, P-R3; 15 P-B5 with a plus for White. Black's development is deficient and his backward King Pawn is a chronic weakness.

$\quad$ 7 **P-N3** $\quad\quad$ . . . .

To transfer the Queen Bishop to an effective diagonal on the left wing.

7 . . . .   **P-B3**

Part and parcel of the Stonewall formation. Black's plan is to build an invulnerable Pawn barrier and then proceed slowly with his men to the King-side. The idea is good, if it works!

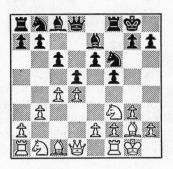

8 **N-K5**   . . . .

White, however, is not without resource. One thing is almost certain: if, in a given position, one side has an advantage, correct play can do no worse than maintain an even balance. White's advantage in the present setup is marked. He controls the greater portion of the center; his hold on K5 cannot be challenged by an adverse Pawn and he has considerable more *Lebensraum*. A Black Knight at its K5 can be driven by a White Pawn. Consequently, at best, Black may achieve only equality.

White's Knight on K5 now dominates the center in all directions.

8 . . . .   **QN-Q2**

Merely to bring out the men and not necessarily to swap Knights.

9 **N-Q3** . . . .

White can afford to leave his Knight on K5. For, if Black exchanges, White's Pawn on K5 exerts a cramping effect on Black's development. In restrained positions, however, every exchange simplifies and, to a small degree, lessens the problem of the defender. That is why White retreats. His Knight on Q3 makes difficult any liberating attempt on Black's part.

9 . . . . **Q-K1**

To swing the Queen over to the King-side, most likely to KR4.

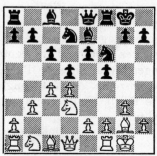

10 **P-B3!** . . . .

More than anything else, this move shows up the weakness of Black's position. Now Black cannot play . . . N-K5. Moreover, White plans an eventual P-K4. Thus, Black's hold on his K5 square has practically vanished.

    10 . . . .   **P-QN3**

To free the Queen Bishop for action via the Queen-side.

    11 **B-N2**   **B-N2**

Development goes on apace.

    12 **N-Q2**   . . .

Readying for P-K4.

    12 . . . .   **P-B4!**

This break is highly necessary. Otherwise, after P-K4-5, Black will remain permanently cramped.

    13 **P-K3**   . . . .

Thus, Black has contained White's threat of P-K4 in the nick of time.

    13 . . . .   **R-B1**

From here on, Black's position is somewhat freer than before. White's advantage now is the weakness of Black's King Pawn, plus the fact that he can occupy his K5 at some later time, unchallenged by an enemy Pawn.

White is for choice.

Conclusions and recommendations

The Dutch Defense falls in the category of the lesser analyzed openings and, as such, grants a player conversant with its details a creditable opportunity to play for a win with the Black men. Theoretically, White's structure is the sounder. Not so much so, however, as to prove fatal.

Chess Movie

THERE OUGHTA BE A LAW

Wᴴᴇɴ Kɴɪɢʜᴛs are developed on the wing and Bishops are swapped for Knights with impunity, sacrosanct tenets are violated. The culprit ought to be punished. Instead, here he is rewarded! Dutch master, S. Landau (White) defeats the inimitable Tartakover in the following game at Rotterdam, 1931. The game begins with *1* P-Q4, P-K3; *2* P-QB4, P-KB4; *3* P-KN3, N-KB3; *4* B-N2, reaching Diagram 1.

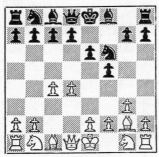

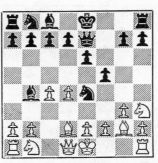

1 Tartakover continues with the old-fashioned check—*4* ... B-N5ch. There follows *5* B-Q2, Q-K2. Now Landau apparently violates general principles with *6* N-KR3, and the learned Doctor plays *6* ... N-K5. For the present, it appears that Black is making progress.

2 Oddly enough, White again violates principles: he plays *7* BxN. To violate *a principle*, we learn, is bad. To violate *principles* possibly is another story. Anyway, the game continues *7* ... PxB; *8* O-O, BxB; *9* NxB, P-Q4. Clearly, White leads in development—all of a sudden.

133

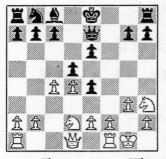

3 The secret is out. White plays *10 N-B4*, and the Knight is no longer on a limb; it is well centralized. Black plays *10 ... P-QB3*, and White increases the pressure with *11 Q-N3*. After *11 ... O-O*, White breaks with *12 P-B3!* There follows *12 ... KPxP; 13 RxP*. White will double Rooks.

4 White's threat to double Rooks on the King Bishop file throws a scare into Tartakover. He plays for simplification. *13 ... P-KN4* is the move. There follows *14 N-N2, RxR; 15 QxR, N-Q2*. The position is somewhat simplified; but Black's King Knight Pawn is a pronounced weakness.

5 Landau plays *16 R-KB1*, and Tartakover attends to his Queen-side with *16 ... P-N3*. Soon, his Bishop will come out on the flank. There follows *17 Q-K3, B-R3; 18 PxP, BPxP*. Thus far, Black has parried the obvious threats. Now his defense is much more difficult. Notably because of his weak Pawns.

6 White trains his guns on the target. *19 N-B3* is the move. Black follows with *19 ... P-N5*, and White penetrates with *20 N-N5*. Among other threats, the King Pawn is attacked. Black defends with *20 ... N-B1*. *21 R-B7* signals the beginning of the final assault. *21 ... Q-Q3* follows.

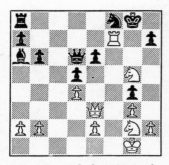

7 Can Black survive the head-on clash? The answer is no! White plays *22 Q-B2* (threatening Q-B6). Black perforce rejoins with *22 ... P-K4*. And White tastes first blood with *23 RxKRP*. Since the Rook is immune from capture, Black responds *23 ... Q-N3*, for defense and counterplay.

8 At first sight, it appears that White was too impetuous. For now, two pieces are *en prise*. But White was prepared. *24 N-R4!* is the proper continuation, and Black is embarrassed. He makes the most of the worst: *24 ... NxR; 25 NxQ, NxN*. A powerful Queen for two lesser pieces is his (forced) deal.

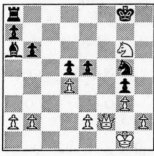

9 It is White's move—fortunately. What a difference one puny move makes! Black could win with ... N-R6ch, but White continues with *26 Q-B6*, and Black is moving out of sheer impetus. Now comes the spite check. *26 ... N-R6ch* is the move. Black can safely resign; but will he?

10 Landau replies *27 K-N2*, and Tartakover hangs on by the skin of his bridgework with *27 ... R-K1*. Now follows *28 NxP*, with a plethora of threats. Q-N6ch, Q-B7ch, NxP, etc., are menacing. White can win a Rook, a Knight or a King. Black resigns. Naturally.

13

Theoretically Important Games

Game 1: CENTER GAME
(Scheveningen, 1913)

	J. MIESES			A. ALEKHINE	
	White			*Black*	
1	P-K4	P-K4	5	N-QB3	B-K2
2	P-Q4	PxP	6	B-Q2	O-O
3	QxP	N-QB3	7	O-O-O	P-Q4!
4	Q-K3	N-B3	8	PxP	NxP

A typical situation in this opening: White's Queen will either be useless or a target during the remaining play.

9	Q-N3	B-R5!		10	Q-B3	B-K3
				11	B-K3	NxN!

In return for the Queen Black gets Rook, Knight, and Pawn —plus a lasting initiative based on the White Queen's inactivity!

12	RxQ	NxPch		17	R-QB1	P-KN3
13	K-N1	QRxR		18	P-N4	B-K5
14	B-K2	N/R7-N5		19	Q-R3	B-B3
15	N-R3	KR-K1!		20	B-B3	BxB
16	N-B4	B-B4		21	QxB	N-K4
				22	Q-K2	P-B4!

This Pawn will play an important role in the final attack. White's Queen is a spectator to the end.

23	R-N1	P-B5		25	NxN	RxN
24	P-R4	N-Q4		26	P-B4	N-Q6!

The brilliant Knight move exploits a new weakness in White's camp, as 27 PxN, RxP; 28 R-N3, B-Q5 does not look inviting to him.

27	Q-B3	R-QN4!		31	P-N5	R/B1-B7!
28	PxN	RxPch		32	K-K1	R-N8ch
29	K-B1	PxP		33	Q-Q1	B-B6ch
30	K-Q1	R-QB1!			Resigns	

A brilliant attack by Black (though 33 ... R-K7ch is more exact). The White Queen has been useless from beginning to end.

Game 2: CENTER GAME
(Postal Game, 1932–33)

M. VON FEILITSCH
White

P. KERES
Black

1	P-K4	P-K4
2	P-Q4	PxP
3	QxP	N-QB3
4	Q-K3	N-B3
5	N-QB3	B-N5
6	B-Q2	O-O

7	O-O-O	R-K1
8	B-QB4	P-Q3
9	P-B3	N-QR4!
10	B-Q3	P-Q4
11	Q-N5	P-KR3!
12	Q-R4	P-Q5

Black has freed himself and soon begins a withering attack. As in the previous game, White's Queen will be little more than an innocent bystander.

| 13 | QN-K2 | BxBch |
| 14 | RxB | P-B4 |

| 15 | P-QB4 | B-K3 |
| 16 | P-QN3 | P-QN4! |

So that if *17* PxP, BxP!; *18* PxB, NxPch; *19* K-B2, NxR; *20* KxN, NxPch!; winning the Queen!

17	N-B4	PxP
18	NxB	RxN
19	PxP	R-N1
20	N-K2	Q-N3!

21	K-Q1	Q-N5
22	Q-N3	N-Q2!
23	R-B2	Q-R6!
24	P-B4	R-KN3!
25	Q-B3	RxP!

Black winds up his brilliant attack with a few-convincing strokes.

26	P-K5	R-QN8ch!	29	QxN	PxQ
27	R-B1	NxBP!!	30	B-B4	Q-R5ch!
28	RxR	N-K6ch		Resigns	

White must lose another piece. Whereas Black's Queen was in the thick of the fight, the White Queen played the inglorious role that is typical of this opening.

Game 3: DANISH GAMBIT
(Baden, 1914)

	G. NYHOLM			R. RETI	
	White			*Black*	
1	P-K4	P-K4	5	BxP	PxP
2	P-Q4	PxP	6	QBxP	N-KB3
3	P-QB3	PxP	7	N-KB3	B-N5ch!
4	B-QB4	P-Q4	8	K-B1	. . . .

A sad decision, but if 8 N-B3, NxB; 9 PxN, Q-K2ch; and White can hardly interpose 10 Q-K2, allowing the exchange of Queens when a Pawn down. It is already clear that White has nothing to show for his minus Pawn.

| 8 | . . . . | O-O! | 9 | Q-N3 | N-B3! |

Sprightly play. He is not afraid of 10 BxN, PxB; 11 QxB? because of 11 . . . R-N1!!; 12 Q-B3, RxB!; 13 QxR??, Q-Q8ch; 14 N-K1, B-R3ch; and mate follows.

10 N-B3	Q-K2!	16 B-K2	B-K3
11 P-QR3	B-Q3!	17 Q-B2	Q-B4!
12 R-K1	N-K4	18 R-B1	KR-Q1
13 NxN	BxN	19 P-N3	P-QR4
14 B-B4	P-B3!	20 Q-N1	R-Q7!
15 P-KR4	P-QN4	21 N-Q5	RxQB!

A nice finish. The idea is that after 22 NxNch, PxN; 23 QxR, BxQ; 24 RxQ, BxP; 25 RxBP, P-N5; the passed Pawns walk in.

| 22 QxR | QxN! | 24 R-B2 | BxQP |
| 23 PxQ | BxQ | Resigns | |

Game 4: DANISH GAMBIT
(Postal Game, 1948)

R. E. HODURSKI *White*		G. M. CROWLEY *Black*	
1 P-K4	P-K4	6 BxQP	N-KB3
2 P-Q4	PxP	7 BxPch!	KxB
3 P-QB3	PxP	8 QxQ	B-N5ch
4 B-QB4	PxP	9 Q-Q2	BxQch
5 BxP	P-Q4	10 NxQ	P-B4

A definite improvement on White's play in the previous game. For many years it was thought that this position favors

Black—because of his Queen-side majority of Pawns. Actually, as we shall see, White has the better of it because of his superior development and because his King Pawn and King Bishop Pawn can advance menacingly if given a chance.

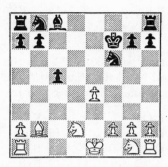

| 11 | KN-B3 | B-K3 | | 13 | NxB | KxN |
| 12 | N-N5ch | K-K2 | | 14 | P-B4 | P-QN4? |

Black does not realize the gravity of the situation. Development with 14 ... N-B3 was his best chance. From this point on, White steadily increases his command of the board until he has a strangle hold.

15	P-B5ch	K-B2		21	R-Q1ch	K-B1
16	P-K5	N-K1		22	R-Q7	R-N1
17	P-K6ch	K-K2		23	P-N4	P-R3
18	N-K4	N-R3		24	N-Q6ch	NxN
19	O-O-O	R-Q1		25	RxN	N-N1
20	RxR	KxR		26	B-K5!	P-B5
				27	P-K7!	Resigns

A tragicomic situation. White threatens to win a piece with 28 R-Q8ch!

Black cannot save himself with 27 ... N-Q2; for then 28 R-B6ch, K-N2; 29 R-B7ch wins the miserable Knight.

Game 5: KING'S GAMBIT
(Stuttgart, 1939)

G. KIENINGER	E. ELISKASES
White	*Black*

| 1 P-K4 | P-K4 | 3 N-KB3 | N-KB3 |
| 2 P-KB4 | PxP | 4 N-B3 | . . . . |

As pointed out on page 33, *4* P-K5 is the move. However, this game is quoted in all the standard opening books, and as the full score is extremely hard to come by, it is given here.

4	P-Q4	9 K-B2	B-KB4
5 PxP	NxP	10 P-B5	N-B3!
6 NxN	QxN	11 B-N5	Q-Q4!
7 P-Q4	B-K2	12 BxP	O-O-O
8 P-B4	Q-K5ch	13 B-K3	B-B3!
		14 Q-R4	B-K5!

Ruthlessly following up his plan of piling up on the weakened Queen Pawn, Black envisages the sacrifice of a whole Rook.

Black has this astonishing line up his sleeve: *15* BxN; QxB; *16* QxP, BxN; *17* PxB, BxP; *18* BxB, RxB; *19* Q-R8ch, K-Q2; *20* QxR, QxQBP!; and White is lost!

15	BxN	QxB		18	KR-K1	BxN!
16	QxQ	BxQ		19	KxB	BxP!
17	QR-Q1	KR-K1		20	BxB	RxR
				21	RxR	RxB

Black has won the weak Pawn as planned, but White has counterplay, with resulting drawing chances.

22	R-K7!	R-Q2		30	R-Q4ch	K-K3
23	R-K8ch	R-Q1		31	R-K4ch	K-B3
24	R-K7	R-B1		32	R-Q4	R-R6ch
25	P-QN4	P-QR3		33	K-K4	R-QB6
26	P-QR4	K-Q1		34	K-Q5	P-N4?!
27	R-K4	K-Q2		35	R-Q2	P-N3?!
28	P-N5	PxP		36	PxP	PxP
29	PxP	R-QR1		37	K-Q6!	R-B4
				38	R-Q5!	. . . .

Curiously enough, Black cannot win the ending. His Queen Knight Pawn is too weak.

38	. . . .	R-B7		43	K-B6	P-B4
39	P-N4	RxP		44	P-N6	R-R1
40	K-B6	P-R4		45	P-N7	P-N5
41	PxP	RxP		46	R-Q6ch	K-K4
42	KxP	K-K3		47	K-B7	P-N6

If now 48 P-N8/Q??, White loses!

48	R-Q8!	R-R2ch		50	R-Q8	R-R2ch
49	R-Q7	R-R1		51	R-Q7	Drawn

A fascinating game.

Game 6: KING'S GAMBIT
(Southsea, 1951)

P. RAVN		A. O'KELLY DE GALWAY	
White		*Black*	
1 P-K4	P-K4	6 O-O	N-QB3
2 P-KB4	PxP	7 P-Q4	P-Q4
3 N-KB3	B-K2	8 PxP e.p.	BxP
4 B-B4	N-KB3	9 R-K1ch	N-K2
5 P-K5	N-N5	10 P-KR3	N-KB3

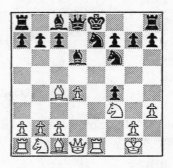

Black has a good development, and he can hold on to the gambit Pawn without compromising his position with ... P-KN4. He has already refuted the gambit.

11 N-B3	O-O	15 P-B4	Q-B3
12 N-QN5	N-N3	16 P-QN4	N-N6
13 NxB	PxN!	17 B-N2	B-B4
14 B-Q3	N-R4	18 P-QR4	KR-K1

Black steadily improves his position.

19 Q-Q2	BxB	21 Q-N3	N/N3-R5!
20 QxB	N-B4	22 NxN	NxN
		23 Q-B2	P-B6!

Beginning the final phase.

24	P-Q5	Q-N4	28 B-B1	Q-B3
25	P-N4	P-KR4	29 R-R3	PxP
26	Q-B1	RxRch	30 K-R2	P-B7
27	QxR	PxP	31 Q-B1	Q-K4ch
			Resigns	

The coming ... Q-K8 will be crushing.

Game 7: KING'S GAMBIT DECLINED
(Maehrisch–Ostrau, 1923)

A. RUBINSTEIN   K. HROMADKA
White   *Black*

1	P-K4	P-K4	7 P-KR3	BxN
2	P-KB4	B-B4	8 QxB	N-Q5
3	N-KB3	P-Q3	9 Q-N3	Q-K2
4	N-B3	N-KB3	10 PxP	PxP
5	B-B4	N-B3	11 K-Q1	P-B3
6	P-Q3	B-KN5	12 P-QR4	KR-N1

Too slow. 12 ... O-O-O (see page 47) is best.

13	R-B1	P-KR3	16 P-B3	B-N3
14	N-K2	O-O-O	17 P-R5	B-B2
15	NxN	BxN	18 B-K3	K-N1

Threatening ... NxP.

19	K-B2	K-R1	20 R-B3	N-Q4?!

This allows 21 PxN, PxP; 22 B-R2, P-K5; 23 B-KB4, PxR; 24 BxB, etc. But Rubinstein prefers to go his own way.

21	B-N1	N-B5	23 P-KN3!	NxRP
22	Q-B2	B-N1	24 RxP!	Q-Q3
			25 Q-N6!!	....

If 25 ... PxQ; 26 PxP dis ch, B-R2; 27 RxBch, K-N1; 28 R/B7xPch, K-B1; 29 B-R6, and Black can resign.

25	R-Q2	27 BxQ	R-B7ch
26 B-B5!	RxR	28 QxR!	NxQ
		29 B-B5!	Resigns

Black must lose a piece. White's Bishops are all-powerful.

Game 8: FALKBEER COUNTER GAMBIT
(Hilversum, 1947)

V. CASTALDI		P. TRIFUNOVICH	
White		*Black*	
1 P-K4	P-K4	3 KPxP	P-K5
2 P-KB4	P-Q4	4 P-Q3	N-KB3
		5 N-Q2	....

This move, strongly recommended in recent years, is by no means so formidable as its reputation.

5	PxP	9 QxQch	KxQ
6 BxP	NxP	10 B-R4	B-KB4
7 N-K4?	N-N5!	11 N-N5	K-K1
8 B-N5ch	P-B3!	12 K-Q1	P-B3
		13 N/5-B3	N/1-R3!

With the troublesome threat of ... N-B4. If White expected relief from the exchange of Queens, he is soon undeceived.

14	P-QR3	R-Q1ch	19	P-N3	K-B2
15	B-Q2	N-Q4	20	R-QB1	B-B2
16	K-K2	N-B4	21	K-B2	B-N3ch
17	B-N3	NxB	22	K-N2	KR-K1
18	PxN	B-Q3	23	P-R3	N-K6ch

Black has increased the pressure relentlessly to drive White into a hopeless situation.

24	K-R2	R-Q6	27	P-N4	B-K5
25	P-QN4	KR-Q1	28	N-K1	R-Q7ch!
26	B-B3	N-Q8		Resigns	

For if 29 BxR, RxBch; 30 K-N3, B-B7ch; 31 K-R2, BxN/K8ch; with devastating effect. A masterpiece of logical play.

Game 9: PETROFF'S DEFENSE
(British Championship, 1938)

C. H. ALEXANDER   H. V. MALLISON
White   *Black*

1	P-K4	P-K4	9	PxP	P-KB4
2	N-KB3	N-KB3	10	P-KR3	B-R4
3	NxP	P-Q3	11	N-B3	N-Q2?!
4	N-KB3	NxP	12	NxN	PxN
5	P-Q4	P-Q4	13	BxP	N-B3
6	B-Q3	B-Q3	14	B-B5!	K-R1
7	O-O	B-KN5	15	P-KN4!	NxQP
8	P-B4	O-O?!	16	B-K6!	....

This is the game that discredited Marshall's dashing counter-attack. (Thus far the variation has been given on page 58.) As two of Black's pieces are attacked, his next move is forced.

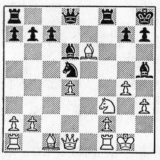

| 16 | .... | B-B2 | 17 | N-N5! | |

Again Black has no choice, for if *17* ... B-N1; *18* BxB, RxB??; *19* N-B7 mate!—or *18* ... KxB; *19* N-K6, winning as in the text continuation.

| 17 | .... | BxB | 18 | NxB | Q-R5 |

An ingenious resource: after *19* NxR, QxRP; Black can force a draw. But now comes the real point of the variation—

by guarding his King Rook Pawn, White threatens B-N5, winning the Queen. This gives White time to win the exchange.

19 Q-N3!!	N-B5	21 NxR	RxN
20 BxN	BxB	22 K-N2	B-Q3

With the exchange to the good, White has an easy win.

23 Q-K6!	Q-N4	31 R-Q7	P-N4
24 P-B4!	BxP	32 P-Q5	P-QR4
25 QR-K1	Q-QR4	33 R-K7	P-R5
26 Q-K5!	QxQ	34 P-R3	B-Q3
27 RxQ	K-N1	35 RxRch	KxR
28 R-K7	P-KN4	36 R-K6	K-N2
29 P-KR4	PxP	37 KxP	B-B5
30 K-R3	P-KR3	38 K-R5	B-B8
		39 R-K2	Resigns

Black has had enough. A game of outstanding theoretical importance.

Game 10: PETROFF'S DEFENSE
(U.S. Championship, 1940)

I. KASHDAN		A. KUPCHIK	
White		*Black*	
1 P-K4	P-K4	4 N-KB3	NxP
2 N-KB3	N-KB3	5 P-Q4	P-Q4
3 NxP	P-Q3	6 B-Q3	B-K2
		7 O-O	O-O

Inexact. The right way is 7 ... N-QB3; and if 8 P-B4, N-QN5; as shown on page 57.

8 P-B4	N-KB3	9 N-B3	N-B3?

Another inexactitude, this time a very serious one that gives White a strangle hold on Black's position. Relatively better was 9 ... PxP; 10 BxP, QN-Q2; followed by ... N-N3-Q4.

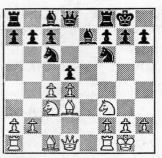

10	P-B5!	B-N5	14	P-R3	N-N1
11	B-K3	Q-B1	15	Q-B2	P-B3
12	R-K1	R-K1	16	N-KN5	P-KN3
13	P-KR3!	B-K3	17	NxB	QxN
			18	B-KN5	Q-Q2

This blocks the development of his Queen Knight—but if *18 ... Q-B1?; 19 RxB, RxR; 20 BxN,* etc. The ultimate goal of White's stifling pressure is to gain undisputed mastery of the open King file.

19	R-K3	B-Q1	22	R-K1	BxB
20	Q-K2	RxR	23	QxB	N-N2
21	QxR	N-R4	24	R-K7	Q-Q1

White has the open file, and the seventh rank as well. Material gain is the next step, with an easily won ending.

25	Q-B6	Q-KB1	31	BxQNP	N-R3
26	RxNP	N-K3	32	BxN	RxB
27	P-QN4	Q-N2	33	R-Q7	R-R1
28	QxQch	KxQ	34	RxP	R-QN1
29	N-K2	P-QR4	35	P-B6	R-N7
30	P-N5	PxP	36	R-K5	N-B2
			37	N-B3	Resigns

Black's faulty ninth move cost him the game.

Game 11: PHILIDOR'S DEFENSE
(Monte Carlo, 1903)

C. SCHLECHTER
White

J. MASON
Black

1	P-K4	P-K4	5	N-QB3	B-Q2
2	N-KB3	P-Q3	6	B-K2	N-B3
3	P-Q4	PxP	7	O-O	B-K2
4	NxP	N-KB3	8	P-B4	....

Black has chosen the easiest, but not the best, way out. The surrender of the center at his third move leaves his opponent with a lasting plus in mobility.

8	....	NxN	11	B-N2	N-K1
9	QxN	B-B3	12	P-N5	B-Q2
10	P-QN4!	O-O	13	N-Q5	P-KB4

Striving for freedom, he only succeeds in opening the King file for White's use.

14	B-Q3!	P-B3	16	NxBch	QxN
15	NPxP	NPxP	17	QR-K1!	PxP
			18	RxP	Q-B3

Now White simplifies into a won ending.

19 Q-B4ch!	Q-B2	25 RxQP	QRxKBP
20 R-K7!	QxQ	26 RxR	RxR
21 BxQch	P-Q4	27 R-Q8	K-B1
22 BxPch	PxB	28 B-R3ch	K-B2
23 RxB	R-B1	29 R-Q7ch	K-N3
24 R-B2	R-B5	30 RxP	R-B5

Black must regain one of the lost Pawns; but meanwhile White sets up a foolproof winning process.

31 R-K7!	N-B3	33 B-N2	RxP
32 R-K2	R-QR5	34 BxN	KxB

Now White's plan is clear: Black's King cannot block the passed Queen Bishop Pawn.

35 K-B2	P-R4	41 K-N4	R-N1ch
36 K-K1!	P-N4	42 K-R5	R-QB1
37 K-Q2	K-B4	43 K-N5	R-N1ch
38 K-Q3	R-R1	44 K-R6	R-QB1
39 P-B4	R-Q1ch	45 R-B2!	K-K4
40 K-B3	R-QB1	46 K-N7	R-B4
		47 K-N6	Resigns

From this logical game it is all too clear that after Black surrenders the center, his prospects are bleak indeed.

Game 12: PHILIDOR'S DEFENSE
(Stockholm, 1912)

A. ALEKHINE		G. MARCO	
White		*Black*	
1 P-K4	P-K4	4 N-B3	QN-Q2
2 N-KB3	P-Q3	5 B-QB4	B-K2
3 P-Q4	N-KB3	6 O-O	O-O

After this colorless move, Black is limited to an unpromising defensive situation. As indicated on page 70, his best course is to try for ... P-KR3 and ... P-KN4—with possibilities of counterplay.

7	Q-K2	P-B3	12	QR-Q1	K-N2
8	P-QR4!	P-KR3	13	N-KR2!	N-KN1
9	B-N3	Q-B2	14	P-B4	P-B3
10	P-KR3	K-R2	15	Q-N4!	PxQP
11	B-K3	P-KN3	16	BxP	N-B4
			17	P-B5!	....

White's position becomes more menacing from one move to the next. If now 17 ... P-KN4; 18 BxN, followed by 19 Q-R5, penetrates Black's defenses.

17	....	NxB	22	N-K2!	R-N2
18	QxPch	K-R1	23	N-B4	Q-K1
19	PxN	B-Q2	24	Q-R4	Q-B2
20	Q-N3	R-B2	25	R-Q3	K-R2
21	N-N4	Q-Q1	26	N-N6	....

With the nasty threat of 27 R-B4 followed by 28 NxRP!, NxN; 29 QxNch!!, KxQ; 30 R-R4ch and mate next move!

26	....	RxN	29	BxB	R-K1
27	PxRch	QxP	30	RxP	Q-N2
28	BxBP	BxN	31	B-B6	NxB
			32	KRxN	Resigns

Black never really had a chance after his faulty opening play.

Game 13: CARO-KANN DEFENSE
(Vienna, 1928)

| | H. KMOCH | | B. HOENLINGER | |
	White		*Black*	
1	P-K4	P-QB3	*5* N-N3	B-N3
2	P-Q4	P-Q4	*6* P-KR4	P-KR3
3	N-QB3	PxP	*7* N-B3	N-Q2
4	NxP	B-B4	*8* B-Q3	BxB
			9 QxB	KN-B3

Even after the more exact 9 ... Q-B2; *10* B-Q2, KN-B3; *11* O-O-O, P-K3; *12* K-N1, O-O-O; *13* P-B4, Black has a lifeless game. See also page 82.

10 B-Q2	P-K3	*11* O-O-O	B-Q3
		12 KR-K1	BxN

Leads to trouble. He should have tried *12* ... Q-B2; *13* N-B5, O-O-O.

13 PxB	Q-N3	*14* N-K5	NxN

Or *14* ... O-O; *15* NxN, NxN; *16* P-KN4, with a strong attack.

15 PxN	N-N5	*17* B-N5	Q-R4
16 Q-KB3	P-KR4	*18* K-N1	NxP

Or *18* ... O-O; *19* B-K7, KR-K1; *20* B-Q6, with winning positional advantage.

19 Q-B4	P-B3

20	BxP!	PxB	22	RxPch	K-B1
21	QxP	N-B2	23	R-Q7	R-R2
			24	RxNch!	Resigns

An unrewarding variation for Black; without offering more than arduous equality, it exposes him to a number of tactical dangers.

Game 14: CARO-KANN DEFENSE
(London, 1947)

R. J. BROADBENT		S. FAZEKAS	
White		*Black*	
1 P-K4	P-QB3	6 N-B3	B-N5
2 P-Q4	P-Q4	7 B-K2	B-Q3
3 N-QB3	PxP	8 O-O	O-O
4 NxP	N-B3	9 P-B4	R-K1
5 NxNch	KPxN	10 R-K1	N-Q2

In the Chess Movie on page 84, Black played 5 ... NPxN and ran into difficulties. The recapture with the King Pawn gives Black a reasonable development, but the resulting Pawn position is against him. For White has four Pawns to three on the Queen-side, and, as we shall see, he knows how to exploit his advantage.

11	B-Q2	QR-B1
12	P-KR3	B-R4
13	B-B3	B-N1
14	N-R4	Q-B2
15	P-KN3	B-N3

16	NxB	RPxN
17	B-B3	P-KB4
18	Q-Q3	Q-Q3
19	QR-Q1	P-R3
20	P-QN4!	....

The Queen-side Pawns are on the way to becoming menacing.

20	....	P-B5
21	P-N4	Q-B3
22	K-N2	Q-R5
23	P-Q5!	P-QB4

24	PxP	RxR
25	RxR	NxP
26	Q-Q4	Q-R3
27	P-Q6	N-K3

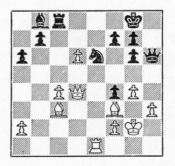

White has acquired his passed Pawn—and a very menacing one too. He can now play 28 Q-Q5 with decisive effect, but the continuation he actually selects is also strong.

28	RxN!?	PxR
29	P-Q7	R-Q1
30	Q-N6	Q-N4
31	QxPch	K-R2
32	Q-B7!	B-K4

33	B-R5	R-QN1
34	P-Q8/Q	RxQ
35	BxR	QxB
36	BxP	P-R4
37	B-Q5!	K-R3

White attacks on two fronts. Black must succumb.

38 P-B5!	K-N4	43 Q-N8	P-N4
39 B-B3	Q-Q6	44 B-K4	P-B6ch
40 P-B6	Q-Q3	45 K-R3	PxP
41 P-B7!	QxP	46 Q-R7ch	K-N4
42 P-R4ch!	K-R3	47 Q-N6ch	Resigns

It is mate next move.

Game 15: NIMZO-INDIAN DEFENSE
(Berne, 1932)

A. STAEHELIN		A. ALEKHINE	
White		*Black*	
1 P-Q4	N-KB3	4 Q-B2	P-Q4
2 P-QB4	P-K3	5 PxP	QxP
3 N-QB3	B-N5	6 N-B3	P-B4
		7 P-QR3	. . . .

White branches off from 7 B-Q2, as played on page 92.

7	BxNch	10 B-K2	P-QN3
8 PxB	N-B3	11 O-O	PxP!
9 P-K3	O-O	12 KPxP?	. . . .

White discards 12 BPxP because it gives Black the Queen-side majority of Pawns. The text is worse, however, as it leaves White with a weak Pawn on the Queen Bishop file.

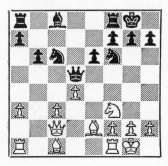

12	....	B-N2	17	N-K1	P-QN4
13	R-Q1	QR-B1!	18	Q-N3	Q-KB4
14	P-B4	N-QR4!	19	B-Q3	B-K5
15	Q-R4	NxP	20	BxB?	NxB
16	R-N1	P-QR3	21	P-B3	N-B6!
				Resigns	

White loses the exchange without compensation.

Game 16: NIMZO-INDIAN DEFENSE
(Margate, 1938)

J. R. CAPABLANCA		M. NAJDORF	
White		*Black*	
1 P-Q4	N-KB3	8 BxB	N-B3
2 P-QB4	P-K3	9 R-Q1	O-O
3 N-QB3	B-N5	10 P-QR3	PxP
4 Q-B2	P-Q4	11 NxP	NxN
5 PxP	QxP	12 RxN	Q-B3
6 N-B3	P-B4	13 P-K4	P-K4
7 B-Q2	BxN	14 R-B4	....

This is the position reached at the end of the model variation on page 94. Black is desperately in need of counterplay.

14	....	Q-K3	16	R-Q5	Q-KN3
15	R-B5	N-Q2	17	P-B3	N-N3!

Black alertly surrenders a Pawn in the hope of stamping
the position of White's Queen Rook as unfavorable. This speculation turns out well.

18	RxP	B-K3	21	R-QN5	P-QN3
19	P-B4	Q-R3	22	B-K2	N-B4
20	P-KN3	N-Q2	23	P-QN4	P-R3!
			24	RxP	B-N6!

A very complicated position. If *25* Q-N2, QxR; *26* PxN, Q-QB3; *27* QxB, QxKP; *28* R-B1, KR-K1; *29* Q-Q1, QR-Q1; *30* B-Q2, R-K2; and White cannot meet the threat of .... R/K2-Q2 or ... R/Q1-K1.

25 RxQ	BxQ	28 O-O	N-Q7
26 R-R5	NxP	29 R-B2	KR-B1
27 B-R1	P-B4!	30 B-Q4	P-N3
		31 R-R4	N-K5

Threatening to tie up the unfortunate Rook for good with ... P-KR4. White therefore decides to give up the exchange.

| 32 P-N4 | NxR | 34 B-B5 | RPxP |
| 33 KxN | P-QR4! | 35 RPxP | B-N6 |

After *35* ... B-K5; Black retains his winning chances.

36 PxP	R-R7	39 R-K3	K-B2
37 PxP!	PxP	40 K-B3	BxBch
38 R-R3	B-B5	41 RxB	RxR
		42 KxR	....

The ending is a draw.

42	K-K3	44 K-K3!	R-KR1
43 K-B3	K-B4	45 K-Q4!	RxP
		46 K-Q5	Drawn

White's Knight Pawn will cost Black his Rook. A difficult, exciting game.

Game 17: GRUENFELD DEFENSE
(U.S. Championship, 1938)

S. RESHEVSKY
White
A. E. SANTASIERE
Black

	White		Black
1	P-Q4	N-KB3	
2	P-QB4	P-KN3	
3	N-QB3	P-Q4	
4	B-B4	B-N2	
5	P-K3	O-O	
6	Q-N3	PxP	

	White	Black
7	KBxP	QN-Q2
8	N-B3	N-N3
9	B-K2	B-K3
10	Q-B2	KN-Q4
11	B-K5	R-B1
12	NxN	QxN
13	BxB	KxB?

As shown on page 103, the correct move is *13* ... Q-R4ch.
The careless text move allows White to get a strong bind on
the position.

	White	Black			White	Black
14	P-QN4!	B-B4		*22*	R-B5	P-K3
15	Q-N2	N-B5		*23*	QR-QB1	P-QR3
16	Q-N3	N-N3		*24*	P-QR4	Q-N1
17	Q-B3	Q-Q3		*25*	P-R3!	BxN
18	P-QR3	N-Q4		*26*	BxB	KR-Q1
19	Q-N2	B-N5		*27*	Q-N3	P-B4
20	O-O	P-QB3		*28*	P-N3	K-B3
21	KR-B1	P-B3		*29*	K-N2	P-R3
				30	P-R4	P-KN4?

Being at a loss for good moves in his cramped position,
Black resorts to bad ones. It does not take White long to engi-
neer a brilliant breakthrough.

	White	Black			White	Black
31	P-K4!	BPxP		*34*	R-K1	K-Q3
32	PxPch	PxP		*35*	BxN!	KPxB
33	BxP	K-K2		*36*	R-K5!	R-N1

White is now ready to smash Black's weakened position.

37 R/B5xQPch!	PxR	39 Q-B5ch!	K-Q2
38 QxPch	K-B2	40 Q-K7ch	K-B3
		41 Q-K6ch	Resigns

Game 18: GRUENFELD DEFENSE
(Match, 1950)

KRYLOV   KOZMA
White   Black

1 P-Q4	N-KB3	5 P-K4	NxN
2 P-QB4	P-KN3	6 PxN	P-QB4
3 N-QB3	P-Q4	7 B-QB4	B-N2
4 PxP	NxP	8 N-K2	O-O
		9 O-O	PxP

The main line on page 106 gives 9 ... N-Q2 here.

| 10 PxP | N-B3 | 11 B-K3 | B-N5 |
| | | 12 P-B3 | N-R4!? |

Inviting the Pawn grab 13 BxPch, RxB; 14 PxB, RxRch; 15 KxR, which leaves Black with the initiative.

| 13 B-Q3 | B-K3 | 15 QxB | P-B3 |
| 14 P-Q5! | BxR | 16 N-Q4!! | .... |

The sacrifice of the exchange, characteristic of this variation, gives White a mighty initiative.

16	B-Q2	*19* P-B5!	KPxBP
17 B-KR6	R-K1	*20* PxP	P-KN4
18 P-B4	P-K3	*21* N-K6!	Q-K2
		22 BxP!	....

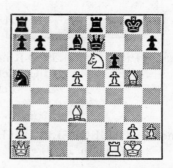

The main point of White's second sacrifice is that if *22* ... PxB; *23* P-B6, Q-B2; *24* NxP, QxQP; *25* P-B7ch, K-B1; *26* NxPch, K-K2; *27* Q-B6 mate.

22	BxN	*26* BxPch!	KxB
23 BxP	Q-B4ch	*27* R-B7ch	K-R3
24 B-Q4	QxP	*28* B-K3ch!	RxB
25 PxB	RxP	*29* Q-B6ch	Resigns

There is a mate in two. This theoretically valuable game shows how important Black's King Bishop is for the defense, and how sadly it can be missed after the acceptance of the exchange sacrifice.

Game 19: BUDAPEST DEFENSE
(Match, 1946)

C. KOTTNAUER   G. MARTIN
White   *Black*

1	P-Q4	N-KB3	8	B-Q3	NxP
2	P-QB4	P-K4	9	BxB	NxR
3	PxP	N-K5	10	N-B3	B-B4
4	Q-B2	P-Q4	11	N-K4	Q-K2
5	PxP e.p.	B-B4	12	B-N5	P-KB3
6	N-QB3!	NxQP	13	O-O-O!	N-R3
7	P-K4	NxKP	14	R-Q7	. . . .

Thus far we have the variation given on page 116.

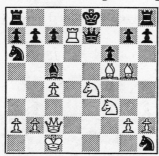

Black must now give up the Queen, for if *14* . . . Q-B1;
15 Q-R4!, P-B3; *16* RxQNP is deadly.

14	. . . .	QxR	22	K-Q2	KR-K1
15	BxQch	KxB	23	QxPch	K-Q1
16	NxBch	NxN	24	Q-N8ch	K-K2
17	Q-B5ch	N-K3	25	QxPch	K-B1
18	N-Q4	QR-K1	26	N-Q3!	R/K8-K5
19	Q-Q5ch	K-B1	27	P-B5	N-B7
20	NxN	PxB	28	NxN	R-K7ch
21	N-B5!	R-K8ch	29	K-B3	RxN
			30	P-QN4	Resigns

He is helpless against the Queen-side Pawns.

Game 20: BUDAPEST DEFENSE
(Berlin, 1918)

	A. RUBINSTEIN			M. VIDMAR
	White			*Black*

1	P-Q4	N-KB3	7	Q-Q5	BxNch
2	P-QB4	P-K4	8	PxB	Q-R6
3	PxP	N-N5	9	R-B1	P-B3
4	B-B4	N-QB3	10	PxP	NxP/3
5	N-KB3	B-N5ch	11	Q-Q2	P-Q3
6	N-B3	Q-K2	12	N-Q4	O-O
			13	P-K3??	....

Here *13* P-B3 is the recommended move. (See page 120.)

13	....	NxN	15	Q-B2	Q-R4ch
14	BPxN	N-K5	16	K-K2	....

Now Black is ready for a promising sacrifice of the exchange, which yields him a powerful attack.

16	....	RxB	21	K-R4	R-K3
17	PxR	B-B4	22	B-K2	R-R3ch
18	Q-N2	R-K1	23	B-R5	RxBch
19	K-B3	N-Q7ch	24	KxR	B-N3ch
20	K-N3	N-K5ch	25	K-N4	Q-R4 mate

Game 21: DUTCH DEFENSE
(Warsaw, 1935)

B. REILLY		R. FINE	
White		*Black*	
1 P-Q4	P-K3	4 B-N2	B-K2
2 N-KB3	P-KB4	5 P-B4	P-Q3
3 P-KN3	N-KB3	6 N-B3	O-O
		7 O-O	Q-K1

Thus far the game has followed the variation on page 130.
The key to White's strategy is an early P-K4.

8 Q-B2	QN-Q2	13 P-Q5!	P-B4
9 P-K4	N-R4?	14 B-Q2	N-N5
10 PxP	PxP	15 N-N5	Q-Q1
11 R-K1!	QN-B3	16 N-K6	BxN
12 N-KN5!	P-B3	17 RxB	....

White's control of the King file and the K6 square gives him
an overwhelming positional advantage.

17	P-QR3	20 N-Q1	P-B5
18 QR-K1!	R-B2	21 B-K4!	P-KN3
19 N-B3	N-K4	22 B-QB3	N-N2

Winning the exchange, but White will have ample compensation.

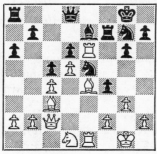

23	BxN!	PxB	27	PxN	Q-K1
24	N-B3!	R-KB1	28	R-Q7	B-B3
25	R-Q1!	PxP	29	B-Q5!	K-R1
26	RPxP	NxR	30	N-K4	B-N2
			31	N-Q6	....

White simply piles on the pressure.

31	....	Q-N1	36	N-Q6ch	K-R1
32	P-K7!	R-K1	37	Q-K4!	B-Q5
33	N-B7ch!	K-N1	38	K-N2	B-B3
34	NxPch	K-R1	39	Q-K6	BxKP
35	N-B7ch	K-N1	40	Q-K5ch	Resigns

A masterpiece of positional play by White.

Game 22: DUTCH DEFENSE
(Venice, 1948)

M. NAJDORF		H. GROB	
White		*Black*	
1 P-Q4	P-K3	6 QxB	O-O
2 P-QB4	P-KB4	7 N-QB3	P-Q4
3 P-KN3	N-KB3	8 N-B3	P-B3
4 B-N2	B-N5ch	9 O-O	QN-Q2
5 B-Q2	BxBch	10 P-K3	PxP?

This foolish capture puts an end to Black's "stonewall" setup. The following play shows in a most instructive manner how Black is harmed by giving up his solid Pawn formation.

11	Q-K2	P-QN4	14	N-R3!	N-Q4
12	N-N5	N-N1	15	P-K4!	NxN
13	P-KR4!	P-KR3	16	PxN	P-QR4

In return for the sacrificed Pawn, White has an enormous lead in development, which is bound to have a decisive effect.

17	N-B4	K-R2	20	PxP!	PxP
18	KR-K1	R-R2	21	P-Q5!	R-Q1
19	P-R5!	Q-B2	22	QR-Q1	P-B4

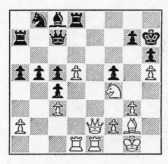

| 23 | P-Q6! | RxP | 24 | B-Q5! | .... |

Threatening a mating attack with 25 Q-K8 or even 25 B-N8ch!

| 24 | .... | Q-Q1 | 25 | Q-K8 | .... |

This leaves Black without a satisfactory reply.

| 25 | .... | B-K3 | 26 | RxB | Resigns |

Black was fittingly punished for giving up his stonewall Pawn pattern.

HOW TO WIN IN
THE MIDDLE GAME OF CHESS

How to Win

IN THE

MIDDLE GAME OF CHESS

BY

I. A. Horowitz

With 143 diagrams

DAVID McKAY COMPANY, INC.

NEW YORK

Contents

v

HOW TO WIN IN
THE MIDDLE GAME OF CHESS

1

Climax of a middle game: *Rubinstein (Black) wins in four* crushing *moves: 1 ... RxN!; 2 PxQ, R-Q7!!; 3 QxR, BxBch; 4 Q-N2, R-R6! and White resigned.*

What Is the Middle Game?

THE MIDDLE GAME is an arbitrary term applied to that portion of the game of chess following the opening and preceding the ending. Since the average game is about forty-five moves and since approximately the first twelve moves cover the opening and perhaps as many the end game, it is clear that the middle game embraces the better part of the whole.

Despite this significant fact, the popular notion prevails with the rank-and-file chessplayer that he is unable to give a satisfactory account of himself during the entire course of the game because he is deficient in opening play. "If I only knew the openings!" is the incessant cry, leaving the listener to sur-

mise that before him stands a Capablanca, nipped in the bud
by some sort of opening bogey. By "knowing" the openings,
incidentally, this person does not mean comprehending them.
He refers to a veritable storehouse of moves of ranking chessmasters, compiled in such works as the voluminous *Handbuch
des Schachspiels* or the tabulated *Practical Chess Openings*.
What he regrets is that he is unable to follow Capablanca or
Lasker or Alekhine or Botvinnik down to the twelfth or twen-
tieth move. Were he able to do so, he thinks his fertile imagination would carry him through the rest of the game to glory.
Little does he realize that if he passed the opening phase with
meticulous perfection, he would now be confronted with the
peripatetic panorama of the enigmatic middle game. Little
does he realize that the "know-why" is of greater importance
than the "know-how." He has yet to learn that imitation without
appreciation is the certain path to defeat in any part of the
game.

With these guiding thoughts in view, we tackle the middle
game. The task is large; the pleasures are great.

The middle game is real chess. Whereas the opening is an
initial development of the forces and the end game scientific
calculation, the middle game embodies every conceivable principle of the magic sixty-four squares, strategical and tactical,
simple, abstract, and profound. Planning and judgment, jockeying and feinting, and a varied assortment of artifices, obvious
and subtle and bludgeon-like, are all here. The art of attack,
the art of sacrifice, the art of combination, the art of defense,
and multifarious skills are required of the player. The middle
game is the art of chess.

The middle game is indeed complex. In a general way, it
covers about a score of strategic motifs and nearly as many
tactical ones. To add to the ramifications, or, better yet, to
multiply them, a single game is a compound of multitudinous
factors, the elements of which rarely appear in pure form.
Mostly, they are in combination with one another. To boot, the
White and Black forces must be in perfect location in relation
to each other for the execution of a given idea. Even the mis-

placement of one puny unit may mean the abrogation of a plan.

In this connection, there is a relevant thought in the study of chess, often forgotten by the uninitiated. According to the laws of chess, Black moves after White, and *vice versa*. With each movement, the position changes. It is not enough to think only in terms of what you are going to do. It is equally essential to burden yourself with your opponent's problems. Then you will be able to anticipate his good plans and encourage his bad ones.

Following is a diversity of positions, selected at random, to give the reader an inkling of what he is to encounter in the middle game.

THE PIN

The first position is a relatively simple one. Among others, there are four striking features about it. (1) Material is even. (2) White's men are better posted. His dominating Knight at Q5 overshadows Black's Knight, out on a limb at R4. (3) White controls the center. (4) White has inaugurated a wing demonstration.

This last contains a latent danger in so far as the assault may boomerang, leaving the White King exposed.

The position is critical, however, in that White has practically reached his maximum potential. He must now do something or soon retreat ignominiously.

WHITE TO PLAY

6

And there is something to be done to penetrate the enemy bastion. It is based on the ever recurring tactical motif—the pin. The win is as follows:

1 P-B6   **PxP**

Forced: for, on 1 . . . B-R1; 2 NxPch decides.

2 PxP   **NxP**

If 2 . . . BxP; 3 RxB, NxR; 4 B-N5, White gains a piece and maintains an irresistible attack.

3 B-N5   . . . .

Black must lose a piece.

Elementary it appears, and elementary it is.

DEMOLISHING THE KING POSITION

WHITE TO PLAY

In this position, the outstanding features are few. White is a Pawn behind; but his position, while tenuous, is far superior. He must, however, make progress fast before Black consolidates.

The play is simple (when you know how).

1 Q-Q5!   . . . .

Threatening 2 QxP mate.

1 . . . .   **P-K3**

Forced.

2 QxKP!!   PxQ

Practically forced, to avoid the threats of 3 Q-K8 mate or
3 QxB.

3 BxPch   Q-B2
4 RxB!   ....

Mate cannot be prevented.

REMOVAL OF THE GUARD

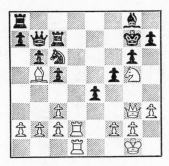

WHITE TO PLAY

In this position, White's development is superior, but
Black's long-term prospects favor him, on account of his mobile King-side Pawn majority. It is up to White to put an
end to the game in the short term. White wins as follows:

1 QxRch   QxQ
2 R-Q7ch   QxR
3 RxQch   ....

Now White picks off Black's Knight and remains with a piece
to the good.

PROVOKING STRATEGY

New York, 1924

QUEEN'S GAMBIT DECLINED

	DR. A. ALEKHINE *White*			DR. EM. LASKER *Black*
1	P-Q4	P-Q4	6	B-B4	P-B3

	DR. A. ALEKHINE *White*			DR. EM. LASKER *Black*
1	P-Q4	P-Q4	6 B-B4	P-B3
2	P-QB4	P-K3	7 P-K3	N-R4
3	N-KB3	N-KB3	8 B-Q3	NxB
4	N-B3	QN-Q2	9 PxN	B-Q3
5	PxP	PxP	10 P-KN3	O-O

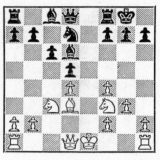

11	O-O	R-K1	24 KR-K1	P-KR4!
12	Q-B2	N-B1	25 P-KR3	N-R2
13	N-Q1	P-B3	26 RxRch	RxR
14	N-K3	B-K3	27 R-K1	R-N1
15	N-R4	B-QB2	28 Q-B1	N-N4
16	P-QN4	B-N3	29 N-K5	PxN
17	N-B3	B-KB2	30 QxN	P-K5
18	P-N5	B-KR4	31 P-B6	P-N3
19	P-N4	B-KB2	32 P-B4	PxNP
20	PxP	R-B1	33 B-K2	PxP
21	Q-N2	PxP	34 B-R5	R-N7
22	P-B5	Q-Q3	35 N-R4	QxP
23	N-N2	B-B2	36 QxQ	BxQ
			Resigns	

It is not within the scope of this work at this time to delineate and discuss the subtle strategy and the exacting tactics of this effort. To be sure, what is involved is far beyond the ken of the vast majority of the chessmasters!

Sufficient it is for the moment to point up its one underlying thematic note. From the diagramed position, where White suffers from an isolated Pawn, we see a series of demonstrations and counterdemonstrations.

At first, White attempts what looks like an overwhelming assault. By timing the pressure on the isolated Pawn, however, Black draws away a vital Knight from the critical sector.

Then it is Black's turn. His general plan is to line up a Queen on Q3 and a Bishop on QB2 and checkmate the opposing King at R7. It sounds simple. Yet the obstacles are many. To begin with, there is a well-sheltered Knight at White's KB3, which guards the important square. Little by little Black hacks away at the stronghold by resorting to "provoking" strategy (17 N-B3, *B-KB2;* 18 P-N5, *B-KR4;* 19 P-N4, *B-KB2*). Having accomplished his purpose, he now lines up Queen and Bishop (22 ... *Q-Q3;* 23 N-N2, *B-B2*). He must, however, still challenge White's guardian Knight. For this, he sets in motion a final Knight maneuver of his own, implemented by fine Pawn piay (24 ... *P-KR4!;* 25 P-KR3, *N-R2;* followed later by 28 ... *N-N4*). When both Knights are in contact, it is the beginning of the end for White.

THE INTUITIVE SACRIFICE

The diagram below, reached after fifteen moves, displays one of the deepest opening sacrifices extant. It is achieved as follows:

Margate, 1938

QUEEN'S GAMBIT ACCEPTED

	DR. A. ALEKHINE *White*			E. BOOK *Black*
1	P-Q4	P-Q4		
2	P-QB4	PxP		
3	N-KB3	N-KB3		
4	P-K3	P-K3		
5	BxP	P-B4		
6	O-O	N-B3		
7	Q-K2	P-QR3		

	DR. A. ALEKHINE *White*	E. BOOK *Black*
8	N-B3	P-QN4
9	B-N3	P-N5
10	P—Q5!	N-QR4
11	B-R4ch	B-Q2
12	PxP	PxP
13	R-Q1!!	PxN
14	RxB!	NxR
15	N-K5	R-R2

To part with a whole Rook, before White's forces are completely developed and when, on the surface, Black seems to enjoy a goodly degree of freedom, shows a sound, intuitive feeling for position.

The game concluded as follows:

16	PxP	K-K2		21	B-KN5	B-N2
17	P-K4	N-KB3		22	N-Q7	RxN
18	B-KN5	Q-B2		23	RxRch	K-B1
19	B-B4	Q-N3		24	BxN	BxB
20	R-Q1	P-N3		25	P-K5	Resigns

The foregoing positions, selected at random, offer food for thought. Each posed its particular problem for the players; each required a different sort of solution. In most, cold reasoning prevailed. But just what is there to indicate in the first that, in a few moves, a fatal pin will wind up the hostilities? Or, for another, that removal of the guard is the correct method? Or that a Queen sacrifice will demolish the King's stronghold? And what is the basis for the intuitive feeling behind the Rook sacrifice in the last position?

These are the types of questions that arise from a study of middle games as actually have been played. And to them all there is a generic answer. The masters who have solved such problems did not do so on a hit-or-miss basis, sufficient for one kind of position but inadequate for another.

Certainly, there is an answer. And it lies in the systematic study of *strategy*—the formulation of plans—and *tactics*—the execution of plans. Clearly, ideas—and plans are ideas—stem from knowledge. So the answer is more knowledge, therefore more ideas.

The appraisal of ideas and their application are part and parcel of the whole. To distinguish between good, bad, and indifferent, to weigh one plan against an alternative or against an opponent's plan and effectively to carry out the plan decided upon—these considerations comprise the subject matter of how to win in the middle game.

2

Checkmate is the goal: *White crashes through the enemy barrier with 1 N-B5ch!, PxN; 2 RxPch!!, KxR; 3 Q-R5ch, K-N2; 4 P-N6, after which Black resigns.*

Middle Game Goal; The Pin; The Knight Fork

In order to comprehend the mechanics of the middle game, it is necessary to know the middle-game goal. Checkmate of the enemy King is the principal goal of the game of chess. It is the ultimate goal of the opening; it is the goal of the ending and, similarly, it is the goal of the middle game. Checkmating ideas, however, do not come to the fore during the early stages of play, unless the opponent exposes his King critically, neglects his development glaringly, or is guilty of some other serious omission. Consequently, checkmating ideas in the opening are subordinated to lesser objectives, more in line with

12

the beginning phase. As the game progresses, however, and most of the men ready for action, checkmating ideas are more pronounced. That is why much of the middle-game play revolves about the King, as a subject both of attack and defense. The primary, long, and short-term objective of the middle game, therefore, is checkmate. All other plans are auxiliary ones in so far as they aid and abet this project.

Material and positional gain, too, are within the realm of checkmate. True, they are subsidiary goals within the principal goal. Material is force, and a preponderance of force brooks little or no interference or resistance in pressing for checkmate. And position is sway, which commands a mighty respect. These plus factors ultimately are converted into checkmate.

MODUS OPERANDI

It is one thing to know the goal; it is another to reach it. And there are no twentieth-century automata or fabled magic words that bridge the vast gap. To get the proper perspective on what is involved in the middle game, it is best to reduce it to its component parts. In a broad sense, the middle game is the science of formulating and executing plans, commonly known as strategy and tactics. Broad, indeed, is this definition, which applies equally well to any part of the game. Since the middle game, however, embraces the better part of the whole, it is clear that strategy and tactics play their greatest role here.

Strategy and tactics

There is the story told of a gentleman who had just had his car repaired. He winced when he was told the job would cost $25. "Twenty-five dollars?" he queried. "Only for hitting a nail on the head. How do you arrive at that figure?"

"Very simply," said the mechanic. "One dollar for hitting the nail on the head, and twenty-four dollars for knowing which nail to hit!"

In chess, too, the all-important questions are what to do and how to do it. Relatively, the "what" carries greater weight than the "how." For a poor plan, even if perfectly carried out, will only lead to a poor result. But the "how" may not be discounted lightly, as in the above tale. For a good plan, if poorly carried out, will lead to a poor result, too. It is abundantly clear, therefore, that correct strategy and tactics are the ideal combination for successful results.

All of the foregoing is by way of an introduction to planning and the execution of plans. Since a plan, as a rule, envisions a series of moves, each single move of which is a supporting factor, the first step in the study of planning is the analysis of tactics. A firm grasp of tactical situations is the sound foundation for synthesized planning.

Common tactical motifs

1. Pin
2. Knight Fork
3. Double Attack
4. Discovered Check
5. Double Check
6. Overworked Piece
7. Removal of the Guard
8. Queening Combinations
9. Underpromotion
10. X-Ray Attack
11. Trapped Man
12. Vulnerable First Rank
13. Interference
14. Surprise Mating Attacks
15. Combined Operations
16. Outcombining the Combiner

It is not within the scope of this study to belabor the excellent tactical presentations in such works as the *Middle Game in Chess* by Fine—and *Winning Chess* by Chernev and Reinfeld. Instead, the strategical side of the game will be emphasized. For the purpose of review, however, the most common tactical motifs are listed above. And examples follow.

In addition to the above, there are innumerable other motifs, rarely encountered in over-the-board play. These will be covered under the caption of Sundry Combinations.

THE PIN

The pin is a piercing attack on hostile men standing on the same line. The man in the direct line of fire of the attacker serves to shield the one behind. The term "pin," undoubtedly, derives from the binding tie between the vulnerable men.

The potency of the pin varies. What we may call the absolute pin exists when a King is the man being shielded. Then the pinned man cannot move and thereby expose its King to capture. Such a procedure would be illegal. Thus, the absolute pin is nearly foolproof.

What we may call the real pin is one in which the front man safeguards a more valuable colleague. The absolute pin is a special example, in a sense, of this; but the usual, real pin is real only in so far as it is unwise to move the pinned man and so lose material. It is only a phantom pin if, for a good reason, the pinned man is able to move.

Winning by pinning

The classic method of exploiting a pin is to pile up attacking forces on the immobile pinned man. Here is a case in point:

The position below has a number of interesting features, the most prominent of which are: (1) Black is a piece minus; and (2) White's Bishop at K4 is already under an absolute pin: it cannot move on the diagonal QN1-KR7, as the White King would be exposed to capture.

(See diagram on page 16.)

Black takes advantage of the absolute pin by establishing a second pin—a real pin.

1 ....   **Q-B4!**

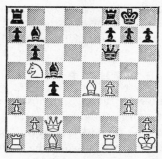

BLACK TO PLAY AND WIN

White's Bishop is now under a double pin. It cannot move in one direction, as the White King would be exposed; it dare not move in the other direction, as the White Queen will fall. Now the pinned Bishop is doubly attacked and defended only once.

　　　　　2 **N-B3**　　　　. . . .

Protecting the pinned piece.

　　　　　2 . . . .　　　　**KR-K1**

Piling on.

　　　　　3 **R-K1**　　　　. . . .

Defending. For the moment, it appears that the power of the pin is spent.

　　　　　3 . . . .　　　　**RxB!**

To remove one of the defenders and, at the same time, to clear the path for another attacker, Black effects a substitution of the piece under pin.

　　　　　4 **NxR**　　　　**R-K1**

At last the pinned piece is doomed. White attempts *a* desperate counterstroke.

　　　　　5 **P-KN4**　　　　. . . .

To draw the enemy Queen away from the critical sector.

5 ....   RxN!!

Final breakthrough by the use of another tactical motif—
the double check.

Resigns

For, if 6 PxQ, RxR double checkmate. White is helpless in
any case.

Key move in the above position is the pin, initiated with
1 ... Q-B4. True, several other tactical motifs enter the picture. In most examples from actual play, however, the single
tactical motif rarely appears in pure form.

The phantom pin

There is nothing so useless as a pin that does not bind. Ex-
cessive reliance on this spurious device has been the downfall
of many a victim. Below, it is seen in all its feebleness in the
shortest game of the 1936 U. S. Open Championship.

F. ARNOLD	M. HANAUER
White	*Black*
1 P-Q4	N-KB3
2 P-QB4	P-K4
3 P-Q5	B-B4
4 B-N5?	....

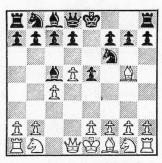

BLACK TO PLAY

To all intents and purposes, Black's King Knight is pinned. But is it?

4 ....   **N-K5!**

It is only a phantom pin.

5 **BxQ?**   ....

Not the best. But White is lost no matter what.

5 ....   **BxP mate**

Pin and counterpin

Just because a player includes the pin in his repertoire, he need not think to use it at every available opportunity. In the following position, for instance, 1 P-B7, R-KB1; 2 QxP settles matters quickly. For Black is at a loss to defend against the threat of a 3 QxP checkmate. White, however, is the type of player who believes "when you've got your opponent down, tantalize him." This is, indeed, a noble sentiment, but——

So White plays:

1 **QxP**   ....

Of course, White sees that Black can pin his Queen. Pinning is his forte.

1 ....   **R-KN1**

Black obliges.

2 **R-Q8!??**   ....

The tantalizer, a counterpin. White's Queen is apparently safe and he threatens the exquisite mate: 3 Q-N7. What a picture!

2 ....   Q-N8ch!

He reckoned without his host. Black's forte is the double attack.

Resigns

White's Queen goes by the wayside.

Establishing a pin

In this summary review of tactical elements we are concerned primarily with defining and illustrating the themes. But it may be said, in passing, that the true mastery of pins—or other tactical motifs—is in foreseeing them in apparently innocent positions. There is no real trick in using a pin already at hand; there is in combining to bring one about—or, defensively, in maneuvering to avoid one.

For the present, the example already given may suffice. On page 10, White's winning method is to establish a pin. To achieve this, White has to understand the value of pins, by second nature as it were, that he may concentrate on this one in the course of analytical ramifications and perceive it as a real and winning pin.

THE KNIGHT FORK

All combinations on the chessboard involve a simultaneous threat on two or more points. Points rather than men, since the target may be the gain of an intangible square (or squares) as well as of a tangible chess piece. The Knight fork, one of the elementary basic tactics, is no exception. It is an attack on two or more points in hostile domain. Because of the Knight's peculiar properties and unique movement, however, the Knight fork is classified separately. Otherwise, it might come under the caption of Double Attack.

The knight's unique move

The Knight's move itself is the delight of the mathematician and the terror of the chess novice—as Chernev and Reinfeld declare in *Winning Chess*.

Compound the Knight's odd angle of movement, its power to hurdle obstructing men (friend or foe), and its surprising propensity for simultaneous attack—and it is small wonder that the Knight fork—a Knight's move one, two, or more times removed—rates as a tactical motif.

Forking ways

WHITE TO PLAY AND WIN

In the above position, the average player of the White men would be content to draw. For White's dangerous-looking passed Pawn at R7 is bound to fall, after it is sufficiently attacked. Yet here the Knight fork spells victory.

1 RxN! . . . .

The sacrifice of the Exchange is the auxiliary motif here.

1 . . . .   **KxR**

Forced, or the Pawn queens.

2 N-B5ch   **K-K1**

If 2 . . . K-B2, 3 N-K6ch (Knight fork) wins. If 2 . . . K—Q3, 3 N-N7ch (Knight fork) wins.

3 N-K6!   . . . .

Preparing the setting for the final Knight fork.

3 . . . .   **R-Q8ch**

Otherwise 4 N-B7ch decides.

4 **K-R2**	**R-QR8**
5 **P-R8(Q)ch**	**RxQ**
6 **N-B7ch**	**Resigns**

The Rook cannot escape the prong of the fork.

Knife and fork

The fork rarely plies its part alone. The check, itself a tactical force, the capture or conversely the sacrifice, the pin, and the threat of mate on the unprotected back rank are all auxiliary motifs here.

(*See diagram on page 22.*)

If anything, Black's position seems supreme here. But the Knight fork, in conjunction with auxiliary tactics, forces the issue to a successful conclusion.

1 **N-R6ch**   **K-R1**

WHITE TO PLAY AND WIN

Using the pin to arrive at a setting for the fork.

        2 QxB!   . . . .

An unusual sacrifice of the Queen. It is based on the following Knight fork.

        2 . . . .   **QxQ**
        3 NxPch!   **RxN**

Otherwise 4 NxQ.

        4 R-Q8ch   **Resigns**

Mate is to follow.

The auxiliary fork

WHITE TO PLAY AND WIN

The above position combines a number of sharp, tactical threats in which Knight forks predominate.

1 Q-N5ch   ....

It isn't often that a player cheerfully parts with his Queen. Here, the parting is pleasant. For, if 1 ... QxQ, 2 N-B6 checkmate.

Since White has, incidentally, trained his sights on the Black Knight, Black's reply is virtually forced.

1 ....   **N-Q2**

Not 1 ... N-B3 2 N-B6 checkmate.

2 KR-K1!   ....

With mate in view by either N-B6dbl ch or N-Q6dbl ch.

2 ....   **B-N5**

Black's choice of defensive plays is limited. He hopes to squirm by attacking White's Rook.

3 N-B6dbl ch   **K-B1**
4 NxNch   ....

The crucial fork. King and Queen are under attack.

4 ....   **RxN**
5 Q-K5   ....

Mate cannot be stopped.

The combination, it will be noted, did not begin or end with the Knight fork. Its perfect cohesion, however, was made possible only by the auxiliary Knight fork.

TACTICS ARE IDEAS

Like a jigsaw puzzle, pins, forks, and all tactical motifs fit into their proper place in the finished product, the chess game. Unlike the selfsame puzzle, where the denouement is predetermined, the final composition of a chess game is the result of a clash of ideas in the imagination of the players. To know more tactics is to be fortified with more ideas.

3

A double-attack complex: *The White Queen, unsupported, threatens
Black's Queen Rook, and, backed by the Bishop, threatens QxRP. But
the attack on the square, KR7, is paramount—threatening mate to the
King.*

Double Attack and Discovered
Attack

THE POWERS of the pieces, by their very nature, are such that
each man attacks in at least two different directions. Each
move, consequently, involves a simultaneous assault on two
or more squares (and whatever happens to be upon them).
The single exception is the puny Rook Pawn, whose scope is
limited by the edge of the board. Hence it attacks only one
square at a time. The double attack, technically, is one which
jeopardizes two or more hostile men. The definition may be
stretched, however, to include critical squares as well as hostile
men.

Because simultaneous attack is intrinsic with the chessmen,

the double attack is a common tactical motif. The most frequent double attacks occur with the most powerful pieces, for
they range over the greatest portion of the playing field and
their geometric proclivities lend themselves to this motif. Thus
the double attack is more apt to occur with a Queen in the
setting than with any other man. A Pawn, on the contrary, is
the least likely to be engaged in this motif. Because checks
and mating threats must be respected, the King is often one
of the butts of double attacks. And, since material is the
physical essence of the game, double-attacking raids on loose,
unprotected men offer abundant prey.

CHECK AND DOUBLE ATTACK

The possibility of the double attack is present in nearly all
positions. When everything appears to be adequately defended,
even then its specter hovers over the board. Particularly is this
true when there is a direct pipeline to the enemy King. That
is the moment to beware.

Black's position in the following diagram presents a picture of solidarity. All is well guarded, yet...

WHITE WINS A PAWN

1 NxP! ....

...All is not what it seems! This temporary forking sacrifice
breaches the bastion and exposes the King. It is the more
powerful here, since the Knight move unmasks White's Bishop

at Q2 for a straightforward attack on Black's Bishop. This auxiliary motif is known as the discovered attack.

1 ....   **PxN**

Forced. Otherwise Black loses a piece.

2 **Q-N5ch**   ....

The double attack, with the King a focal point.

2 ....   **Q-Q2**

3 **QxB**   ....

White has netted an important Pawn.

DOUBLE, DOUBLE

The double attack is indeed a powerful weapon. It is not necessarily, however, the be-all and end-all of the game. Many, many other indispensable ideas and attributes make up a chess game.

Black is a Pawn to the good in the following position. He may reasonably expect to win, but only after much resistance by his opponent, as the Bishops of opposite colors may introduce drawing chances. He observes that White is threatening a double attack (double, discovered attack) by playing his Rook to Q2, after which White's Rook menaces the adverse Bishop and White's Bishop, the adverse Rook.

BLACK TO PLAY AND WIN

1 ....   **PxP!**

Black is impervious to the threat.

2 **R-Q2**   . . . .

The double (discovered) attack.

2 . . . .   **PxPch**

Creating a setting for a counter double attack.

3 **KxP**   . . . .

If 3 K-N2, R-KR6, threatening to promote the Pawn, gains time to save both pieces. Now how does Black save a piece?

3 . . . .   **B-B2!!**

Resigns

The secret is out. If 4 BxR, RxPch forks King and Rook. With three Pawns behind, White has no chance.

Here we have examined the mechanism of two double attacks. One failed; the other succeeded. Failure may not be attributed to the lack of force of the double attack so much as to the desperate plight in which White found himself before engaging upon this last resort. Success by Black, on the other hand, deserves the crowning reward. In White's case, the double attack was a setup. In Black's, it had to be created. It required basic knowledge, fertile imagination, a clear conception, and faultless execution.

A ROYAL DOUBLE

Whenever the King enters into the reckoning of a combination, all fundamental values momentarily change. So long as checkmate is in the offing, the chessmen are no longer themselves. A Queen may be just another piece of wood. And a lowly unit, plus a mate in sight, may assume great proportions. Checkmate needs no further accounting.

When the King is the target, as in the diagram below, the attacker can afford to be generous with his forces—if he is reasonably certain the onslaught will succeed. If he is uncertain, or if the attack will not succeed, he must bear in mind that he will be called upon for a strict accounting.

Here the attacker uses a mating threat as a lever to pick up material, employing pinning and double-attacking motifs.

WHITE TO PLAY AND WIN

1 B-B7!! . . . .

A tricky, devastating move, attacking the Knight Pawn and unmasking a concealed Rook battery, now facing the opposing Rook. Even though Black's Rook is actually defended, it is affected by the initial double attack, which will be followed by another one.

1 . . . . KxB

Black's choice is wide but sad. If 1 . . . RxR, for example, White has 2 QxPch, K-B1; 3 Q-N8ch, K-K2; 4 Q-K8ch, K-Q3; 5 Q-K6 checkmate.

If 1 . . . QxB; 2 RxR, White has gained the Exchange. For Black's Bishop is pinned.

2 RxR QxR

Black's Bishop suffers from an absolute pin. Therefore the text.

3 Q-N7ch . . . .

The second double attack. Black's Rook must fall. The game continued:

3	K-N1
4 QxR	P-K5
5 R-K3	B-Q5
6 RxP	Resigns

AN INTANGIBLE TARGET

It is a common failing over the chessboard to think only in terms of immediate material gain. Rarely does one invest a sizable principal to yield a definite but intangible dividend, which can be converted to something real. Yet opportunities of this kind abound in nearly every game.

The following position is a case in point. Material is even and Black hopes to swap off a pair of Rooks and maintain the balance. The moment, however, is at hand for action.

WHITE TO PLAY AND WIN

1 NxP! . . . .

The reason for this sacrifice is not apparent for some time.

1 . . . . KxN

Forced, as White threatens to capture the Queen with check and also to shatter the King's barrier.

2 RxR QxR

Transition moves to arrive at the anticipated setting.

3 Q-K3!!   . . . .

The double attack. Why double, however, when only the Rook is at stake?

It is double because not only is the material Rook attacked but also the intangible square, K5. Black's vulnerability on this square is the cause of his defeat.

3 . . . .   **Resigns**

Odd, indeed, is the resignation. Superficially, White's threat is unclear. A scrutiny of the position, however, discloses that there is no defense. For example, if 3 . . . R-R8; 4 Q-K5ch, K-K2; 5 R-N8, White threatens 6 RxQ as well as 6 Q-N5ch, K-Q2; 7 Q-Q8ch, K-B3; 8 Q-Q6 checkmate. And Black cannot contain the threat. For example, if 5 . . . Q-R5; 6 R-N7ch and Black is mated shortly. So at the juncture of resignation, Black had to lose his Queen and resigned in deference to the ability of his opponent.

DISCOVERED ATTACK

One move at a time is axiomatic in chess. When one move, however, does the work of two or more moves, it is per se a vigorous offensive weapon. Such is the discovered attack. It is the discharge of a battery of two or more men standing in a straight line. The front man, moving—and checking, capturing, or threatening—unmasks the action of the rear man (or men) which may strike from any of various possible directions. Thus, like buckshot, their potent sting bites on a number of targets simultaneously. And, as a rule, only one target can be defended at a time.

Simplicity is the keynote

The discovered attack need not be a labored effort. In the following example it works like a charm.

White's Queen is subject to capture. But—

WHITE TO PLAY AND WIN

1 **B-R6!!** . . . .

Unmasking the Rook for a concerted attack against Black's King Knight Pawn. Now there is no way to defend against the triple attack on the Pawn.

1 . . . . **Resigns**

For, if 1 . . . NxQ; 2 BxPch, K-N1; 3 BxNdis ch, followed by checkmate. The mating net is the auxiliary motif.

Stock attack

This type of position occurs time and time again and, as such, is a stock attack.

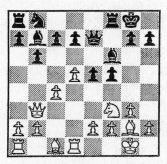

WHITE TO PLAY AND WIN

When two opposing Bishops are fianchettoed, as in the preceding diagram, the stage is set for the discovered attack. That the position appears innocuous because two White men intervene between the Bishops is only an illusion. The "interventionists," as a matter of fact, are part and parcel of a nefarious scheme to conceal the latent danger.

1 N-R4   ....

Clearing one piece out of the path of the opposing Bishops. By doing so with a threat on the Bishop Pawn, White makes the subsequent, menacing discovered attack all the more forceful.

1 ....   BxN?

Best is 1 ... P-Q3, conceding the loss of a Pawn.

2 P-Q6!   ....

The discovered attack in operation. The Pawn advances with a peremptory threat on the Queen and leaves the Bishops *vis-à-vis*. Now White must gain material.

2 ....   PxP
3 BxB   Resigns

The Rook must fall.

It is to be noted that the auxiliary motif here is the trapped Rook at the tail end of the discovered attack. The discovered attack, however, is the primary motif.

Combined operations

When a number of men are lined up on a diagonal, with the front man shielding the rear one, the position has the makings of a discovered attack. Such potentialities are rife in the following diagram. White's Knight and Rook, for example, mask the action of White's Bishop at Q3 in the direction of the enemy King. His Pawn at Q4 masks the action of his Bishop at N2. Black's Knight at Q4 eclipses his Bishop at R1.

But it is White's move.

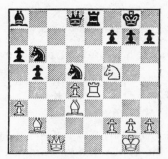

WHITE MATES IN SEVEN!

1 Q-N5! . . . .

Threatening 2 QxP mate.

1 . . . . P-N3

Of course not 1 . . . QxQ; 2 RxR mate.

2 Q-R6 . . . .

Having forced a hole in the opposing Pawn array, White penetrates. Mate is now threatened on N7.

2 . . . . PxN

Forced. Having served its purpose, the Knight is expendable.

Now Black's Pawn at KB4 and White's Rook limit the scope of White's valuable King Bishop.

3 R-N4ch . . . .

The discovered attack. The Rook moves, attacking in one direction, unmasking the Bishop, which attacks in another direction.

3 . . . . PxR

Forced, but clearing the Pawn out of the way.

| 4 BxPch | K-R1 |
| 5 B-N6dis ch | .... |

Discovered check, a subsidiary of discovered attack.

5	K-N1
6 Q-R7ch	K-B1
7 QxP checkmate.	

In the seven moves, possibly a dozen tactical motifs were used to arrive at the final solution. Paramount, however, was the discovered attack.

Attack on a square

The goal of a discovered attack is gain—material or otherwise. Even a vital square is considered gain. In the following diagram, for example, material gain is of secondary consideration. But it is of sufficient import to link itself directly with the positional considerations.

BLACK TO PLAY AND WIN

| 1 .... | RxKP! |

The discovered attack. The Rook move frees the Black Queen to reach out on the long diagonal in the direction of the White King.

1 ... RxQP would work even better—except for 2 QxR CHECK.

Resigns

For if 2 QxR, Q-B6ch; 3 Q-B2, QxQ mate; and there is no other defense at all adequate: 2 RxB, Q-R8ch; 3 K-B2, RxQch, etc.

TACTICS ARE IDEAS

With an ever increasing repertoire of tactics at your command, be certain to employ them at all times under favorable circumstances. Use them again and again and again until they are, so to speak, second nature. In this way you will fortify your ability and establish a bullish confidence in yourself—a necessary attribute of good chess. On the other hand, do not let your imagination run riot. Contain it. Do not try "to discover America." Remember, Columbus got there first.

4

A near-maximum discovery: *Discovered check by White's Knight unmasks attacking thrusts by four pieces in as many different directions. Moreover, the Knight can add attacks on two men from KB3, and might attack a total of seven on its own move.* °

Discovered Check, Double Check, and the Overworked Piece

SUBSIDIARY OF THE discovered attack, yet even more cogent, is the discovered check. Like its parent, it permits, in one fell move, two or more pieces to hit out in separate directions. Only here one of the targets is the enemy King—hence the cogency.

° A further curiosity and complex discovery is that by PxP *en passant* when the Pawn taken has just interposed against a check and the Pawn taking discovers check! New, potentially attacking lines may be unmasked by each Pawn—and the capturing Pawn also hits two squares. Just for fun, try setting up a maximum attacking complex from the PxP e.p. dis ch theme.

In the pure form of this mechanism, the front man strikes at whatever is vulnerable, while the unmasked one takes a bead on the opposing King. And since "A check must be respected," the front man may make off with its booty, unmolested.

Using the front man as the focal point, moreover, it is even possible, though unlikely, to unmask four distinct thrusts simultaneously (as in the photo). Add to these thrusts the independent action of the front man, and it is clear that the potential magnitude of the discovered check is something enormous. It can wreak havoc.

Elementary discovered check

In the position below, White is probably happy. He is a Pawn to the good, enjoys a Queen-side Pawn majority, and secures Black's advanced King Pawn by the well-known blockade. But he is in for a rude awakening!

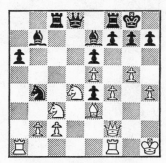

BLACK TO PLAY AND WIN

It's elementary.

1 ....   **QxN!**
Resigns

For, after 2 BxQ, P-K6dis ch recovers the Queen, and White is out a piece.

For example, 3 Q-N2, BxQch; 4 KxB, NxP; 5 QR-Q1, RxN!; 6 BxR, P-K7. Or 5 R-R4, KR-Q1; 6 B-N6, R-Q7ch; 7 K-B3, RxN!; 8 PxR, P-K7. Either way Black wins a piece. Black's lurking Queen Bishop on the same diagonal as the White King was portentous.

Threat of discovered check

An embellishment on the discovered check—the threat of the discovery—plays its role in the position below. And White is fortunate that that is so. For, otherwise, Black's King-side Pawns assume menacing proportions.

WHITE TO PLAY AND WIN

This win is a grade or so above the elementary.

1 R-K7! . . . .

The Rook is immune.

1 . . . . **K-N1**

Naturally not 1 . . . QxR; 2 P-B6dis ch, for the Queen goes.

2 RxRP **Resigns**

White's penetration to the seventh rank, based on the threat of discovered check, and now the constant harassment of the Black Monarch, take all the fight out of the second player.

The climactic discovered check

BLACK TO PLAY AND WIN

Deceptive is the word for the above position. White's forces appear well disposed. But it is Black's move!

1 ....   **RxPch!!**

The beginning of a combination involving the sacrifice of two Rooks in order to execute a discovered check—and what follows in its wake.

2 KxR   **RxPch!**

Black now breaks the blockade of the King Pawn.

3 BxR   **P-K6dbl ch**
Resigns

For any King move allows mate; and the interposition of the Rook, 4 R-Q5, ends in disaster after 4 ... QxBch; 5 K-R1, QxRch; 6 K-N2, Q-B7ch; 7 K-R1, P-K7.

All jells perfectly.

A compound combination

Everything in White's camp, as shown below, appears well guarded; and, superficially, the chances might be rated even. Yet with startling clarity Black picks the opposing position apart and flings his men to the four winds.

BLACK TO PLAY AND WIN

Though the discovered check, our theme, is to come, Black resorts first to another combinational motif.

1 ....   **NxQP!**

The motif is the destruction of a guard—to unhinge White's Queen from its moorings!

2 **QxQ?**   ....

White's move loses outright, but he undertakes it in a desperate effort to maintain complications whereby Black might go wrong. For, though 2 Q-K2 is better, still Black's extra Pawn and superior position insure him a win. On 2 Q-K2, P-K5 is strong.

2 ....   **NxN!**

Introducing a second motif. Black's threat is a double, discovered checkmate, by ... N-B6. This is one of the most powerful threats extant.

3 **K-B1**   ....

After any other move, White is hopelessly lost.

3 . . . .   **N-B7dis ch**

Discovered check comes in as the third motif.

4 **B-B1**   . . . .

For, on 4 K-K2, N-Q5ch, the fork, regains the Queen, leaving White a piece minus.

4 . . . .   **RxBch**
5 **K-K2**   . . . .

The point of White's Bishop interposition is now clear; it has brought Black's Rook into a pin.

5 . . . .   **N-Q5ch**
6 **K-Q2**   . . . .

Curiously, however, it makes no difference now where the White King goes. Black is able always to secure his Rook while recapturing the Queen. Thus, 6 K-K3, NxQch—or 6 K-Q3, R-Q8ch followed by 7 . . . NxQ(ch).

6 . . . .   **N-N6ch**

Thus, Black secures his Rook by a *Zwischenzug* (another tactical motif that may be translated as "in-between move").

Resigns

For White remains two pieces behind.

That at least seven comparatively popular tactical motifs are used in such a simple position and in so few moves is incredible. Yet there they are.

With almost discouraging candor, this position elucidates the requirements of a good chessplayer.

DOUBLE CHECK

Another offspring of the discovered attack and close kin to the discovered check is the double check. In the double check, the front man of a battery moves, giving check to the opposing

King while, at the same time, unmasking the rear man, which checks, too. In so far as immediate checkmating plans are concerned, this tactical motif is a commandeering one. The enemy King, in the crossfire of two separate units, must move. The resource of interposing one of his own men to the check is denied the player thus harassed. Nor can he reply by capturing a checking man. For only one of these checks can be curbed by such means, whereas two checks prevail.

The double check is really a double, discovered check. The front man attacks in the usual straightforward manner; the rear one attacks only by virtue of having its line of attack uncovered.

Double trouble

One of the neatest examples of the efficacy of the double check is the following brevity.

CARO-KANN DEFENSE

	RETI *White*		TARTAKOVER *Black*
1	P-K4	P-QB3
2	P-Q4	P-Q4
3	N-QB3	PxP
4	NxP	N-B3

	RETI *White*		TARTAKOVER *Black*
5	Q-Q3	P-K4
6	PxP	Q-R4ch
7	B-Q2	QxKP
8	O-O-O	NxN

Under the impression that his forceful play has merited a reward, Tartakover accepts the tribute of a piece. He is soon to be disillusioned.

1 Q-Q8ch   ....

A Queen sacrifice, no less, is the auxiliary motif to set the stage for the following double check.

1 ....   KxQ
2 B-N5dbl ch   ....

Double, discovered check, Bishop and Rook check simultaneously. The King must move.

2 ....   K-B2

And now it is revealed that there's not only a double check but also a double mate: if 2 ... K-K1; 3 R-Q8 mate.

3 B-Q8 mate

Note that it is the double cogency of the double check which makes it so peremptory. To the Bishop check there are many possible interpositions and two captures; to the Rook check, several more interpositions—any of which would leave Black materially ahead. To the two checks combined, however, there is but one resource: *the King must move.*

A near doubleton

The selfsame tactical motif was shrewdly dodged by Botvinnik who might otherwise have doubled for Tartakover as in the preceding example. It (almost) happened in an encounter with Keres in a 1948 tournament for the World Championship.

FRENCH DEFENSE

KERES		BOTVINNIK	
White		*Black*	
1 P-K4	P-K3	5 Q-N4	N-KB3
2 P-Q4	P-Q4	6 QxNP	R-N1
3 N-QB3	B-N5	7 Q-R6	....
4 B-Q2	PxP		

Here Botvinnik continued with 7 ... N-B3. Had he played, instead, 7 ... QxP, the following might conceivably have occurred: 8 O—O—O, N-N5; 9 Q-R4, NxBP; 10 NxP! QxN (see diagram).

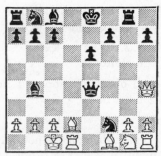

WHITE (*Variation*) MATES IN THREE

1	Q-Q8ch!	KxQ
2	B-N5dbl ch	....

Double, discovered check by Bishop and Rook. The King must move.

2	....	K-K1
3	R-Q8 mate	

These combinative twins point a significant moral and a like lesson. The moral—merely an aside—is that "Virtue is its own reward," but only the virtuous appreciate the consideration. All others must control their predatory instincts.

The lesson is also a fundamental one. We have seen practically the same idea derive from entirely distinct beginnings: a Queen sacrifice and a double check as prelude to mate in both a Caro-Kann and a French Defense. In chess, basic ideas occur again and again and again. It is for the learner to absorb these and apply them in his own games. The opportunities will arise.

The immortal game

The double check is indeed a powerful bludgeon. It does not, as a rule, occur by sheer accident. Subtle refinements in planning precede its action. The following position from Anderssen's Immortal Partie illustrates its crafty foundation.

WHITE TO MOVE

Not only is White a piece behind but Black threatens ... QxN and then mate. It is, however, White's move.

1 QR-Q1!!!   ....

One of the deepest moves in the history of chess. Its meaning will become clear as the game progresses.

1 ....   QxN

A natural reply but perhaps not best.

2 RxNch   NxR

Virtually forced. If 2 ... K-B1, White soon forces mate after 3 RxQPdis ch, K-K1; 4 R-K7ch, K-Q1; 5 B-B5dis ch.

If 2 ... K-Q1, White wins with 3 RxPch, K-B1; 4 R-Q8ch!! for, on 4 ... RxR, 5 PxQ since the pin has been broken. Or 4 ... NxR; 5 Q-Q7ch, KxQ; 6 B-B5dbl ch!! (double, discovered check!), K-B3 (or K-K1); 7 B-Q7 mate. Or 4 ... KxR; 5 B-K2dis ch, winning the Queen.

3 QxPch!!   ....

Compelling the anticipated setting. This is all part and parcel of White's diabolic first move.

3	KxQ
4 B-B5dbl ch	....

Double, discovered check. The King must move.

4	K-K1

If 4 ... K-B3; 5 B-Q7 mate.

5 B-Q7ch	K-B1
6 BxN mate	

The auxiliary double check

The double check is often the means to the end of the game. It is not necessarily the end in itself. In the position below, White had just played 1 R-KN1, with threat of establishing a double checking combination. Black defended with 1 ... N-N3, and eventually White won in a blaze of glory with different combinational themes.

Had it not been for the threat of the double checking combination, White's first move, which served in the subsequent combinations, would not have been possible. But that threat was potent as we see if we imagine that Black captures White's Queen.

1	NxQ
2 RxPch	K-R1
3 R-N8dbl ch	....

Double, discovered check. The King must move.

3 ....   KxR
4 R-N1ch   Q-N4
5 RxQ mate

THE OVERWORKED PIECE

A quite different, tactical motif is that of the "overworked piece." This term suggests rather a fault on the part of the opponent than a winning maneuver by the player. So be it; for the arts of winning in chess lie in seeing how to capitalize on errors by the opponent, and a game played perfectly by both sides must be a draw.

On the other hand, the term need not suggest that the player must wait for an outright blunder by the opponent. In the delicate and complicated balance of give and take in chess play, the "overworked piece" may come about, as it were, by force. As we have seen, all units of the chessboard, save the Rook Pawn, strike out in at least two different directions. And, for reasons of economy—even a wise economy—each unit may be employed on two or more of its lines of force.

When such employment is compatible with the position, these units, so to say, augment the power of their side. And that side which displays the most power prevails.

As the complications grow greater and more delicate, however, such a unit may become burdened rather than useful. And, in just such an instance, it may be that the imposition of a single extra, even measly, chore is enough to snap the backbone of the entire structure. The minute increment may be like the last straw that broke the camel's back.

Hence placing an additional load on an overworked unit is another strong tactical motif.

A futile double guard

Here is a case in point where two units barely manage to hold the position together. An extra burden on each, simultaneously, and the game falls apart.

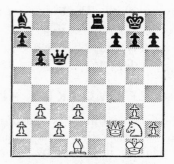

BLACK TO MOVE AND WIN

| *1* .... | **R-K8ch!** |

Both the Queen and the Knight guard K1, yet neither can capture the Rook, for both are overworked. The Queen also guards the Knight; so 2 QxR permits 2...QxN mate. And the Knight also obstructs the diagonal; so 2 NxR allows 2... Q-R8 mate.

An uncovered square

The diagram below illustrates how a unit may be overworked with guarding a square as well as material.

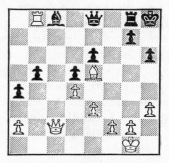

WHITE TO MOVE AND WIN

| *1* **RxB!** | **Resigns** |

Black's Queen was overburdened; for, if 1 ... QxR; 2 Q-N6, there is no defense to the threat of 3 QxRP mate. Guarding both the Bishop and Black's KN3 square, the Queen had to relinquish control over one or the other.

Overtaxation

The following position gives the impression of a long struggle ahead. White's advanced passed Pawns seemingly ought to net him a piece. But Black levies a tax that leaves White bankrupt.

BLACK TO MOVE AND WIN

1	N-B6!
Resigns	

White's Bishop is taxed to guard the White Knight and is now called upon simultaneously to obstruct the Rook on the seventh rank. It cannot do both. So the threat, to which there is no defense, is 2 ... RxNch, followed by 3 ... RxP mate.

Setting up the motif

The theme of the overworked piece is a few moves removed from the diagram setting below. But White visualizes the potentialities and cleverly sets up the motif.

(See diagram on page 50.)

1 BxP!	PxB
2 NxP!!	....

50

WHITE TO MOVE AND WIN

The threat of mate at N7 is an auxiliary motif.

2 ....   **R-KN1**

The Rook guards against the mate, but thereupon, working on the file, it becomes overworked on the rank!

3 **R-K8!!!**   **Resigns**

The threat of mate at N7 is renewed, for now the Rook at KN1 is pinned, and Black is helpless. He dare not play 3 ... RxR, of course. And he may not play 3 ... QxR, for he then allows the threat of 4 Q-B6ch, with mate to follow.

TACTICS AND STRATEGY

Tactics, the masters agree, are about 99 per cent of the game; strategy only 1 per cent. Yet, strangely enough, the highest degree of the art of chess is reached by the perfect blend of the two. There is no question, however, where the emphasis is placed.

5

Removal of a guard by a check: *The Black Queen is lost after 1 BxPch as the Queen's protection is removed by the attack on its guardian King.*

Removal of a Guard, Queening Combinations, and Underpromotion

THE FORCES of the chessboard are interlinked in varying degrees, either directly or remotely. Hence even a single move affects the correlation of all the units. Between certain units, too, there is sometimes a close, direct tie: one protects the other or the movement of one clears a path to the other. In just these circumstances, the tactical motif, the removal of a guard, is born.

The dynamics of this motif are simple: attack a defending unit, compel its retreat (or capture), and then pick off the defenseless unit.

In the application of this motif, particularly, there come to the fore those elementary tactics: the capture, the check, and the threat. Such forcing moves set off the combination after it has been prepared.

Removal of a guard is close kin to the motif previously discussed, the overworked piece. In fact, the distinction between them is hairline. In the case of the overworked piece, the defending unit is not necessarily attacked; it is simply overtaxed, with at least one more burden than it can handle. In the removal of a guard, the defending piece is actually impelled away (or removed) from its ward.

The vulnerable guard

The following position from a master game is a setup. Black's Rook defends the the Bishop which is under attack by White's Knight. The course is easy.

WHITE TO PLAY AND WIN

1 K-N3   Resigns

As the Rook cannot be protected, it must move. If it abandons the Bishop, the removal of the guard has been accomplished, and 2 NxB follows.

The combination is augmented here by a second motif; for 1 . . . R-Q5, the only move to protect the Bishop, fails against 2 N-B5ch (both Knight fork and discovered attack, either of which is quite sufficient to win).

Out at first

This setting looks like the beginning of a struggle. Lo and behold! It is the end. White cannot make first base.

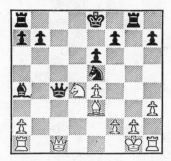

BLACK TO PLAY AND WIN

Black wins with one pitch:

| 1 .... | QxN!! |

Resigns

White's Knight has been guarding a most vulnerable square in his camp—KB3. Without his Knight, White's game is lost; yet, if White strikes back, he strikes out: 2 BxQ, N-B6ch!; 3 K-B1, B-N4ch; 4 Q-B4, BxQ mate.

Preparing the motif

In the following position there is no vulnerable guard, and White is, moreover, in deadly peril of 1 ... QxPch and 2 ... QxP mate. Time, it seems, is of the essence.

Yet, strangely enough, White is able successfully to project a maneuver which seems elaborate enough. Our theme is the removal of a guard, but here the tie that binds must first be constructed and then destroyed.

It is all done, both the construction and the destruction, not by mirrors, but by that most forceful of elementary tactics: the check.

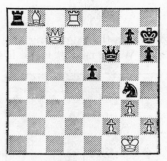

WHITE TO PLAY AND WIN

1 Q-B2ch   Q-N3

Black does not play 1 . . . P-N3 as the further exposure of his King leads to an even clearer loss. One way of winning is 2 R-Q7ch, K-N1; 3 Q-B4ch, and mate follows.

Now, however, Black's King and Queen are tied to each other.

2 R-R8ch   Resigns

For, on 2 . . . KxR; 3 QxQ. The guard has been destroyed.

Piercing an illusion

The motif of the removal of a guard is a simple one in essence; but, for some instances, the eye must be trained to see it. The following setting is not difficult but illusive.

Black's King-side barrier seems unyielding. Yet it is actually vulnerable on the obviously open King Bishop file.

(See diagram on page 55.)

The winning method becomes manifest when, despite appearances, one analyzes the defense, Black's Knight at Q1, and seeks the means to remove that guard.

1 N-K6!!   . . . .

WHITE TO PLAY AND WIN

This is a direct attack on the guard, supplemented by one on the Queen (an elaborate use of the Knight fork).

1 .... **Resigns**

Black's best, if not strongest, move. For, if he moves his Queen, then 2 NxN removes the guard and the Bishop Pawn falls, and Black's position falls with it. If 1 ... PxN, Black falls in with a tactical motif known as line clearance, leading to 2 Q-B8ch, K-R2; 3 Q-R6ch, K-N1; 4 R-B8 mate. And if 1 ... NxN; 2 QxPch, followed by 3 QxN/6, leaves Black's position in shambles.

QUEENING COMBINATIONS

When a Pawn reaches the eighth rank, according to the laws of chess, it must be promoted. It must become an added piece of the same color (any piece, except of course a King). While this law is mandatory, it is indeed a blessing. For greater material gain can hardly be wrought in any other way than to convert a Pawn into a Queen.

Hence, when a Pawn can advance unmolested, it normally does so, and queens. And when a Pawn is passed (i.e., is unimpeded by adverse Pawns) or far advanced, it sets the stage for queening combinations. These embrace a number of ideas in which the key is to clear the path for the Pawn. The nature of the ideas ranges from the seemingly elementary, effecting a final Pawn push on a comparatively unobstructed board, to the surprisingly complex, securing the new Queen by sacrificial combinations on a cluttered board. An example from each extreme will suffice to indicate the types and their diversity.

Elementary queening

White's problem in the following position is to queen his Pawn. For all the apparent simplicity of the position, it is a mighty task.

WHITE TO PLAY AND WIN

On the move and but one square from queening, White yet has a subsidiary problem to solve: to escape checks without prejudice to his Pawn.

1 K-B6   R-R3ch

Black must check. For, on 1 ... R-R1; 2 R-B8, and there is no way to prevent the Pawn from queening.

2 K-B5!   ....

Important. On, say, 2 K-K5, Black has 2 ... R-KN3, followed by ... K-R3, and the Pawn falls.

2 ....   R-R4ch

Forced. Against 2 . . . R-KN3, there is a mating gimmick: 3 P-N8(Q), RxQ; 4 R-R7 mate.

3 K-B4!   **R-R5ch**

Against 3 . . . R-KN4, there is another gimmick: 4 R-B5 pins Black's Rook, and the Pawn queens.

4 K-B3   **R-R6ch**

On 3 . . . R-KN5, White enforces a different pin: 4 R-B5ch, K-R5; 5 R-B4, and then the Pawn queens.

5 K-N2   **R-R7ch**

6 R-B2!   **Resigns**

The subsidiary problem is solved and, with it, the primary one. For, after 6 . . . R-R1; 7 R-B8, again Black can only check, and White can now counter with the standard routine, an advance upon the Rook by the King (e.g., K-B3-K4-Q5, etc.). Then, after the checks have been exhausted, the Pawn will queen.

In this example the new Queen may indeed be taken (if Black switches his Rook to the King Knight file) but then White wins the capturing Rook for a decisive material gain.

Complex queening

In the following position, White has a deficit of Rook versus two pieces, and he can reckon only on his advanced Pawns.

Yet, if ever a Pawn appeared to be dead in its tracks, White's Queen Pawn is that one. White's Q8 is under adequate surveillance: a Black Bishop blockades at Q1; a Black Rook observes at QN1; and a Black Knight commands Q7—surely, an insuperable barrier. And White's Queen Rook Pawn seems to play no part in this scene (e.g., 1 PxP, RxP; 2 R-B8, R-Q2, and Black holds everything).

A little legerdemain, however, and Black's men go poof!

WHITE TO PLAY AND WIN

Forced.	*1* R-B8!!	**RxR**
	2 R-K8ch!!	**NxR**

Now Q7 has been cleared.

| | *3* P-Q7 | **N-Q3** |

But Black still covers the queening square.

| | *4* PxR(Q) | **NxQ** |
| | *5* PxP!!! | **Resigns** |

Note the potency of the *double* queening threat. This rare attribute of the Pawn makes good a combination in which a double Rook sacrifice and a Pawn fork with the threat of queening cleared the path for the puny Rook Pawn.

UNDERPROMOTION

So potent is the Queen that, in the normal course of affairs, a Pawn is unhesitatingly promoted to a Queen. But there are times—few and far between—when it is advantageous to *underpromote* a Pawn—to a Knight, a Bishop, or a Rook, instead of a Queen.

These instances arise out of various special considerations. For one, a Queen may be too much force—or just enough, that is, to create a stalemate. In others, the promotion of a Pawn to a Knight may lead to a check and hence to the gain of a necessary *tempo*. Or it may lead to a fork and material gain.

The examples below illustrate the diversity of this rare tactical motif.

Winning by an eyelash

The first position is a classic. White has but a puny Pawn against a Rook. Surely, a loss! But not so; for the Pawn is far advanced and, if White succeeds in promoting it to a Queen, he is certain to win. For a Queen beats a Rook. Well, maybe. Let's see!

WHITE TO PLAY AND WIN

1 P-B7   R-Q3ch

Black's defense is limited; he must stave off queening as long as possible.

2 K-N5! . . . .

Necessary. On any other move, Black at least secures the draw: e.g., 2 K-N7, R-Q2, pinning and winning the Pawn for the Rook. Or 2 K-R5, R-QB3, and Black actually wins. Or 2 K-B5, R-Q8, followed by 3 . . . R-QB8(ch) and a sure draw.

2 . . . .   **R-Q4ch**

3 K-N4   . . . .

Again, no other move will do for White. If King back to N5, Black repeats the position and no progress has been made. On other moves, Black employs the same defenses as above.

3 . . . .   **R-Q5ch**

4 K-N3   **R-Q6ch**

5 K-B2   . . . .

Now it appears that all is over; for Black is out of checks, his Rook is *en prise* and the Pawn must queen. But——

5 . . . .   **R-Q5!!**

An elegant defense! If 6 P-B8(Q), Black forces the issue with 6 . . . R-B5ch; 7 QxR *stalemate!*

6 P-B8(R)!!!   . . . .

An unusual example of winning by underpromoting. By making the Pawn a Rook, White forestalls the stalemate defense and also threatens 7 R-QR8 mate. Black has no choice; he must play:

6	**R-QR5**
7 **K-N3!**	**Resigns**

For White threatens 8 KxR as well as 8 R-B1 checkmate. The Rook must fall!

Winning by an idea

At first sight White's position looks lost in the following diagram. Black has an extra piece and can mount mating threats. But Black is lost! For it is White's move.

WHITE TO PLAY AND WIN

With his move, White enforces a combination both profound and subtle.

1 **R-B8ch!**	**RxR**

If 1 ... KxP; 2 RxR decides; but now 2 PxR(Q)ch simply loses the new Queen (or a Pawn net), doesn't it?

2 **QxPch!!!**	....

This nearly inconceivable idea wins. And yet the Rook and Queen sacrifices serve merely to set up a modest underpromotion!

2	**KxQ**

On 2 ... K-B2, 3 PxR(Q)dbl ch nets a Queen plus for White.

3 PxR(N)ch!   Resigns

Now White picks off the Queen, then wins with his two Pawns plus.

THE RIGHT PERSPECTIVE

Time and again the question arises: what is the best method of acquiring tactical proficiency? Is it essential to fortify oneself with tomes? The answer is a simple "no." The best way to learn chess is to play, play, and play. Book lore helps. But there are literally at least a hundred tactics in the average game of chess, and it is clear that a few games will cover more than a library of volumes. Books stimulate ideas; play crystallizes them. There is no substitute for play.

6

A Royal X-Ray Attack: *Black's King and Queen are both in the line of force of White's Queen. As Black's King is by law his indispensable man, it must move, letting the Queen fall.*

X-Ray Attack and Trapped Man

THE LINES of force of the major pieces, the Queen and the Rook, and of the Bishop are continuous to the very edge of the board. A Queen on KR1, for example, attacks every square on the file, from KR1 to KR8, every square on the diagonal, from KR1 to QR8, and every square on the rank, from KR1 to QR1. When a unit obstructs such a line of force, it merely interrupts it; and the force automatically persists when the obstructing unit moves.

Because of this characteristic of Queen, Rook, and Bishop, the tactical motif, the X-Ray Attack, comes into being. The X-Ray, called by some authors the skewer, is really a piercing attack, directly striking upon a front man and penetrating beyond, in its effect, to a rear man on the same line of force. Thus, when the front man gives way, the rear one is vulnerable.

In a way, the X-Ray is like the pin. The main difference between the two is the comparative values of the front man under attack and of the rear man. In a pin, the front man is generally the less valuable. Hence it stands by necessity to shelter its more important colleague, and so becomes pinned. In the X-Ray, the opposite condition obtains. So the front man is perforce moved, letting the rear man fall in a choice of the lesser evil.

The x-ray in reserve

The position below has occurred time and time again.

WHITE TO PLAY AND WIN

White wins with ease because he can summon to his command an effective X-Ray attack.

1 R-R8!   **Resigns**

White threatens 2 P-R8(Q) and, if 1 ... RxP; 2 R-R7ch (the X-Ray Attack), followed by 2 RxR.

It is interesting to note that, if Black's King were at his KR2 or KN2, White could not win.

The x-ray that failed

White has a clear-cut win in the next position, by straight-forward means. But he is imbued with the power of the X-Ray, or thinks he is. So he advances.

1 **P-R7?** . . . .

Better is 1 R-R6, retaining both Pawns.

1	**RxP!**
2 **R-R7ch**	**K-Q3**
3 **RxR**	**Stalemate!**

Had White omitted capturing Black's Rook, the position would have been a theoretical draw. Interestingly enough, a leading grandmaster mismanaged the White men.

Stalemate, one of the tactical motifs to be discussed later, invalidates many a plan.

An x-ray finale

White seems to be in a sorry mess in the following position. But again all is not what it seems. It is White's move.

(*See diagram on page 66.*)

Where there's a will, there's apt to be something relative. Here White works from clause to clause to codicil.

1 **R-N1ch!!**   **N-N5**

WHITE TO PLAY AND WIN

Clause 1 is that the Rook on B8 is immune: if 1 ... KxR; 2 R-N8 mate. And likewise, if 1 ... K-R2; White has another saving clause: 2 B-N8ch, K-R1; 3 B-Q6dis ch, K-R2; 4 B-B5 mate.

So 1 ... N-N5 was virtually forced, and White proceeds from there:

2 RxNch!!	QxR
3 R-N8ch	Resigns

White comes out a piece ahead after a mating net, a discovered check, and an X-Ray attack all play a part. What is noteworthy, however, is that, the other factors aiding, White creates his X-Ray attack practically out of thin air.

A beam of x-rays

Here again White's position is all too perilous. It is either mate or be mated.

(*See diagram on page 67.*)

Fortunately, however, with the aid of one pin, White succeeds in fixing Black's King under a whole beam of X-Rays.

1 RxPch!!   . . . .

WHITE TO PLAY AND WIN

Taking advantage of the pinned Knight, White inflicts his first X-Ray, also a bludgeonlike sacrifice.

> *1 ....*   **KxR**

Forced; else the Black Queen goes.

> *2* **Q-K7ch**   **K-N3**

On 2 ... K-R3, another X-Ray, 3 R-R8ch, wins the adverse Queen.

> *3* **R-N8ch**   **K-B4**

Black can avoid further X-Ray by the Rook only by this move.

> *4* **RxNch!!**   *....*

Setting the stage for the final X-Ray.

> *4 ....*   **KxR**

If 4 ... PxR; 5 Q-Q7ch(X-Ray) decides.

> *5* **Q-N7ch**   **K-B4**

If 5 ... K-R4; 6 Q-R7ch (X-Ray again).

> *6* **Q-Q7ch**   **Resigns**

For now the X-Ray penetrates, and the Black Queen must fall.

TRAPPED MAN

Many factors govern the moves of the chessmen. In general, however, the scope of each move is to enhance the potentialities of the player's side while reducing those of the opponent. When we analyze these two aims, it is difficult to speculate on which is paramount: expansion or restraint.

In actual play, however, specific positions require specific treatments. The proper move in a given position may aim to expand or to restrain, or it may strive to control, thus holding the balance momentarily. Or it may aim for a combination of any of these.

Such actions are leveled, as a rule, at whole sectors of the board or at men in concert. Rarely, indeed, is a single man the target, excepting, of course, when it is the opposing King —in which case we have a mating attack.

Yet, occasionally, for one reason or another, a piece strays into a net. It is then that theoretical refinements should be cast aside. To shanghai the man is the business of the moment.

A venerable example

The most familiar trap in the books is "Noah's Ark"—so called in humorous allusion to its antiquity. Yet it beguiles countless victims. In it, a Bishop is the target.

RUY LOPEZ

	White			Black	
1	P-K4	P-K4	6	R-K1	P-QN4
2	N-KB3	N-QB3	7	B-N3	P-Q3
3	B-N5	P-QR3	8	P-Q4?	PxP
4	B-R4	N-B3	9	NxP??	NxN
5	O-O	B-K2			

Even here all seems well. White simply regains his piece.

10 **QxN** . . . .

BLACK TO PLAY AND WIN

But no! In two moves, White is hopelessly lost.

10	**P-B4**
11 **Q-K3**	**P-B5**

The Bishop is impaled.

A royal debacle

The trapped man is most apt to fall into his sorry plight when the board is still crowded. So, though such cases may occur later in the game, a large share of opening traps involve a trapped man. Nor are all of them old, familiar traps like "Noah's Ark." The following miniature game is to the point.

KING'S INDIAN DEFENSE

1 P-Q4	N-KB3	*6* N-B3	P-B4
2 P-QB4	P-KN3	*7* B-K2	PxP
3 N-QB3	B-N2	*8* NxP	N-B3
4 P-K4	P-Q3	*9* N-B2	Q-N3
5 P-B4	O-O	*10* B-K3	....

In his efforts to exploit the weakness, White's diagonal, KN1-QR7, and prevent White from castling, Black played his Queen to N3. He now faces a loss of time or of his Queen after White's 10 B-K3. But Black was under the impression that that Bishop was tied to the defense of the Queen Knight Pawn. Hence—

10	QxP?

White must be punished for leaving the Pawn unguarded, Black thinks.

11 N-R4	Resigns

The Queen is trapped. There is no retreat.

The above example is reminiscent of the story of the legatee whose inheritance consisted of the advice: "Never take the Queen Knight Pawn with your Queen."

Miracle of Main Street

On the side of the board, out on a limb, as it were, it is not too surprising for even the Queen to become enmeshed in a trap. Wandering in the byways is never as safe as promenading the highways. In the center of the chessboard, with so many diversified avenues of escape, lies safety.

But not always!

CAMBRIDGE SPRINGS DEFENSE

1 P-Q4	P-Q4	8 Q-B2	P-K4
2 P-QB4	P-K3	9 QPxP	N-K5
3 N-QB3	N-KB3	10 N/2xN	PxN
4 B-N5	QN-Q2	11 B-K2	O-O
5 N-B3	P-B3	12 O-O	BxN
6 P-K3	Q-R4	13 PxB	P-B3
7 N-Q2	B-N5	14 B-B4	NxP

Of course White is anxious to be rid of his doubled Pawns and sees Black's King Pawn as a fair exchange for his Queen Bishop Pawn. So—

15 QxP	B-B4!!

He now discovers that he is in for more than he bargained.

16 Q-Q4	....

For 16 QxB sells the White Queen cheap to 16 . . . N-B6ch!.

16	QR-Q1
Resigns	

The Queen is trapped!

Snared on the first rank: *owing to the snug position of the Black King, White forces mate by the brilliant "sacrifice" of 1 Q-K5! If Black captures, 2 R-Q8ch and mate in two. If Black defends, the White Queen captures Queen or Rook, and only resignation can forestall a mate.*

Vulnerable First Rank and Interference

THERE IS A variation of chess, called cylindrical chess, in which the board is an imaginary cylinder. In these circumstances, a King at its KR1 can step sedately to its QR1 in its normal, short-gaited pace. Needless to say, therefore, in cylindrical chess it is difficult to fix an opposing King as a target: he has additional escape squares at QR1 and, unless its Queen Rook Pawn impedes, at QR2.

Even in cylindrical chess, however, the King's lateral flight (to QR1 when a Pawn stands at QR2) is futile against a lateral check by Queen or Rook on the first rank.

In orthodox chess, all the more so. Since the King begins its reign on the first rank and usually remains there, surrounded or at least hedged in by its Pawns, the strategic Achilles' heel of the chessboard is the first rank. And particularly so after the prerogative of castling has been invoked—for then the King is snugly tucked away behind the barrier of its Pawns. While a particularly nervous player may strive immediately for "air" with some such move as P-R3, to permit egress of his King, most abstain, knowing that that very move may prove, at some later stage of the game, to be a fatal weakness. And often time and circumstances permit no such dallying with P-R3.

So the King is more often than not circumscribed by the limitations of the board and its own Pawns, and hence original combinations abound which utilize the vulnerability of the first rank as their thematic motif.

Elementary first rank

This position appears even and is so, as a matter of fact, so far as material is concerned. Positionally, too, Black's Rook on the seventh rank must be deemed strong, so it seems. But all is not what it seems. Black is vulnerable on the first rank.

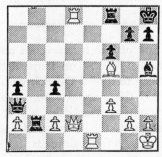

WHITE TO PLAY AND WIN

The proof is in one move:

1 Q-B3!!   Resigns

1 ... QxQ loses to 2 RxR checkmate. And 1 ... Q-B4 is met by 2 RxRch, QxR; 3 QxR. The Rook on the seventh was no asset. Instead, it was a liability.

Second sight

WHITE TO PLAY AND WIN

Not all combinations involving the vulnerable first rank are setups. This position, despite the unguarded first rank, looks uncrackable because ... R-Q1, with the Bishop protecting that square, too, apparently defends. But the combination here is easy, when you know it.

The move is a familiar one to the lovers of chess problems.

1 B-K6   Resigns

It is a combination of line interference and line clearance with respect to Black's Rook. The immediate threat on the Rook is combined with that of 2 Q-R8ch with mate to follow. And, if 1 ... RxR; 2 Q-K8 is checkmate.

Often combination play works by a sort of inversion of logic. Here, on first sight, the unguarded rank seems to cry out for a 1 Q-R8—but 1 ... R-Q1 defends. So, on second sight, we get an inversion of ... R-Q1 beforehand and can then strike at K8—as it might have gone: 1 B-K6, R-Q1; 2 RxRch, BxR; 3 Q-K8 mate.

The first rank incognito

From the looks of this position, it appears that White is more vulnerable than Black on the first rank. Verily, if it were Black's move, 1 ... Q-B8ch spells finis. But it is White's move.

WHITE TO PLAY AND WIN

What then? Black's King is not enclosed by Pawns.

$$1 \text{ R-B8ch!!} \qquad \text{BxR}$$

Forced; for, if 1 ... K-B2; 2 Q-B7ch decides.

$$2 \text{ Q-K8ch} \qquad \text{R-B1}$$
$$3 \text{ RxPch!!} \qquad \text{KxR}$$

Now, if 3 ... K-R1, White mates by 2 R-R7ch, K-N1; 3 Q-N6 mate.

$$4 \text{ Q-N6ch} \qquad \text{K-R1}$$
$$5 \text{ Q-R7 mate}$$

In this instance Black is mated on the first rank, without his own Pawns blocking. The King cannot flee from the edge of the board. A double Rook sacrifice is the auxiliary motif, leading to the vulnerable first rank.

INTERFERENCE

Attack and defense are the direct consequences of the lines of force of the chessmen. During the course of the game, these lines of force are constantly flowing in the various directions of the powers of the pieces.

For example, in the following diagram, the lines of force of Black's King Bishop reach from its KB1 to KR3 and from KB1 to QR6. If Black should play 1 . . . N-K2, the latter line of force would still be coursing through K2 in ultimate, theoretical effect but would be cut off temporarily for immediate practical effect.

Often in a game a situation arises in which it becomes necessary so to cut off a line of force of an enemy piece that cannot be subdued either by capture or by diversion. In such case, of course, one's own piece will be subject to capture; but the interposition of the piece on the enemy's line of force may serve an immediate objective. Such an interposition is called interference.

Interference is one of the rarer tactical motifs. It occurs frequently enough, however, to warrant a special study.

Elementary interference

In the following position, if the Black Queen were not on the board, White could checkmate in one move by 1 QxP. But the Black Queen is on the board. So——

WHITE TO PLAY AND WIN

Extreme measures are justified.

1 R-B5!!   ....

The interference of the Rook cuts off the line of force of the Black Queen operating over the squares, KB4, KN4, and KR4. It is as though the Queen were not there.

1 N-B5 is also interference of a sort. But it is not so powerful as the Knight does not attack Black's Queen and also, in abandoning its observation of K6, it allows Black's King a flight square after 1 . . . PxN.

1 ....   PxR

Under the combined threats, including 2 RxQ, Black was helpless; but now Black's own Pawn interferes. So——

2 QxP mate

Team play

Any interference theme in chess is a form of team play. In our last example, White's Rook threw a block that allowed the White Queen to go on for a touchdown. In this one the quarterback has to call for a more complicated play. Black on the move calls the play, but first he must determine exactly what he wants to do, then how to do it.

If Black tried 1 . . . Q-K6ch in this position, he would have to have his head examined. For, obviously, White would reply 2 QxQ. But if . . . Q-K6ch were feasible, it would be a sockdolager. This is the clue to the setting.

(See diagram on page 78.)

How can White's Queen be taken out of the play?

1 ....   R-N6!!

Interference—an interposition on the line of force of White's Queen, guarding the third rank. Black now threatens . . . RxQ.

2 QxR   ....

BLACK TO PLAY AND WIN

For 2 PxR leaves a block on the third rank, permitting 2 ... Q-K6ch.

2 ....   **B-R5!!!**

Now White's Queen, jostled from one side by the Rook, is hit at another angle by a second piece. As White's Queen is pinned by the Bishop, it cannot move except to capture.

3 **QxB**   ....

But now the road is clear for the Black Queen.

3 ....   **Q-K6ch**

Mate follows.

Thus, the first sacrifice, that of the Rook, was direct interference, leading only to a second sacrifice to clear White's third rank of the defensive power of White's Queen. Two tactical motifs were employed to achieve the denouement.

The road to roam

In the following position, White can threaten to end the game by mate with a Queen check on the Knight file. But he won't get there because Black has ... B-KN3.

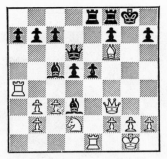

WHITE TO PLAY AND WIN

But the long way round can be the shortest way home. It is here.

1 N-K4!   ....

White interposes on the Bishop's line of force. 1 R-K4 is also good.

1 ....   BxN

Forced. Black must be able to interpose when White checks.

2 RxB   Resigns

For now Black is helpless against the impending Queen check. Thus, the interference by 1 N-K4 compelled the vital defending Bishop to move to where it could be removed by capture.

CONFIDENCE IS AN ASSET

During the course of the game any number of opportunities will arise for combinations, simple, complex, and speculative. Successfully to cope with these, it is imperative to believe in yourself, take what you see at face value, banish vague fears, and trust your judgment. Be confident!

8

A Typical Surprise Mating Attack: *Material is virtually even in the above position. White has the advantage of the Exchange; Black, two extra Pawns. But White, on the move, has the opportunity for a decisive mating attack, initiated by a surprise sacrifice: 1 RxRPch, PxR; 2 QxPch, K-R4; 3 P-N4ch, BxP; 4 PxBch, KxP; 5 R-N8ch, and mate soon follows.*

Surprise Mating Attacks and Combined Operations

Chess is a form of logic expressed in terms of movement. Since logic is the science of pure reasoning, its conclusions are self-evident objectively, devoid of the element of surprise.

Chess is also, however, a game played by human beings. And because of the human equation which enters into the reckoning of every game of chess, other factors, such as incompetence, diffidence, or dissidence, in respect to pure reason, make for many unexpected or surprise turns.

Most often, when these surprise attacks occur, the King is involved, either directly or remotely. Since the King is the principal target of the game and all sorts of actions are leveled at him—some planned, some rash, and some even desperate —more often he is directly involved.

When such actions are all out, they are apt to be surprise mating attacks.

Point of view

Undoubtedly, what occurs in the following position is a surprise—for White, not for Black. As Black is a piece and two Pawns behind, he might as well have headed for the showers, unless he had an inkling of what is about to happen.

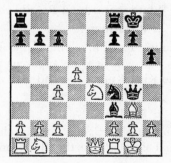

BLACK TO PLAY AND WIN

Black's design is diabolic.

1 . . . .   Q-R6

Resigns

There is nought to be done about 2 . . . QxNP mate; for if 2 PxQ, NxP mate. Pert!

Double surprise

Both White and Black were surprised by the "surprise mating attack" in the following position. In fact, neither player saw it until after the game.

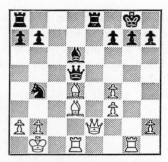

WHITE TO PLAY AND WIN

The first move is routine.

1 RxPch	K-B1

If 1 ... K-R1, White mates by 2 RxPdbl ch, K-N1; 3 R-R8.

2 R-N8ch!	....

An unusual tactical motif involving a line and square clearance. For reasons that will become apparent it is essential for White to clear the King Knight file and also the square, KN7.

2	KxR
3 R-N1ch	....

While the ultimate objective is not yet clear, the immediate short-term goal is to utilize the Rook on the open King Knight file.

3	K-B1

4 B-N7ch	....

Now a reason why the Rook was jettisoned from KN7 is manifest. White's Bishop pre-empts that square.

4	**K-N1**	
5	**B-B6dis ch**	**K-B1**

The stage is set for a new and climactic motif.

6	**R-N8ch!**	....

To force the Black King into the open so White's Queen can draw a bead on it *with check*.

6	....	**KxR**
7	**Q-N2ch**	**K-B1**
8	**Q-N7 mate**	

Curiously enough, Black won the actual game, in which this surprise mating attack was overlooked!

The surprise as a climax

Often the surprise mating attack is truly the climax of a profound and well-calculated "Combined Operation." It is then the far-seen stinger on the tail of a combination or series of combinations. In the following position, Black has manifestly sacrificed earlier.

BLACK TO PLAY AND WIN

White is doing everything within his power to repel the enemy invasion. But it is too late. His King's stronghold has already been breached. It is now only a question of how Black is to proceed.

1 ....   **N-K7ch!**

Involving several tactical motifs—for one, the Knight sacrifice is a line clearance; for another, it is an interference.

2 RxN   ....

Else the interference works and 2...Q-N7 is mate. But now the Rook at K2 serves as a block in what is to follow—another tactical motif out of the line clearance.

2 ....   **R-B8ch!!**

As in our previous example, the first sacrifice clears the path for a second.

3 **KxR**   ....

Otherwise, mate at R1.

3 ....   **Q-R8ch**

4 **K-B2**   **N-N5 mate**

A pretty picture. Note how White's Rook at K2 blocks its King from exiting on that square.

The logic of the illogical

Surprise mating attacks are not necessarily born of desperation. They may well be the natural procession of moves, appearing desperate and surprising because they involve the sacrifice of material. As we said originally, "Checkmate of the enemy King is the principal goal of the game of chess." When checkmate is possible, everything else is subordinate. And many times when a surprise mating attack is possible, it is the only way to win. In a move or two, the chance may pass, never to return.

The following position is somewhat typical. Indeed, White may well win in the long run, anyway. But the process will be arduous, to say the least; whereas the surprise mating attack is immediately decisive.

WHITE TO PLAY AND WIN

Black's pieces are cramped. His vital peril, as will be seen, is the blocked and blocking position of his Bishop. In a few moves that might be remedied. But White is on the move!

1 N-B5ch!   . . . .

Penetrating the bastion of the Black Monarch.

1 . . . .   **PxN**

If 1 . . . K-B2; 2 RxPch is a decisive blow; and, on 1 . . . K-R1; Black is mated soon after 2 RxPch, KxR; 3 Q-R1ch.

2 RxPch!   . . . .

These sacrifices had better be correct or White will be in for a surprise.

2 . . . .   **KxR**

Not 2 . . . K-N3; 3 Q-R5 mate.

3 Q-R5ch   **N-R3**

Not 3 . . . K-N2; 4 P-N6 as then there is no defense to the check at R7.

4 QxNch	**K-N1**
5 Q-N6ch	**K-R1**
6 B-K3	**Resigns**

Mate cannot be averted.

COMBINED OPERATIONS

The elements of combination play, the check, the capture, and the threat, and the various motifs, such as the pin, the fork, and the double attack, make up the structure of the mechanism for executing plans.

On occasion, when the plan is a simple one, a singularly independent tactical operation may suffice. More often than not, however, the administration of the plan involves tactics in concert, in effect, a compounding of the motifs. Such is the nature of what we call combined operations.

Combining to an end

Innumerable tactical ideas govern the play in the following setting. Yet a cursory appraisal leaves the impression that it is nothing more than a Knight fork.

How many motifs are employed? At least six are obvious. They are (1) the threat of mate, (2) the mating net, (3) interference, (4) the overworked piece, (5) the sacrifice, and (6) the Knight fork. And many of these recur.

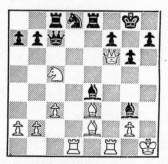

WHITE TO PLAY AND WIN

The ultimate objective is hardly apparent at the outset.

1 B-KR6   ....

First, a simple move, threatening mate (1) by means of a common mating net (2).

Black can defend in various ways. If 1 ... N-K3, the Knight interferes (3) with the defense of the Bishop by its Rook, and White continues with 2 NxB.

If Black attempts a counterattack by 1 ... BxPch, it fails after 2 KxB, RxBch; 3 K-B3; for, if 3 ... Q-K4 (defending against the mate at N2) the Queen has relinquished the protection of the Knight (4), and White wins with 4 RxNch.

If Black plays 1 ... Q-K4 at once, 2 NxB wins; for the Queen cannot recapture (4) and still guard N2.

Hence——

    1 ....   **B-K4**

The Bishop guards against the mate threat by a counterattack on White's Queen; but it shuts off the defense of the other Black Bishop (3).

Since White's Queen is attacked, it does not appear to matter that Black's Queen Bishop is *en prise*. Yet that is just the difficulty.

    2 NxB!!   ....

Material sacrifice (5), a prelude to the end, the Knight fork (6).

    2 ....   **BxQ**

More or less forced, as otherwise Black is out a piece.

    3 **NxBch**   **K-R1**
    4 **B-N7ch!**   ....

Another sacrifice (5) to draw the Black King into the culminating Knight fork (6).

    4 ....   **KxB**
    5 **NxRch**   **Resigns**

For, after White picks off the Queen, he has achieved his end, a vast material superiority.

Combining to promotion

BLACK TO PLAY AND WIN

Material is approximately even in the preceding position. But Black's Pawns could become easy targets. So it is up to Black to do something to alleviate that prospect.

Curiously, at least four different tactics are employed in this comparatively simple position.

1	**N-N6ch!**

Material sacrifice to bring about a preconceived setting.

2 PxN	....

Practically forced as, after 2 ... NxR, Black is a piece to the good.

2	**PxPdis ch**
3 **K-N1**	**N-B7**

Black sets up a mating net.

4 RxN	....

Forced.

4	**R-R8ch!!**

To draw the King away from its present square.

5 **KxR**	**PxR**
Resigns	

For the Pawn queens by force.

Thus, we have seen a Knight sacrifice, a discovered check, a Rook sacrifice, a mating net, and a Pawn promotion.

Operation mate

For beauty, the following combination has few peers, and in the combined operations there are interference, a triple sacrifice, and a mating net to bring about the denouement.

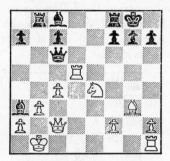

WHITE TO PLAY AND WIN

The first move must predict the rest.

> **1 B-Q6!!** ....

Interference, even at the expense of a piece. Black's Queen is blocked out of a vital sector.

> **1 ....** **PxB**

Black must take or lose material, and 1 ... BxB is no better. Mate still results in the ultimate sequel.

> **2 N-B6ch!!** **PxN**

Another sacrifice, to breach the King position.

> **3 R-N1ch** **K-R1**
> **4 QxPch!** ....

And here White renews his process of expenditure with a third sacrifice, to establish a mating net.

$$4 \ldots \quad \text{KxQ}$$
$$5 \ \text{R-R5 mate}$$

The end-all

There are combined operations that seem more like "swindles," so complete is the magic of the combinations. Such is the one that evolves from the following position, the end of a game between Mason and Winawer in the Vienna Tournament of 1882. Mason was no slouch if the pyrotechnics employed here are any evidence.

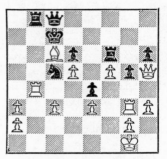

WHITE TO PLAY AND WIN

"Look on my works, ye mighty, and despair."

$$1 \ \text{RxNP!} \quad \ldots$$

A Rook sacrifice, merely to clear the path for the entry of White's Queen to the seventh rank.

$$1 \ldots \quad \text{PxR}$$

Otherwise, the Rook enters itself, with fatal effects.

$$2 \ \text{Q-R7ch} \quad \text{N-Q2}$$

Not 2 ... K-Q1; 3 Q-R8ch after which White wins quickly.

$$3 \ \text{BxN} \quad \ldots$$

With critical threats of discovered check.

3	**Q-N1**

Not 3 ... QxB; 4 QxQch, KxQ; 5 RxR after which White's material superiority is established and decides.

Now, indeed, Black can reply to any discovered check with 4 ... QxQ. It seems that White has miscalculated.

4 **R-N7ch!!!**	....

One of the cleverest sacrifices to grace the game of chess.

5	**KxR**

Not 5 ... RxR; 6 QxQ, a case of the overworked piece. Nor 5 ... K-Q1; 6 QxQch, an example of interference.

But now the Black King is in position for what is to follow.

5 **B-B8dbl ch**	**Resigns**

Double, discovered check, with interference. Because of the double check, Black's King must move and because of the interference, Black's Queen must go. To boot, White picks off another Rook shortly.

CHESSIC DYNAMICS

Not a single action of the chessboard, no matter how minute or ineffectual, is self-contained. Its reactions reverberate to the farthest ends of the playing field. Hence, it is always well to remember that there are sixty-four squares on the board.

9

Outcombined: *Black tries 1...B-B3, a simple but faulty forking combination. For White then surprises with 2 QxPch!, RxQ; 3 RxBch, K-N2; 4 NxPch (or 3...R-B1; 4 RxRch, KxR; 5 NxPch) for a clear net gain after he recaptures with NxQ. A fine example of a countercombination to refute a combination.*

Outcombining the Combiner and Sundry Combinations

Dʀ. Tᴀʀᴛᴀᴋᴏᴠᴇʀ's burlesque, "All the little errors are there waiting to be made," is equally true, only in a more serious way, of the combinations. They are part and parcel of the game.

In the making of combinations, too, the "little errors" can figure. Since each combination is a series of White and Black moves, it is clear that both players are responsible or culpable for its respective success or failure. Success, as a rule, will crown the effort of the player whose knowledge is greater or who is more alert to the potentialities of the position.

In a given game, many combinations will be complex: that is, they will branch off into variations, sub-variations, and even, at times, sub-sub-variations. Hence accuracy and the ability to see ahead will be at a premium. In these instances, it is well to bear in mind that one bad move nullifies possibly forty good ones.

Errors, on the other hand, are bound to occur because the human factor enters into the calculations. Sometimes the errors will be glaring; but often enough they will be subtle.

Yet errors, run-of-the-mill errors, are hardly worth a study. What is, is a type of error germane to making combinations.

It is the combination that goes awry because its tail end contains a stinger, overlooked by the combiner. In such a case, the combiner is hoist by his own petard, particularly when the opponent may have been oblivious of any saving resource until near the end. And there is the combination which the opponent foresees and allows only because he has also foreseen the ultimate miscarriage. Whether or not the opponent is originally aware of the flaw in the combination hardly matters. The result is the same whether the combiner has outcombined himself or whether the opponent has deliberately enticed him into the combination.

A threefold study

BLACK TO PLAY AND WIN

In *The Pleasures of Chess,* illustrating how the mind works on a combination, a trinity of positions is given. Position No. 1 pinpoints the pattern for queening a Pawn by a Rook sacrifice which draws away the White King from the queening square, never to return.

Black appears lost, but ——

1	**R-R8ch!!**
2 **KxR**	**PxP**
Resigns	

For Black threatens 3 ... R-R1ch, resulting in mate, and 3 ... PxR(Q)ch, and White is without defense.

Position No. 2 has all the earmarks of No. 1.

BLACK TO PLAY AND LOSE! ! !

Having fixed the previous combinative pattern in his mind, Black gleefully continues:

1	**R-R8ch??**
2 **KxR**	**PxP**

He now confidently expects White to resign. But he is rudely awakened.

3 **R-KB5!!**	**KxR**

Now, the Black King has been drawn into position to allow for ——

4 **P-N4ch!!**	....

Thereby creating an approach square for the White King.

| 4 .... | KxP |
| 5 K-N2 | Resigns |

For White's Pawns march on to easy victory.

The next position is a composed ending that contains all the essential elements of the two previous positions.

WHITE TO PLAY AND WIN

| 1 R-Q8ch! | .... |

If 1 PxP, KxP, the resulting position is a book draw. If 1 P-N7, K-B3, White must lose his advanced Knight Pawn. The text move forces Black's reply.

| 1 .... | KxR |
| 2 P-N7! | .... |

Now, as in position No. 1, the Pawn threatens to go on to queen.

| 2 .... | R-QN5 |

And, as in position No. 2, Black seems to have the saving clause.

| 3 KxR | P-B4ch |

And, as before, Black creates an approach square. But ——

| 4 K-N5! | .... |

Failure to capture the Pawn grants White a win, thus:

4	**K-B2**
5 **K-R6**	....

White threatens 6 K-R7, which insures the queening of his Pawn.

5	**K-N1**
6 **K-N6**	**P-B5**
7 **P-R4**	**Resigns**

Black is in a mating net: 7 ... P-B6; 8 P-R5, P-B7; 9 P-R6, P-B8(Q); 10 P-R7 mate.

Thus it can be seen that what appears to be the tail of a combination may not be the tail at all. Or, looking at it another way, there may be a tail to the tail, and even a tail to the tail's tail.

The forlorn hope

The next position is the near conclusion of a game. Black is a piece behind, which he has sacrificed. He has worked up what appears to be a terrific attack and hopes to recover his piece or give checkmate.

BLACK TO MOVE

Who wins, that is the question.

1	**B-N6!**

Black plans to continue with 2 . . . Q-R2ch, which will not do at once as White has the rejoinder of Q-Q4ch.

After the text move, the threat of 2 . . . Q-R2ch becomes promising since White will be unable to interpose at Q4. This motif is a line clearance as Black's Rook now covers his Q5.

2 **RxB**   **Q-R2ch**

What is White to do? If 3 K-R1, N-B7ch wins the Queen. If 3 K-B1, Q-B7 checkmate. If 3 K-N2, Q-B7ch; 4 K-R3, QxRPch; 5 KxN, Q-R4 mate. If 3 N-Q4, RxN.

Shall White resign? NO!

3 **N-N6!!**   . . . .

Black's combination is subject to a tail-end stinger which he has overlooked. White's move creates a setting in which Black's Rook and Queen will be on a line with White's Rook.

3 . . . .   **QxNch**

For, on 3 . . . RxN; 4 Q-Q4ch, White picks off Black's Rook.

4 **Q-Q4ch!**   **Resigns**

For Black's attack peters out with much material minus after 4 . . . RxQ; 5 RxQ — and, if 4 . . . QxQch; 5 NxQ, RxN; 6 BxN, White remains a piece ahead.

SUNDRY COMBINATIONS

The specific tactical motifs reviewed thus far are the ones that most frequently occur over the board. There are, by far, many, many more tactical motifs, and there are variations of these for which there is a niche in the repertoire of the master. It is not within the bounds of practicality to cover every conceivable motif. Suffice it to say that they do exist and that their study will be well rewarding to the aspiring chessplayer when, as, and if he enjoys the opportunity to analyze and later synthesize the mechanism of the unique theme.

For the record, we give brief examples of some of the lesser prevailing motifs.

The cross check

This motif can aptly be termed a variant rather than a motif in itself. For example, it is a variant of the forcing element, the check; and it is also a variant at times of the discovered check. In essence, the theme is to answer the powerful compulsion of check, with another check, in turn.

The following examples are given in brutal simplicity the better to illustrate the theme.

1. BLACK TO PLAY

In the position above, White's Pawns insure a win unless Black's Queen can administer a perpetual check. But Black is stymied in any such try: for example:

| *1* .... | **Q-N4ch** |
| **2 Q-K2ch** | .... |

And, in the face of this cross check, Black must swap Queens, and then the loss of the game is inevitable.

(*See diagram on page 99.*)

Whereas in the first position White's maneuver was, in a sense, defensive—a simplification to consolidate his advantage—the cross check can be and usually is an aggressive motif when in the form of a discovered check.

Here White threatens to win by discovery. For example,

2. BLACK TO PLAY

by R-QN7dis ch. And 1 . . . K-Q1 is hopeless in view of 2 Q-Q5ch with a winning attack; and 1 . . . N-K2 permits another discovery: 2 R-B6dis ch. So the forceful measure of an aggressive check is Black's only hope.

1	**Q-N7ch**
2 **R-B2dis ch**	. . . .

But here the check is crossed by another discovery, and Black's Queen is lost.

The self-block

A glance at the following position discloses that material is about even but that Black is constricted, in fact, in a mating net. A more careful scrutiny, however, emphasizes the difficulty that confronts White, if he is to win. He dare not let Black's King escape to N1. If he does, then Black will be in position to advance his King Rook Pawn the moment White's Bishop moves and so puncture the mating net.

(*See diagram on page 100.*)

In short, White must threaten to mate at once when Black has . . . K-N1 available.

1 **N-N4** . . . .

WHITE TO PLAY AND WIN

This move turns the trick by tying down Black's Rook.
For on any Rook move there follows: 2 B-N7ch, K-N1; 3 N-R6
mate.

1 ....   **P-R3**

If 1 ... P-R4; 2 K-R4, Black is compelled to move his Rook,
permitting the aforementioned mate.

2 **K-R4**   ....

To exhaust Black's moves. Temporizing to exhaust an opponent's moves is of itself one of the rarer tactical motifs.
2 N-K5 also wins in the long run, but with far less *élan*.

2 ....   **P-R4**

Now it seems that White must beat a retreat, in which case
Black will draw. For if 3 KxP, R-R1ch permits ... K-N1 safely
thereafter. But here the self-block comes to the rescue!

3 **B-N7ch**   ....

Compelling the setting for the self-block.

3 ....   **RxB**
4 **N-R6**   ....

Observe now that White threatens nothing, at least nothing
that will win the game. But Black faces *zugzwang* (the dis-

agreeable necessity to move): he must perforce occupy the King's sole escape square with his Rook.

4	**R-N1**
5 **NxP mate**	....

Black has self-blocked himself into a mate.

THE WILL TO WIN

Anything and everything that can be used to promote the flow of ideas is helpful in chess. We garner ideas in such studies as these. But to recall the ideas under the stress and tension of serious tournament play is often another story. Grit and determination to win are important factors—and confidence. It may help to think: How can anyone with a head shaped like my opponent's hope to outthink me?

10

The Castling Motif as a Stinger: *White combines to win a Pawn with 1 P-R5, BxB; 2 KxB, N-Q2; 3 RxP? But Black, preparing the way with a Knight fork, 3 ... N-B4ch, threatening to win a whole Rook, then answers 4 PxN by castling with check for a material plus and a winning position: 4 ... O-O-Och!*

More Sundry Combinations—
Castling and Zugzwang

As MENTIONED before, there are many, many sundry tactical motifs. As with those already given, however, it must suffice simply to indicate the possibilities. The first given hereunder, for example, is seen very rarely indeed; yet it is a natural concomitant on the moves of the pieces involved. The second is frequent enough to deserve special study; and it reflects, too, a peculiarly strategic facet of tactics.

CASTLING AS A TACTICAL MOTIF

The active king

A few single moves on the chessboard engage the services of more than one unit. Discovered attacks are the chief exception to this rule. There is, however, another important exception. It is the move of castles (O-O and O-O-O). Implicit in castling is the use of two units: King and Rook. As it is a combination move in fact, it may well be on occasion a combinational move in tactics, establishing dual actions in two distinct sectors of the board.

It has been said that the basis of every combination is a double attack. And when both King and Rook are left attacking after the act of castling, the latter must rank as a tactical motif. One fine example of this theme is given with the photograph.

The passive king

The dual move in castling still makes for a combinational motif even when no check occurs, as above, or even when the castling King does not wind up attacking an enemy unit. Since two distinct sectors of the board are affected, castling still has a radical effect on the disposition of the over-all lines of force. The point is apparent in the following gamelet.

NIMZO-INDIAN DEFENSE

	H. STEINER *White*		A. ROTHMAN *Black*	
1	P-Q4	P-K3	8 QxB	R-K1
2	P-QB4	N-KB3	9 P-QN4	P-K4
3	N-QB3	B-N5	10 PxP	PxP
4	Q-B2	N-B3	11 B-N2	B-N5
5	N-B3	P-Q3	12 P-N5	BxN
6	P-K3	O-O	13 PxB	N-Q5
7	P-QR3	BxNch		

Black's last move is highly ingenious. As matters stand, the Knight is immune to capture, because of the recapture with a discovered check, after which White's Queen goes. And Black threatens also 14 . . . NxPch.

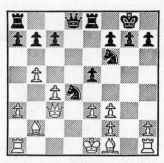

14 **O-O-O**   **Resigns**

Alas for ingenuity! By moving two units at once (can this be legal?), White simultaneously parries the threat to his King (by transferring the King to a different sector) and also introduces a winning pin, whereupon Black's Knight must fall.

ZUGZWANG

The right to move, which is endowed, according to the Laws of Chess, to White and Black in their respective turns, curiously enough also carries an obligation—the obligation to move. Small distinction is made between the right and the obligation, since the players think usually in positive terms. And the right to move is thus translated into the right to enhance one's position. To be able to forfeit or to pass up a move would be construed as a spurious privilege.

Yet there are times, not often, to be sure, when any move in a given position not only does not promote one's prospects but definitely harms them. In such cases it would be an unmitigated blessing to be able to forfeit the move. For the move is a liability. Mandatory laws, however, insist upon a move. In these circumstances, when a player is compelled to move against his will, he is said to be in *zugzwang*, a German term meaning "move-compulsion."

In problem chess, a *zugzwang* theme is referred to as a "waiter," meaning that the solution is accomplished by a waiting move, one without a threat, or, in players' terminology, a "quiet move," which compels, nonetheless, an overt, losing response.

'Ware the exceptional!

Chess runs from move to routine move on the basis of straightforward logic, until tactics introduce the exception. And then it's too late for logic. So, in the following position, Black has mobilized a potent material plus, and the day is his, by all logic. White is two full Pawns behind in a simple sort of position that has no earmarks of the exceptional.

WHITE TO PLAY AND WIN

Yet—a second look—and *zugzwang*, and Black's game goes poof!

1 Q-K7ch   Q-N4

Black's reply is forced. On 1 ... P-N4; 2 Q-K1ch, he gets mated.

2 Q-K4ch   . . . .

2 Q-K1ch can lead to a draw by perpetual check.

2 . . . .   Q-N5

White seems to have made no progress.

3 Q-K3   . . . .

The *coup de repos*. If Black could now pass up his move, all would be well for him. But he must move. He is in *zugzwang*.

3 . . . .   **Resigns**

For mate follows shortly.

Repletion

If it weren't for *zugzwang*, White would be a dead pigeon in this ending. What with an Exchange and two Pawns behind, he could hardly hold out long.

WHITE TO PLAY AND WIN

But the onus of having to make a move falls upon Black just when he isn't ready for one.

1 **RxR**   **RxR**
2 **P-KR4!**   . . . .

White prevents Black from freeing himself with . . . P-KN4 and . . . K-N3.

2 . . . .   **P-R3**
3 **K-N2**   **P-KN4**
4 **P-R5!**   **Resigns**

For after Black's Pawn moves have been exhausted he must abandon his Rook. *Zugzwang*.

Achieving the impossible

Everyone knows that it takes at least two minor pieces to achieve a mate—nor will two Knights avail, either. So what duffer would not settle for a draw for White in the following position?

WHITE TO PLAY AND WIN

But White can accomplish with one lone Knight what he could hardly do with two in most positions, and all because Black is compelled to move against his will.

> *1* **N-B6!** ....

Of course not 1 N-N3?? stalemate.

> *1* **K-R8**
> *2* **N-K4** ....

White prepares for 2 ... P-R7; 3 N-N3 mate.

> *2* **K-R7**
> *3* **N-Q2** ....

White maneuvers into the *zugzwang* setting.

> *3* **K-R8**
> *4* **N-B1** ....

Here Black is in *zugzwang:* he must move his Pawn against his will.

$$4 \ldots \ldots \qquad \text{P-R7}$$
$$5 \ \text{N-N3 mate}$$

A typical "Zugzwanger"

In the following position all of the Black men are adequately defended, or defended at least as many times as they are attacked.

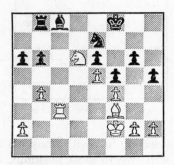

WHITE TO PLAY AND WIN

White makes one move, and Black is embarrassed for a reply.

$$1 \ \text{R-B7!} \qquad \text{Resigns}$$

While White has no immediate threat, Black has no immediate move. Black cannot move his King without losing his Knight. He cannot move his Bishop, except to give it away. He cannot move his Knight without losing his Bishop. And he cannot move his Rook to a safe spot. As soon as his Pawn moves are exhausted, he will suffer fatal material loss.

Zugzwang is one of the rarer tactical motifs. It occurs often enough, however, so that any aspiring chessplayer must be on the lookout for a chance to use or to avoid it.

LOOK FURTHER

The Will to Win is part and parcel with a fluent sequence of ideas. Logic can be pursued so far, then further; and, as we have just seen *zugzwang* overturn an apparently hopeless position, so one more little tactical conception may upset all our logical planning, or our opponent's. Generally, the one who wins in chess is the one who has the most and the best ideas. If it is to be the most, then don't step short—look further!

11

A Perp at Need: *White threatens mate on the move; so Black had better take a perpetual check—or else. He does so by 1 ... N-R7ch; 2 K-Q1, N-B6ch; 3 K-B1, N-R7ch; 4 K-N1, N-B6ch; and, having tried both sides, White settles for a draw. (Note: if 5 K-R1??, R-QR7 mate!)*

Drawing Combinations— Perpetual Check and Stalemate

THOUGH ONE cannot win a game by a *drawing* combination, one does "win" considerable satisfaction by saving the half-point after being faced by the dismal prospect of an outright loss—and there can be no doubt that drawing tactics have their uses.

Even the greatest of masters have erred. And the lesser fry continually stumble and falter. So, though this is a series on "How to Win," nonetheless and "irregardless," we offer here two standard drawing resources that any aspiring student of the game must know well.

PERPETUAL CHECK

Among the various tactical motifs, perhaps most prominent is the perpetual check. It is nothing more than an endless series of checks, which is resolved according to the Laws of Chess into a draw, whereby each contestant is awarded one half-point. Most likely perpetual checks would fall into one of the drawing categories of the Laws of Chess, such as the threefold repetition of position or the fifty move rule.

Since perpetual check or "a perp," as it is commonly called, occurs often enough during the course of play, it is definitely a worth-while subject for study.

Know the exceptions!

Every chessplayer knows or ought to know that a Queen generally beats a Rook. The position below, however, is the exception that proves the rule.

WHITE TO PLAY AND DRAW

An instructive ending.

1 R-N2ch   K-R6

Black's best try is to approach the White King with his own, with a view to delivering checkmate.

2 R-R2ch!   . . . .

A star move. For White's Rook is immune on account of 2 ... KxR Stalemate.

2 ....   **K-N6**

Now White can force the draw immediately by 3 R-R3ch. Still another, even more picturesque method is:

3 R-N2ch   **K-B5**

Black avoided 1 ... K-B6 and now avoids 3 ... K-B6 because of White's resource: R-N3ch; KxR (or else RxQ follows) Stalemate.

4 R-B2ch   **Draw**

Black cannot escape a perpetual check. So long as he remains on the Rook, Knight, or Bishop files, White will continue to check (except, as mentioned, if ... K-B6, then R-N3ch) and, if the King plays to the King file, then R-K2 pins and wins Black's Queen for the Rook, which also draws.

Drawn by perpetual check, with stalemate and pin as auxiliary motifs.

Despite any opposition

Black is a Pawn behind in this position. A Pawn is not so much under ordinary circumstances.

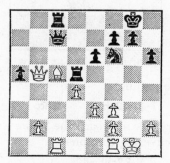

BLACK TO PLAY AND DRAW

The circumstances here, though, involve young Alekhine, future champion of the world, as White. So a draw, from Black's point of view, is more than satisfactory.

$$1 \ldots \qquad \textbf{QxPch!!}$$

It didn't usually matter much whether the opponent was a Pawn or a Queen behind Alekhine. The result was the same. Here, however, Black actually has an idea!

2	KxQ	R-R4ch
3	K-N3	R-N4ch
4	K-B4	R-B4ch
	Drawn	

Perpetual check on the Rook, Knight, and Bishop file is the answer.

The long way round

Most perpetual checks are of the short variety; for in no time flat a player can see that there is no way out. Occasionally, however, the "perp" is long and arduous. Take the following case, for example.

WHITE TO PLAY AND DRAW

It is well to bear in mind that if White fails to check, he is doomed.

1	N-N4ch	K-K2
2	N-B5ch	K-Q2
3	N-K5ch	K-B1

Black tries to escape into any nook or cranny.

4	N-K7ch	K-N1
5	N-Q7ch	K-R2
6	N-B8ch	K-R3

The merry chase continues.

7	N-N8ch	K-N4
8	N-R7ch	K-N5
9	N-R6ch	K-B6

Well, there's almost a whole board open before the King.

10	N-N5ch	K-Q6
11	N-N4ch	K-K7
12	N-B3ch	K-B7

Or is there?

13	N-Q3ch	K-N6
14	N-K4ch	K-N5
15	N-K5ch	K-B4

Almost completing the tour.

16	N-N3ch	K-B3

This is where we came in.

17	N-N4ch	**Draw**

Or shall we waltz around again?

STALEMATE

At rare intervals, if it were only legal, it would be advantageous to forfeit the right to move (see *Zugzwang,* page 105). By the same token, it is profitable at times not to be able to move at all. When a legal move is not possible, and the King is not in check, a condition of stalemate exists. By definition, according to the Laws of Chess, a stalemate is a draw; and, since a draw grants to each player one half-point, it is easy to see that one player will gain from the result in certain otherwise unfavorable circumstances.

Stalemate, as a rule, is the last resource of the player whose plans "gang agley." To bring it about, however, requires diabolical cunning, a hope, and a prayer, and often a little cooperation from the opponent.

Avoid the stalemate!

Stalemate occurs infrequently in the game only because most games are not played to a finish. Nearly every King and Pawn versus King endgame which results in a draw by agreement does so because both players foresee the stalemate as inevitable.

In the following position White wins only because he can avoid the stalemate. It would be so easy and so unwise for White to reach the square QB7, for example, or even QB6 (by 1 K-B5, K-R1; 2 K-B6 Stalemate—or 2 K-Q6, K-N2; 3 K-Q7, K-R1; 4 K-B7 Stalemate).

(*See diagram on page 116.*)

Instead, White wins easily by sidestepping the stalemate.

1 **P-R8(Q)ch!**   . . . .

As so often the solution is: Give till it hurts—your opponent!

1 . . .   **KxQ**

Forced.

2 **K-R6**   . . . .

WHITE TO PLAY AND WIN

If Black were allowed to stall just this once, White would have no better than 3 P-N7ch, K-N1; 4 K-N6 Stalemate. But Black cannot stall.

2	....	K-N1
3	P-N7	K-B2
4	K-R7	Resigns

For the Pawn goes on to queen.

The saving clause

When all seems lost, stalemate may yet be the auspicious finale. To all intents and appearances here, White doesn't enjoy the vestige of a chance.

WHITE TO PLAY AND DRAW

But it is all deceptive.

1 P-N8(Q)	BxQ
2 B-N1!!	....

White has contrived an ingenious and saving clause.

| 2 .... | PxB(Q) |

Otherwise, White continues simply by capturing Black's Pawn, after which a draw comes about by mutual exhaustion of forces, or lack of mating force.

Stalemate!

The surprise element

The following position will make a well-known grandmaster wince. He should have played 1 R-R8 and then, with careful play, he could have nursed his Pawns along to victory.

Instead, he played:

| 1 R-KB6?? | .... |

And so he set the stage, by a slim oversight, for a surprise.

| 1 .... | R-B6ch! |

2 **K-N2** . . . .

Else 2 . . . RxP; 3 RxPch, KxP and Black can draw after
. . . K-N5 and possibly . . . R-KB6 and . . . RxP. Or 2 KxR, Stalemate!

2 . . . . **RxPch**

And Black draws; for if the Rook is captured, it is again
stalemate, and, if it is not, Black manages to pick off all of
White's Pawns.

Another long way round

Rare indeed is a stalemate defense. Rarer, by far, is a
long-drawn-out stalemate defense in which the defender thinks
ahead a good many moves to the nullifying denouement. Consider:

WHITE TO PLAY AND DRAW

The defense here consists in secreting the White King in a manhole and then pulling the lid over his head.

1 **K-Q7** . . . .

It is clear that White will lose if he chases the Rook Pawn. The text move, curiously, threatens to chase the Pawn, yet at the same time bears also on the other wing.

1 . . . . **P-R4**

Forced. Otherwise, 2 K-K6 enables White to overtake the stray Rook Pawn and then even win.

2 **K-B7** **P-R5**

If Black attempts to anticipate the stalemate defense, say, by 2 . . . P-N3, he will lose after 3 P-R4. For after 4 P-R5 the Black Monarch will find himself in a mating net.

3 **K-N6** **P-R6**
4 **K-R5** **P-R7**

If 4 . . . P-N3ch, White continues with 5 K-R4, P-R7; 6 P-R3, P-R8(Q); 7 P-N3, Any; and then Stalemate!

5 **P-N6** **P-R8(Q)**

Curiouser and curiouser is this position. Black has a Queen, and White has a few moves to spare, and yet there is no way to prevent the inevitable stalemate.

6	**P-N5**	**Q-QN8**
7	**P-R4**	**Any**
8	**P-N4**	**Any**
	Stalemate!	

12

BLACK

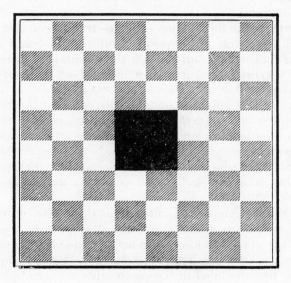

WHITE

Strategically, the central hub of the chessboard is the most important part. The control of the center, therefore, is the first principle of middle-game strategy.

Strategy in the Middle Game—
The Center

THE MIDDLE GAME is only a fraction of the game of chess. Sometimes it is the greater part of the whole; sometimes, the lesser. It is apt, however, to be the significant part.

The middle game ranges over a wide variety of actions,

from the purely scientific and logical, embodied in strategy and tactics (the planning and the execution of plans), to the psychological, or the creation of impressions which in fact do not count.

Strategy—the formulation of plans—it has been said, plays a much lesser role in the result of an over-the-board contest than its concomitant part—tactics—the execution of plans. That a plan is subsidiary to its execution is indeed odd. Yet chessmasters agree that more than 90 per cent of games are decided by tactics. This appraisal undoubtedly can be tempered. For all positions clearly are the result of strategy, good or bad, and certain ones lend themselves to something other than perfect management because of their strategic base. A tactical blunder, therefore, may superficially be chargeable to tactics, whereas in reality it is the background condition that prompts the blunder.

As an example of the latter idea, think of a position in which one side is deficient in material and nearly hopelessly lost. The prospective loser in an act of desperation launches a sudden, unsound onslaught. In so doing, he injects a note of insecurity into the mind of the prospective winner. And things happen. The prospective winner loses his composure, errs, and boots the game. The tactical error here is the overt losing action. The strategic concept, however, is the desperate attack that is the inducing action. To ignore the role of strategy in such a case is to draw a false conclusion.

An example bearing on points made above may be helpful since too generalized a statement may not register or may even be suspect.

Applied psychology

Logical strategy, as mentioned above, may be readily understood. The psychological, happily, is well illustrated from an actual game.

Black is a Pawn behind and should lose against grandmaster Flohr. But he sets up a threat of mate in one, supplemented by an attack on White's King Bishop (see the following diagram). H. Grob played:

1 . . . .   Q-N4
Resigns

Lo and behold! Mesmerized by the threat, Flohr resigns. He could have saved everything with one simple move (Do you see it?) but succumbed to an impression that in fact did not count.

Prerequisites of planning

Plans are conceived ideas evolving from experience or drawing upon imagination. They fall into various categories, grand and subordinate, general and specific. A grand and specific plan, for example, is the adoption of an opening that leads to a certain favorable pattern. In the execution of this plan, obstacles may have to be surmounted that call for supporting or subordinate plans. In contradistinction, a general plan might be the conformation to some general principle, such as: development promotes position; or, it is important to control the center.

There are plans that may be identified only with the middle game. Other plans begin actually in the opening, course through the middle game, and wind up in the endgame. Since the middle game is the connecting link of opening to endgame, an academic knowledge of all branches of the game is required for successful middle-game planning. Emphasis should be laid particularly on the endgame. For in the middle game any number of opportunities arise to reduce the forces, to set up an endgame. These opportunities must be by-passed unless the player knows how to determine with reasonable certitude that he will be working into a favorable endgame, not into an unfavorable one. Knowledge of the endgame is foresight in the middle game.

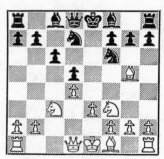

A GRAND AND SPECIFIC PLAN

The Exchange Variation of the Queen's Gambit Declined might readily lead to the position in the next diagram.

Note Black's weak and backward Pawn. The plan began in the opening, coursed through the middle game, and wound up in the ending. A game of this type and its consequences will be discussed later on. (See page 182.)

A GENERAL PLAN

White conforms to general principles, brings out his men, controls the center.

Strategic principles

There are about a dozen broad principles of middle-game strategy, and many lesser ones. The scope of this work will be to outline the major plans with suggestions and recommendations for continued study of the plans less frequently encountered.

Topical headings will cover:
1. The Center
2. Better Development
3. Advantage in Space
4. King-side Attack
5. King in the Center
6. Queen-side Attack
7. Pawn Majorities
8. Weak Pawns
9. Strong Squares
10. Material Advantage
11. Sundries

THE CENTER

When chessmasters play against each other, the odds are that neither will present the other gratis with a Queen, a Rook, a Knight, or even a Pawn. For the difference of one puny Pawn, all other things being equal, is sufficient to determine the outcome of the game. How, then, does one master proceed to defeat the other? The answer lies in a fight for squares. For it is not humanly possible in a game of chess, in which every move is give and take, to maintain an even balance of all the factors, particularly the squares.

There are 64 squares on the board. Half are white, and half black. Except for that distinction of color, to all appearances, they are very much alike. Yet some squares are more valuable than others. Which are the more important squares, and why?

As indicated on the diagram at the beginning of this chapter, the squares in the center of the board are the more important ones. The reason they are becomes apparent when the squares are considered in terms of a network of interlinked paths. It is clear that the player who controls the hub of the network can send his men from one side of the board, directly through that hub, to the other side with ease. On the other hand, the player who does not control the hub must traverse devious routes, time-consuming routes. Time is an important factor in chess—that is, it is important to reach objectives in the least number of moves. It follows that it is important to control the central squares.

Such control of the center is the first positional advantage of opening play. What is its significance in the middle game? What is its true worth in terms of material? How does one capitalize on it in the middle game?

To assay the value of the control of the center in terms of material is indeed difficult. For one thing, the value is relative, affected by many considerations. The reader may, however, draw an inference from the numerous gambits in which one side offers a Pawn in return for control of the center. As a rule, the offer is speculative and, in most cases, with perfect play, unsound. Hence it seems that, at best, control of the center is worth no more than one Pawn. Generally, it is worth less.

This appraisal is a useful guide when we have to choose between alternative lines that may follow from a position in the middle game. It is a *modus operandi*.

The ultimate goal of the game is checkmate, or the gain of material which may ultimately be translated into checkmate. Therefore any factor that bears on that goal is important. Control of the center is such a factor. It is not an end in itself; it is a means toward an end. As such, its value varies. If that control can be exchanged, say, for the gain of a Pawn with no untoward considerations in the offing, the exchange should be viewed favorably.

In order to capitalize on control of the center, it is generally necessary to effect such an exchange as the game progresses. Thus it is a mistaken notion to regard control of the center as an end in itself. Most often it is only the beginning of a chain reaction, each step of which is intended to add an infinitesimal plus to one's position. The cumulative total of all the small pluses often proves to be decisive.

What generally derives from the control of the center? Material gain, the launching of sound wing demonstrations, occasionally even mating attacks, and a host of intangible advantages. It is far beyond the scope of this work to outline all in detail. In the examples that follow, however, these advantages will be pointed up as they occur.

A rarer example

Hardly ever is control of the center the beginning and the end of the game. Yet one cannot say, "never." Below, a few deft moves monopolize the center, and the game is over.

This example, to be sure, is from an opening that is famous for the critical struggles that evolve from the very first moves.

ALEKHINE'S DEFENSE

1	P-K4	N-KB3
2	P-K5	N-Q4
3	P-QB4	N-N3
4	P-Q4	....

This position is typical of hyper-modern openings in which Black purposely cedes the center. The idea is double-edged, however, as Black discovers on his very next move.

4 .... **N-B3?**

Correct is 4...P-Q3 with a view to hacking away at White's center.

5	P-Q5	NxKP
6	P-B5	N/3-B5
7	Q-Q4	....

White must win a piece. He threatens 8 BxN, as well as 8 P-QN3. The game is over for all practical purposes.

A typical example

The following game was played in the final round of the world's team championship at Prague, 1931. It is typical of the step-by-step processes essential for converting dominance in the center into final victory.

RETI OPENING

	I. A. HOROWITZ *White*		D. PRZEPIORKA *Black*
1	N-KB3	N-KB3	9 R-Q1	P-B4
2	P-B4	P-K3	10 P-K4	Q-N1
3	P-KN3	P-QN3	11 P-N3	PxP
4	B-N2	B-N2	12 NxP	P-QR3
5	O-O	B-K2	13 B-N2	Q-B2
6	P-Q4	P-Q3	14 P-B4	QR-B1
7	N-B3	O-O	15 Q-K2	KR-Q1
8	Q-B2	QN-Q2	16 QR-B1	B-B1

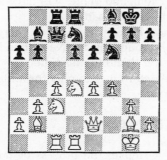

White's position is ideal. He has complete control of the center, ceded him by Black, who is following a "hold the line" and "come and get me" plan. Observe that nearly every one of White's men bears on the center.

Still the position is not a "pianola." It will not play itself. How is White to progress? As he does control the center, he can amass his forces in any direction—in the center, on the Queen-side or on the King-side—much more rapidly than Black. Where shall he strike? Is there any clue in the position?

Black's Pawn position is almost entirely sound, structurally. His Queen Pawn is backward on a half-open file. Yet, if White gangs up on it, by doubling Rooks on the Queen file, it avails him nothing, for the backward Pawn is adequately defended now and, if necessary, can be defended further. The Queen

Knight Pawn is also backward; but White has no ready avenue of approach to it, does not even have it under surveillance at the moment.

Black's King-side seems to offer the greatest prospects for White since Black's main forces are clustered on the Queen-side. And it is difficult for Black to regroup them.

Hence, the King-side it is. But what is the next step there? White can attempt a breakthrough by a Pawn assault, beginning with 17 P-KN4 and 18 P-N5. But Black can counter 17 P-KN4 with 17 . . . P-K4; and, since White's King Bishop Pawn is unprotected, 18 PxP necessarily follows. But then Black opens up his game by 18 . . . PxP, rids himself of his backward Queen Pawn, and White will have left no lasting impression on the vulnerable wing.

If White wishes, he can most likely reorganize his forces to effect the breakthrough by P-KN4-5. For Black meanwhile can do nothing better than bide his time.

Instead, White determines to play for an immediate breach in the Black King-side.

17 P-KB5 . . . .

Here is the first step in the process of translating and attempting to add to small advantages. White's move, to be sure, grants Black control of his K4, which White had previously been contesting. But it is hardly possible to make headway without relinquishing something. White is giving and White is taking. The question to consider is, "Is White getting more than he is giving?"

The text move poses a pressing problem for Black. His King Pawn is under direct attack. Since he cannot well defend it, he must exchange or advance it. Each alternative has its pros and cons. Yet, since Black has no way to build up from the occupation of his K4 and White can persist in his assault, White is deriving the greater benefit from his move.

17 . . . . PxP

On 17 . . . P-K4; 18 N-B2, followed by 19 N-K3, Black is reduced to marking time, while White continues with the Pawn assault, P-KN4-5, eventually exposing the Black Monarch to painful threats. Moreover, a gaping hole remains at Black's Q4.

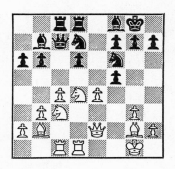

18 **N-Q5**   . . . .

A *Zwischenzug* (in-between move). As Black's Queen is under fire, White is not jeopardizing the Pawn which he has temporarily omitted recapturing.

White's purpose is to open the line of his Queen Bishop, bearing in the direction of the Black Monarch, and, at the same time, to remove some of the Monarch's defenders so he will become an easier target.

18 . . . .   **BxN**

Black is loath to part with his King Knight and weaken his forces on the King-side. He is comparatively happy to trade off his feeble Queen Bishop. But there is more involved in the transaction than is immediately apparent.

Black has given up a Bishop for a Knight. A Bishop is infinitesimally more valuable than a Knight. So White has drawn blood in the first tangible step of the transition from control of the center to slight material plus.

19 **BPxB**   . . . .

A continuing *Zwischenzug:* as White opens an attack on Black's Queen, he assures the recovery of his Pawn.

19	Q-N2
20 NxP	N-K4

Now the center is locked, and Black has staved off any immediately disastrous result. The next step is for White to translate the advantage of having the two Bishops into something more tangible, if possible.

21 B-QR3	N-K1
22 Q-K3	R-Q2
23 B-R3	....

White operates by training his sights on scattered Black weaknesses.

23	RxR
24 RxR	R-B2

By swapping down, Black takes the sting out of any prospective attack. But he must still reckon with White's edge in having the two Bishops.

25 K-N2	....

White aims to avoid a Knight fork in the event of Q-N5.

25	P-N3
26 N-R6ch	....

26	BxN

Here Black cedes another Bishop for a Knight, adding to White's infinitesimal plus. In positions with fixed Pawns, however, as against mobile Pawns, Knights often are superior to Bishops, and Black is prompted by that idea. Moreover, 26 . . . K-R1; 27 B-N2 sets up an annoying pin on Black's Knight at K4. And, if Black breaks the pin by . . . P-B3, the mobility of his minor pieces is practically nil.

27	QxB	N-Q6
28	RxR	QxR
29	Q-Q2	N-K4
30	Q-B1	. . . .

White challenges the only open file.

30	. . . .	QxQ

If Black refuses to exchange, White can continue favorably with 31 Q-B8, allowing for possibilities similar to those which actually occur.

31	BxQ	N-KB3

Now it seems that White is going to lose a Pawn. But—the Bishops to the rescue.

32	B-B8	P-QR4
33	B-K3	N/3-Q2

Black cannot afford to capture the King Pawn and give White a Pawn majority on the Queen-side. Such a majority, supported by the two Bishops, is easily enough to decide.

(*See diagram on page 134.*)

34	B-Q4	. . . .

The next step is to translate the advantage of the two Bishops against two Knights into something still more tangible.

34	. . . .	K-B1
35	K-B2	K-K2
36	K-K2	K-Q1
37	BxN/7	. . . .

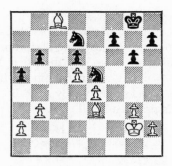

The beginning of that translation. Note that Black's Knights have been virtually immobilized since 34 B-Q4 and 35 K-B2.

37 ....   **NxB**

Forced. If 37 ... KxB, 38 BxP.

38 **K-Q3**   **N-K4ch**

Otherwise, White's King heads for QN5, and Black's game must fall.

39 **BxN**   ....

Now the second Bishop goes, but White has a winning Pawn ending.

39 ....   **PxB**

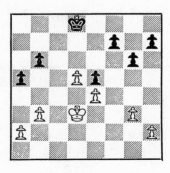

One of the earmarks of the position is that White has a *protected* passed Pawn.

40 P-KN4 . . . .

White prevents Black from breaking through with an eventual . . . P-KB4 which could lead to Black's having a protected passed Pawn, too.

40 . . . .   P-B3
41 P-KR4 . . . .

White is angling for P-N5. For then, if Black exchanges, White's one Pawn on the King's wing will hold two of Black's. Or, if Black by-passes with . . . P-KB4, White can capture and then soon establishes two passed Pawns, one of which must march through to victory.

41 . . . .   P-R4
42 PxP   PxP

Has Black now secured the draw? Or can White still make progress?

43 K-B4   K-Q2
44 K-N5   K-Q3

If 44 . . . K-B2; 45 P-R3, K-N2; 46 P-Q6, Black loses.

Now, in view of Black's threat to break through with . . . P-B4, does White dare to capture the Knight Pawn?

45 KxP!   P-B4

Otherwise White captures the Rook Pawn, too, and returns
with his King to the center for an easy win.

| 46 | PxP | P-K5 |

The tempting 46 ... KxP loses: 47 P-B6, K-K3; 48 KxP, and
White is able to return to Q2 with his King in time to stop
Black's Pawn from queening. Then his two Queen-side Pawns
decide.

47	P-B6	P-K6
48	P-B7	K-K2
49	P-Q6ch	....

White's Pawns are jockeying their way down. This is a close
race.

49	....	KxBP
50	P-Q7	P-K7
51	P-Q8(Q)	P-K8(Q)

Now the task begins anew. White has a Pawn plus. With
Queens on the board in a wide-open field, the danger of perpetual check is always present.

| 52 | Q-Q5ch | K-N2 |
| 53 | QxKRP | .... |

If 53 QxQRP, Black may play for a perpetual or for capture
of the King Rook Pawn. In the latter case, Black's single
passed Pawn is just as menacing as White's two.

53	Q-B7ch
54 K-N5	QxQRP
55 Q-N4ch	K-R2
56 Q-QB4	. . . .

This way White holds on to his advantage. But how can he progress?

| 56 . . . . | K-N2 |

Black marks time.

| 57 Q-B3ch | K-R2 |
| 58 Q-KN3 | Q-R6 |

Now Black plays either for perpetual check or to exchange off the Queen-side Pawns.

| · 59 K-B6 | . . . . |

White's plan is a long-drawn-out one. It is to attempt to force the exchange of Queens by marching his King into the vicinity of the Black King. Then, by mating threats, he hopes to embarrass Black into a position in which he cannot avoid the exchange of Queens.

| 59 . . . . | Q-N5? |

A blunder. It is to be noted, however, that Black cannot dissolve the Pawns by 59 . . . P-R5. For then follows 60 Q-Q3ch and eventually White forks Black's King and Queen Rook Pawn and wins it. The process is possible only because Black's King cannot closely approach White's Rook Pawn: e.g., 60 . . .

K-R3; 61 Q-K3ch, and Black cannot play 61 ... K-R4 on account of 62 Q-N5 mate.

Now White forces the exchange of Queens.

60 Q-Q3ch   K-N1

Not 60 ... K-R3; 61 Q-Q6ch.

61 Q-Q8ch   Resigns

For now the exchange can be forced by the Queen zigzag: 61 ... K-B2; 62 Q-Q7ch, K-N1; 63 Q-B8ch, K-B2; 64 Q-N7ch. If Black's King goes to the third rank on move 62, then of course 63 Q-Q6ch forces the issue.

Thus the contest ends. The final denouement is a far cry from the original proposition, to wit, that control of the center wins games. Yet the transitions from the beginning may be observed, step by step: (1) control of the center; (2) Kingside assault; (3) gain of Bishop for Knight; (4) gain of second Bishop for Knight; (5) better Pawn endgame. These all began with the control of the center.

LOOK FIRST!

Planning alone, as has been said, will not win games. For the tactical execution or a deficiency in it can upset the best-laid strategy. But it is certainly foolhardy to pursue a "strategy" which sets up a loss! And to drift without a plan at all is nothing more than foolsofty.

13

IN THE OPENING   IN MIDDLE GAME

   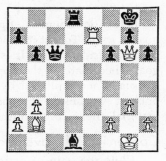

BLACK TO MOVE   BLACK TO MOVE

*Numerically, development is
approximately even; but potentially Black leads (1 . . .
N-K6!; 2 PxN, Q-R5ch, etc.),
as Black's Knight is posted to
better advantage.*

*The middle-game position
is qualitative. White has a
mating threat; but Black
mates (1 . . . Q-R8ch!!; 2 KxQ,
B-B6ch; 3 K-N1, R-Q8ch,
etc.). Quality prevails.*

Better Development

ALL OTHER THINGS being equal, better development wins
games. "Better development," however, does not refer merely
to the number of pieces brought out. It means the posting of
forces to better advantage. The fewer pieces left undeveloped
the better; yet a half dozen innocuously clustered in a sector
far removed from the critical scene of activity, for example,
weighs less at a given moment than minimal opposing forces,
directly bearing on vulnerable targets. *The advantage clearly
rests with the forces in active positions.*

As a rule, better development is both quantitative and
qualitative in the opening. That is, the player who has more

139

men commanding the central squares is sovereign. In the middle game, better development is usually qualitative. Here an irresistible mating attack far overshadows all other considerations. Or a preponderance in any vital sector is significant.

Better development, though an important factor, is not a goal in itself. To put it another way, it is not the primary goal; it is a subsidiary one. It is a step in the way to the ultimate goal—checkmate of the opposing King. And, since checkmate is usually accomplished by overwhelming force, better development is a link in the chain reaction leading to the gain of material, thence to the ultimate goal.

Conversion of advantages

While the gain of material is usually the result of better development, yet, paradoxically, the sacrifice of material often leads to better development. The interplay of the intangible, development, and the tangible, material, is implicit in the process of converting one type of advantage to another.

In this connection it is well to note the rule of thumb that governs such conversions. Most authorities hold that a gain of three *tempi* is the equivalent of a Pawn. *Tempi* naturally refers to time to do things, to accumulate force, to develop. In the middle game particularly, where the mustering of forces quickly in a given location is at a premium, this evaluation is apt. In the process of exchanging tangibles for intangibles, or vice versa, however, the all-important point is that the conversion result in a net profit, to something more lopsided than a Pawn for three *tempi* or the inverse.

Where one side enjoys a superior development, the question arises: How shall he exploit that advantage? The answer lies in striking on the King-side, in the center, on the Queen-side, wherever the clues (preponderance of force versus likely targets) for that given position indicate. Unfortunately, there is no twentieth-century automaton to supply a ready answer to such questions. The targets in the field may be many or few, apparent or concealed, and sometimes even nonexistent.

Yet the logic of the game is infallible. When development is unbalanced, the side with a clear lead can translate that advantage, with correct play, to some other advantage, eventually into something more tangible, probably into material gain, possibly into checkmate.

Specific gains from development

When a player can muster a majority of force in a given sector, it is easy to see that he can then gain something. Yet, as the sector is only a fraction of the playing field, he must also determine what advantage will accrue to him in terms of the over-all picture.

If the enemy King is on the agitated scene, then the reward for a successful incursion will be greater. For checkmate leaves no weaknesses in its wake. When lesser targets, on the other hand, are susceptible to attack, that action must be surveyed again and again in the light of broader considerations.

From all this it may be gleaned that the primary and direct target of all actions should be the opposing King, in so far as is feasible. With the King itself lending a hand in the defense, however, it is not always feasible to rally a superior development in that direction. Then the projects resulting from better development may be limited in scope. They may encompass the gain of much material, of little material, or of just the control of critical terrain. They may even be designed merely to provoke weaknesses where none exist as yet.

An instructive example

The following game points out specifically the uses of better development. There are many weaknesses that may be provoked, many that may be attacked as a result of better development. Some are delineated in the course of this game. Others will be as they crop up in subsequent game studies. For no one game can possibly illustrate all these factors of development.

Similarly, any game must include numerous other strategical motifs bearing on how to win in the middle game. Hence such will be touched upon here, indicated by references in italics.

Hastings, 1895

RUY LOPEZ

DR. EMANUEL LASKER		WILHELM STEINITZ	
White		*Black*	
1 P-K4	P-K4	8 R-K1	B-K2
2 N-KB3	N-QB3	9 QN-Q2	O-O
3 B-N5	P-QR3	10 N-B1	Q-K1
4 B-R4	P-Q3	11 B-B2	K-R1
5 O-O	N-K2	12 N-N3	B-N5
6 P-B3	B-Q2	13 P-Q5	....
7 P-Q4	N-N3		

Up to this point the play has been possibly exemplary, certainly nothing to arouse grave criticism. But now a strange trend manifests itself.

13	N-N1	16 P-KN4	N-K2
14 P-KR3	B-B1	17 N-N3	N-N1
15 N-B5	B-Q1		

What a picture! Black does not have a single piece off the first rank after seventeen moves. One would think the game belonged to two anonymous duffers. Yet each of these contestants monopolized the world championship for nearly three decades.

There it is. The most abject retreat in the history of chess. As one commentator was wont to remark: "This completes the grand withdrawal ... too bad the Pawns cannot retreat, too."

Development. It is abundantly clear that White's development is supreme. Yet the procedure for utilizing this advantage is far from clear. For there is not a single organic weakness in Black's Pawn configuration nor in any sector of his front.

Since White has more men in the field and since he has a better hold on the center (his Pawn at Q5), he must now formulate a plan to utilize these advantages in time and space. To begin with, he may complete his development with some such moves as 18 B-K3 and 19 Q-Q2. Or he may undertake more positive action at once.

Because of Black's lagging development there is no imminent danger that he may open the game by liberating counteractions, such as ... P-KN3, ... N-K2 and ... P-KB4. If he does, he only opens lines that accrue to White and boomerang in Black's camp (that is just what you will see happen later on to the game). Under the circumstances, White can build up at a leisurely pace, while Black must bide his time.

Two long-range plans suggest themselves for White, and it is possible that he may operate them in concert or independently. One plan calls for expansion on the Queen-side, by a Pawn demonstration supported by major and minor pieces. The intermediary goal is to reach P-QB5, stifle Black on that wing, and then penetrate for material gain. To execute this plan requires considerable skill. For a misplay may permit Black to punch a hole in White's Pawn configuration and so check any of his ambitions in that direction forever.

The other plan is to concentrate the White men on Black's King, lurking, as it were, for an opportunity to penetrate in mass.

18 K-N2 ....

Motive? This move appears to be out of context. It does not seem to fit into either plan. It has the earmarks of a "wait and see" policy. With such a lead in development, Lasker could afford the luxury of a passive play.

At all times, however, it is essential to comprehend the motive of any given move and ascribe a correct meaning to it. Such information is vital for appraising a situation or for a clue as to what the opponent has in mind. It may be the basis for the proper countermeasures.

Why K-N2? That is the question. Outside of any long-range plan, the King at N2 defends both the Rook Pawn and the Knight. Hence it may be considered as a consolidating move. Yet, as the Pawn and the Knight are not under attack and the prospects of such attack are dim, to say the least, the King move can hardly be justified on that ground.

At N2 the King has cleared the first rank so that the King Rook can swing to KR1. From there the Rook may lend impetus to an advance of White's King Rook Pawn for a piercing maneuver. This plan is so farfetched, however, so difficult to enforce, so uncertain of results, that the move can hardly be justified on that ground.

Hence the point of the King's move is not clear.

18		**N-Q2**
19 **B-K3**		....

White completes his development and also lines up for a possible Queen-side Pawn demonstration.

Constricted as he is, it is difficult for Black to formulate a good plan. He might try 19 . . . P-QR4 to anticipate White's Queen-side Pawn advance; but that is only palliatory.

Black's next move is not purposeless. It is the first move of a maneuver to swing his Queen Knight, via B1, to K2, to reinforce . . . P-KB4 when, as, and if it is feasible.

19		**N-N3**
20 **P-N3**		....

Restraint. White's alternative plans are well defined; yet he need not rush pellmell into them. He takes time out to keep

Black's Knight from his QB5 where it might be disconcerting. Restraint and progress are the sequence.

20 ....   B-Q2

21 P-B4   ....

Bishop for Knight. Here it is just as well to assess 21 BxN, swapping the Bishop for the Knight, though neither side has seemed concerned on that point.

A Bishop, as has been pointed out, is slightly more valuable than a Knight. So the first tally on the exchange is a minus for White. Against that, Black's Pawns become doubled —a plus for White. Hence the exchange is about level. Yet there are other considerations: by capturing White opens a file for Black whence pressure develops on White's Queen Bishop Pawn and Black obtains a modicum of freedom. To boot, the absence of the Bishop accentuates the Pawn hole at White's KB4. All in all, the BxN exchange is unprofitable.

21 ....   N-B1
22 Q-Q2   N B-K2
23 P-B5   ....

White now dominates the entire Queen-side. But the advantage is still intangible.

White's future course will be determined by Black's procedure.

| 23 .... | **P-KN3** |

Psychology. Black apparently feints a breakthrough via . . .
P-B4, which has much of the speculative about it. While the
move is possible, White must consider it in his reckoning, even
if it is bad. This is a good bit of psychology.

| 24 **Q-B3** | .... |

Again restraint. The move is intended to prevent . . . P-B4.

| 24 .... | **P-B4??** |

Hold—or Break? Black's 23d was no feint. It was the real thing
as now appears. But his calculations are inaccurate.

It is understandable that, in a cramped position, it is difficult for even a Steinitz to maintain an even calm. So he gambles
on a break.

Better is the consolidating 24 . . . P-B3, continuing the policy
of watchful, hopeful waiting. But then White continues to
press on the Queen-side.

(*See diagram on page 147.*)

| 25 **NxKP!** | .... |

Tactics. Up to now, the game has been fought along positional
lines. Now tactics come to the fore. White sacrifices material
to force open an avenue to the enemy King.

25	PxN
26 QxPch	N-B3
27 B-Q4!	....

Zwischenzug. The point. Black had expected 27 P-N5 to which he'd reply with 27 ... NxQP, relieving his game considerably. But the quiet intervening text move maintains a grip of iron. Now there is no adequate reply to the threat of (28) P-N5.

27	PxNP
28 PxP	BxP

On 28 ... P-R3; 29 P-N5, PxP; 30 QxNP, White's threats on the pinned Knight and also on the open King Rook file are decisive.

It is interesting to note that, in this last line, White actually is able to utilize the open King Rook file and so lends point to White's 18th move, which appeared pointless at the time. It does not follow from this, however, that White anticipated the present position at that move. Almost all plays on the chessboard are remotely related to each other; and the better player, as a rule, ties up the relationship at the propitious moment.

29 Q-N5!	....

White simultaneously attacks Bishop and Knight; he must recover a piece.

29	Q-Q2
30 BxNch	K-N1

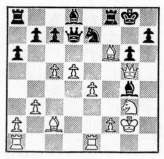

31 **B-Q1**   . . . .

Counterthreat. White perceives and parries a subtle threat.
Black had intended 31 . . . NxP!; 32 BxB, N-B5ch; 33 K any,
QRxB after which he has recovered his Pawn.

31 . . . .   **B-R6ch**

31 . . . BxB, with the same threat in view, fails because
32 QRxB activates a Rook on Black's Queen (e.g., 32 . . . NxP;
33 BxB, N-B5ch; 34 QxN, and, however Black replies, he remains a piece down).

Similarly, 31 . . . NxP at once fails also because of 32 B/1xB
(32 . . . BxB; 33 BxQ, BxQ; 34 PxN—or 33 . . . N-B5ch; 34 QxN).

32 **K-N1**   **NxP**

Pure desperation: Black is at a loss to free himself in any
case.

33	**BxB**	**N-B5**
34	**B-B6**	**Q-Q7**

(*See diagram on page 149.*)

35 **R-K2!**   . . . .

Keep Track of Material. White is well ahead in material and
can afford to part with a little to retain his edge. He meets
Black's feeble threats by giving back the Exchange.

35	. . . .	**NxRch**
36	**BxN**	**Q-Q2**

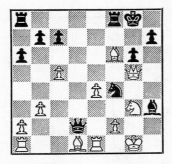

Black avoids the exchange of Queens which would permit a longer, though equally futile, resistance. He is the equivalent of nearly two Pawns behind.

37 **R-Q1**   . . . .

Even quicker is 37 B-B4ch, B-K3; 38 N-B5!

37	. . . .	**Q-B2**
38	**B-B4**	**B-K3**
39	**P-K5**	**BxB**
40	**N-B5**	**Resigns**

Thus, what started out to be a discourse on better development embraces what seems nearly the entire roster of middle-game motifs. Nor is this denouement odd; for on move 18 Black had not a single piece developed, while White had a slew of them on all-important squares.

Hence the lesson to be learned is that better development, of itself, like control of the center, is only one of many important factors. It is sufficient, though, to set in motion the chain reaction of converting one plus into another, adding fractional advantages in the process.

PLAN WELL!

Strategy embraces the conversion and accumulation of advantages. But you must plan solidly from the very first in order to acquire the initial advantage from which to work.

14

1. *Control of center and lead in development are both advantages in space. The freer play of White's forces is evident. Such an advantage may not win in itself but lends itself to the conversion of advantages with net gain or might conceivably lead to an endgame win as in position 2.*

2. *By the time the endgame is reached, such advantage can win. White's advantage (his King's position) does so by superior mobility: 1 K-B7, K-K1; 2 K-Q6, K-B2; 3 K-Q7, K-B1; 4 K-K6, K-N2; 5 K-K7, and White wins. Black to move is no help: 1 ... K-B2; 2 K-Q6 or 1 ... K-B1; 2 K-Q7, and White wins.*

Advantage in Space

THE TERMS space, terrain, squares, and *lebensraum* are synonyms for room in which to move. An advantage in space, like control of the center, like better development, is one of the governing factors in the outcome of a contest. It means more maneuverability, more chance to exercise the powers of the pieces.

Indeed, control of the center is merely a special instance of an advantage in space. Center control means an advantage in the qualitatively most important sector of the board. If the opponent does not control extra space elsewhere, it is of course a net advantage; and, even if he does, it is still a net advantage far more often than not. Better development, also, by its very nature, implies an advantage in space. For it means command of the avenues of approach to the various targets—command of space on possibly different fronts.

IN THESE EXAMPLES, AN ADVANTAGE
IN SPACE IS NO ADVANTAGE!

3. Stalemate is one of the prime exceptions in chess. It is so, too, for the advantage in space. Here White controls seven squares, contests three; but, with Black to move, White has no advantage. White surely does, though, if he is on the move.

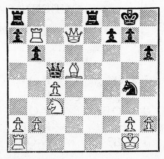

4. A converse exception is advantage in qualitatively better space (here the King field). White holds theoretical advantages in all else, but Black mates: 1 K-R1, N-B7ch; 2 K-N1, N-R6dbl ch; 3 K-R1, Q-N8ch!; 4 RxQ, N-B7 mate. Mate is a grip on better squares.

The control of space is thus an asset, regardless of its source. The command of open files, of long diagonals, of sprawling ranks, of squares for maneuverable Knights, means greater potential mobility of the pieces. The outcome is likely to be material gain.

In some instances, to be sure, such control may be nebulous in value. Rooks on an open file that leads to nothing, for example, are merely Rooks enjoying the open breeze. Yet even such mobility cannot be altogether discounted; and, under no circumstances, save only stalemate, is command of space a disadvantage.

The examples at the beginning of this chapter illustrate some of the effects of advantage in space, and exceptions. The real exception is stalemate, which is so by definition. The last stresses quality over quantity.

The following game, played in the International Correspondence Championship of 1930, is a typical example of the conversion of an advantage in space to a final mating net.

QUEEN'S GAMBIT DECLINED
Tarrasch Defense

| F. BATIK | DR. E. DYCKHOFF |
| *White* | *Black* |

	White			Black
1	P-Q4	P-Q4	6 P-KN3	N-B3
2	P-QB4	P-K3	7 B-N2	B-K2
3	N-QB3	P-QB4	8 O-O	O-O
4	BPxP	KPxP	9 PxP	P-Q5
5	N-B3	N-QB3		

Black has essayed the Tarrasch Defense, which was consistently advocated by the good doctor after whom the defense was named, as being the only valid defense to the Queen's Gambit.

After White's last move (9 PxP), Black can continue with 9 ... BxP and maintain an even balance of material. In that event, the game most likely goes 10 N-QR4, B-K2; 11 B-K3. White retains an iron grip on his Q4, accentuating the weakness of Black's isolated Queen Pawn and, at the same time, threatening to make inroads into Black's camp via QB5 and the opened Queen Bishop file. As against this plan, Black has no constructive one. To be so saddled at the begininng of a contest is onerous for most players.

So Black prefers to yield a Pawn in return for an advantage in space. His Queen Pawn, now on the fifth rank, exerts a restraining influence on White's forces.

10 N-QR4 ....

Else Black recovers his Pawn by 10 . . . BxP and still dominates the center.

Now the issue is drawn. White has a Pawn; Black, advantage in space. Note the cramping effect of Black's Queen Pawn on White's position, also the White Knight out on a limb.

The position must be viewed objectively for a clue as to how to proceed. White must try to batter down Black's Queen Pawn, exchange it off and press his three-for-two Pawn majority on the Queen-side. Or, if exigencies demand it, he may try just to press that Pawn majority. Black must prevent White from furthering those plans and, at the same time, attempt to create targets. He will utilize his advantage in space to shift his forces quickly from one point to another.

10 .... B-B4

Develop and Restrain. A key move, the omission of which collapses Black's game. The move is directed specifically against White's plan to play P-K3 and rid himself of Black's ingrown Pawn, as will soon become evident. The Bishop at B4 bears along the entire diagonal (. . . KR2-QN8) with purpose and intent. But it acts also as a prop for Black's . . . N-K5, which may follow. Thus, the move develops and restrains.

(See diagram on page 154.)

11 N-R4 ....

Why not 11 P-K3? If it is so important for White to rid himself of that Queen Pawn, why not do so at once? The

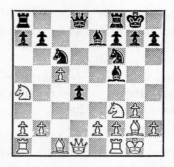

answer lies in a combination which White must anticipate. On 11 P-K3, PxP; 12 QxQ, PxPch! followed by 13 . . . QRxQ, Black recovers his Pawn and remains with a free-and-easy game. On 12 BxP?, QxQ!; 13 RxQ, B-B7! Black forks Rook and Knight and wins.

White's eleventh aims to cut down the opposing material so that, in the long run, his extra Pawn will tell.

An alternative plan begins with 11 B-B4. It leads to all sorts of dubious complications with an unclear result.

Finally, the immediate attempt to put the Pawn majority into effect with 11 P-QR3 and 12 P-QN4 fails: e.g., 11 . . . N-K5; 12 P-QN4, N-B6; 13 NxN, PxN; 14 QxQ, QRxQ; 15 B-N5, BxB; 16 NxB, N-Q5 after which Black's passed Pawn must net at least the Exchange.

11 . . . .   **B-K5**

Black is willing to fall in line with White's plan, to the extent of swapping Bishops. He reasons that the absence of White's King Bishop perceptibly weakens the defense of the White King. On 12 BxB, NxB, moreover, Black threatens to disrupt White's King-side Pawns by . . . BxN, also to recover his Pawn. Hence, White's next move.

12 **P-B3**   . . . .

Gain of a Tempo. Apparently, White now gains a *tempo,* as the Bishop is attacked and must move. Such a gain can be meaningless, however, unless it enhances the position of one side at the expense of the other. Here that outcome is doubtful. For while Black must expend a move, White's Pawn at KB3 does not enhance his position. On the contrary, it weakens it. In reality, White has not gained a *tempo*. He has fallen victim possibly to Black's provoking strategy. Now a hole exists at White's K3.

| 12 .... | B-Q4 |
| 13 N-B5 | .... |

The Books. All of the moves thus far are so-called book moves. Since "book" is the double-distilled essence of master practice, the odds are that the game has been reasonably well played to here. It does not follow, however, that the book moves are always the best ones. Nor, for that matter, are the books static. Ideas and moves keep changing all the time. Good moves at one era are relegated to limbo in the next. And virtue is discovered in once so-called bad moves.

Present-day book calls for 13 P-K4, B-B5; 14 R-B2, P-KN3, and White is supposed to enjoy the better position. That conclusion, however, is subject to debate. For by no means has Black's advantage in space been dissipated.

| 13 .... | B-K3 |

| 14 NxBch | .... |

If, instead, 14 P-K4, Black may continue with 14 ... BxN, thereby minimizing his material disadvantage by doubling

White's extra Pawn. Also, Black's Queen Pawn assumes greater significance as it becomes a passed Pawn.

14	QxN
15 B-N5	....

Swapping Down. Up to now White has been bent on exchanging men. With a Pawn plus, this is generally good strategy. Generalizations, however, rarely rule in specific cases. The question to be considered here is, how will the absence of White's Queen Bishop affect the position? The answer seems to be that it will make more gaping the Pawn hole at White's K3.

Thus far White has made no progress with the long-term plan of putting his Queen-side three-for-two majority to work. Mainly because the plan has not been feasible. At this juncture Black can thwart 15 P-QR3 (preparing for P-QN4) by 15 ... B-B5 (threatening White's King Pawn) and 16 ... P-QR4.

On the other hand, there is another alternative open to White: to continue 15 P-K4, to set up a mobile King-side Pawn majority. He must reckon here, however, with Black's newly passed Queen Pawn.

Incidentally, if Black attempts to recover his Pawn in this line by 15 ... PxP e.p., he will be disappointed. White need not submit to 16 BxP, BxP! but can play 16 R-K1 instead, whereafter he regains the Pawn momentarily sacrificed, is rid of Black's Queen Pawn, and utilizes his extra Pawn freely to decide.

Hence 15 P-K4 seems to offer the best prospects. True, Black may recover his Pawn: 15 ... B-B5; 16 R-B2, B-N4, as there is now no way of preventing 17 ... BxN, followed by 18 ... QxBP. But White meanwhile can play 17 B-N5, continue with 18 BxN, destroying Black's King-side Pawn formation.

15	B-B5

Now Black presses on White's K2 and compels an awkward defense.

16 **R-K1**   **P-KR3**

Black's move is based on desire to rid himself of White's Queen Bishop and point up weaknesses of the Black squares in White's camp—or, as alternative, to free Black's King Knight from the annoying pin.

17 **BxN**   . . . .

White pursues the principle of swapping down material. If 17 B-R4, P-KN4 wins a piece; and, if 17 B-Q2, Black penetrates with 17 . . . N-Q4.

17 . . . .   **QxB**
18 **P-N3**   . . . .

Now White aims to consolidate and follows this policy tenaciously. 18 P-K4 is no longer tenable: e.g., 18 . . . PxP e.p.; 19 RxP, QR-Q1; 20 Q-K1, Q-Q5; 21 Q-B3, B-N4; 22 QxQ, NxQ; 23 N-B3, N-B7, and Black wins.

18 . . . .   **B-R3**
19 **Q-Q2**   . . . .

This seems to be White's last opportunity to play P-K4. Evidently, he is not concerned about liberating his King Pawn but places great stock in the long-term potentialities of his

Queen-side Pawn majority. Most likely this is the definite turning point of the game.

19		**KR-K1**
20 **N-N2**		**R-K6!**

Now White is reduced to play in the first two ranks, and Black's pressure mounts against the backward King Pawn.

21 **QR-B1**   ....

21 P-QN4, with the idea of instituting the Pawn majority attack, offers greater prospects; but Black ought to come first: e.g., 21 ... QR-K1; 22 B-B1, Q-K2; 23 K-B2, N-K4; 24 P-QR4, P-QN4; and Black's Bishop soon occupies the long diagonal at QN2 with an ovewhelming attacking position.

21		**QR-K1**
22 **B-B1**		**N-K4**

Black's Queen Pawn is immune: 23 QxP, NxPch. And, curiously enough, among the various possibilities, White must reckon with ... QxP and ... RxP.

(*See diagram on page 159.*)

23 **P-B4**   ....

This move further weakens White's King-side and grants the Knight ready access to the opposing King. But White was

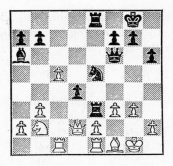

at a loss for a better continuation: e.g., 23 K-N2, NxP!; 24 PxN,
BxBch; 25 KxB (or 25 RxB, R-K7ch!), QxPch; 26 K-N1, R-K7,
and Black wins. Or 26 Q-B2, Q-R8ch; 27 Q-N1, RxRch.

23	**N-N5**
24 **N-B4**	....

White's Knight has maneuvered and maneuvered to join
the fray. Now his career is short lived.

24	**BxN**

Bishop for Knight. Black readily parts with a Bishop for a
Knight as the latter was assuming a powerful role.

25 **RxB**	**Q-KN3!**

Black threatens 26 ... NxP, unhinging the King Knight Pawn and placing the White King in a mating net. The same idea prevails after the next move.

26	**B-N2**	**NxP!**

King Field Sacrifice. A pretty example of this kind, to expose the King.

27	**KxN**	**QxPch**
28	**K-N1**	**P-Q6**

And the Pawn, which has played its greatest role, takes a bow as the curtain is about to fall. It is evident here that advantage in space has become paramount.

29	**R-B3**	....

There is nought else to be done against the threat of 29 ... RxP.

29	....	**R/1-K3**

Threatening 30 ... R-N3.

Resigns

White has only palliatives: e.g., 30 P-B5 (to prevent ... R-N3), R/3-K5, and Black threatens 31 .. R-N5. If 31 R-B4, RxP wins on the spot.

Thus, after a number of vicissitudes, the advantage in space decides. The chain reaction of conversion, beginning with the sacrifice of a Pawn on Black's ninth turn, has run its course and winds up in the form of a mating net.

This game is not only a lesson in what to do when an advantage in space exists. It illustrates also how to gain such an advantage. Usually, it comes about as a result of arduous thrusting and parrying until one side gains the upper hand. Sometimes it comes about merely as a gift. Here it involves the sacrifice of material—the sacrifice of a valuable Pawn in return for control of certain key squares.

SPIRIT OF THE GAMBIT

When a player essays a gambit, he assumes a calculated risk. He gives up material for an advantage of some other kind. In effecting this exchange, the deportment of the gambiteer must be beyond reproach. He must not betray a single qualm, immediately or during the future course of the game. Every action, every gesture is a reflection of his own appraisal of his position. Gambits are for the strong.

15

King-side Attack;
Queen-side Attack;
King in the Center

I F ALL THE force on the chessboard could be mustered at a given moment against a single target, clearly the charge would be leveled at the opposing King. For when the King falls, the game ends. The premium on the King is so great, consequently, as to invite rife speculation—sacrifices of material, swift utilization of advantages in time and space.

It is, of course, hypothetical to conceive all the force of the chessboard concentrated on one point. It is by no means visionary, however, to build a preponderance of force in any critical sector, even at the cost of neglecting less important areas.

The usual positional or close game begins with a fight for the center, for better development, for a more advantageous pattern. It embraces the give-and-take of the strenuous struggle, where an infinitesimal plus, step by step, may be converted into something more tangible—into final victory. The open game, on the other hand, is often the steppingstone or direct approach to the enemy King. In this encounter, the subtle nuances—the careful appraisal of time versus space versus material—are often sidetracked and give way to heavy sledgehammer blows where all the force is spent in a boom, boom, boom. And, in the following calm, if no actual mate occurs, the pieces are picked up. Whose pieces? The defender's, of course, if the attack is successful. Or the attacker's, if he has shot his bolt and missed his mark.

KING-SIDE ATTACK

The following examples show the attacks in all their glory.

London, 1915

DUTCH DEFENSE

DR. ED. LASKER		SIR GEORGE THOMAS	
White		*Black*	
1 P-Q4	P-K3	6 P-K4	PxP
2 N-KB3	P-KB4	7 NxP	P-QN3
3 N-QB3	N-KB3	8 N-K5	O-O
4 B-N5	B-K2	9 B-Q3	B-N2?
5 BxN	BxB		

This opening is similar in many ways to the contemporary hypermodern debuts. Black has given up immediate occupation of the center for long-term control. The fianchettoed Queen Bishop presages (in Black's opinion) the coming struggle for command of the mid-section of the playing field. All is more or less quiet in Black's camp.

White, for his part, has violated some elementary principles. First, he has parted early with a Bishop for a Knight. Then he has moved his King Knight twice in the opening, while his other men remain to be developed.

In all justice, Black's position ought to be superior. And possibly it would be, in the long run, if there were no Kings on the board. Observe, however, that most of White's minor men point in one direction, the direction of the Black King. White is building a King-side preponderance for an immediate decision.

10 **Q-R5**   . . . .

Now two Knights, a Bishop, and a Queen take a bead on the Black Monarch, with the Bishop concealed to some extent by the shielding Knight at K4.

10 . . . .   **Q-K2?**

Black is evidently oblivious of the overwhelming force aimed at his King.

11 **QxPch!!!**   . . . .

This violent sacrifice forces the Black King into the open. White checkmates in eight moves!

11	KxQ	15 P-N3ch	K-B6
12 NxBdbl ch.	K-R3	16 B-K2ch	K-N7
13 N/5-N4ch	K-N4	17 R-R2ch	K-N8
14 P-R4ch	K-B5	18 O-O-O mate	

Syracuse, 1943

TWO KNIGHTS' DEFENSE

W. M. P. MITCHELL		I. A. HOROWITZ	
:---:		:---:	
White		*Black*	
1 P-K4	P-K4	6 B-N5ch	P-B3
2 N-KB3	N-QB3	7 PxP	PxP
3 B-B4	N-B3	8 Q-B3	PxB!?
4 N-N5	P-Q4	9 QxR	B-QB4
5 PxP	N-QR4		

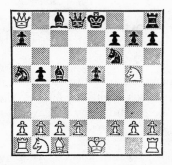

This fulminating position arises out of an opening variation that has been popular for several centuries. Black gives up a Pawn and the Exchange in order to control the center and gain better development, with a view to bringing matters to a head by a King-side attack.

Black's sacrifice is speculative in the sense that if the attack peters out and he has not recovered his material loss, he will lose the game.

10 **Q-B3** ....

In order to bring the Queen into safety against the threat of ... O-O followed by ... Q-B2 and ... B-N2, and consequent incarceration.

10	**B-N2**
11 **Q-K2**	**O-O**
12 **P-QB3**	....

White's last has a dual purpose. It menaces P-QN4, forking two pieces, and, at the same time, creates a possible exit for the White King at QB2 if the King-side becomes too turbulent.

12	P-KR3
13 N-B3	N-B5
14 P-QN4	P-K5
15 N-Q4	....

White cannot afford 15 PxB, PxN, for then the King file is open and this offers a direct approach to the White King.

15	BxN
16 PxB	QxP
17 N-B3	N-K4
18 O-O	....

White has managed to retain the advantage of the Exchange and now seeks seclusion on the right wing, behind what appears to be a solid array of Pawns.

18	N-B6ch!

All is not what it seems. Black's last penetrates the King-field.

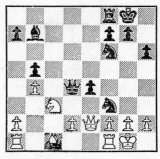

19 K-R1	....

If 19 PxN, PxP, attacking the Queen and threatening ...Q-N5ch, followed by mate.

19	N-N5

Now Black gangs up on the enemy King en masse, with a preponderant force.

20 QxNP   ....

This diversion is of no help. There was, however, nothing to be done against the threat of .... Q-K4, followed, if necessary, by ... Q-KR4 and a critical penetration of White's defenses.

20 ....   QxBP!

Threatening 21 ... Q-N8ch!; 22 RxQ, N-B7 mate!

21	**Q-K2**	**Q-R5**
22	**PxN**	**PxP**
	Resigns	

White must lose much material and/or get mated.

The following position occurred in the game Bronstein-Najdorf in the team match, Argentina-U.S.S.R. After much jockeying and feinting, White has managed to secure a preponderant force in the neighborhood of the Black King. At this juncture White embarked on a burst of sacrificial orgies, all intended to expose the Black King to devastating blows.

Black, under duress, accepted everything that came his way and then—White resigned.

Curiously, White can win by force with the correct procedure.

1 BxP!	NxB
2 RxNch!	KxR
3 Q-R4ch	K-N2

All forced. If 3 ... K-N3; 4 Q-N4ch, K-R2; 5 R-Q3, B-B1; 6 R-R3ch, B-R3; 7 PxP and White's threat of mate at N7 decides.

4 N-B5ch!	....

This move has manifold purposes. For one thing, it compels Black to build a barrier around his own King after the capture of the Knight. For another thing, it is the beginning of a clearance idea which opens up the path of White's King Bishop (now at QN3) for future operation.

4	PxN

Otherwise, Black gets mated.

5 R-Q3	....

Threatening 6 R-N3ch, with mate to follow.

5	NxKP

No other move will do. If, for instance, 5 ... PxP; 6 R-N3ch, B-N4; 7 QxBch, K-B1; 8 R-R3 and Black cannot stop mate. If 5 ... QxP; 6 R-R3 and Black is defenseless.

6 R-R3	N-N3
7 Q-R6ch	K-N1
8 NxQP!	....

Threatening 9 NxBch, QxN; 10 QxNch, K-B1; 11 R-R8 mate—and in addition Black's Queen is attacked.

	8	**RxN**

Forced.

	9 **BxR**	....

Again threatening 10 QxNch, etc.

	9	**B-Q1**

The only move.

10 **QxNch**	**K-B1**
11 **Q-R6ch**	**K-K2**
12 **R-K3ch**	**K-Q3**

If 12 .... K-Q2; 13 Q-B8 and White must at least recover his material and leave the Black King's defenses in tatters.

13 **B-B3**	....

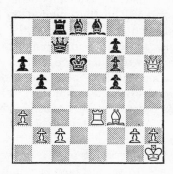

Now, despite the fact that White is a piece down, he should win. There is no valid defense.

For example, if 13...B-Q2 (to save the Bishop); 14 Q-B8ch mates quickly. Or if 13...B-B3, 14 Q-B4ch wins: 14...K-Q2; 15 QxPch, K-Q3; 16 Q-B4ch, K-Q2; 17 B-N4ch, etc. Or, in this line, if 14...K-B4; 15 R-B3ch, followed by 16 RxQ, decides.

Any other Black play should be equally fruitless.

True, this ending does not culminate in what may be termed a King-side attack. But the King-side attack is the vehicle to bring material gain.

Now, what is the lesson to be learned from the foregoing examples? In all of them it is evident that a majority of forces were brought to bear against the opposing King.

In the first case (Lasker-Thomas) this was achieved by straightforward means, with only a minor investment. White gave up a Bishop for a Knight in order to remove one of the defenders from the area of the Black King, and later moved a Knight twice in the opening in order quickly to dominate the vulnerable squares around the opposing King. In this game, White set up a pattern (with Black's cooperation) that was favorable for a quick incursion.

In game No. 2 (Mitchell-Horowitz) the White King was subdued by an overwhelming concentration of force. Here, however, Black gambled an Exchange—that is, he gave up a Rook for a Bishop early in the opening—in order quickly to rush sufficient material to the sector of the adverse King. In these negotiations, speculation or a calculated risk was implicit, since there was no guarantee that Black could achieve his goal after parting with a sizable chunk of material.

In position No. 3 (Bronstein-Najdorf) White established a superiority of force against the opposing King after a long, arduous struggle. (At the crucial moment, however, he failed to observe the correct procedure and lost.) An important point of this tussle was that the proper procedure would have utilized the King-side attack to bring about a winning position. The attack, *of itself*, was not conclusive.

These games clarify the proposition that an overwhelming force is essential to subdue the enemy King. "Overwhelming," incidentally, is a relative concept. If a King is defended a half-dozen different ways but attacked ten times, that King is not secure. On the other hand, a King may be without a single defender and be relatively safe if the enemy pieces are unable to reach him.

What is there in any given position that prompts a King-side attack as against some other operation? To begin with, of course, it is the unique value of the King. This motive explains the attacker's desire, though not necessarily his ability. *The ability to reach the enemy King with superior force* is the real signal for the shift to the King-side attack.

Sometimes the King-side attack has its very foundation in the opening. Gambits, such as the King's Gambit, the Evans Gambit, the Scotch Gambit, and a host of others, by the sacrifice of a Pawn, are designed to further developments, to open lines quickly leading to the opposing King. Sometimes the attack is the result of a natural build-up. And at other times the attack may be sheer bluff, an act of desperation. At all times, however, the King-side attack is fraught with danger for both sides.

KING IN THE CENTER

When the King becomes a ready target in the center of the board, he is subject to flailing blows from so many directions that his chances of survival are slim indeed. That is why the privilege of castling is valued so highly. For castling supplies an easy avenue of escape. And that, too, is why a player is willing to sacrifice all kinds of material to ferret out and pinpoint the enemy King in the center.

This strategic motif—pinpointing the enemy King in the center—usually comes into play at the tail end of the opening, and courses through the middle game. Since it mostly involves great sacrifices of material, it places a heavy burden on the aggressor and demands of him sharp and even spectacular tactics.

The following game highlights this method of approach to the enemy King.

New Orleans, 1858

TWO KNIGHTS' DEFENSE

	P. MORPHY		AMATEUR
	White		*Black*

1 P-K4	P-K4	5 N-N5	P-Q4
2 N-KB3	N-QB3	6 PxP	NxP
3 B-B4	N-B3	7 O-O	B-K2
4 P-Q4	PxP		

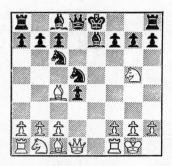

Black's position has the earmarks of a good, sound structure. His pieces are happily developed with excellent prospective mobility and, to boot, he is a Pawn to the good. Soon he will castle and take the initiative....

8 NxBP! ....

But White has ideas of his own. Black will not castle, even if it costs White a piece!

8 .... **KxN**

Forced, since White's last move forked Queen and Rook. Now Black's King is slated to remain in the center of the board.

9 Q-B3ch **K-K3**

A better chance is 9 ... B-B3. In that case, White can settle for a Pawn plus after 10 BxNch, B-K3; 11 BxN, PxB; 12 QxP.

Or White can keep the Black King in an awkward post by 10 BxNch, B-K3; 11 BxBch, KxB; 11 Q-N3ch, when he can pick off the Queen Knight Pawn at will.

With the text move Black retains the piece.

10 **N-B3!**   . . . .

This is one of those spectacular moves demanded of the aggressor. The idea is to open lines quickly at any cost leading to the target King.

    10 . . . .   **PxN**
    11 **R-K1ch**   **N-K4**

Forced. If 11 . . . K-Q2; 12 QxNch, K-K1; 13 Q-B7ch, K-Q2 and White has a fielder's choice of decisive continuations.

    12 **B-B4**   **B-B3**
    13 **BxN**   **BxB**
    14 **RxBch!**   . . . .

White gives up nearly everything to reach the Black Monarch. But he still retains sufficient mating force.

    14 . . . .   **KxR**
    15 **R-K1ch**   **K-Q5**
    16 **BxN**   . . . .

White can afford this relatively quiet move in order to remove an important defender. In the involvements of the combination, White naturally strives for mate. But at all times he is willing to settle for less than that, if necessary, providing he winds up with a good plus in material.

16	R-K1

Black has no good move. If 16 ... QxB; 17 QxP mate. And if 16 ... PxP; 17 R-K4ch soon mates.

17 Q-Q3ch	K-B4
18 P-N4ch	KxP

18 ... K-N3; 19 Q-Q4ch, K-R3; 20 Q-B4ch and mate in two more moves.

19 Q-Q4ch	K-R4

White announced mate in four.

20 QxBPch	K-R5
21 Q-N3ch	K-R4
22 Q-QR3ch	K-N3
23 R-N1 mate	

And what is the lesson here? Does it mean that whenever the opponent is getting ready to castle a player should prevent him from doing so, at all or any cost? Definitely not. It means (1) that the King in the center of the board is a comparatively easy target; (2) that if there is sufficient immediate and reserve striking force within his range a sacrifice is to be considered; (3) that the onus of accuracy rests with the aggressor. If all the conditions are favorable, then sacrifice. The attack will work out successfully or there will be a lesson to be learned.

QUEEN-SIDE ATTACK

Usually a player will castle on the King-side, leaving Queen-side castling to those exceptional cases where it facilitates either the rapid and advantageous occupation of the Queen file by the Queen Rook or the effective advance of the King-side Pawns in a King-side attack.

The dangers of Queen-side castling greatly outweigh the occasional benefits. There is a broader front to defend; the King must often make a time-wasting move to QN1 to protect the Queen Rook Pawn and/or get out of the way of the opponent's rather easily opened Queen Bishop file; the opponent's Queen can often take up a menacing position on the Queen-side, in many instances moving directly to QR4 from her original square; and the opponent's Queen-side Pawns may start rolling forward any moment in a charge to open lines against the castled King.

The game below may be found more than ordinarily instructive in so far as it illustrates some aspect of all these themes.

New York, 1936

QUEEN'S GAMBIT DECLINED

A. W. DAKE		I. A. HOROWITZ	
White		*Black*	
1 P-Q4	N-KB3	7 P-K3	N-R4
2 N-KB3	P-Q4	8 B-KN5	B-K2
3 P-B4	P-K3	9 BxB	QxB
4 N-B3	QN-Q2	10 Q-B2	O-O
5 PxP	PxP	11 B-Q3	KN-B3
6 B-B4	P-B3	12 O-O-O	P-B4

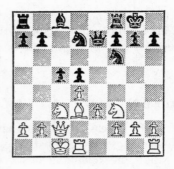

Anticipating a King-side Pawn advance, Black seeks counterplay by opening the Queen Bishop file. An alternative was 12 ... R-K1 with the idea of following up with 13 ... N-K5.

13 P-KN4 ....

Threatening 14 P-N5, but Black is able to parry this. If 13 PxP, NxP; 14 NxP, NxBch (not 14 ... NxN; 15 BxPch, followed by 16 RxN); 15 QxN, NxN; 16 QxN, B-K3 and Black regains his Pawn or gets a strong attack.

13	P-B5
14 B-B5	N-N3
15 N-K5	....

If 15 P-N5, BxB; 16 QxB, N-K5; 17 NxP, NxN; 18 QxQN, NxBP.

15	BxB!

The crux of the position. This move, which is in fact a liberating one, apparently invites a terrific onslaught on the open Knight file. But this is only superficial reasoning. A closer examination shows that Black has enough defensive resources for the protection of his King, while at the same time is able to conduct a Queen-side attack.

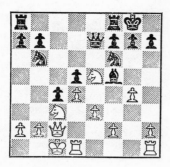

16 **PxB** ....

If 16 QxB, Q-K3; 17 Q-B3, N-K5!; with a good game. White, of course, dare not play in this variation 18 NxN, PxN; 19 QxP, because of 19 ... P-B3!

16 .... **QR-Q1**

Preparing for 17 ... N-K5 which, if played at once, fails because of 17 NxQP, NxN; 18 QxN attacking the other Knight.

17 **KR-N1** **N-K5!**

From this point Black assumes the offensive. The threat is now 18 ... NxN, and if 19 QxN, N-R5 and ... P-QN4 with a mobile Pawn majority to assail the adverse King.

18 **NxN** ....

If 18 P-B6, QxP; 19 NxN, PxN; 20 QxKP, N-Q4 followed by ... Q-QR3 with favorable prospects.

18 .... **PxN**
19 **QxKP** ....

Not an oversight, but rather faulty judgment. Better, perhaps, was 19 K-N1, although even then after ... R-B1 Black's position is superior.

19 .... **P-B3**
20 **Q-R4** **P-B6!**

21 R-N3	PxPch

Not 21 ... Q-N5? because of 22 RxPch! and Black gets mated.

22 K-N1	R-B1

Threatening 23 ... R-B8ch; 24 RxR, PxR(Q)ch; 25 KxQ, Q-B2ch winning the Knight.

23 N-Q3	Q-R6
24 Q-N4	....

Forced, otherwise the White Queen Rook is unprotected in some of the ensuing variations.

24	R-KB2
25 NxP	....

There is nothing better. The threat was 25 ... N-R5.

25	N-Q4	28 Q-K2	R(2)-B2
26 P-K4	N-B6ch	29 P-QR4	P-QR3
27 RxN	QxR		

Simpler was 29 ... Q-N6 and if then 30 Q-N5, Q-B7ch followed by ... QxKP. Black, however, was under the impression that after he prevented White's Q-N5 the first player would be helpless.

30 Q-Q3	Q-N5
31 P-K5	R-B6
32 Q-K4	....

For now comes the realization that if 32 ... Q-N6; 33 PxP, R-B7; 34 Q-K6ch! But Black has a winning alternative.

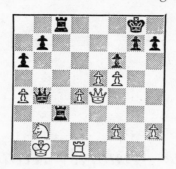

| 32 .... | R-B7 | 34 KxR | PxP |
| 33 QxR | RxQ | 35 P-Q5 | .... |

The only chance is to force this Pawn through.

35	K-B2	41 PxP	PxP
36 P-Q6	K-K1	42 N-Q1	Q-B5
37 P-Q7ch	K-Q1	43 K-B2	P-R4
38 R-Q3	Q-KB5	44 N-B3	P-R5
39 P-B3	QxPch	45 N-K4	P-R6
40 K-B3	P-QN4!	46 N-Q6	....

If 46 N-B5, Q-B5ch; 47 R-B3, QxRch followed by ... P-R7.

| 46 .... | KxP | 48 N-R7ch | K-N2 |
| 47 NxNPdis ch | K-B3 | Resigns | |

16

The Minority Attack

W_{HEN} Philidor long ago uttered his famous phrase about
Pawn play as the "soul of chess," he meant to stress the fundamental, if sometimes unobtrusive, role of the Pawns in practically everything that is done on the chessboard.

Great, indeed, is the art of Pawnpushing, and here we
must content ourselves with mentioning just a few of the major
motifs. Among these is the topic of Pawn majorities. When a
player has a preponderance of undoubled Pawns on one side
of the board, he is said to have a Pawn majority, the chief
advantage of which is that it usually involves the existence
or potentiality of one or more passed Pawns. The advantage is
more pronounced when it occurs on the side opposite to the
adversary's castled King, because the King may be too distant
to play his part in halting any queening threat in the endgame.

Pawn majorities on the Queen-side are proverbially more
menacing than on the other wing for the simple reason that
most players castle on the King-side. Note in this connection
that a player who has castled King-side can advance a Queen-
side Pawn majority any time during the game without worry-
ing about loosening a cordon of protective Pawns around his
King.

It must not be inferred from what has been said above that

a Pawn majority *automatically* confers an advantage. So far is this from being true that a special and very important case arises in which a Pawn majority is vulnerable to an undermining action by a Pawn minority. Specifically, a position sometimes occurs on the Queen-side in which Pawns on QN2, QB3, and Q4 are confronted by an adverse Pawn on Q4 while forming a target for an advancing Queen Knight Pawn. The attacking side lacks a Queen Bishop Pawn. In the typical formation, both players also have Queen Rook Pawns, but these have subsidiary roles.

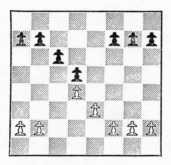

Mechanics of the minority attack

White advances his Queen Knight Pawn to N5, threatening PxP. If Black allows this and replies with . . . PxP, he leaves the Black Queen Bishop Pawn backward on an open file and therefore difficult to defend. A similar weakening of the Black Bishop Pawn ensues if Black seeks to stop P-QN5 with . . . P-QN4, unless, as occasionally happens, he can block the Queen Bishop file by sinking a piece into his QB5. The third possibility, . . . PxP as soon as the White Knight Pawn reaches N5, is perhaps the least satisfactory of all from Black's point of view. The Black Queen Pawn becomes isolated and, after White recaptures with a piece, the Black Queen Knight Pawn is exposed to pressure on the Knight file.

So critical is the plight of the defender against the minority attack that he must seek counterplay on the King-side at all costs. Experience shows, however, that White usually has little trouble warding off tactical threats while tightening the vise on the Queen-side.

Here is a modern game that has become famous as a blueprint for conducting the minority attack. More than this, it embodies an astonishing Knight's tour and a precisely played ending, showing once more how a well-planned chess battle is an organic whole with interrelated parts.

Dubrovnik, 1950

QUEEN'S GAMBIT DECLINED

LARRY EVANS		OPSAHL	
White		*Black*	
1 P-Q4	N-KB3	5 P-K3	B-K2
2 P-QB4	P-K3	6 Q-B2	O-O
3 N-QB3	P-Q4	7 PxP	....
4 B-N5	QN-Q2		

The Exchange Variation, played thousands of times, which gives White the opportunity for the minority attack.

7	PxP	10 O-O	N-B1
8 N-B3	P-B3	11 QR-N1	N-K5
9 B-Q3	R-K1	12 BxB	QxB

13 **P-QN4** ....

The attack begins! White's every move hereabouts is a model of precision.

13	....	**P-QR3**
14	**P-QR4**	**NxN**

Black might have tried 14 ... P-KB4 to reinforce the position of his Knight at K5, but then he would have abandoned his K4 to White's Knight.

15	**QxN**	**B-N5**
16	**N-Q2**	**Q-N4**

With this and the next few moves, Black tries to create chances on the King-side. As usual, however, in this type of position, ordinary care by White suffices to scotch Black's hopes, while Black has no way of ridding himself of his organic weaknesses.

17	KR-B1	R-K3		20	P-N3	QR-K1
18	P-N5	RPxP		21	PxP	PxP
19	PxP	B-R6				

An ideal setup in the prosecution of the minority attack. Black's Queen Bishop Pawn is a shining target on the open Bishop file, and the necessity of defending it leads to further disadvantages.

22	B-B1	BxB		29	NPxQ	P-N3
23	NxB	N-N3		30	N-Q2	R-Q3
24	R-N6	N-K2		31	K-B1	K-N2
25	Q-N4	P-R4		32	R-R1	R-Q2
26	R-N8	RxR		33	N-N3	R-N2
27	QxRch	K-R2		34	N-B5	R-N7
28	Q-B4	QxQ	

If 34 . . . R-B2, White can play R-R8 and follow with an incursion of the King at QN6. Or he can prepare a breakthrough with P-B3 and P-K4.

35	**R-R7**	**K-B3**
36	**R-R6**	. . . .

The winning plan could start here with 36 N-Q7ch, but White must reckon with the clock and so temporizes until he can work out all the details.

36	. . . .	R-N8ch		39	R-B7	R-QR8
37	K-N2	R-N7		40	N-Q3	K-K3
38	R-R7	R-N8	

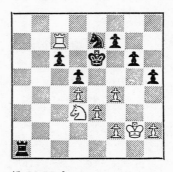

41	**N-B5ch**	. . . .

The beginning of an amazing Knight's tour, the end result of which is material gain.

41	. . . .	**K-B3**
42	**N-Q7ch**	**K-K3**

Not 42 ... K-N2 because of 43 N-K5, winning a Pawn.

43	**N-B8ch**	**K-B3**
44	**N-R7ch**	**K-K3**
45	**N-N5ch**	....

Thereby completing a nearly circular journey.

45	....	**K-Q3**

If 45 ... K-B3; 46 P-B3, and P-K4-5ch.

46	**R-N7**	**P-B3**
47	**N-R7**	**K-K3**
48	**N-B8ch**	....

Returning with the Knight, as it were, counterclockwise.

48	....	**K-B2**
49	**NxP**	....

A Pawn is gone, but the win is still extremely difficult.

49	....	KxN	53	K-N3	R-B7
50	RxN	K-B4	54	P-R4	K-B4
51	R-QB7	R-QB8	55	R-KR8	K-N3
52	R-B8	K-N3	56	P-B5ch	....

Securing a passed Pawn. The rest is given without comment, as it would be going too far afield for the purposes of this book to annotate the remainder of the ending. White's goal is to force a won King and Pawn ending by returning his extra Pawn.

56	....	KxP	65	R-R1	K-B4
57	RxPch	K-N3	66	K-N3	K-N4
58	R-R8	K-B4	67	R-R4	K-B4
59	R-KN8	R-B8	68	R-B4ch	K-N4
60	K-N2	R-QR8	69	R-N4ch	K-B4
61	P-R5	R-R2	70	K-R4	R-R1
62	R-N3	R-R2	71	R-N7	R-R1
63	R-R3	K-N4	72	P-R6	R-R8
64	K-B3	R-R3	73	R-N3	R-R8ch

74	R-R3	R-KN8	78 K-N4	K-N3
75	R-B3ch	K-N3	79 K-B4	K-N2
76	R-N3ch	RxR	80 K-B5	K-B2
77	KxR	KxP	81 P-B3	Resigns

If 81 . . . K-N2; 82 K-K6, and White wins the Queen Bishop Pawn, and Queen Pawn. If 81 . . . K-K2; 82 K-N6, K-K3; 83 P-B4, K-K2; 84 P-B5 wins the King Bishop Pawn.

17

Weak Pawns and Strong Squares

In observing how the minority attack can develop a target in the form of a backward Pawn, we have anticipated in some measure the subject of Pawn weaknesses. Apart from Pawns doubled or tripled on the same file, which may suffer from restricted mobility, the only other major type of Pawn weakness is the isolated Pawn, that is, one incapable of being protected by a fellow Pawn or Pawns on adjoining files. The isolated Queen Pawn in particular presents a recurrent strategic theme.

It should be emphasized that the "isolani" is not necessarily and invariably a weakness. On the contrary, the isolated Queen Pawn, through its sphere of influence over the squares K5 and QB5, helps to control the center and threatens at times to advance effectively to Q5. Nevertheless, the central square Q5 directly in front of it may often be occupied strongly by an enemy piece, and there is always the isolated Pawn's inherent lack of anchorage.

The following game is an example of what can happen to an "isolani" in an unguarded moment.

187

St. Petersburg, 1909

QUEEN'S GAMBIT

A. SPEYER
White

A. RUBINSTEIN
Black

	White		*Black*
1	P-Q4	P-Q4	7	BxP	N-B3
2	P-QB4	P-K3	8	O-O	Q-B2
3	N-QB3	PxP	9	Q-K2	B-K2
4	N-B3	P-QR3	10	B-Q2	O-O
5	P-QR4	P-QB4	11	QR-B1	R-Q1
6	P-K3	N-KB3	12	B-Q3	....

Allowing an isolated Queen Pawn for the sake of play in the open Queen Bishop file and in the center.

12	....	PxP
13	PxP	B-Q2

Black cannot play 13 ... NxP? forthwith because of 14 NxN, RxN; 15 N-N5.

14	N-K4	QR-B1
15	N-K5	B-K1

Stopping 16 NxNch, BxN; 17 BxPch, KxB; 18 Q-R5ch with at least a draw.

Capture of the White Queen Pawn is still bad: 15 ... NxP;

16 NxNch, BxN (if 16...PxN; 17 Q-N4ch); 17 Q-K4, QxN;
18 QxPch, K-B1; 19 B-N4ch.

16 **B-B3** . . . .

16 . . . . **NxP!**

Now the Pawn falls relatively early in the game. If 17 BxN,
QxR; 18 B-B3, RxQB; 19 NxR, Q-R3 is sufficient.

17 NxNch	BxN	*20* QxB	RxB
18 Q-K4	N-B4	*21* QxQ	RxQ
19 P-KN4	BxN!	*22* PxN	PxP

As the smoke clears, Black emerges two Pawns ahead.
Despite Bishops of opposite colors, White can have only the
faintest hopes of drawing. The rest of the game is a finely
played ending by one of the great masters of all time.

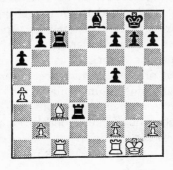

23	P-R5	P-B3	40	B-Q4	R-K5ch
24	KR-Q1	R(2)-Q2	41	K-Q3	B-B3!
25	RxR	RxR	42	P-N4	B-N4ch
26	R-K1	B-B3	43	K-B3	P-B5
27	R-K3	R-Q8ch	44	B-B5	K-B4
28	R-K1	R-Q2	45	K-Q2	P-R4
29	P-B4	K-B2	46	K-B3	B-K7
30	K-B2	B-K5	47	R-N2	P-B6
31	R-K2	P-KN4!	48	R-N7	B-N4
32	R-Q2	B-Q4	49	R-N3	R-B5ch
33	K-N3	K-K3	50	K-Q2	K-K5
34	R-K2ch	B-K5	51	B-N6	RxP
35	R-Q2	R-N2!	52	R-R3	R-N7ch
36	PxP	RxPch	53	K-B3	P-B7
37	K-B4	R-N5ch	54	R-K3ch	K-B5
38	K-K3	R-R5!	55	R-K6	K-B4
39	R-KB2	B-Q4		Resigns	

STRONG SQUARES

Much of the battle in chess rages about the occupation and/or control of strong squares. Practically speaking, of course, one cannot be strong everywhere; it is enough of a problem to be strong in the center, on important files and diagonals, and in all areas involving the safety of the King.

A strong square almost defines itself as one that is difficult or impossible to attack. Thus, as we have already noted, the square in front of an isolated Pawn is a strong point for the opponent in so far as he can seize it with a piece that cannot be driven off by a Pawn. Similarly, a "hole" in the adverse position, which may be described as a square for which the enemy lacks Pawn protection, may become a gaping wound in his side if we can lodge an unassailable piece in it.

Often control of certain complexes of white or black squares depends on our retention of one or both Bishops. For example, by exchanging or otherwise losing the services of his Queen Bishop, White may easily become weak on vital black squares.

This is just another way of saying, of course, that Black may become strong on them. By the same token, absence of White's King Bishop may result in loss of an important white diagonal and a corresponding gain by Black, who may then acquire command of strategic white squares.

This whole matter is clearly no isolated theme, since every game of chess is played on a board of sixty-four squares which are variously weak or strong, as the fortunes of war ebb and flow. Some games, however, such as the one that follows, portray in exceptional relief how the possession of strong squares can lead straight to clear-cut victory.

Baden-Baden, 1925

QUEEN'S PAWN OPENING

A. RUBINSTEIN		DR. K. TREYBAL	
White		*Black*	
1 N-KB3	P-Q4	6 B-N2	B-Q3
2 P-Q4	P-K3	7 QN-Q2	N-QN5
3 P-K3	N-KB3	8 B-K2	Q-K2
4 B-Q3	P-B4	9 P-QR3	N-B3
5 P-QN3	N-B3	10 N-K5	BxN

While it is true that the White Knight was powerfully placed on K5, Black pays too high a price for ridding himself of it. The disappearance of the Black King Bishop means a serious weakening of the black squares which that piece normally controls.

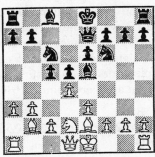

11	PxB	N-Q2
12	P-KB4	P-B4
13	P-B4	....

With an eye to forcing open the Queen file and exploiting Black's weak square, Q3. Naturally, what is Black's weakness is White's strength.

13	....	O-O
14	O-O	N-N3
15	Q-B2	PxP

Sooner or later White's QR-B1 would have compelled this move.

16	NxP	NxN	19	QR-Q1	B-Q2
17	BxN	N-Q1	20	PxP	PxP
18	P-K4	K-R1	21	R-Q6	....

Now White has the open Queen file and the long diagonal QR1-KR8, occupies the strong square Q6, and boasts a formidable passed Pawn which he threatens to push at any moment to K6 in order to increase the scope of his Queen Bishop. This combination of advantages—a centralized position coupled with complete domination of a plethora of strong squares—soon results in an overwhelming triumph.

21	....	B-B3	24	P-K6	Q-K2
22	KR-Q1	N-B2	25	QxQBP	....
23	BxN	QxB			

This simple capture is decisive. It would be a mistake to play 25 R-Q7 because of 25 . . . BxR; 26 RxB, QxP, and White cannot continue with 27 RxKNP by reason of the mating threat at K1.

25	....	QR-Q1
26	B-K5	P-QR3
27	P-QN4	....

Threatening RxR.

27	....	QR-K1	30	B-Q4	R-B3
28	R/1-Q3	K-N1	31	RxB	Resigns
29	R-KN3	P-N3			

SIMPLE SUCCESS FORMULA

Strive to tear holes in your opponent's defenses. Occupy the gaps in his line. His weak points are your strong ones. At the risk of oversimplification, one may paraphrase a famous quotation and say that winning is a matter of "gettin' thar fustest on the strongest squares."

18

Material Advantage
and Sundries

THE OBJECT of the game is to checkmate the opponent's King. But in chess, as in so many other things, the most direct approach is not always the most workable. Bearing in mind that to force mate requires at least a Rook (plus the King), we can see how a material advantage of one or two Pawns or even a minor piece is not in ordinary circumstances sufficient *per se* to win the game. The fundamental rule here is to use a relatively small material advantage as a lever with which to bring about further material gain until enough has been accumulated to effect mate. Thus, if one can effectively attack an adverse unit—a Pawn, for example—with two pieces while the opponent can muster only one piece for the defense, the Pawn will fall and one's material advantage will have been used to increase itself to that extent. Obviously this can be thought of as an accelerative process, which, if systematically pursued, will lead more and more quickly to the win.

Exchanging when one has a material advantage is usually desirable because it simplifies and clarifies the situation, thus tending to deprive the opponent of fortuitous chances that may be lurking in complications. Fewer upsets are likely when the margin of superiority is 2:1 than when it is 8:7. It should be stressed that the player who is ahead should be careful to exchange pieces rather than Pawns. Such exchanges will do more to eliminate "fishing in troubled waters." Besides, a decimation of Pawns may deprive the stronger side of queening (and therefore of winning) possibilities.

Of countless examples in master chess of turning material advantages to account, the following game is one of the most instructive by virtue of its simplicity.

Monte Carlo, 1903

PHILIDOR DEFENSE

C. SCHLECHTER		J. MASON	
White		*Black*	
1 P-K4	P-K4	6 B-K2	N-B3
2 N-KB3	P-Q3	7 O-O	B-K2
3 P-Q4	PxP	8 P-B4	NxN
4 NxP	N-KB3	9 QxN	B-B3
5 N-QB3	B-Q2	10 P-QN4	....

Somewhat unusual, but serving the dual purpose of fianchettoing the Queen Bishop while threatening a strategic advance to N5.

10	**O-O**
11 **B-N2**	**N-K1**
12 **P-N5**	**....**

Intending to play N-Q5 without permitting BxN.

12	B-Q2	18 RxP	Q-B3
13 N-Q5	P-KB4	19 Q-B4ch!	Q-B2
14 B-Q3	P-B3	20 R-K7!	QxQ
15 NPxP	NPxP	21 BxQch	P-Q4
16 NxBch	QxN	22 BxPch	PxB
17 QR-K1	PxP	23 RxB	....

Now White is a Pawn ahead and it remains to be seen how he proposes to turn this material advantage to account.

23	R-B1	27 R-Q8	K-B1
24 R-B2	R-B5	28 B-R3ch	K-B2
25 RxQP	QRxKBP	29 R-Q7ch	K-N3
26 RxR	RxR	30 RxP	R-B5

Temporarily two Pawns ahead, White must give back one of them. Which will it be—the Queen Bishop Pawn or the Queen Rook Pawn? In situations of this kind, clarifying maneuvers are often available, and this proves to be the case here.

(*See diagram on page 197.*)

| 31 R-K7! | N-B3 | 33 B-N2 | RxP |
| 32 R-K2 | R-QR5 | 34 BxN | KxP |

White has exchanged relentlessly, and has now achieved a winning position thanks to his extra Pawn and the strategic

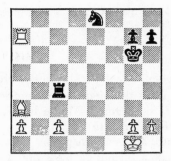

placement of his Rook in cutting off the Black King from the Queen-side. Now all he has to do is march his own King to the Queen-side to support the advance of the passed Pawn.

35	K-B2	P-R4	42	K-R5	R-QB1
36	K-K1	P-N4	43	K-N5	R-N1ch
37	K-Q2	K-B4	44	K-R6	R-QB1
38	K-Q3	R-R1	45	R-QB2!	K-K4
39	P-B4	R-Q1ch	46	K-N7	R-B4
40	K-B3	R-QB1	47	K-N6	Resigns
41	K-N4	R-N1ch			

White's Bishop Pawn marches on relentlessly to the queening square.

SUNDRIES

We have covered briefly and concisely both the common tactical motifs and the broad strategic principles that enter into a well-played middle game. More elaborate discussions are beyond the scope of this text, nor are they necessary for a good working knowledge of how to handle middle-game positions. Nevertheless, for the sake of rounding out the discussion and providing information for those who may wish to probe more deeply into the inexhaustible subject of chess theory, it may be useful to mention various topics investigated by Nimzovich and others under such headings as restriction, prophylaxis, blockade, the outpost, Pawn chains, and hanging Pawns.

Restriction and prophylaxis

Restriction, which involves a prophylactic or preventive element, simply means the hindrance or prevention of a broad Pawn advance. If, for instance, White has Pawns on Q5, K4, and KB4, poised for a push to K5, Black may be in a position to stop permanently any such thrust by stationing a Pawn on Q3, a Knight on Q2, a Bishop on KN2, and a Rook on K1.

Blockade

The blockade is a somewhat related theme. Often a passed Pawn in the middle game or ending is satisfactorily stopped by a Knight planted directly in front of it. The Knight is an excellent blockader because his mobility reaches beyond the frustrated Pawn and is in no way hampered by it.

In connection with placing Knights in good posts, it may be pointed out that a time-honored device for maintaining a Knight on a frequently occupied square, such as KB4 or QB4, is to station a watchful Pawn on KR4 or QR4. The opponent will then be unable to move immediately either of his Knight Pawns to N4 without submitting to PxP in reply, which would obviate any attempt to drive off the Knight. If P-N4 is prepared for by a preliminary P-R3, the answer in ordinary circumstances would be P-R5, after which P-N4 would permit N-N6.

The outpost

When a piece, supported by one or more Pawns, takes up a position in an open file in the heart of the opponent's terrain, it is referred to as an outpost. Its function is to exert pressure and to induce weaknesses. Assuming a boardful of men, an illustration of an outpost would be a White Knight established in an open King file at K5, protected by a Pawn at Q4. If Black has Pawns at K3 and KB2 and plays . . . P-B3 to dislodge the

Knight, the Black King Pawn has become loosened as a direct result of the outpost's nuisance value.

Pawn chains

Pawn chains comprise two interlocking series of Pawns in a diagonal pattern. An example would be White Pawns on QB3, Q4, and K5 confronted by Black Pawns on QB5, Q4, and K3. The base of White's chain is the Pawn at QB3; Black's base is the Pawn at K3. If an attempt is to be made to undermine a Pawn chain, the logical point of attack would be the base or foundation.

Hanging pawns

These are two Pawns abreast, say, at Q4 and QB4, containing elements of both strength and weakness which can be properly assessed only by examining the details of the position.

POINTS TO REMEMBER

Familiarize yourself with your tools—tactical motifs and strategic principles. At first you may need to make a conscious effort to recall them as you play. Eventually they'll become second nature.

Make consecutive and coherent plans. Don't be a grasshopper.

Play with self-confidence. It pays to be optimistic. Of course don't make the mistake of underestimating your opponent.

Relax. After all, chess is meant to be enjoyed. If you don't get a kick out of it, you should probably be doing something else.

HOW TO WIN IN THE
CHESS ENDINGS

How to Win

IN THE

CHESS ENDINGS

BY

I. A. Horowitz

With 171 diagrams

DAVID McKAY COMPANY, INC.

NEW YORK

Library of Congress Catalog Card No.: 57-11085

Contents

HOW TO WIN IN THE
CHESS ENDINGS

1

Why the End Game?

THE GAME OF CHESS is divided into three parts—the opening, the middle game, and the end game. Because the flow of ideas begins in the opening, courses through the middle game, and winds up in the end game, it may seem that the study of chess should pursue the same sequence. Curiously, and precisely, it should not.

In the beginning, to be sure, there are thirty-two units on the chessboard. It is only reasonable to assume, however, that a player who cannot manage two or three units correctly is at a complete loss when confronted with thirty-two. Hence, it is easy to see the need for learning the powers and properties of the single units in relation to each other before embracing the combined, progressive potentiality of the many.

3

The end game, moreover, contains basic positions akin to the axioms of mathematics. To know these positions is to acquire a storehouse of fundamentals which are part and parcel of nearly every game. This knowledge is really the solid groundwork of foresight, the prime requisite of planning.

Foresight in the opening, for example, is nothing more than a predisposed knowledge of the middle game, and possibly the end game. Foresight in the middle game is knowledge of the end game. Foresight is the essential attribute for favorably projecting the future.

To crystallize the thought, let us assume one of the usual variety of middle-game positions. In it we find innumerable continuations, many alternate choices. To attack, to defend, to stall, to swap: these are vexing problems. If one could foresee with certainty a favorable result by one of these actions, he would know what to do. There would be no problem.

Rarely, however, is the issue so cut and dried. Almost always there is present an element of speculation. Yet it goes without saying that a favorable result brought about with a minimum of risk is the correct procedure. And here is where knowledge of the end game is the answer. Because the end game has so few units, it is often possible to calculate its consequences without fear of contradiction—without risk. Thus the first course of action to be considered is that which leads to an end game.

Even so we need *knowledge* of the end game. It is one thing to be able to handle a winning end game when placed actually in it. It is quite another thing, starting from our middle-game position, to be able to judge if the end game will be a favorable one. Rare is the talent that can run out mentally the moves which bring about the end game and then superimpose another mental reckoning of whether or not that position is a winning one. Our essential foresight in the middle game must then include a sure knowledge of what end-game positions are winning ones.

Now that we have established the need for learning the end game, let us proceed to the task.

KING VERSUS PAWN

When a Pawn reaches the eighth rank, it is a well-known fact that it will promote to a piece of its own color, most likely a Queen. This power to expand is one of the most decisive factors of the entire game. That is why it is necessary in the end game to watch every enemy Pawn advance with surreptitious caution.

Because the general run of end games is garnished with a lot of material and because even one puny move may affect the final result, the calculations are generally deep, profound, and exacting. It is rather a tedious procedure, in any given position, to count the number of moves it requires for a Pawn to Queen in order to determine whether the Pawn can be stopped by the opposing King. It is even more tedious mentally to observe: "I go here; he goes there; I go here; he goes there, etc." The chance of error or of a miscount is too great. Considering, moreover, that the calculation usually comes at the tail end of other maneuvers not yet made but only in the imagination, the total number of moves to be observed are many—often too many for the average chess player. Under the circumstances, a short cut is desirable to avert tortuous analysis. Fortunately, for one type of position, there is such a device. There is an easy way of calculating the relationship of a King to an enemy Pawn so that you can determine with exactitude whether or not the Pawn may be stopped.

With White on the move in this position, can the Black Pawn be prevented from queening?

In order to make the calculations step by step, we observe the following moves:

1	K-B6	P-R4
2	K-Q5	P-R5
3	K-K4	P-R6
4	K-B3	P-R7
5	K-N2	....

The Pawn queens—to no avail!

The Pawn can be stopped. But we have been taxed with calculating five accurate moves. Since the diagrammed position may be part of earlier calculations still in the mind of the player, we note the player is compelled to look ahead for a number of moves, possibly beyond his ken. There is a much more simple way of doing the same thing.

Here is the very same position. Only this time we have used a device for determining whether the Pawn can be stopped. We draw a line on the diagonal of the Pawn, extending from Black's KR3 to QB8. Then we extend the line straight upward to the same rank on which the Black Pawn stands. We have described a triangle. Now we describe a second triangle from Black's KR3 to KR8 to QB8 and back to KR3. Together, these triangles form a square. If the White King can enter the square, the Pawn can be stopped.

At first sight all of this effort appears to be greater than the

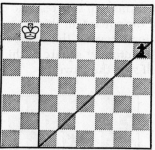

troublesome calculations above. After a while, however, the eye can be trained to envisage the square of the Pawn at a glance, and the calculations will be made in a split second.

Here Are a Few More Examples:

 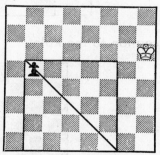

With White on the move, can the Pawn be stopped?

No. The White King is out of the square.

What is the square of the Black Pawn?

The Black Pawn forms two squares, one on its right and one on its left. Parts of the square, in this case, are actually imaginary since they extend beyond the scope of the board. If the White King can get into any square within the square of the Pawn, the King will stop the Pawn.

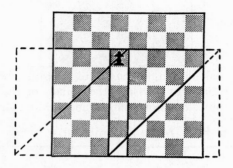

Exception to the Rule

Can the White King stop the Black Pawn?

When a Pawn is on the second rank, its advance of two squares on the first move must be taken into account. Hence, for the purposes of quick calculation, the Pawn must be considered as on the third rank. In this position, the White King cannot stop the Pawn, appearances to the contrary notwithstanding.

We may represent the "Pawn square" diagrammatically in this wise:

HOW TO STUDY THE END GAME

Rarely will an exact book position occur in a game. The positions that will occur, however, may embody the self-same principles as the book position. In order to make assurance doubly sure that you understand the principle rather than the given diagrammed position, set up your own exercises. Compose positions similar to the ones you are studying and ask yourself what difference, if any, exists between the given position and the ones you have composed. You will be surprised at the answers and your knowledge and proficiency at handling end games will increase immeasurably.

2

The Power of the King

SOME GAMES OF CHESS never leave the opening: the "brilliancy" is short and sweet. Between players of approximately equal strength, however, a game is more than likely to reach an ending. And it is in the ending that the game is won, lost, or drawn.

The story is told about two beginners, completely ignorant of the primary end-game concepts, continuing play in an end game featuring Kings—and nothing else! A master watched the absurd struggle for some time but finally gave up waiting for them to abandon it. When he returned later and asked if they had agreed to a draw, one of the beginners replied: "No—he mated me."

This incident is hardly typical of chess players, even begin-

10

ners. Yet it is surprising to learn how little some nonbeginners know about such really basic positions as even King and Pawn end games.

In King and Pawn endings, the position of the Kings is often the decisive factor. King and Pawn versus King and Pawn may be a win or a draw, depending on how far advanced the Pawns may be, on whether one or both Pawns can be stopped from queening, or on whether one King can force the other King out of the way, or in end-game terminology, "gaining the opposition," and so gobble up the enemy Pawn.

Often one King is able in a materially even position to reach and capture the opponent's Pawns, while the opposing King cannot. The "King position" is thus a simple demonstration of a "positional" advantage being converted into a "material" one.

Let us now turn to a study of the movement of the King in King and Pawn end games.

REACHING A FIXED GOAL

After you have become familiar with the short-range movements of the King, you are ready for the next steps. They include King and Pawn (or Pawns) versus King (with and without Pawns).

Consider this position.

The basic concept involved here is the movement of the King. It is important to realize that, as the King moves toward a fixed goal, it has several equally short routes. One of these will be a straight line more often than not; but other equally short routes will not be straight lines. In chess, the old adage of mathematics comes a cropper: the shortest distance between two points may *not* be a straight line. The following examples will demonstrate.

It most certainly seems that, to reach the fixed goal, KB3 (that is, to capture the Pawn on KB3—and we're assuming the Pawn is *fixed*: i.e., cannot move), White must play: *1* K-B3, *2* K-Q3, *3* K-K3, *4* KxP—four moves.

Indeed, there is no shorter—with the factors shown. But that route can be an illusion, given other factors, say, an opposing Bishop controlling the diagonal which cuts through White's QB3. In such a case, even the odd way of *1* K-B4, *2* K-Q5, *3* K-K4, and *4* KxP is effective—and still only four moves.

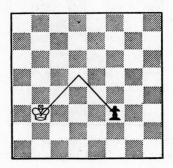

So it is important to understand that the King has many routes. Consider the zigzag one: *1 K-B2, 2 K-Q3, 3 K-K4,* and *4 KxP.*

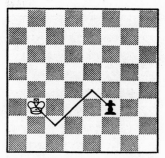

Here we refer you to the bit of advice previously given under "How to Study the End Game." Set up your own exercises for the King's approach, to be sure you understand the principle and not just the diagrammed examples. Actually, a King going from QB3 to KB3 has more than twenty different "shortest" routes! Work them out; then, for a given position, you will be intelligently able to answer the question which you must frequently ask yourself: "Which route?"

OVERTAKING A PAWN

It is seldom that the Pawn is "fixed." More often, in the end game, the Pawn is apt to be pushing resolutely on to queen —and win.

You can extend the principle of reaching a fixed goal, nonetheless, and so reapply the lesson just learned. The goal now will be the Pawn's queening square—or, if possible, some square along the route before it queens.

Having determined the square, you proceed again to study how it can be approached, and to this end the following problem becomes important. It is a wonderful example of how vital that question: Which route? can be.

The problem is a difficult one. Do not feel too bad if, as a beginner, you cannot solve it. But do try it first before reading the solution. As one important clue, consider that your King can have one of two totally different objectives.

White to Play and Draw

Stop! At this point study the position, try to determine what must be done for White to draw, and work out your solution(s) till you are sure. If you cannot succeed, then read on.

1 KxR! . . . .

Perhaps we could safely forego any comment here. And yet White's move represents a first crucial decision. Taking the Rook permits Black's Pawn to escape beyond the pale. Or, conversely, we may phrase it that the capture puts White's King hopelessly outside of the Pawn's square.

Suffice it to say, however, that the Rook must be taken: else, e.g., *1* K-R6? R-QB1, and Black has ample means for winning after *2* KxP, RxP; or even more hopeless is *1* K-R6? K-N3, and Black has made vital progress while White has resolved nothing at all.

1 . . . . **P-R4**

The dreaded Pawn advance. Still, the position is now one of King and Pawn versus King and Pawn. You can profit by reconsidering the current lesson—plus the clue mentioned.

Our clue was that White's King has two goals. One is to try to stop the Black Pawn. The other is to try to queen his own Pawn. The achievement of either goal will suffice to draw.

A brief consideration shows that neither goal can be attained by direct means. For example, the pursuit of the Pawn fails: 2 K-R7, P-R5; 3 K-R6, P-R6—and alas! the King can never re-enter the Pawn's square. And, as Black's King is within the White Pawn's square, 2 P-B7, K-N2 is equally futile.

As our clue suggests, however, we must try to use the White King to support its Pawn. On the face of it, this procedure also seems futile: 2 K-N7, P-R5; 3 K-B7, K-N3! and Black picks off the White Pawn with utmost ease, while his own Pawn will go on, unhampered, to queen.

White simply cannot draw, it seems!

The Solution(s)

Curiously enough, however, White can draw. His failure in the tries above results from his employing only the apparently shortest, the straight-line routes of approach. For the correct solutions (for White tries lead to more than one solution), you must fall back upon that vital question: *Which route?*

As White's King has two goals, the question now becomes which route will best serve both goals. By employing a route that advances the White King upon both its possible objectives in the shortest number of moves you can attain one goal or the other—and draw.

Here, then, is a striking demonstration of the value of the King's diverse routes to a given goal.

First Solution

Let us consider the correct route.

(Continue from last diagram)

2 K-N7! . . . .

By using a diagonal move, the White King advances with equal gain on each of its goals: to overtake Black's Pawn and to reach and support its own.

2 . . . . **P-R5**

Definitely Black's best try at the moment: his unstoppable Pawn hurries on to queen whereas White's queening is still out of consideration.

3 K-B6! . . . .

Again, a diagonal move, equally directed toward both goals.

3 . . . . **P-R6**

Black still presses on to queen. His alternative tries will be discussed presently.

4 K-K7! . . . .

Here, then, we see a use for the apparently senseless zigzag route described early in this lesson! The consequences now become fairly clear: White can reach and support his own Pawn, at need.

4	P-R7
5 P-B7!	P-R8(Q)
6 P-B8(Q)ch	Drawn

For with Queens on both sides only a gross blunder can lead to a win now.

Second Solution

Admittedly, White has demonstrated a draw; but was it against Black's best play? What if Black tries to stop the White Pawn from queening?

(Continue from last diagram)

2 **K-N7!**   **P-R5**
3 **K-B6!**   **K-N3**

Black moves on the White Pawn before its King can arrive to support it. The Pawn is lost, surely?

4 **K-K5!**   . . . .

Again, a diagonal move of the King is the shortest approach to its two goals!

4 . . . .   **KxP**

White's Pawn is gone, indeed; but now White's King is able to enter the square of Black's Pawn!

5 **K-B4!**   . . . .

Within the queening square White's King soon overtakes and captures the Black Pawn: 5 ... P-R6; 6 K-N3, P-R7; 7 KxP. In an actual game, the draw would be conceded now, if not sooner.

Other Solutions

These two main lines do not exhaust the possibilities. But enough has been stated to guide the way. You will do well here again to review "How to Study the End Game," as you should again and again in each end-game lesson.

For example, in the last line, note how White still draws after 4 ... P-R6; 5 K-Q6! by reverting to the goal of supporting his own Pawn on to queen: 5 ... P-R7; 6 P-B7! K-N2 [6 ... P-R8(Q); 7 P-B8(Q)ch is also a draw]; 7 K-Q7! P-R8(Q); 8 P-B8(Q)ch, Drawn.

And another interesting study is the solution with 2 K-N7, K-N3 in which Black goes after White's Pawn immediately.

Work out each possibility for yourself. The effort will repay you by instilling an instinct, as it were, for all such positions.

Principles in the Solution

Having worked out all the possibilities, your next step is to sum up the principles involved. Then try to remember the principles, rather than the moves—which may prove evanescent.

In this problem the outcome is a draw because White selects that King route which permits him to switch, at need, depending on Black's moves, from one to the other of two saving goals. Thus, in answering the question: *Which route?* the White King moves on the diagonal route: K-N7-B6 as it is quite as short an approach to Black's Pawn as is K-R7-R6 and has the added advantage of being a short approach to White's own Pawn.

The Diagonal Approach

In the question of the shortest routes to either of two goals, the King's diagonal move is most important. The beginner must realize, therefore, that the more "diagonal" the direction to a goal, the fewer shortest routes there are.

Imagining, of course, that the Pawn is "fixed," i.e., cannot

How many shortest routes are there?

move, there are only four "shortest" routes: (1) *1* K-N8, *2* K-B7, *3* K-Q6 and *4* KxP; (2) *1* K-N7, *2* K-B7, *3* K-Q6 and *4* KxP; (3) *1* K-N7, *2* K-B6, *3* K-Q6 and *4* KxP; (4) *1* K-N7, *2* K-B6, *3* K-Q5 and KxP.

In the following position there is only one shortest route, the direct diagonal: K-N7-B6-Q5-K4-B3-N2-R1 (KxR).

HOW TO STUDY THE POWER OF A KING

Put a White King and a Black Pawn on the board at random, and try to count the number of shortest routes.

When you reach a King and Pawn ending in one of your own games—*stop!* Try to visualize all the possible shortest routes. Decide whether there is any difference between these King routes and, if so, which is the most efficacious.

3

King Versus Pawns

THE MOST UNDERRATED MAN in the ending is the ubiquitous King. For a piece that reflects the climate of every move on the length and breadth of the sixty-four squares and for one with a powerful potential of its own, its appraisal is far below par. This is comprehensibly so.

In the opening and in the middle game a venturesome King is buffeted from pillar to post, and as often as not never reaches the post. In the ending, however, when most of the major pieces are gone and the risk of checkmate is therefore remote, the King can and ought to share the burdens of the ever-recurring problems. It is well, consequently, to establish the relationship of the King and other forces in terms of end-game powers.

In these terms, as an offensive and defensive unit, the King approximates the value of a Bishop or of a Knight, subject, of course, to the law that it may not be captured. While it does not exercise the long range of the Bishop or the devious hop of the Knight, the King attacks eight squares simultaneously in eight different directions. It is indeed, a weighty force, not to be discounted lightly or to be ignored in the culminating activities.

KING VERSUS THREE PAWNS

It is a curious fact, though seldom put to the test, that a King can stand off and even capture three opposing, connected Pawns under given circumstances.

In the following diagram we must assume that Black's other forces, including his King, are somehow deadlocked. In such case, White's King, opposing three Pawns, must succeed in capturing all of them.

1 . **K-N3** . . . .

This is the best move, although some others may lead to the same result.

1 . . . . **P-B4**

After *1* ... P-R4, much the same denouement results in mirror image as it were with 2 K-R4. But *1* ... P-N4 loses at once: e.g., 2 K-N4, and Black, being compelled to move, must advance either the Bishop or Rook Pawn to be taken. Thereafter, Black is again compelled to move, and all his Pawns are mopped up.

2	**K-B4**	**P-R4**
3	**K-N5**	....

Now Black's Pawns are stymied. Black must pitch a Pawn and soon relinquish the others as well.

So much for the example. It is hardly, it must be admitted, of theoretical value. For positions in which the Pawns are so utterly on their own are few and far between. In this example it is to be noted that the Pawns fail only for want of one puny *tempo*.[1]

For example, after *1* K-N3, P-B4; *2* K-B4, P-R4; *3* K-N5, if Black's King could make one move, White's would then be compelled to retreat (obviously, *4* KxNP puts White's King out of the "square" of either of the remaining Black Pawns). Then a repetition of the procedure would lead ultimately to the promotion of the Black Pawns.

Because such positions are so very rare in which one side is so tied up that it cannot contribute even a *tempo* to the sustenance of its Pawns, it is safe to draw the general conclusion: three Pawns on different files will beat an opposing King.

KING VERSUS TWO PAWNS

Again, assuming the assistance of a *tempo* at need, two Pawns generally can hold the King at bay, although they cannot progress by force to the queening square.

[1] A *tempo* is the value of one move.

1 **K-Q3**   . . . .

1 KxP is out of the question as the Queen Pawn runs on to queen.

	1	**Tempo**
	2 **K-B4**	**Tempo**

The Pawns dare not advance so long as the King holds contact with the advanced Queen Pawn. It is a standoff.

In the previous diagram the Pawns were connected, i.e., on adjacent files. Here they are separated by a file. Yet they can still maintain each other with the assistance of a *tempo* at need.

	1 **K-Q4**	**Tempo**
	2 **K-B5**	**P-K4**

The advance of the further Pawn prevents the King from capturing the nearer: 3 KxP? P-K5, and the Pawn runs on to queen.

By jockeying the Pawns properly Black can always manage to prevent their capture. Indeed, *Black* makes progress if the King tries too hard: 3 K-B4, *tempo;* 4 K-Q3, P-B4; 5 K-K4, P-B5, etc. To hold his own, White must play 3 K-B4, *tempo;* 4 K-B5: another standoff. Black can't stand 4 . . . P-K5; 5 K-Q4!

Exception to the Rule

When the Pawns are separated by a file, as we have just seen, they can sustain themselves against the King (with the assistance of a *tempo*). It goes without saying that distant Pawns, the two Rook Pawns, for example, can do even better. The King cannot chase down one without letting the other queen. So it appears at first sight that a separation of two files is even more favorable than of one. Oddly, that is an optical illusion.

1 **K-K4**   **Tempo**

On *1* . . . P-QB4; 2 K-Q5, P-B4; 3 KxP, White's King is still in the "square" of the remaining Pawn and so can return and capture it.

2 **K-B5**   **P-B4**

Now the Pawns hold as before, as 3 KxP, P-B5 leaves White's King outside the "square."

3 K-K4! . . . .

Now that the Queen Bishop Pawn has been induced to advance, the King returns, and for a purpose.

3 . . . . **Tempo**

If either Pawn moves, it can be captured safely enough.

4 K-Q5 . . . .

Harking back a lesson, here we see most definitely that a straight line is not the King's most effective route. In a circuitous course, the King has vanquished the Pawns: 4 . . . P-B4; 5 KxP or 4 . . . P-B5; 5 KxP, and the King is within the square of the remaining Pawn. It will return and capture it.

A Practical Example

Theoretical exposition, no matter how interesting, is valueless unless some practical use can be found for the subject matter. Here is the case in point anent the foregoing discussion.

At first sight Black appears to enjoy whatever advantage is in the position. For it is clear that Black has checked the advance of White's Pawns for good. But it is not clear that White has checked or can check the advance of Black's Pawns.

White, strangely, wins.

1 K-R5 . . . .

Threatening 2 KxP and staying within the square of Black's other Pawn.

1 . . . .   **P-K4**

Preventing the capture of the Rook Pawn. If now 2 . . . KxP, White is outside of the square of Black's King Pawn. White's feint at the Rook Pawn seems to be in vain. Is it?

2 **K-N4**   . . . .

After having provoked the advance of the King Pawn, the King returns.

2 . . . .   **K-N4**

Black cannot advance either Pawn without losing both.

3 **K-B5**   . . . .

In any case, White wins both Pawns. The continuation might be 3 . . . P-R4; 4 KxP, P-R5; 5 K-B4, and White picks off the remaining Pawn.

Exception to the Contrary

In most cases, with two passed Pawns on one side, counter-balanced by two on the other side, with each King within the square of the adverse Pawns, the game is drawn. This is so regardless of whether the Pawns are connected or separated by a file. The one marked exception is the position below. The point is: how far advanced can the Pawns be?

White loses as he cannot check the advance of the Black Pawns. As soon as it is his move, he must give ground. The King cannot hold separated Pawns which have already advanced so far as the sixth rank.

PAWNS VERSUS PAWNS

The most decisive factor in Pawn endings is the ability to establish a passed Pawn, that is, a Pawn unimpeded in its advance by an adverse Pawn. Where the Pawn position is unbalanced, that is where opposite colored Pawns are on different files, the positions abound with opportunities for creating passed Pawns. Where, however, the position is balanced, it is next to impossible to effect a passed Pawn.

Here is the classic exception to the rule.

With Black to move, the Pawns can restrain each other after *1* ... P-N3. But it is White's move.

1 P-N6! . . . .

This sacrifice effects a breach in the opposing Pawn array.

1 . . . . **RPxP**

If *1* ... BPxP, Black fares no better. *2* P-R6, PxP; *3* P-B6, and presumably the Bishop Pawn goes on to queen.

2	**P-B6**	**PxBP**
3	**P-R6**	. . . .

The Pawn is passed.

WHY STUDY THE END GAME?

It is an axiom that one bad move nullifies forty good ones. As this applies only to the end game—after forty moves have been made—Q. E. D.

4

Know your endings! *Here it is White to play and win, not draw. Try to work out the win, first, then read text on "King and Two Pawns." Grow to know such endings as by instinct.*

King Versus King and Pawns

THE POWERS and proclivities of King and Pawns are strong and varied. We have already observed a few cases of their foibles. In the realm of chess, the oddities and curiosities relating to King and Pawn are many. They are, however, beyond the scope of this work, although by no means so for the scholar who aims for proficiency.

We expect to cover all the fundamental, elementary tasks and principles relating to the end game in the order of ease of assimilation. That is why we have begun with Kings and Pawns.

In this connection we begin with the proposition that King and two Pawns (or more) almost always will beat a lone King. The winning procedure is so simple that it requires but little explanation.

The object is to promote one of the Pawns to a Queen whereafter King and Queen can mate the lone King with consummate ease.

Hence, the Pawns must be advanced until one of them reaches the eighth rank, without being subject to capture. It does not matter, with two Pawns, if their King is not in the vicinity. The Pawns are self-sustaining (as was shown earlier), and there is always adequate time to maneuver the King to the required area. The first step is to bring the King to the support of the Pawns. Then the defense is helpless to deter their victorious march. Slight caution must be observed to avoid stalemate.

KING AND TWO PAWNS

The position pictured on page 29 illustrates the technique for promoting a Pawn, and the single hazard in it.

1	K-Q5	....

The King approaches to support its Pawns.

1	....	K-R1
2	K-B5	....

Trap. 2 K-B6 is stalemate.

2	....	K-N2

White's sole problem is how to approach without creating stalemate.

3	P-R8ch!	KxQ
4	K-B6	K-N1
5	P-N7	Resigns

After 5 ... K-R2; 6 K-B7, there is no stopping the Pawn from queening.

KING AND ONE PAWN

In the studies of King and Pawn versus King, the principle of the opposition plays a major role. It is important to understand it thoroughly.

Vertical Opposition

Horizontal Opposition

Diagonal Oppositions

Distant Horizontal Opposition

The Principle of the Opposition

One situation that occurs very frequently in the end game is that of the Kings being directly opposed. They may be opposed in various ways, as shown in the preceding diagrams:

Three are all forms of simple opposition, with merely one square between the two Kings. If many squares separate the

Kings, they are said to be in distant opposition, as in the last diagram.

The critical point in any case of opposition is that that side which must move must give ground. Thus, in the diagram on vertical opposition above, if it is White's move, the King must either retreat to the first rank and so permit Black's King to penetrate to its sixth rank, or the White King must sidestep to the Rook or Bishop file and so allow Black's King to make headway on the Bishop or the Rook file respectively: e.g., *1* K-R2, K-B6 or *1* K-B2, K-R6. And therewith Black advances from the fifth to the sixth rank.

Or, in horizontal opposition, White to move, Black similarly can bull his way from the King file to the Queen file: *1* K-B5, K-Q6 or *1* K-B3, K-Q4.

So it is with all cases of opposition. The diagonal and the distant can be translated with due procedure into the simple vertical or the simple horizontal forms. In short, the side that must move must give ground; and, conversely, the side that has just taken the opposition is said "to have the opposition." Thus, taking the opposition is to secure an advantage and is often the surest and, in fact, the only way to make progress in the end game.

One Example

The importance of the opposition is well illustrated in the following position.

White to Move and Draw

Here we have conflicting aims. White is a Pawn behind; hence he strives for the draw. Black is a Pawn ahead; and he naturally tries to convert the Pawn to a Queen and victory. With Black's King behind the Pawn and the White King in front, the correct play leads in nearly all cases to a draw. Here is the procedure.

1 K-K3 . . . .

This move is not the only drawing move. *1* K-Q3 or *1* K-B3 will also draw, with the correct follow-up. But this is the best move, for it enables White to take the opposition no matter where Black's King advances.

1 . . . . **K-B4**

To make progress, Black must play either *1* . . . K-B4 or *1* . . . K-Q4. If he temporizes with *1* . . . K-Q3 or *1* . . . K-B3, White returns (*2* K-K4), and Black has not enhanced his chances.

2 K-B3 . . . .

White takes the opposition and prevents the Black King from making further headway. It is to be noted in passing that any other move loses for White. The exact winning method on another move will be discussed later on.

If Black plays *1* . . . K-Q4, White now plays *2* K-Q3, and the mirror image of the text occurs. The basic program remains the same.

2 . . . . **P-K5ch**

Again, this is Black's only means of making progress. A retreating King move permits White to return (*3* K-K4).

3 K-K3 . . . .

Here, too, this is not the only drawing move. Since it restricts Black's King, however, it is the best move.

3 . . . . **K-K4**

There is no way to prevent Black from advancing. Fortunately, however, there is a way to prevent him from winning.

| 4 K-K2 | .... |

Again, the best move, but not the only one. The idea is the same as before. White is in position to take the opposition no matter which way Black's King advances.

| 4 .... | K-Q5 |

This time Black tries his luck on the Queen file. But it is of no avail against the correct defense.

| 5 K-Q2 | .... |

Taking the opposition. Black cannot progress without advancing his Pawn.

| 5 .... | P-K6ch |
| 6 K-K2 | .... |

Here White's move is important as a misstep might be fatal. It is best to restrict the movement of Black's King.

| 6 .... | K-K5 |

Now again it is White's turn, and this time he must make the one and only correct move. Any other loses.

| 7 K-K1! | .... |

So that White can take the opposition no matter where the Black King advances.

7	K-B6
8 K-B1!	P-K7ch
9 K-K1	K-K6
Stalemate!	

It is interesting to see what would happen if White made an incorrect seventh move. Instead of playing 7 K-K1, let us suppose he played 7 K-B1. Now White loses: 8 ... K-B6; 9 K-K1, P-K7 and, unfortunately, it is White's move. He must abandon the queening square by playing 10 K-Q2 and Black decides by 10 ... K-B7, followed by Pawn, queens.

Thus, it can be seen that the ending is no place to make even a slight slip of the finger. The difference between one square and the next may be the difference between a draw and a loss.

LEARN THOROUGHLY

It is not sufficient of itself to learn the drawing method we have just discussed. The type of position and the procedure ought to be so impressed in the mind of the learner that it is second nature. Only a fraction of a second at most should be required to determine the result. In this way all the profound calculation is circumvented, and a player is able to calculate a result with ease, even though he is far removed from the final denouement.

5

Know your endings! *Here, with an obvious advantage in space, White's King looks a sure bet to win the Black Pawn and promote its own. But see page 42!*

More on Kings and Pawns

BASIC CHESS endings are many. Roughly, they number about six or seven hundred. Because a goodly number of these are more or less on the elementary side, they ought to be mastered by a reasonable degree of application. Yet such is not necessarily the case.

For every principle in chess and for every method there are numerous exceptions. Unfortunately, it is the exceptions rather than the general principles that rule. Sure knowledge of the exceptions is the line of demarcation between the chess player and the would-be chess player.

In the following general rule exceptions abound. Yet it is a good starting point for determining the result in King versus King and Pawn endings. *The King in front of its Pawn defeats a lone King.*

THE GENERAL RULE

The main idea is: the King in front of its Pawn promotes its advance.

White to Move and Win

White's goal here is to advance his Pawn to the eighth rank and promote it to a Queen. The method employed is straightforward and simple. The King clears the path and drives the opposing King from the queening square.

1 **K-Q5** . . . .

White takes the opposition. Black must give ground.

1 . . . . **K-K2**

1 . . . K-B2 is no better. Then White progresses with 2 K-Q6, pursuing the mirror image of the following text.

2 **K-B6** . . . .

Here is a major point within the main principle. When the King reaches the sixth rank, ahead of its Pawn, the Pawn will queen by force. It is important to remember this point to be able to foretell such winning positions from innumerable examples in earlier end-game and even middle-game setups.

2 . . . .   K-Q1

Whatever Black does, he is lost: e.g., 2 ... K-K3; 3 P-Q4, K-K2; 4 P-Q5, K-Q1; 5 K-Q6, and White wins presently as in the text.

3 K-Q6   . . . .

Here is the key square for the King, for the King can move later to either the King file or the Bishop file.

3 . . . .   K-B1

After 3 ... K-K1, White continues as in the text.

4 P-Q4   . . . .

White need make no calculations. With his King on the sixth rank, in the key square in front of his Pawn, all White need do is push. Push the Pawn as far as it will go.

4 . . . .   K-Q1
5 P-Q5   K-B1
6 K-K7   . . . .

White queens by marching 7 P-Q6, 8 P-Q7, and 9 P-Q8(Q).

ANOTHER APPLICATION

It is to be noted that, once White's King occupies the key square, Q6, it does not matter who is to move. White will win. In the previous line, Black was to move. Now assume White moves.

White to Move and Win

   1 **K-B6**   . . . .

Or *1* K-K6 pursuing a mirror image sequel.

   1 . . . .   **K-B1**

On *1* . . . K-K2, White immediately assumes control of the queening route and queening square with 2 K-B7.

2 **P-Q6**	**K-Q1**
3 **P-Q7**	**K-K2**
4 **K-B7**	. . . .

The Pawn queens.

FIRST EXCEPTION

In the following position Black's King is in front of its Pawn; and, according to the general rule, Black ought to win. With correct play here, however, White draws.

White to Move and Draw

1 K-K3   . . . .

White takes the opposition, and Black can make no headway. Skipping mirror image lines, the text illustrates the general procedure.

1 . . . .   **K-B4**
2 K-B3   . . . .

By taking the opposition, White restrains Black from any progress. Now, if Black's King shuttles to and fro, White continues, holding the opposition: *2* ... K-K4; *3* K-K3, K-Q4; *4* K-Q3, etc.

3 . . . .   **P-K4**

Now Black's King is no longer in front of the Pawn.

4 K-K3   **Drawn**

THE RULE MODIFIED

From the foregoing we can adduce what amounts to a primary modification of the general rule: besides being in front of its Pawn, the King may need a free square between it and the Pawn. The modification applies when the adversary may otherwise secure the opposition.

White to Move, Black to Win

Between this position and the previous one there is but one slight difference: the position of the Black Pawn.

It is the slight difference, however, that makes all the difference in the result. Now Black wins!

1 K-K3   P-K3!

The Pawn advance places the onus of moving on White. With this extra *tempo*, Black secures the opposition, White must give ground, and Black goes on to win in the manner just discussed.

THEORY AND PRACTICE

Judging from what we have learned, the following position seems to be a win for White.

Black to Move and Draw

True, both sides have a Pawn; but, clearly, White's King will approach and pick off the Black Pawn. Then the King will remain in front of its Pawn, and White will win.

All is not what it seems, however. It is Black's move, and he has a resource also based on what we have just learned. By a deft stroke he can draw.

(As a secondary lesson, bear in mind that, although end-game combinations are comparatively rare, they do exist!)

1 . . . .   P-Q6!

Since the Pawn must fall anyway, it offers itself immediately and so turns the table. White must now either capture the Pawn, by-pass it, or retreat his King. The other options are worse; so he captures.

2 PxP   K-B3!
3 K-K4   . . . .

Or 3 P-Q4, K-K3, and White's King is no longer in front of the Pawn. Then Black draws as already demonstrated.

3 . . . .   K-K3

Now Black maintains the opposition and draws.

SECOND EXCEPTION

In almost all phases of the end game the proverbial exception crops up when there is a Rook Pawn on the board. It constitutes here another exception to our general rule.

When the King is in front of the Rook Pawn, the result is not a win if the opposing King can reach its R1.

1 K-N1   **Draw**

White's King shuttles back and forth between R1 and N1, and Black can do nothing to disturb these movements. Eventually, when the Black Pawn reaches the seventh rank, protected by the Black King, White will be stalemated (unless, of course, Black abandons his Pawn).

Try it!

AGAIN THE ROOK PAWN!

That pesky Rook Pawn figures yet another way in King versus King and Pawn endings. Here Black's King is in front of its Pawn, nor can White easily get his King to R1. In fact, it looks like clear sailing for Black.

White to Move and Draw

It would be, indeed, if it were Black to move. But it is White's move.

1 K-B5!   . . . .

White not only heads for R1, the ultimate drawing goal, but also boxes in Black's King. (Look always for such dual-purpose moves in endings!)

1 . . . .   K-R5

1 . . . K-R3 is futile: White makes for R1. Nor does 1 . . . P-R3 change matters: White heads for R1 with 2 K-B4, and a draw results in similar fashion to the following text.

2 K-B4   P-R4

After 2 . . . K-R6, White has options: 3 K-N5, and he picks off the Pawn or 3 K-B3, continuing the policy of maintaining the opposition and boxing in Black's King. Either line draws.

3 K-B3   K-R6
4 K-B2   . . . .

White still heads for N1 and R1.

| 4 .... | K-R7 |
| 5 K-B1 | P-R5 |

If Black at any time abandons control of White's KN1, White secures his draw with K-N1. But, it seems, Black can progress comfortably enough with his Pawn.

| 6 K-B2 | P-R6 |
| 7 K-B1 | K-R8 |

Black cannot allow 8 K-N1; but he ˉ ın make way for his Pawn.

| 8 K-B2 | P-R7 |
| 9 K-B1 | Stalemate! |

Even though a Pawn ahead, Black is stalemated!

ULTERIOR GOAL

When studying the endings, the learner cannot help but chafe over one goose egg after another harvested from mistakes in opening or middle game. It is difficult to see how improved end-game technique can remedy those errors.

To those who suffer from such sense of futility the only advice is: "Be patient." Perfect end-game technique will not only win end games. Eventually it cannot help but osmose to the other departments.

6

Know your endings! *Here it is White to play and win, not draw. Try to work out the win first, then read text on "Queening with Check." Do likewise, for that matter, with each diagrammed position, and the lesson will "take" more effectively.*

Hold That Pawn!

T HE CHEAPNESS of the Pawn is proverbial. Annals of all time are punctuated with such statements as "But lower Slobonia was sacrificed as a mere Pawn in the current game of politics." Masters of the chessboard, on the other hand, speak differently. One of the earliest great authorities, Philidor, declared that Pawn play is "the soul of chess." And Paul Keres told a member of the United States team only last summer: "The older I grow, the more I value Pawns."

Probably neither spoke solely in respect to the end game. But we must dwell upon play, both with and against the Pawn, in the end game. For here it is that the greatest power of the Pawn comes cogently into effect. In two senses you must hold that Pawn! You must preserve your Pawn to have winning chances, or block an opposing Pawn to avoid losing.

PAWN VERSUS PAWN

All other things being equal, Pawn versus Pawn results in a draw. The likelihood of complete balance, however, between the Kings and other factors is too remote. That is why it is essential to comprehend and appraise all routine and even apparently extraneous factors.

Who Queens First?

Who queens first is probably the most important factor. The race is generally decided on this proposition. When Pawns queen simultaneously, that is, one queens immediately after the other, the usual result is a draw. For Queen versus Queen with lone Kings on the board is a no-decision contest.

When one Pawn reaches the eighth rank and promotes to a Queen and the opposing Pawn reaches only the seventh rank, the Queen ought to win. Here is an example of the technique:

White to Move and Win

White's problem in this position is to prevent the Black Pawn from queening with immunity. To do so, White requires the assistance of his King, for a lone Queen cannot drive the enemy King from the defense of its Pawn.

White's goal, of course, is to capture the Black Pawn.

In the text position White dare not approach with his King, for Black will queen, and the game will end in a draw. So the first step is to reach a position in which the White King can approach the Pawn safely. To do so, White must immobilize the Pawn.

There are various ways of accomplishing this objective. The quickest, however, is to bring the Queen in close contact with the enemy King.

1 Q-Q2   . . . .

Any move giving check and approaching the Pawn is good enough. The shortest route, however, begins with the text move, which exercises a pin on the Pawn.

1 . . . .   **K-B8**

This reply is forced. On any other move, White stations his Queen in front of the Pawn by playing Q-K1, approaches the Pawn with the King, and then picks it off.

2 Q-B4ch   **K-N7**

Black, on the other hand, keeps open the threat of queening the Pawn. 2 . . . K-K8 is a move which Black will make only under compulsion, for that move allows the White King to move.

3 Q-K3   . . . .

White attacks and threatens to pick off the Black Pawn. Note that White is utilizing various motifs to achieve his objective —the pin, the check, and the direct attack. Any one of these tactical weapons of itself would be insufficient for White's purpose.

3 ....   **K-B8**

Forced, to defend the Pawn.

4 Q-B3ch   K-K8

At last Black's King is shunted to blockade the Pawn.

5 K-B3   ....

At long last White's King is able to approach.

5 ....   **K-Q1**

Forced.

6 K-Q3   ....

Because Black's Pawn is pinned, White is again able to move in with his King. Now, whatever Black does, the Pawn falls.

6 ....   **K-B8**

If 6 ... K-K8, 7 QxP mate.

7 QxP   ....

Because the White King in the text position was on QN4, in the vicinity of the Black Pawn, the winning procedure was comparatively short. Had the White King started, say on QR8 or KR8 or on any square a long way from the Black Pawn, the procedure would be longer. But the method would be the same: (1) Force the Black King in front of its Pawn by the pin, check or direct attack. (2) Approach the Pawn with the White King, whenever the Pawn cannot move. (3) Pick off the Pawn.

In this connection it is worthy of note that a Queen will win with consummate ease against a Pawn which has not reached the seventh rank, except, of course, if the Queen is subject to immediate capture.

Queening with Check

Another factor that often upsets the simple calculations of a Pawn ending is that one side queens with check. The check, which must be respected, acts as a brake in the routine procedure of the adversary. Here is a case in point.

White to Move and Win

There is more to this ending than meets the eye. Appearances favor a draw, but such is not the case. White has a way of jockeying the Black King into an unfavorable post which will cost him a move. And that move will be enough to decide for White.

1 K-Q4! ....

Clearly, if White advances *1* P-R6, Black follows suit with *1* ... P-B6, and both Pawns queen with a resulting draw. White's King move does not appear to affect the issue. But it does.

1 .... K-N5

If instead, *1* ... P-B6; *2* K-K3, White's King reaches B2, blockades the Pawn and then White queens his own Pawn.

2 P-R6 P-B6

Black has little choice. He cannot afford to lose time by moving his King.

3 K-K3 K-N6

Forced.

| 4 P-R7 | P-B7 |
| 5 K-K2! | K-N7 |

Forced. Now we see the point of White's King moves. He has maneuvered the Black King onto an unfortunate square.

| 6 P-R8(Q)ch | . . . . |

Check. Black's Pawn remains on the seventh and soon falls by the wayside.

Tail-end Combination

Another factor to be considered in the Pawn race for Queens is a tail-end combination. Often, after both sides have queened, a nasty check by one of the Queens results in the gain of the other. The decisive check may be administered on the diagonal, file, or rank, depending upon the position. Here the setting is in proper alignment for just such a conclusion.

Whoever Moves First Wins

If Black moves first, he wins as follows:

1	P-R4
2 P-R4	P-R5
3 P-R5	P-R6
4 P-R6	P-R7
5 P-R7	P-R8(Q)
6 P-R8(Q)	K-B7dis.ch

Black's last move, discovering check, brings about the tactical motif known as the X-ray. White's King must move, after which Black picks off White's Queen.

With White to move, the win is considerably more difficult, requires an exceptional knowledge of technique. But the win is there.

1	P-R4	P-R4
2	P-R5	P-R5
3	P-R6	P-R6
4	P-R7	P-R7
5	P-R8(Q)	....

If Black now queens, White moves his King and discovers check, and Black's Queen goes by the wayside. Hence, Black tries to avert the discovery and hopes to promote his Pawn later.

5	....	K-B7

We now reach a tough position, somewhat ahead of schedule. In most respects it is similar to Queen versus Pawn on the seventh, already discussed. But there are some salient differences. Black's Pawn is a Rook Pawn, and this factor gives Black somewhat more leeway in the defense.

6	K-Q4	....

White's King approaches the Pawn and readies for Q-KR1, blockading the Pawn.

6	....	K-N8

Preventing the blockade.

7	Q-N8ch	....

Beginning a methodical approach to the Black King and Pawn.

7	....	K-R8

In the previous Queen versus Pawn on the seventh position, the King dared not move in front of its Pawn. Because Black has a Rook Pawn, however, White's King, as yet, dare not approach, for the result would be stalemate. Still, White has other means.

8	Q-Q5ch	K-N8
9	Q-N5ch	K-R8
10	Q-B4	K-N7
11	Q-N4ch	K-R8
12	Q-B3ch	K-N8
13	K-K3!	. . . .

The star move. Curiously, White could not prevent Black from queening.

13	. . . .	P-R8(Q)
14	Q-B2 mate	

Even more curious is it that Black could offer more resistance by underpromoting with 13 ... P-R8(N). Queen versus Knight, however, offers no serious problem for the Queen. Here the game is resolved by 14 K-K2, K-R7; 15 Q-N4, N-N6; 16 K-B3, and Black must relinquish his Knight and be mated.

7

Know your endings! *Here it is White to play and win. Try to work out the win first, then consult the text on the last example in this chapter.*

Two for One

THE REAL POWER of the puny Pawn is so great that the advantage of a single Pawn—all other things being equal—is usually sufficient favorably to determine the outcome of the most cluttered-up position. Barring blunders, an opening Pawn plus can be nursed through the middle game and turned into a potent, usually decisive factor in the ending.

It is in the last department particularly that expert treatment is required to avoid the snares, pitfalls, and swindles implicit in the position. It is at this time that the right procedure, even the right move, means so much, for one thoughtless move will nullify all the preceding laborious efforts.

The following examples will serve to indicate types of methods that can come up again and again. They are well worth knowing thoroughly.

THE LEAD PIPE CINCH

When two united Pawns, as in the following position, are pitted against a lone Pawn blockaded by the opposing King, the result is a foregone conclusion. The two Pawns will win with consummate ease.

White to Move and Win

The method is to advance the Pawns in a way in which they support each other, threaten in due time to queen, and draw the adverse King into their orbit. As the last action causes the King to relinquish its guard over the single Pawn, that Pawn is then picked off. In turn, the other King is freed to join in the queening operation, and the rest is what is described as "a matter of technique."

A DELUSORY PERIL

Even when the two united passed Pawns are apparently stopped dead in their tracks, as in this position, and the White

King is out of the "square" of Black's passed Pawn, all is not lost.

White to Move and Win

Even a couple of Pawns and a King can effect a mating net to win or at least to gain time by a well-directed jostle.

1 K-N6   . . . .

It is clear that an attempt to reach the Black Pawn is futile. K-B4 is met by . . . P-N6-7-8(Q).

1 . . . .   P-N6

The Pawn cannot be stopped. White must act fast.

2 P-B7!   . . . .

This is not the only winning move. 2 P-Q7ch ought to win, too. But this is the prettiest.

2 . . . .   P-N7

What else? 2 . . . K-Q2; 3 K-N7, and White queens *with check*.

3 K-B6!   P-N8(Q)
4 P-Q7 mate   . . . .

The foregoing position illustrates one of the rarer occasions with simplified Pawn endings in which strategy rather than tactics is the dominating force.

AN ESSENTIAL DIFFERENCE

Here it is to be observed that, if neither of the King Knight Pawns were on the board, the game would be a draw. But they are on the board, and this factor makes the difference.

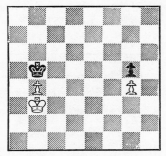

White to Move and Win

A Pawn plus is usually a win in the ending, and the additional Pawns, even though well balanced, add to the winning chances. Hence the rule: when swapping down for a winning ending, exchange off pieces but not Pawns so far as possible.

Here it is two versus one, but the two White Pawns are separated. The general idea then is to draw the adverse King away from the support of its own Pawn. After that, the single Pawn is "easy pickin's," and the resultant position is a simple win.

1 K-B3	K-N3

Black has little choice.

2 K-Q4	. . . .

White dashes for the other Pawn, while Black's King must keep the Queen Knight Pawn under close observation.

2	K-N4
3 K-K5	KxP
4 K-B5	K-B4
5 KxP	. . . .

Black is miles out of bounds. So he resigns.

YET ANOTHER DIFFERENCE

Here is the very same position, with one notable difference. The opposing Pawns are on the Rook file, instead of the Knight file. Note we have mentioned that the Rook file is almost always an exceptional case. It changes the complexion of things completely here. The best White can do, with correct play, is to draw.

White to Move, Black to Draw

1	**K-B3**	**K-N3**
2	**K-Q4**	. . . .

Curiously, 2 K-B4, followed by 3 P-N5 or 3 K-Q4, gains no time.

2	. . . .	**K-N4**
3	**K-K5**	**KxP**
4	**K-B5**	**K-B4**

Black heads immediately in the general direction of his KR1. If he reaches KB1 in time, he can hold the game.

5	**K-N5**	**K-Q3**
6	**KxP**	**K-K2**
7	**K-N6**	**K-B1**
	Drawn	

There is nought to be done. On 8 K-R7, K-B2 draws as we have previously demonstrated; and, otherwise, Black reaches his KR1 and draws.

It is to be noted, however, that, if the position had been modified by placing Black's Rook Pawn on R3, and White's on R5, White would win. Black's King could not then reach any of the key squares in time.

By the same token, with Black's Pawn at R3 and White's at R4, White's only winning move would be *1* P-R5. If it were Black's move, his only drawing move would be *1* ... P-R4.

To determine the odds of any of these positions coming up exactly in a game would require the calculations of a Univac. Hence this study is meant to suggest a course of action for any similar position. It is not a static expedient just for the ones explained.

A BLACK DILEMMA

When two united passed Pawns advance upon an opposing Pawn and King, the result also is usually a win. The technique, however, must be flawless. Here is a classic example.

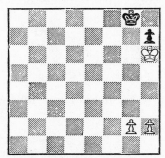

White to Move and Win

Clearly in this position there is no way of driving Black's King from the support of its Pawn. Hence, the winning plan must be to promote one of White's Pawns. The first step is to advance one of them to the fifth rank. It does not matter which Pawn.

1 P-R4   K-R1

Here is Black's dilemma. At a given move it will matter vastly whether his King is on R1 or N1. Actually, his moment of dilemma is past, as White can now force the creation of the correct position. And, in syllogistic terms, it would have been a true dilemma; for if Black had foreseen and chosen to have his King at R1 at the start, likewise White could still bring about the desired position by force, or rather timing.

| 2 P-R5 | K-N1 |

Now comes time for accurate timing. The right move will win; the wrong one will draw. The point is that White must eventually play P-N6 and exchange off Pawns. When he does so, he must be sure that Black's King is at R1, not N1. Here White has the choice of moving the Knight Pawn one or two squares. Which is correct?

| 3 P-N3! | . . . . |

The only winning move. (Try the position, also, with Black's King at R1, and work out the results both with 3 P-N3 and 3 P-N4.)

3	K-R1
4 P-N4	K-N1
5 P-N5	K-R1
6 P-N6	PxP

Nor does 6 ... K-N1 help. There follows: 7 P-N7, K-B2 8 KxP, etc.

| 7 PxP | . . . . |

Now White has canceled the drawing outcome of a lone Rook Pawn. 7 KxP leads only to that draw.

7	K-N1
8 P-N7	K-B2
9 K-R7	Resigns

Here we see the final result of the correct 3 P-N3! With 3 P-N4, the subsequent play would have offered Black the chance of 7 ... K-R1; 8 P-N7ch, K-N1; 9 K-N6, stalemate!

A FINAL FINESSE

Here is another example of two for one, with White's Pawns united. Unless White is able to utilize the theoretical information which he has gleaned from our studies, he can fiddle away his win.

White to Move and Win

The first move is the star move!

	1 P-Q6ch!!	PxPch

Black can do no better. If he moves his King, White cleans up with 2 P-Q7(ch), walks his King to KB7, with appropriate timing, and garners Black's Pawn for an easy win.

	2 K-Q5!	K-B1!!

Trap.

	3 K-B6!!	....

Not 3 KxP which draws, after 3 ... K-Q1. Now the threat is 4 P-K7.

	3	K-Q1
	4 KxP	....

Now White has won the Pawn while taking the opposition, and the latter makes all the difference.

	4	K-K1
	5 P-K7	Resigns

8

Can White win? Work on this position for yourself first, then see page 71.

Pawn Plusses and Minuses

A MATTER of technique" is the phrase which, curiously enough, is applied to the hopelessly lost ending that requires no technique at all. Simple, direct, routine play, devoid of subtlety and finesse and brooking no opposition, is what this phrase depicts. To be sure, many Pawn endings culminate in such a manner.

Many Pawn endings, on the contrary, are full of tricks and traps and sagacious strategy. Sometimes their general contour is a carry-over from the middle game, when the strategic conception of the ending is already mapped out. Sometimes the strategic motif is introduced in the finale. In all cases, however, certain clear, identifiable characteristics predominate. And they direct the ensuing play.

THE PASSED PAWN

A Pawn unimpeded in its advance by an opposing Pawn is a significant characteristic. It is a dangerous Pawn, for it threatens to queen. Hence, it bears constant surveillance by the opposing King in King and Pawn endings. Thus it diverts the attention of the King from sundry other affairs. A passed Pawn, as a rule, is a strategic plus.

When such a Pawn is protected or capable of being protected by another Pawn, it is technically called a protected, passed Pawn. It carries a lot of weight.

Here is a position with such a Pawn. Units, it will be observed, are even. Black has a passed Pawn; White a protected, passed Pawn. The weight is by far in favor of the protected Pawn.

White to Move and Win

The first idea is direct. White heads in the direction and square of Black's passed Pawn. And Black is helpless to defend.

1 **K-B3**   **P-N5**

If Black temporizes with his King, say by *1 . . .* K-Q4, White keeps on approaching the passed Pawn, until he is in direct contact with it. At no time is the Black King able to defend the Pawn without stepping out of the "square" of White's passed Pawn.

2 **K-Q3** **P-N6**
3 **K-K3** **P-N7**
4 **K-B2** . . . .

Now White picks off the Pawn and returns to the other side to win. While the win is comparatively easy, there are still some obstacles which must be hurdled. (See following diagram.)

White to Move and Win

1 **K-Q5** **K-B2!**

There is a bit of jockeying here in order for Black to put up the strongest resistance. He strives for *2* K-B5, K-N2; *3* P-N6?, K-R3; *4* K-B6, stalemate. *2 . . .* K-N2 will not do on account of *3* K-B5, K-B2; *4* P-N6ch, K-N2; *5* K-N5, after which Black's Rook Pawn falls by the wayside.

White's goal is to queen his Knight Pawn or (first) pick off Black's Rook Pawn.

2 **K-K6!** . . . .

White must drive Black from QN3. *2* K-B5, K-N2; *3* K-Q6 fails versus *3 . . .* K-N3, maintaining the opposition: *4* K-Q7,

K-N2; 5 K-Q8, K-N1. After the text move, White gains the
opposition.

    2 ....   **K-N2**

    3 **K-Q7**   ....

White has the opposition. Observe the difference.

    3 ....   **K-N3**

If *3* ... K-N1; *4* K-B6, K-R2; *5* K-B7, K-R1; *6* K-N6, Black's
Pawn falls.

    4 **K-B8!**   ....

Thus White circumvented the Black King and drives it from
the critical field.

    4 ....   **K-R2**

If *4* ... K-B4; *5* K-B7, White's Pawn marches on.

    5 **K-B7**   **K-R1**

    6 **K-N6**   ....

The rest is "technique."

This simple ending illustrates any number of points. To
begin with, it clearly exemplifies the power of the passed
Pawn. Here both passed Pawns—White's and Black's—command attention. Only because the White King can reach the
square of Black's isolated passed Pawn is the Pawn easy prey.

Because White's passed Pawn is protected and cannot be
captured, it is both a latent and a potent threat. Yet, still there
is Black's last hope, the stalemate trap to be surmounted.

THE OUTSIDE PASSED PAWN

A passed Pawn, as we have seen, demands constant surveillance by the enemy. An outside passed Pawn, or an outside
Pawn, as it is sometimes called, is one which is even more
dangerous than the usual passed Pawn. It is a Pawn outside
of the squares of critical hostilities. Since it threatens to queen,
it draws the opposing King away from any all-important sector
and leaves that sector vulnerable to enemy penetration.

Here is a position with an outside passed Pawn in the making.

Black to Move and Win

A cursory glance will grant White the advantage, for he is about to win a Pawn. A second glance will give Black the advantage, for he can establish an outside Pawn. A third glance will only reveal the problems.

1 .... **K-Q4**

It seems that Black ought to make a dash to queen by establishing an outside Pawn with *1* ... P-R4. For after *2* PxP, PxP, White's King cannot prevent Black from queening; whereas Black's King can prevent White from queening. This action, nonetheless, is superficial, illusory, and ill-advised, for after *1* ... P-R4, Black does not win; he loses! White turns the tables with *2* P-B5, and it is he who establishes an outside Pawn: *2* ... NPxP; *3* PxRP. Hence, Black must exercise caution.

2 **KxP** ....

On other moves Black wins with either *2* ... P-R4 or *2* ... K-K5, depending upon White's play.

2 .... **P-R4**

The purpose of Black's King move becomes clearer.

3 **P-B5** ....

On other moves, Black's Rook Pawn gets there first. And Black wins easily.

3 . . . .   **P-R5**

3 . . . PxNP will also do. The point is that Black's King can now take care of White's Bishop Pawn.

Thus we see how an ill-timed advance may convert a potential outside Pawn to an inside Pawn.

In the following position, White's Queen Rook Pawn is an outside passed Pawn. It cannot queen by force by advancing, for Black's King is within its square. But its threat to queen is sufficient to demand the attention of the Black King, which, in turn, leaves the Black Pawns as booty.

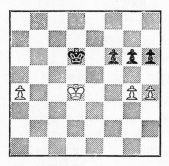

1 **P-KR5**   . . . .

This move effects a breach in Black's left wing.

1 . . . .   **PxP**

Black has little choice. He must either capture, as in the text, advance his Pawn to N4, or counter with 1 . . . P-B4. The counter is easily disposed of by 2 RPxP, K-K3; 3 PxP, after which Black's position is hopeless.

After 1 . . . P-N4; 2 K-K4, Black cannot prevent the eventual penetration of K-B5. Then all of Black's Pawns fall by the wayside.

2 **PxP**   . . . .

Now it is a question of timing. White's plan is to draw the Black King away from his own Pawns, and Black has no choice but to submit.

$$2\ \ldots\ \ \ \ \text{K-B3}$$

The moves of 2 ... K-K3 and 2 ... P-B4 only delay the inevitable. Black's Pawns are doomed, and he must abandon them and hope that he can return in time to draw against a Rook Pawn.

3	K-K4	K-N3
4	K-B5	K-R4
5	KxP	KxP
6	K-N6	K-N4
7	KxP	K-B3
8	K-N7	....

Black cannot return in time.

THE BACKWARD PAWN

A Pawn that is behind its own Pawn on the file to the left or right and which cannot advance because it is immediately subject to capture and loss by an opposing Pawn is a backward Pawn. It is a chronic weakness in the Pawn array. Unless it can be dissolved, it usually creates a situation tantamount to being a Pawn behind, for then one opposing Pawn holds two in tow.

Here, with White on the move, he wins handily because Black's Queen Pawn is backward.

1	K-K4	K-K2
2	K-Q5	K-Q2
3	P-N5	....

Black is hopeless. His King must stop the Knight Pawn and abandon the others.

In the very same position, with Black on the move, the game is a draw, for Black can dissolve the backward Pawn with *1* ... P-Q4.

THE DOUBLED PAWN

Doubled Pawns, that is, two Pawns of the same color on the same file, are weak in the ending because the Pawns cannot defend each other. For practical purposes, the weakness need not be fatal when all the Pawns—both White and Black—happen to be in the same sector. When the Pawns, however, are separated, they are a serious handicap.

In the following example from actual play (Flohr—Capablanca), Black, on the move, draws by a quick dissolution of the Pawns.

1	....	K-K4
2	K-K2	K-K5
3	K-B2	P-R5!

This Pawn sacrifice is the key plan.

> 4 PxP . . . .

4 K-K2, PxP grants White no headway.

> 4 . . . . P-B5

Dissolving all the Pawns. White remains with a doubled Rook Pawn which is of no consequence. "The rest is a matter of technique."

With White on the move in the very same position, White wins: 1 K-K2, K-K4; 2 K-B3, K-Q4; 3 K-B4, K-K3; 4 P-R3, and Black must abandon his Pawns. Thus we observe that at best the doubled Pawn is rarely a virtue.

OTHER FACTORS

In Pawn endings, any number of factors, significant and extraneous, play an important role. Quantitative and qualitative Pawn structures, superior King positions, correct timing —all are part and parcel of the whole.

It is not within the scope of this work to document each and every one of them. One factor, however, which crops up sufficiently to demand attention is the Pawn mating net and the corollary threats which stem from this source.

An example to the point is given.

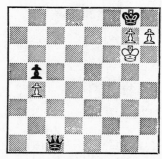

A Queen Ahead; Black Is Mated

The above position is a singular clue to the next one which is quite involved. A hasty appraisal discloses (1) White is a Pawn ahead. (2) White has two protected passed Pawns. (3) Black has a protected passed Pawn. (4) The White King is quite a distance away from its passed Pawns and will most likely not be able to assist in their advance.

White to Move and Win

The denouement rests on this last point.

1	**K-Q4**	**K-N5**
2	**P-R4**	**K-R4**

So far, so good. White has made a little progress.

3	**K-K4**	**K-N5**

Now it seems, however, that White is stymied. What is the next step?

4	**K-K3!**	**K-R4**
5	**K-B3!**	. . . .

In connection with White's last moves there are some observations. First, it is to be noted that the White King is still within the square of Black's passed Pawn: 5 . . . P-B6; 6 K-K3, P-B7; 7 K-Q2, and the Pawn goes by the wayside.

Again there is a principle called triangulation.[1] White wishes to reach his KB3 to assist in the Pawn advance. Black, momentarily, prevents this action. White succeeds, however, by describing a triangle with his King—3 K-K4, 4 K-K3, 5 K-B3. This action places the onus of moving on Black, and White is able to make headway.

Triangulation is often an effective procedure for gaining or losing a move.

5	....	K-N3
6	P-N4	K-R3
7	P-R5	K-N4

Again White's Pawns are stymied. But the process of triangulation to the fore!

| 8 | K-K3 | K-R3 |
| 9 | K-B4 | .... |

White has again described a triangle with his King—K-B3, K-K3, K-B4—to place the onus of moving upon Black. Black must give way. Observe, too, that White's King is still in the square of the Black Passed Pawn.

9	....	K-N3
10	P-N5	K-R2
11	P-N6ch	....

White's Pawns have made rapid strides. As he approaches the goal of queening, the task becomes harder.

Here this question arises: Why did White advance his Knight Pawn to N6? Why did he not advance his Rook Pawn to R6? The answer is that White was acquainted with this type of position. The specific play does not originate with a principle. It originates with knowledge.

| 11 | .... | K-R3 |

[1] In order to understand triangulation, it is well to remember that a move can be gained or lost only if one King is in a to-and-fro groove while the other is able to move about freely. In the above position Black's moves were circumscribed.

Again White's Pawns are stymied. And again triangulation!

12 K-K3!   . . . .

This is not a retreat, appearances to the contrary. It is the beginning of triangulation.

White wishes to reach the position which just existed, only with Black to move.

12 . . .		**K-N2**
13 **K-K4**		**K-R3**
14 **K-B4**		. . . .

And so White achieves his goal. It is Black's move.

14 . . . .   **K-N2**

Up to this point White has made much progress without risk. At no time has the King been out of the square of the Black passed Pawn. Now, however, if White is to win, he must be certain of what he is doing, for a misstep can be fatal.

15 **K-N5!!**   . . . .

The King is outside of the square of Black's Pawn.

15 . . .		**P-B6**
16 **P-R6ch**		**K-N1**
17 **K-B6**		**P-B7**

Black's Pawn is enough to chill the ardor of an expert.

18 **P-R7ch**   **K-R1**

If *18* . . . K-B1, *19* P-R8(Q) mate.

19 **K-B7**   **P-B8(Q)**

White mates in three.

20 **P-N7ch**		**KxP**
21 **P-N8(Q)ch**		**K-R3**
22 **Q-N6 mate.**		

9

Can White win?—or draw? Study this problem first. Don't look now! *Not even at the page or titles. But it is covered in the next to last example on page 81.*

Knight Versus Pawns

THE TABLE of relative values of the chessmen gives a Knight as approximately equal to three Pawns. This is, of course, a rule of thumb, for the formula is variable. In the opening and middle game, a Knight, more often than not, exceeds three Pawns. Its versatility in leaping from one side of the board to the other in attack or defense is a plus trait. In the ending, however, three Pawns are usually superior. This is so as the position simmers down because latent factors take on an active role. The promoting powers of the Pawns, for example, assume great proportions. And, conversely, the Knight's mating ability diminishes to nearly nothing as it becomes a sole survivor. Even the single Pawn looms menacingly as it enjoys a clear approach to the eighth rank unimpeded. In such positions, Knight versus a single Pawn, the question is can the Knight stop the Pawn by direct means by holding or blocking its advance? Or by indirect means which involve combinations? Usually, if the Pawn can be stopped by the Knight, one way or another, the result is a draw.

THE PAWN ON THE SEVENTH

When a Pawn is on the seventh rank, it is decidedly most dangerous. In the following type of position, however, the draw is easy. The Knight can hold the Pawn and stave off the intermittent sniping of the enemy King, even without the assistance of his own King (except for an occasional *tempo*).

Draw

1 K any	K-K5
2 K any	K-B6
3 N-K1ch	K-B7
4 N-B2	. . . .

Black can make no progress. The Knight will continue to swing, as needs be, between QB2, K1 and KN2.

When the lone Pawn is on the Knight file, the Knight movement is restricted to some extent. Here, for example, the Knight
heads for N1. Should it get there, it will not be able to describe
the previous motions. With proper play, however, the game
will still end in a draw.

Draw

| 1 | N-Q2ch | K-B7 |

If *1* ... K-B6; 2 N-N1ch, K-B7; 3 N-R3, the Knight cannot
be driven from focusing on N1.

| 2 | N-B4! | .... |

The trick clause. The Knight must abandon control of N1.
Yet the result is the same. White threatens 3 NxP.

| 2 | .... | P-N8(Q) |

Of course Black can promote to a Knight, but to no avail.

| 3 | N-R3ch | K any |
| 4 | NxQ | Draw |

The above position and this one are similar except for the
location of the Black King. With the King controlling the
queening square of a Knight's Pawn, the Pawn frequently
wins. Here is one example.

White Loses

1 **N-Q2ch**	**K-B8!**

Black must be careful and actually permit the next check rather than avoid it. For on *1* ... K-B7 White has *2* N-B4, as we have previously seen.

2 **N-N3ch**	**K-Q8**
Resigns	

THAT ROOK PAWN AGAIN

The pesky Rook Pawn, as usual, introduces exceptions to the general rule. Here, however, despite the limitations of the Knight by the edge of the board, the Knight can hold the Pawn, even though it is already on the sixth rank.

White Draws

1	**N-N4**	**K-N6**
2	**N-K3!**	**K-B6**

If 2 ... P-R7, 3 N-B1ch, followed by NxP, draws.

3	**N-B1**	**K-B7**
4	**N-R2**	**K-N7**
	Draw	

The Knight and the King can continue to play ring-around-a-rosy.

When a Rook Pawn is on the seventh, the Knight by itself cannot keep the Pawn in check against the incursion of the opposing King. Here White is helpless.

Black Wins

White can do nothing about ... K-B6, ... K-N7 and ... KxN.

Even against a Rook Pawn, however, there are tricks and traps, if the King can join the Knight in the defense.

Draw

Here, as before, the Knight is doomed. But another factor comes in.

1	K-B2	K-B6
2	K-Q1	K-N7
3	K-K2	KxN
4	K-B1	Stalemate

Thus we see that, if the defending King can land on B1 or B2 in the critical sector, the position can be held to a draw.

ON THE TIGHTROPE

In actual play the Knight and Pawn positions can be very profound. With all the knowledge gained in the preceding positions applied here, White can draw. But one misstep is fatal.

Draw

1 N-B7!!   ....

1 N-N6 loses. *1* ... P-R6; *2* N-B4, P-R7; *3* N-K2ch, K-Q7; *4* N-N3, K-K8, and White cannot avoid the loss of the Knight.

1 ....   P-R6

Necessary. Otherwise the Knight parks in front of the Pawn with 2 N-N5 and 3 N-R3.

2 N-N5   P-R7
3 N-K4ch   ....

This is the key move. Observe in the note to White's first move that *1* N-N6 loses. The reason for the loss is that Black's King can reach K8 before White has time to set up for any kind of defense. Now the Black King is barred from that square for a sufficient length of time to grant White a defensive maneuver.

3 ....   K-B7

If *3* ... K-Q5, White sets up a barrier with *4* N-B2, for then Black cannot progress with *4* ... K-K6 on account of *5* N-N5ch, followed by 6 NxP. Nor can Black progress with 4 ... K-K4 (to be followed by ... K-B5) on account of 5 N-N5ch, followed by 6 NxP. And, on other tries, the White King approaches the critical sector.

4	**N-N3**	**K-Q8**
5	**K-Q6**	**K-K8**

Reaching K8, after all. But one move too late.

6	**K-K5**	**K-B7**
7	**K-B4**	**Draw**

A KINGDOM FOR A HORSE

It is a well-known fact that a single Knight is insufficient mating force, if it is the only unit on the board (in addition to the Kings). It is equally well known that two Knights cannot mate by force, if they are the only survivors on the board. Paradoxically, if the adversary is left with some material, a Pawn or two, there are occasions even when a single Knight is a decisive advantage. Below is such a position.

White Wins

This is the rare exception to the rule. If Black were barren of material, the game would be a draw. But Black, unfortunately, has two Pawns and he is literally hoist by his own petard.

| 1 N-B6 | K-R8 |

1 ... P-N4 leads to the same denouement.

2 N-N4	P-N4
3 K-B1	P-R7
4 N-B2 mate	

A PAWN TO THE BAD

This is another variation of the same theme.

White Wins

Black loses because he has a Pawn.

| 1 N-K4 | K-R7 |

Obviously, if 1 ... P-R7, 2 N-N3 mate.

2 N-Q2	K-R8
3 N-B1	P-R7
4 N-N3 mate	

Can White win? *Here is a very nice exercise in end-game ingenuity. Alekhine solved this position in a matter of mere seconds; but it is not really that easy. Strengthen your own ability by working out the possibilities thoroughly; then, and only then, consult the text on pages 93–94.*

More on Knight and Pawns

O F THE MEN on the chessboard, the Knight is peculiarly unique. It leaps over all and sundry units, landing, as it were, on either black or white squares. Its singular leap taxes the imagination and renders the simplest position difficult of calculation.

One trait resulting from the Knight's leap is that the Knight cannot gain a *tempo*. Any of the other pieces, Bishop, Rook, or Queen, in relation to the King, can often steal a move, by correct, technical manipulation. Not so the Knight. If the Knight tours the length and breadth of the entire board a number of times, while the opposing King moves to and fro, every time the Knight approaches the King, their relationship is exactly the same—and the same side is on the move.

This characteristic is not an asset for the Knight; it is, in fact, a liability. Yet it is something to remember in the final reckoning of the give and take of the essential computations.

EXCEPTIONS COMBINED

As we have seen, the Rook Pawn contributes a goodly share of the many exceptions to the general rules of chess. When the peculiar Knight is involved with a Rook Pawn, the exceptionals clash head on, and the men fail to cooperate.

White Draws

In this position Black is a Knight and a Pawn to the good. If there were any justice in chess, Black ought to win. But who said there was? Here there is no prodding White's King from its haven at R1. The approach of the Black King to R6 or to N6 terminates hostilities in a stalemate. And the Knight cannot move without abandoning the Pawn.

In regard to this and similar positions it is well to note the pertinent details. The Rook Pawn is on the seventh rank, guarded by the Knight. With the Pawn on the sixth and so guarded, Black wins. But even if the Knight defends the Pawn on the seventh from either B6 or B8, the result is still a draw.

QUITE ANOTHER INSTANCE

Now let the above position be inverted, so to speak, with Black's King in front of its Rook Pawn on the seventh rank, and a spare Knight in the offing. There ought, it seems, to be no question about the result. Yet there is a definite question.

How to Tell the Result?

Offhand, it seems Black wins. Actually, however, it depends on whose move it is. With Black to move, for instance, the result is a draw:

1	....	N-B5
2	K-B1	N-Q6ch
3	K-B2	N-K8ch
4	K-B1	N-B6
5	K-B2	N-Q5ch
	Drawn	

The moves can continue *ad infinitum* and *ad nauseam*. But as the Knight cannot gain a *tempo* over White's King, the result must be a draw.

With White to move in the same position, the story is different:

1	K-B1	N-B5
2	K-B2	N-K7
	Resigns	

White loses control of B1, must abandon that square, and free Black's King, whereafter Black queens his Pawn and wins.

The Easy Way

All well and good. Yet how is one to know the result of this type of position without going into extensive analysis?

Fortunately, there is an easy mechanical way. If the Knight can check the opposing King, the result is a draw. If the Knight cannot check, the lone King loses. When Knight and King are far separated, it is still easy to determine the result at a glance. If Knight and King are on the same colored squares and the Knight is to move, the result is a draw; if the King is to move, the result is a loss for the King. Conversely, if Knight and King are on opposite colored squares, the Knight wins if it is to move; and the result is a draw if the King is to move.

All this stems from the fact that the Knight cannot gain a *tempo*. A Knight on a white square moves to a black square and gives check to a white one. So, if the Knight is on a white square and the King is, too, with the Knight to move, no matter how far removed the Knight is from the King, the Knight will check the King as soon as it comes within checking distance. That is the guiding principle.

A One-move Pay-off

Often it is an exaggeration to say that the result of a game depends on one move. Here it is no exaggeration. It is the "honest" truth.

With the foregoing in mind it is clear that White must move both to confine Black's King and to a square on which it can

White Moves. Result?

be checked by the Knight eventually. Here, since the Knight is on a white square, White's King must move to a white square. *1 K-B2 draws; 1 K-B1 loses. Try it.*

KNIGHT VERSUS THREE PAWNS

It is exceedingly difficult to generalize on an ending of Knight versus three Pawns. One thing, however, is certain: since the Pawns can hardly lose, the real question is: Can they win?

When the Pawns are separated and not subject to immediate capture, they are dangerous indeed. One or two Pawns tie down the opposing King, and the third Pawn, with the help of its own King, manages to trade itself for the Knight, leaving a winning result.

When the Pawns are together, as in the diagrammed position, they are dangerous, too. To determine the result, however, requires the most accurate calculation. Here, with White on the move, White wins; with Black to move, Black draws.

1	P-B5ch	K-N2
2	P-N5	N-Q4
3	P-R5	N-B6
4	K-B4	N-K7ch
5	K-K5	N-N6
6	P-B6ch	K-N1
7	P-R6	N-R4
8	P-N6	N-N6
9	P-R7ch	K-R1
10	P-B7	Resigns

With Black to move, he can draw with 1 ... N-Q4. The variations, emanating from this move, are long and laborious —as are, too, the variations from the winning procedure above.

It is beyond the ken of the average player to work out such positions to a conclusion, with so many moves to go and so many variations and sub-variations. The best advice is to figure the three Pawns as a win, particularly if two are already on the fifth rank. Then play the game on a move-to-move basis. Merely grasp as much of the position as you can and hope (and pray) to draw the game if you are the one who has the lone Knight.

A TRICK POSITION

When a King occupies a Rook square behind a barrier of Pawns, it is frequently impossible to drive it out. Hence, despite a preponderance of material, the result is a draw. Here is a type position.

White Wins

Superficially, it seems that White should win with ease. As a matter of fact, he does when he follows the correct procedure. But, then, what is the correct procedure?

At first glance the idea seems to be to sacrifice the Knight for one of the Pawns, then win with the extra Pawn. But try this on your pianola: *1* N-Q4, K-N1; *2* N-B5, K-R1; *3* NxRP, PxN; *4* K-B6 (not *4* K-B7, stalemate!), K-N1; *5* P-N7, K-R2 —and White must yield his extra Pawn, say, by *6* K-K7 or else *6* K-B7, stalemate, anyway.

There are other ways to mismanage to a draw; but White wins as follows:

1 **N-B4**	. . . .

Not the only move, but on the track of the only winning plan.

1	**K-N1**
2 **N-Q5**	**K-R1**
3 **N-B6!**	**PxN**

Forced.

4 **K-B8**	**P-B4**
5 **P-N7ch**	**Resigns**

The point was to get to B8 (or B7) with the White King without stalemating.

THEORY VERSUS PRACTICE

This position from the recent Rosenwald Tournament exemplifies the winning procedure in an ending of three Pawns vs. a Knight.

Evans

Reshevsky

1	K-B4	N-Q7
2	K-K5	N-B6ch
3	KxP	N-R5
4	P-R8(Q)ch	KxQ
5	K-B7!	N-B4
6	P-K4	N-R3ch
7	K-B8	N-B4
8	P-K5!	N-N2
9	K-B7	N-B4
10	P-K6	N-R3ch
11	K-B8	N-N1
12	P-B4	N-B3
13	K-B7	Resigns

And here is the finale of another game in which White is a clear Knight ahead and ought to win. Yet his apparently valiant steed is nought but a pompous ass.

Nimzovich

Rubinstein

1 N-Q3? . . . .

The idea behind this move is excellent. Its execution, however, is poor. White anticipated *1 ... KxP; 2 N-B5, K-B5; 3 N-Q7* after which the Knight retains an iron grip on the position. White's King then marches over to the critical sector and picks off all of Black's Pawns. But now the game takes another turn.

1	. . . .	P-B3!
2	PxP	KxP
3	N-B2	K-N4

With a clear Knight ahead, it still seems White ought to win. But soon an unusual position is reached.

4	K-N4	P-K4
5	K-B4	P-K5
	Drawn	

For there is nought to be done about *6 ... K-B5*, followed by *7 ... P-K6*.

This is the way in which the game should have proceeded:

(See last diagram)

1 K-N4! . . . .

This is the key and star move. The point, as will be seen, is that White's King joins the fray a move sooner. This gain of a *tempo* makes all the difference in the outcome of the game.

| 1 .... | **K-B5** |

After *1* ... P-B4; *2* PxP e.p., KxP; *3* N-K4ch, followed by *5* P-N5, it is all over, for the Knight is immune, and White's King joins the action and decides.

| 2 **N-Q3ch** | **KxP** |

Or *2* ... K-K5; *3* K-B4—the point of *1* K-N4!

| 3 **N-B5** | **K-B4** |
| 4 **N-Q7** | **Resigns** |

For Black is helpless against the incursion of the White King.

This delicate Knight versus Pawn end game could have arisen in a variation of a postal game between the strong Texas amateur, Homer Hyde, and his opponent, William Taber, former champion of several states.

Taber

Hyde

With White to move, there are yet a number of obstacles to be hurdled. The play would have gone as follows:

| *1* **K-Q5!** | .... |

The key move. On *1* N-B2, K-B6 is sufficient; and, on *1* K-Q3, K-B6, White makes no progress.

1 . . . .   **K-B4!**

On *1* . . . K-B6; *2* K-K5, K-N7; *3* N-N5, Black is soon shunted from the defense of his Rook Pawn.

2 **N-B3!!**   . . . .

The apparently meaningless gyrations of the Knight are the most purposeful part of the winning strategy.

2 . . . .   **K-B5**
3 **N-K2ch**   **K-B6**

Black's only chance: e.g., *3* . . . K-B4; *4* K-Q4, and White soon infiltrates.

4 **N-N1ch!!**   **K-N7**
5 **K-K4**   **KxN**
6 **K-B3!!!**   **Resigns**

Five star moves, and now it's all over, for Black's Rook Pawn goes, and the rest is easy. (Note, however, that *6* K-B4 permits a draw by *6* . . . K-B7.)

This miniature ending illustrates the Knight to advantage when used with precision technique.

White Wins

Before proceeding with the solution, let us analyze the problems involved. Black threatens ... K-N5, followed by ... P-R4-5-6 and the exchange of Pawns, leading to a draw. In the event that White by-passes ... P-R6 with P-N3, Black, of course, continues with ... P-R7 and P-R8(Q).

There are two ways to meet the threat. On the face of it, White's first try seems to be the answer.

1 K-K7	K-N5
2 K-Q6	P-R4
3 K-Q5	P-R5
4 N-B4	. . . .

The further advance of Black's Pawn is checked. With a clear Knight ahead, the rest ought to be "a matter of technique." Yet even the combined brilliance of Alekhine, Capablanca, and Lasker will not win the game against best play for Black.

| 4 . . . . | K-N4 |

Black takes the opposition and maintains it. And White can make no progress. For example, consider:

5 K-Q4	K-N5
6 K-Q3	K-N6
7 K-Q4	K-N5
Drawn	

Any Knight move allows the eventual exchange of Pawns.

The Right Way

There is another way to check the advance of the Black Pawn.

(Resume from next to last diagram)

1 **N-N3**   . . . .

This move appears to be way out of context. Yet it is the only way. The idea is to continue with 2 N-R1. Then, when Black's King is at N5, Black cannot play   P-R6; for White has N-B2ch, followed by PxP, with an easy win.

Hence, the Knight maneuver successfully staves off Black's prime threat.

But Black has plenty of fight left.

1 . . .   **K-B5**

Since that prime threat can be met, Black attempts an incursion from the rear.

2 **N-R1**   **K-Q6**
3 **K-K7**   . . .

Even though far removed from the critical sector, White's King can join the fray in the nick of time.

3 . . . .   **K-Q7**

The alternative 3 . . . P-R4 fails: 4 K-Q6, P-R5; 5 K-B5, K-Q7; 6 K-N4, K-B8; 7 K-R3, K-N8; 8 N-N3! and White wins.

4 **K-Q6**   **K-B8**
5 **P-N4!**   **K-N7**
6 **K-B6!!**   . . . .

White can still go astray. Curiously, on 6 K-B5, Black draws by . . . K-B6.

6 . . . .   **K-B6**
7 **K-B5**   **Resigns**

Now Black can do nought to prevent K-N6 and the eventual fall of his Rook Pawn: 7 . . . K-Q6; 8 K-N6, K-B6; 9 K-R5!

Know your endings! *Obviously, White cannot lose in this position. The real question is: Can he win? Study the problem first, for that is the best way to learn. But you will find the answer on page 105 in case of need.*

Bishop versus Pawns

THE TABLE OF relative values of the chessmen gives a Bishop as the equivalent of three Pawns. The formula is, of course, only a rule of thumb, to be modified by circumstances. In the opening and middle game, for example, the Bishop is usually more valuable. As an aggressive weapon, it can inflict greater damage than Pawns. And defensively, too, its rapid strides in reaching critical sectors quickly rule in its favor.

In the end game, as mating threats have vanished, the stature of the Pawns grows and that of the Bishop diminishes. Clearly, the lone Bishop, as opposed to Pawns, is at a disadvantage. The chance of administering checkmate is exceedingly remote, if not impossible. The only question is how much of a disadvantage.

Generally, a Bishop will hold one Pawn surely; two Pawns, likely; and three Pawns, possibly. As the Pawns grow in number, the task of the Bishop grows, too.

THE LONE BISHOP

The cases in chess history where a lone Bishop administers mate are extremely rare. But they do exist. Here is an illustration in point.

White Mates in Three [1]

1 **K-B3!**   . . . .

The star move, releasing the stalemate. Without it, White cannot win.

1	. . . .	**P-N8(Q)**
2	**N-B2ch**	**QxNch**
3	**KxQ mate**	

---

[1] This position is a composed problem. One of its curious features is that the movement of the Black Pawns can be reversed—and it is still mate in three! Only this time, the mate will be administered by a lone Knight. Try it.

THAT ROOK PAWN AGAIN

It is common knowledge that a lone Bishop, without other material on the board, cannot effect checkmate. It is not so well known, however, that a Bishop and a Pawn, opposed to a lone King, cannot win under certain circumstances.

Draw

As usual, the Rook Pawn plays its part in this grotesque result. Despite the preponderance of material, the White King cannot be budged from its haven at KR1. Any effort to prod him from that square by force will result only in a stalemate.

The features that make for the draw are to be noted: (1) The extra Pawn is a Rook Pawn; (2) The Bishop is of the opposite color of the queening square of the Rook Pawn; (3) The lone King occupies or is able to occupy the queening square. This combination of factors spells draw.

SIMILAR CASES

The following positions are all variations on the same theme. Despite material preponderance, the result is a draw.

Draw

There is no Rook Pawn in this position. But the Pawn juxta-position forms a barrier that is tantamount to the same thing. White's King merely moves to R1 and back, and there is no way to dispossess him from these quarters. The advance of the Black King to KB7 creates a stalemate. And the sacrifice of the Bishop for the Knight Pawn will lead to a drawn King and Pawn ending.

Draw

Here again Black remains with a Rook Pawn. This time, however, Black's Bishop does control the queening square. Normally, this position would be a win. White's Rook Pawn, however, prevents the Black King from approaching at N6.

Hence there is no way of prodding the White King from N1.
Result: draw.

Draw

This position is unusual. The result is a draw because Black's
Bishop is incarcerated. There is no way to promote its activity,
and Black is helpless to make progress without creating a stalemate.

WHERE THE ROOK PAWN RULES

The following position has some of the earmarks of the
previous ones. White has a Rook Pawn, and his Bishop does
not control the queening square. But the Black King does not
occupy R1, and with correct play cannot reach that square.
This factor makes all the difference.

White Wins

1 **K-Q4!** . . . .

White's plan is profound. He is prepared to counter the advance of the Knight Pawn to N3 or N4 with 2 P-R6, keeping the Black King from reaching R1. This is the tactical basis of the move. Strategically, he intends to drive the Black King from the defense of the Knight Pawn, which he will pick off with his King. Then it will be clear sailing.

1 K-B5 will not do, for Black counters with ... P-N3ch, and no matter which way White captures, he will be in one of the drawing positions above.

1 K-B4 will not do. For ... P-N4ch creates the necessary access for the Black King to R1.

1 ....   **K-B3**

In addition to the text move, Black has at his command the following moves: *1* ... P-N3, *1* ... P-N4, and sundry King moves.

After *1* ... P-N3 or *1* ... P-N4, White immediately plays 2 P-R6, keeping the Black King from R1, via N2. White then maneuvers his King to pick off Black's Knight Pawn and drive Black's King away from the critical sector: thus: *1* ... P-N4; 2 P-R6, P-N5; 3 K-B4, P-N6; 4 KxP, K-B3; 5 K-N4 (arriving in the nick of time to prevent Black's ... K-N4), K-B2; 6 K-B5, K-B1; 7 K-B6, followed by 8 K-N7 and the eventual queening of the Pawn.

Or *1* ... P-N3; 2 P-R6, K-B3; 3 K-B4, K-B2; 4 K-N5, followed by the capture of the Pawn by the King and leading to the same denouement.

Or *1* ... K-B1; 2 K-B5, K-Q2; 3 B-N8, K-B1; 4 B-B4, followed by K-N6, KxP, etc.

2 **B-N6**   **K-Q2**

If *2* ... K-N4; 3 K-Q5, followed by K-Q6-B7 and the capture of the Knight Pawn, with clear sailing for a Queen.

3 **K-B5**   **K-B1**
4 **B-R7**   ....

Keeping the opposing King from R1.

4	....	K-B2
5	K-N5	P-N3
6	P-R6	K-B1
7	KxP	....

Black is driven from the critical sector.

EXCEPTION UPON EXCEPTION

The following position brings up some interesting points.
With no Black Pawns as we have already observed, the result
is a draw. If Black has only one Pawn, the result is a draw.
But Black has two Pawns—too much wood for his own good.
And that changes the picture.

White Wins

1 **B-K1!** ....

The key move here is based on tactical considerations.
Black's King threatened to go to R4-5-6 and capture White's
Rook Pawn or exchange it off.

1 .... K-B2

Now *1* ... K-R4 is met by *2* P-R3, followed by *3* PxP and
an easy win, for the extra Bishop decides in any but problem
positions.

Black is not concerned with losing one or both of his Pawns, for he would normally reach a stock drawing position.

| 2 B-R4 | .... |

The basis of this move is tactical and strategical. If Black returns to N3, White wishes to be in position to check at Q8 and keep the King from R4.

Strategically, White has two things in mind. If he succeeds in either one of these, he wins. First, he attempts to stalemate the Black King. If he succeeds, Black must advance his Pawn to N6. White then captures, PxP, converting his Rook Pawn into a Knight Pawn, with a resulting easy win. Secondly, he attempts to drive the Black King out of the critical sector (its QR1) and to a point where he is unable to return in time. Success here grants White time to capture both Pawns before Black can reach the drawing position.

2	....	K-Q2
3	K-B5	K-B2
4	B-N5	K-B1

Black is putting up the strongest resistance.

| 5 | K-N6 | K-N1 |
| 6 | B-B4ch | K-B1 |

If 6 ... K-R1, a Bishop *tempo* compels 7 ... P-N6, after which 8 PxP wins handily.

7	B-N3	K-Q2
8	KxP	K-B1
9	K-N6	K-Q2
10	K-N7	K-K3

Black has been compelled to abandon the critical sector.

11	K-B6	K-K2
12	B-Q6ch	K-Q1
13	K-N7	....

Now White picks off the Pawn and wins easily.

The foregoing is only a rough outline of the possibilities of the position. To give every conceivable defense is beyond the scope of this work. Suffice it to say that with correct play, White wins.

WHAT, AGAIN?

By comparison, this position is an easy win, that is, easy if you know how.

White Wins

Curiously, without the Knight Pawn, Black draws. But he has it!

1	K-Q7	K-N1
2	K-K7	K-R1
3	B-B7	K-R2

If 3 ... P-N3 (or ... P-N4); 4 PxP (e.p.), K-N2; 5 K-K6, followed by K-B5-N4-R5 and the removal of Black's Pawn with an easy win.

4	K-B8	K-R1
5	B-N8	P-N4
6	PxP e.p.	P-R4
7	P-N7 mate	

BISHOP VERSUS TWO PAWNS

As a general rule, a Bishop can hold two Pawns. This position, at first sight, seems to be no exception. But it is.

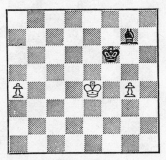

White Wins

1 **P-R5**	**B-B1**

So that 2 P-R6 will be met by B-B4 with an easy draw.

2 **K-Q5**	. . . .

To prevent the . . . B-B4 defense. The threat now is P-R6.

2	**B-R3**

In order to stop the Rook Pawn by . . . B-K6.

3 **P-N5ch!!!**	**BxP**

If *3* . . . KxP, *4* P-R6 as the Black King interferes with the Black Bishop.

4 **K-K4**	**Resigns**

For now the King interferes with the Bishop on another diagonal. There is no way to stop the Rook Pawn.

12

Know your endings! *Study this Reti position with care* before looking at text below. *How does Black win? Simply? Now take up the first example in the text below.*

Bishop(s) and Pawns

IF THE STUDY of chess could be reduced to axioms and principles, a twentieth-century automaton would make a mockery of the grand master. In less time than it takes to set up the chessmen the answers to the most perplexing problems would be produced with certainty and with accuracy.

Such, however, is not the case. Even what appears to be the simplest end game may, in fact, be a series of tortuous moves, embodying multifarious devious ideas interwoven in a plan which is yet part of another plan.

Take the positions with the Bishop and Pawns. On the surface it may seem that a few guiding principles should wrap them up. But there are principles and exceptions, and exceptions to the exceptions, so much so that it is better to withhold judgment. Particular positions are seldom wholly subject to generalizations. Specific situations have to be decided specifically.

A TYPICAL EXCEPTION

By all the laws of the Medes and the Persians and of chess, White is hopelessly lost in the photographed position above. His King cannot stop the Black Pawn from queening, while Black's Bishop can stop White's Pawn. Yet it is all an illusion.

1 K-K7!! . . . .

How this move affects the issue is decidedly unclear. The King even blocks the advance of its own Pawn.

So much for appearances. White now threatens 2 K-B6 which wins Black's Pawn, for 2 . . . B-Q6 is countered by 3 P-K7. Black's reply is forced.

1 . . . . **P-N4**
2 K-Q6!!! . . . .

This move raises a question: Is White a member of the Dodgers? For home plate is in the opposite direction.

But White is really on the right track, threatening 3 K-K5 to approach Black's Pawn. That Pawn must scamper.

2 . . . . **P-N5**
3 P-K7 **B-N4**
4 K-B5!!! . . . .

The secret is out. By attacking the Bishop, White gains a precious *tempo*. If the Bishop is not saved, White can queen. If it is, then White's King is in the "square" of Black's Pawn and makes a timely return to catch it.

| 4 | .... | B-Q2 |
| 5 | K-Q4 | K-N3 |

Or 5 ... P-N6; 6 K-K3, P-N7; 7 K-B2.

6	K-K4	K-B4
7	K-B4	K-Q3
8	P-K8(Q)	BxQ
9	KxP	Drawn

A neat object lesson on how the shortest distance between two points may not always be a straight line in chess. If you really absorbed that lesson you could have solved this ending at the outset.

IRONIC INSTANCE

This Bishop and Pawn ending has a unique twist. Without the Bishop Pawn, Black draws. But there it is!

White to Move and Win

| 1 | B-R3 | .... |

It is essential to blockade the Bishop Pawn at once. Failure to do so results in a draw: e.g., 1 K-Q7, P-B7; 2 B-R3, P-B8(Q); 3 BxQ, drawn.

1	....	P-B7
2	B-B1	K-R1
3	BxP!	....

The trick play.

3 .... **PxB**

On any other move the win is simple.

4 **K-B7**   **P-B8(Q)**
5 **P-N7ch**   **K-R2**
6 **P-N8(Q)mate**

It will be noted that the extra Bishop Pawn was a liability. It prevented a stalemate and, in turn, gave White the opportunity to build up a mating net.

UNDER TWO FLAGS

There is an expression that crops up in chess time and time again. It is "Bishops of opposite colors." It refers to one Bishop controlling white squares and the enemy Bishop controlling black ones.

"Bishops of opposites" is the boon and bane of the expert, depending upon which side of the fence he is sitting on.

Here, with two Pawns plus, because of "Bishops of opposites," Black is unable to make any progress.

Drawn

The Pawns are fixed on the wrong squares. White simply goes to and fro with his Bishop, and there is nought to be done.

Here is why "Bishops of opposites" are dreaded. With two Pawns plus, apparently on the right squares, White cannot win.

Drawn

Black shuttles back and forth with his Bishop. If the White King abandons the King Pawn, it will be captured. If White's Pawn advances to Q6ch, Black plays ... BxP, and White remains with a lone Bishop plus, for a draw.

AGAIN, THE EXCEPTION

This position is similar in some respects to the previous one, but there are some vital differences, sufficiently so to affect the result of the game.

White to Move and Win

For one thing, the Pawns are on the sixth, where they are extremely dangerous. For another, White's King can join the fray.

1	B-N5	B-R6
2	K-N6	B-N5
3	K-B7	Resigns

Black cannot prevent P-K7-8.

With Black to move in the diagrammed position, the outcome is the same. For example *1 . . .* K-K1; 2 B-N5ch, K-B1, and White wins by infiltrating with his King on the Queen side: *3* K-K4, *4* K-Q5, *5* K-B6, *6* K-Q7, and the advance of the King Pawn. While all this is going on, Black is able only to temporize.

LIKE COLORS

When Bishops are of the same colors, that is, they control the same colored squares (in the diagram, black), an extra Pawn often is sufficient to decide the game.

White to Move and Win

First glance here gives the impression of a draw. For Black's Bishop controls the queening square of the Pawn, and there doesn't seem to be a way of driving the Bishop from the diagonal. But there is!

1 B-R4	K-N3

Black's move is forced, for White was threatening B-B2-R7-N8, challenging the Black Bishop and driving it off the diagonal. Then Black has no defense: e.g. (Place White's Bishop at N8), *1 ... B-N8; 2 B-N3, B-R2; 3 B-B7!* and White must queen perforce.

2	**B-B2ch**	**K-R3**
3	**B-B5!**	....

The point of this move will become clear later on. Now, if Black could pass, White could make no headway. But Black is in *zugzwang:* he must move.

3	....	**B-N6**

Or other squares on the diagonal.

4	**B-K7**	....

Threatening *5 B-Q8*, followed by *6 B-B7*, etc.

4	....	**K-N3**

To prevent that threat.

5	**B-Q8ch**	**K-B3**

Reaching almost the same position as the diagram, with one vital difference. Black's Bishop is now at N6, instead of R7.

6	**B-R4!**	....

Thus White is able to challenge the Bishop and swing over to the other side by the gain of a *tempo.*

6	....	**B-Q3**
7	**B-B2**	**Resigns**

As previously mentioned, there is no defense to *8 B-R7-N8*, etc.

A FUTILE BISHOP

As a rule, a Bishop can check two Pawns with the assistance of its King. Here the White King is on the borderline, just outside the critical sector. With precision play, Black can win.

Black to Move and Win

1 . . . .   **P-Q5!**

The star move. It is curious that the tempting 1 . . . P-R4 will not do: e.g., 1 . . . P-R4; 2 K-N6, P-R5; 3 K-R5, K-N6; 4 B-K3, P-R6; 5 K-N5, K-B6; 6 K-B5, K-Q6; 7 B-Q4, K-K5; 8 B-B6, P-R7; 9 P-N4, and White draws.

The text move compels White to seek play on the other wing, for 2 K-N7 loses a *tempo*: e.g., 2 K-N7, P-R4; 3 K-N6, P-R5, and Black jockeys one of his Pawns down to a Queen. The loss of the *tempo* exists in White's playing K-N7 and K-N6, instead of being able to play K-N6 directly. And the loss of the *tempo* is sufficient to turn the tables.

2	K-Q6	P-R4
3	P-N4	P-R5
4	P-N5	P-Q6

White is a move too late.

5 K-K7   P-R6!

6 BxP   . . . .

If 6 KxP, P-R7 wins. The winning procedure is an exercise
in itself. Try it.

6 . . . .   P-Q7
7 KxP   P-Q8(Q)
8 B-K7   K-Q4

This last bit of play on Black's part is worthy of observation.
Strictly speaking, it is not within the scope of Bishop endings.
Since it has come about, however, it is well to absorb the
technique that is required.

9 P-N6   Q-B6ch
10 B-B6   Q-B4!
11 P-N7   . . . .

What else? If 11 K-N7, K-K3 wins in short order. Other
moves will cost the Bishop.

11 . . . .   Q-K3ch
Resigns

For White must lose his Bishop or permit the Queen to go
to KN1. When the Queen lands on N1, the Black King joins

in the fray and White is helpless to resist for any length of time.

REPRISE

Here is another example of the triumph of two Pawns over a lone Bishop, when the King is cut off from cooperating in the defense.

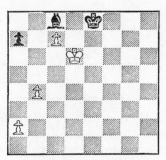

White to Move and Win

1 **K-B6!**   . . . .

This is the all-important move. On other moves, Black plays *1* . . . B-N2 and is able to set up a blockade.

1	**K-K2**
2 **P-N5**	**K-K3**
3 **P-R4**	**K-K4**

Black tries to reach the vital sector with his King.

4 **P-R5**	**K-Q5**
5 **P-N6**	**Resigns**

Black is out of bounds. There is no defense.

A PRACTICAL EXAMPLE

All the basic theory in the world hardly touches the experience of over-the-board play. The following position occurred between two masters, and more than twenty hours of analysis were spent over it, before the final winning procedure was discovered. Almost inconceivable in such a simple setting.

A study of the position discloses that White cannot force his passed Pawn to a Queen. Hence, he must capture Black's Pawn. In doing so, however, he will necessarily relinquish his own passed Pawn. Then the question will remain, will White's last remaining Pawn be sufficient to win?

The first question for White to decide in capturing Black's Pawn is where the White King belongs, for it might be stationed at K5, at B6, at N5, or even at N6. If one decided merely by intuition, rather than by cold analysis, the answer would be the King belongs on N6, before effecting the capture of the Black Pawn. For N6 is closer to the queening square of the Bishop Pawn. Yet that would be the incorrect answer.

1 K-K5   . . . .

Attacking the Pawn, and with a winning threat. White threatens 2 B-N2 and, while Black temporizes, 3 K-B6, 4 K-N5 and 5 B-K4. Then Black is in an embarrassing position, for if he captures the Bishop, he is in a losing Pawn ending. And if he fails to capture the Bishop, White plays BxP, and gains a vital *tempo* by attacking Black's Bishop.

1 . . . .   B-R6

To prevent White's threat.

$\qquad$ 2 **B-K6** $\qquad$ ....

White plays immediately to win the Bishop Pawn for his Knight Pawn.

How does he know that he shouldn't play his King to some other square before winning the Pawn? He knows only because he has analyzed the position. His King belongs on K5 for a reason that will become apparent many moves later.

$\qquad$ 2 .... $\qquad$ **K-N2**
$\qquad$ 3 **BxP** $\qquad$ **B-B8**

Of course not 3 ... B-N7 because of 4 B-K4ch forcing the exchange of Bishops.

$\qquad$ 4 **B-Q6!!** $\qquad$ ....

All part and parcel of the winning plan.

$\qquad$ 4 .... $\qquad$ **B-Q6**

This seems to be the best try for Black, yet the game is soon over. The line offering the most resistance is 4 ... KxP. Then, however, White wins by advancing his Pawn to B5 and B6, placing his Bishop at B7 so as to prevent the adverse King from getting to KB1 and following through by getting his King to KN7, reaching a position similar to the previous one. All this is a long and arduous procedure. But White wins.

$\qquad$ 5 **K-Q4!** $\qquad$ ....

The secret is out. Why K-K5, when capturing the Pawn? Because now the White King can attack the Black Bishop. From any of the other squares—B6, N5, N6—he couldn't attack the Black Bishop. And why attack the Bishop?

$\qquad$ 5 .... $\qquad$ **B moves**
$\qquad$ 6 **K-B5** $\qquad$ **Resigns**

White, by the attack on the Bishop, has gained the necessary *tempo* to defend his second Pawn. With two Pawns up and with Bishops of the same color, the win is easy.

Q. E. D.

13

Know your endings! *Exceptions and counter-principles seem to rule in chess, in the endings as well as elsewhere. Here the long-range Bishop traverses the path of White's Pawn, a point in its favor. Can, then, the short-stepping Knight reinforce the Pawn decisively? See last example in text.*

Bishop versus Knight

Theory has fluctuated on the relative merits of Bishop and Knight. About a century ago the Knight in all its pristine glory was in favor. As the science of chess progressed, the trial-and-error method evoked a reappraisal, and the Bishop ruled supreme. Contemporary experts lean toward the Bishop, though not so radically.

The Bishop is a long-range piece. It attacks and defends

118

from a distance, crossing the length and breadth of the board in a single move. The Bishop is restricted, however, to one color. On the white squares it is always on the white squares; or, if it starts on the black, it must remain on black.

The inimitable Knight's move is akin to a hop and skip. It is capable, however, of covering both black and white squares. A vital difference.

To level off the comparison, it is important to note that the Bishop is able, more often than not, to gain a *tempo* in relation to the Knight or to a semi-restricted King. The peculiar leap of the Knight does not embrace this quality.

THE THESIS

That the Bishop is infinitesimally stronger than the Knight is, after all, a matter of opinion, for there is no mathematical formula which leads to this conclusion. Only the test of grueling over-the-board play is a confirmation.

PART 1—PRO BISHOP

A Critical Example

The following position is an excellent example to make the point. It is well balanced in that each side has an equal number of Pawns in the east and west sectors. It is from the game, Stoltz-Kashdan, The Hague, 1928.

1 . . . .   K-B1

Black moves first. As a matter of good strategy, he begins to centralize his King, from which point of vantage the King will have easy access to either side of the board.

2 **K-B1** . . . .

White follows suit.

2	. . . .	**K-K2**
3	**K-K2**	**K-Q3**
4	**K-Q3**	**K-Q4**

Black arrives first, and White is on the defensive.

It may be argued here that the important distinction of the position is not the Bishop versus the Knight but, instead, the initiative of the first King move. There is, of course, much truth in the argument. If White had moved first, to be sure, White would not lose. Neither would he win. Yet Black is able to convert the slim advantage of the first move to a win!

From here on Black must make progress. The general plan is to weaken White's King-side Pawn configuration, invade and rout it, and tie on to White's Queen Knight Pawn and cause it to fall.

Because the Bishop is able to gain a *tempo* over the Knight, when needed, White cannot maintain the present position. He will be compelled to give ground, permitting Black's King to enter at its K5 or on the Queen side at a critical moment.

5 **P-R4** . . . .

White may assume any number of different Pawn formations, each of which is implicitly weak. The text move aims to cut down on Black's Pawn *tempi* and, at the same time, put the Pawn on black, where it is less vulnerable to the Bishop.

5 . . . . **B-B1**

This inane-looking move is actually purposeful. To begin with, it throws the onus of the move on White, who becomes more and more hard pressed for good moves. In other words, Black is able to stall, and White is not. In addition, Black threatens ... B-R3 and an incursion from the rear.

6 **N-B3**	....	

There is no good way of keeping the Bishop out. If 6 P-QN4. B-R3ch; 7 P-N5, B-N2, White's Queen Knight Pawn is doomed.

6	**B-R3ch**	
7 **K-B3**	....	

Or 7 K-K3, K-B4; 8 N-N5, K-N5; 9 NxBP, KxP and Black's Queen Rook Pawn will march on unimpeded.

7	**P-R3**

To prevent 8 N-N5.

8 **N-Q4**	**P-N3**

To prevent 9 N-B5.

9 **N-B2**	**K-K5**

At long last, a step forward.

10 **N-K3**	**P-B4**
11 **K-Q2**	**P-B5**
12 **N-N4**	**P-R4**

White's defense gets more difficult.

13 **N-B6ch**	....

13 N-R2 seems to offer more resistance. Even then 13 ... B-N4; 14 K-B3, B-K7 leaves White at a loss.

13	**K-B4**
14 **N-Q7**	**B-B1!**
15 **N-B8**	....

White is pinning on to any target...

<table>
<tr><td>15</td><td>....</td><td>P-N4</td></tr>
</table>

... but it is of no avail. Now there is danger of the Knight going lost.

<table>
<tr><td>16</td><td>P-N3</td><td>....</td></tr>
</table>

Necessary. 16 PxP, KxP, and the Knight is lost.

<table>
<tr><td>16</td><td>....</td><td>PxRP</td></tr>
<tr><td>17</td><td>PxRP</td><td>K-N5</td></tr>
<tr><td>18</td><td>N-N6</td><td>B-B4</td></tr>
</table>

Now a Pawn goes by the wayside. It is practically over.

<table>
<tr><td>19</td><td>N-K7</td><td>B-K3</td></tr>
<tr><td>20</td><td>P-N4</td><td>KxP</td></tr>
<tr><td>21</td><td>K-Q3</td><td>K-N5</td></tr>
</table>

Black must exercise a bit of care and precision.

<table>
<tr><td>22</td><td>K-K4</td><td>P-R5</td></tr>
<tr><td>23</td><td>N-B6</td><td>B-B4ch</td></tr>
<tr><td>24</td><td>K-Q5</td><td>P-B6</td></tr>
</table>

To avoid 25 N-K5ch, followed by 26 N-B3.

<table>
<tr><td>25</td><td>P-N5</td><td>P-R6</td></tr>
<tr><td>26</td><td>NxP</td><td>P-R7</td></tr>
<tr><td>27</td><td>P-N6</td><td>P-R8(Q)</td></tr>
</table>

White shortly resigned.

Thus the peregrinations of the Bishop have won out. But only by the slimmest of margins.

Range as a Factor

The long-distance range of the Bishop often can be utilized not only to further the advance of the Pawn, but also to tie up the Knight completely. Here is a case in point.

1 **B-Q5**   ....

Thereby stalemating the Knight.

    1 ....   **K-K2**
    2 **K-B5**   ....

With the Bishop and Knight off the board, the Pawn ending is a simple draw. But they are on the board, and the Bishop performs an additional function.

    2 ....   **K-K1**

In this instance the Bishop holds Black's KB2 square and enables White to obtain the opposition and a winning Pawn ending. In any case, however, White wins by advancing his Pawn to the seventh, supported by the King. For under no circumstances is Black stalemated.

    3 **K-K6**   **K-B1**
    4 **K-Q7**   **Resigns**

The Pawn queens.

Reversing an Exception

An extra Rook Pawn ahead is often a tremendous advantage in the Bishop versus Knight endings, as here, for the Knight suffers its limitations when approaching the edge of the board and meets with great difficulties in stopping the Pawn.

| | 1 K-N5 | N-B7 |
| | 2 P-R4 | N-K5ch |

If 2 ... N-N5; 3 P-R5, Black is in *zugzwang*.

	3 K-N6	NxB
	4 P-R5	N-B5
	5 P-R6	N-K4ch

Black attempts to re-enter the orbit of the Pawn.

| | 6 K-N7 | K-N5 |
| | 7 P-R7 | Resigns |

Black is too late.

PART 2—PRO KNIGHT

Merely Exceptional?

In general, a Bishop can exploit a material advantage somewhat more easily than a Knight. There are, of course, exceptions to the rule. This is one of them.

1 N-N3	B-K4

Not 1 ... BxN stalemate. The thematic stalemate defense occurs more often with the Bishop because of its excess power, concentrated in the critical area.

2 N-B1	K-K7
3 K-N2	B-B5

It now appears hopeless for White.

4 K-R1!!	....

Again on the same theme.

4	K-B6

Not 4 ... KxN stalemate.

5 N-N3!	B-K6

Again the Knight is immune on account of stalemate.

6 K-R2	Draw

There is no way to make progress.

The Exceptional Extended

Without the assistance of the adverse King, the extra Pawn wins for the Knight if the Bishop can be shunted to the short diagonal, where its maneuverability is limited.

1 N-Q6	....

Threatening 2 P-B6 and 3 P-B7.

1	B-N8
2 P-B6	B-N3

The Bishop is now on the short diagonal.

3 K-K6	....

The threat is 4 K-Q7 and 5 N-B4.

3	B-B2
4 K-Q7	B-N1
5 N-N5	K-N7

The Bishop may not move on account of the return of the Knight to Q6.

6 N-B7	K-B6
7 K-B8!	....

Observe how the Bishop's moves are circumscribed.

	7	**B-R2**
	8 **N-N5**	**B-N3**

If 8 ... B-K6, 9 N-Q6!

	9 **N-R3!**	**K-K5**
	10 **N-B4**	**B-B7**
	11 **K-Q7**	**B-N6**
	12 **N-Q6ch**	**Resigns**

The Pawn cannot be stopped.

Additional Force

This position has all the earmarks of the previous one, except that White has an additional Pawn.

Here the win ought to be simpler because of White's additional Pawn. But the Bishop is on the long diagonal, and this creates some problems. It need not be surprising if the same technique, applied to this problem as the previous one, is sufficient. But there is another way.

	1 **K-B8**	**B-Q3**
	2 **N-K7!**	**K-B5**

If 2 ... B-K4; 3 N-Q5, K-N6; 4 N-K3, K-B5; 5 N-B1, White wins. For now White's Knight Pawn is immune from capture and all that is necessary is for White to win the Bishop for the Bishop Pawn.

3 **K-Q7**   **K-K4**

If *3* ... B-N1, White has *4* N-Q5ch, K-K5; *5* N-B3ch, K-K6; *6* N-K2! Then White's Knight is immune on account of the threat of P-N4. White proceeds to pick off the Bishop for the Bishop Pawn, and it is over.

4 **P-N4**   **B-N1**
5 **P-N5**   **Resigns**

For White continues with P-B7, and the rest is easy.

Still Exceptional

When the extra Pawn is on the side of the Knight, it is usually more difficult to force it to the eighth rank, particularly when the Bishop controls or is able to control one of the squares over which the Pawn must go. Given a special case, as here, the Knight wins with precision play.

1 **N-B3**   **B-Q1**
2 **N-K5**   **K-R2**

If 2 ... B-R5; 3 N-N4, B-Q1; 4 N-B6 wins.

3 N-N4	K-R1 [1]
4 N-B6	Resigns

The Bishop must abandon the all-important diagonal.

Observe the feature of this end game which makes the win possible. It is Black's King, incarcerated in the corner. If, at the critical moment, the King were able to move, White could not force the win. But because of this, Black is literally in *zugzwang*.

CONCLUSION

In the greater number of instances here the Knight has prevailed. Lest we mislead the reader, we hasten to state that, in the general rule, the Bishop holds the edge.

As the general rule is more easily stated, it is readily absorbed and then taken for granted. So its instances become less noteworthy. Nonetheless, the general rule—here the Bishop—does prevail.

Still, in chess the exceptional is important. And instances in which the Knight prevails, like the irregular verbs in French, crop up in so many different guises that one must never unthinkingly underestimate the power of the Knight.

[1] 3 ... B-N4 may hold the game!

14

Know your endings! *White on the move; who wins? Try to solve position first, then see last example.*

Rook versus Pawns

IT IS A well-known fact that a Rook is much stronger than a Pawn. Five times as strong, to be exact, in the normal position. When an ending is reached, however, and mating threats are subdued, the Pawn comes into its own. With each advance toward the eighth rank, the Pawn looms as a greater menace, for the eighth rank usually means the conversion from Pawn to Queen; and there is no greater power on the chessboard than the Queen. It is this potential, ever-changing value which

ennobles the Pawn and so creates conflict between units of
such unlike stature.

When two or more Pawns oppose a Rook in an ending, the
play is often tenuous. The difference between a win, a draw,
and a loss is the location of the adverse Kings. When the
superior King is within the orbit of the opposing Pawns, the
King and Rook, operating in concert, mop up the Pawns. When
the superior King, however, is on the borderline or out of
reach of the Pawn(s), and when, above all, the inferior King
lends support to the Pawn(s), the play is treacherous and
exacting.

PART 1—ROOK VERSUS PAWN

A Model Ending—and a Refinement

The usual way of ending the career of an ambitious Pawn
is to bring the superior King within its "square" and pick it
off. That method works here by *1* K-N5, *2* K-B4, *3* K-Q3 heading for KN2. But it happens to be the arduous way. There is
a simpler.

1 **R-N1ch!** ....

The essence here is to gain time by forcing the adverse King
back. As it must then return to further the advance of the
Pawn, White's net gain is one of several moves.

1 .... **K-B4**

To be able to protect the Pawn in the event of 2 R-KR1.

| 2 | R-KR1 | K-N3 |

The Pawn is protected but Black's King is set back two squares.

3	K-N5	P-R4
4	K-B4	K-N4
5	K-Q3	K-N5

White's gain of time enables him to reach the goal with a move in hand.

6	K-K2	P-R5
7	K-B2	P-R6
8	R-R1	Resigns

For Black's King is soon driven from the defense of the Pawn.

The Model Ending

Still, as an exercise, it is important to know what happens in the model ending with a direct approach.

(Start from previous diagram)

1	K-N5	P-R4
2	K-B4	P-R5
3	K-Q3	K-N6

Or 3 ... P-R6; 4 K-K2, K-N6 reverts to the same position as in the next note.

| 4 | K-K2 | K-N7 |

On 4 ... P-R6, White's job is comparatively simple: 5 K-B1, P-R7 (or 5 ... K-R7; 6 R-R3 and mate next); 6 R-R3ch, and Black's Pawn must fall.

| 5 | R-R8 | P-R6 |
| 6 | R-N8ch | .... |

Note the classic use of the Rook: it works from behind the King and Pawn.

6	....	**K-R8**
7	**K-B2**	**P-R7**
8	**K-N3!**	....

White releases the stalemate.

8	....	**K-N8**
9	**K-R3dis.ch**	**K-R8**
10	**R-QR8**	**Resigns**

For, after *11* R-R1ch, White picks off the Pawn.

Another Pawn Pursuit

Here is another version of a Pawn chase by an enemy King and Rook.

But because the Pawn is on the third rank, the winning technique is much simpler than first appears.

1	**R-R5!**	....

This is an attempt to fix the opposing King on its third rank. On this rank it cannot support the Pawn on the sixth rank and beyond.

1	....	**P-N4**
2	**K-Q7**	....

The White King approaches, and it is a matter of time before the Pawn is picked off.

2 .... **P-N5**

Black is lost no matter how he proceeds: e.g., 2 ... K-N3 (to use the Pawn as a shield for crossing over at Black's KR4); 3 K-K6, K-R4; 4 K-B5 after which the Pawn is a "gone gosling."

3 **K-Q6** ...

White need not be perturbed about any further advance of the Pawn. For after 3 ... P-N6; 4 R-R3, P-N7; 5 R-KN3, the Pawn falls.

3 .... **K-N3**

Black only marks time, since he cannot advance the Pawn.

4 **R-K5** ....

Other moves will do, too, but this one is thematic. White's plan is to pick off the Black Pawn with the King. 4 K-K5 interferes with the Rook and permits Black's King to go to N4. After the text move, Black's King is still fixed on the third rank.

4 .... **K-B3**
5 **K-Q5** **Resigns**

For, as already noted, 5 ... P-N6 is met by 6 R-K3, P-N7; 7 R-KN3. On other temporizing moves, White gets his King, via Q4, to the opposing Pawn.

A Finesse

There are many ways of skinning a Pawn in Rook versus Pawn endings. Here, for example, the White King is out of bounds, or apparently so, and the Black King is in position to support the advance of the Pawn. By delicate tactics, however, the Rook can triumph.

1 R-Q2 . . . .

It is clear that the Rook must move. Why to Q2 is the perplexing question. The point will become clear as the play progresses.

1 . . . . **P-Q5**

Not *1* . . . K-K5; *2* K-Q6, P-Q5; *3* K-B5, P-Q6; *4* K-B4, as the Pawn goes lost.

2 R-Q1! . . . .

The point. White actually took two moves—on purpose—to reach Q1, when he might have done so in one move. In this way he obtains the position he is seeking while he still maintains the opposition with his King. The King opposition is essential to make successful progress.

2 . . . . **K-Q4**

Black tries to circumscribe the White King from the critical sector.

3 K-Q7! . . . .

By maintaining the opposition, White forces Black to give ground. Observe that, if Black could maintain the opposition,

White's King could not advance soon enough to count in the immediate proceedings.

Observe, too, that 3 K-B6 will not do. *3* ... K-K5; *4* K-K6, P-Q6, and Black has the opposition.

	3	**K-K5**

Or *3* ... K-B5; *4* K-K6. In either case, the Pawn soon falls.

4	**K-B6**	**P-Q6**
5	**K-B5**	**K-K6**
6	**K-B4**	**P-Q7**

One move too late.

7	**K-B3**	**Resigns**

PART 2—ROOK VERSUS PAWNS

A Critical Point

This position points up the danger of two connected passed Pawns pitted against a Rook. When the Pawns are on the sixth rank, the Pawns will beat a Rook, generally, when both Kings are out of the critical sector.

White Wins

1	**P-B6**	**K-B2**
2	**P-N7**	**R-KN4**
3	**P-B7**	**Resigns**

For there is no way of preventing queening; and a Queen wins against a Rook with a reasonable degree of ease.

An Exception to the Point

To be sure there are exceptions to almost every principle in chess. This position contradicts the previous one. Black has two Pawns on the sixth, which ought to beat the Rook. Yet the Rook wins.

The Pawns and the Rook are, indeed, the overshadowing factors of this position. But the positions of the Kings, too, play a leading role. Here, curiously, the Black King is at a disadvantage.

White Wins

1 R-Q2ch!! . . . .

To force the King to the first rank.

1 . . . . K-N8

Obviously, if King to the sixth rank, then 2 R-Q3ch, followed by RxP, etc. And if *1* . . . K-R8; 2 K-N3, Black is mated next move.

2 K-B3!!! . . . .

This move places the White King in the proper position for subsequent action, as will be seen.

2 . . . . K-B8

Of course, if 2 ... K-R8; 3 K-N3, mate follows, as already noted. If, however, 2 ... P-N7; 3 R-Q1ch, K-R7; 4 R-KN1, P-R7 (4 ... K-R6; 5 R-R1 mate); 5 RxPch, followed by RxP, etc. Also, if 2 ... P-R7; 3 R-Q1ch, K-R7; 4 R-KR1, P-N7; 5 RxP, the Knight Pawn is pinned and falls.

3 R-QR2   K-Q8

If 3 ... K-N8; 4 R-K2 forces the variations given in the note to Black's 2 ... K-B8.

4 K-Q3   K-B8

Black is wriggling and squirming out of the mating threat. If 4 ... K-K8 instead, 5 K-K3, threatens mate, and the White King then approaches the Black Pawns and is able to pick them off.

5 K-K3   . . . .

Approaching the Pawns with a view to capturing them.

5 . . . .   P-R7

Or 5 ... P-N7; 6 K-B2, and White's King controls the Pawns.

6 R-R1ch   K-N7
7 R-R1!   K-N6

For, if 7 ... P-N7; 8 RxP, the remaining Pawn is pinned.

8 K-B3   Resigns

Illusion

The following position has all the earmarks of a mopping-up operation. White's Pawns apparently are doomed, for the

White King seems to be too far away to lend support. All is not what it seems!

White to Move and Draw

> *1* **K-B4** . . . .

Given time, of course, White aims to protect the Pawns.

> *1* **R-KB2**

Soon, it seems, there will be no Pawns. . . .

> *2* **P-R7!** . . . .

. . . but White has other ideas on the subject.

> *2* . . . . **RxRP**
> *3* **K-Q5** . . . .

White's last Pawn move has sidetracked the Rook just enough to give the King time to defend the remaining Pawn.

Drawn

For after *4* K-K6 and P-B7, the Rook must fall for the Pawn.

Another Illusion

Three Pawns can be mighty dangerous even against a Rook. Here, curiously, even without the assistance of the King, they are self-sustaining.

White to Move and Draw

1 P-K6	R-QB6

The Rook heads for the first rank. For, anywhere else, the Rook cannot inflict any real damage. Thus, if *1 ... R-K6; 2 P-K7.* The Pawns then protect themselves, for the Bishop Pawn is immune to capture by the Rook or King, since a capture will allow one of the other Pawns to Queen.

2 **K-N5**	**R-B1**
3 **K-N6**	....

Not now *3 P-K7* because of *4 ... R-K1*, followed by ... K-B2 and ... KxP.

3	**K-R2!**

Black threatens *4 ... R-K1*, after which Pawns will fall.

4 **K-N7**	....

It seems that White is too late, but a neat trick turns the tables.

4	**R-K1**
5 **P-N8(Q)ch!**	....

Not 5 P-K7, K-N1; 6 K-B7, K-B2; 7 K-Q7, R-QR1, as the Pawns then fall.

	5	RxQ
Forced.		
	6 P-B7	R-KB1
Otherwise 7 P-K7.		
	7 K-B6!	K-N2
	8 P-K7	KxP
	Drawn	

A Flock of Finesses

This Rook versus Pawns ending combines a number of diverse ideas to bring about the final denouement.

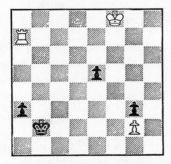

White to Move and Win

It is evident that Black threatens to queen the Rook Pawn in two moves. Hence, White must make haste.

1 **K-K7** ....

White's strategic plan is to trade off his Rook for the Rook Pawn, providing he can pick off both of Black's remaining Pawns. Then, with his extra Knight Pawn, he hopes to win.

The reason for the original King move is not clear at this juncture. It will become clear, however, as the play progresses.

There are a certain number of finesses based upon the King sortie.

1	**P-R7**
2 **K-Q6!**	....

White answers 2 ... P-R8(Q) by 3 RxQ, KxR; 4 KxP, followed by 5 K-B4 and 6 KxP.

2	**P-K5**
3 **K-B5!**	....

The oblique movement of the King is the only way, for a reason which is not yet apparent. It does provide at the moment, however, for 3 ... P-R8(Q) by 4 RxQ, KxR; 5 K-Q4 and the mopping up of both remaining Black Pawns.

3	**P-K6**
4 **K-N4!!**	....

All part and parcel of the same plan. The King belongs on N4, as will be seen in the next play. Of course if here 4 ... P-R8(Q), White is able to give up the Rook and gain both of Black's other Pawns with an easy win.

4	**P-K7**

Now for the point. Observe that both of the Kings are in opposition. This allows the following finesse.

5 **R-K7**	**P-R8(Q)**
6 **RxPch**	....

Because the Kings are in opposition, the Black King cannot escape. The newly created Queen is forfeit.

6	**K-N8**
7 **R-K1ch**	**K-R7**
8 **RxQch**	**Resigns**

The rest is easy.

15

Know your endings! *Is the position in the photograph above the usual draw of Rook against Bishop? Or can you contrive a win for White? Tackle the problem first. Then see last example, page 151.*

Rook versus Bishop

THERE is a vast difference, according to the table of relative values, between a Rook and a Bishop. A Rook is the equivalent of five Pawns, a Bishop of only three. That is why a Rook and other material will generally prevail over a Bishop and like material with consummate ease.

143

When the position simmers down to a lone Rook versus a lone Bishop, however, that is another story. The result is usually a draw. The manifest injustice of the denouement is only one more example of the absence of complete equity in the game of chess.

The rule of thumb then is that a lone Rook only draws against a lone Bishop. Like all such rules, however, this one, too, is subject to exceptions. By the exceptions shall you know the rule.

THE "OPPOSITION" BROOKS NO OPPOSITION

In lone Rook versus lone Bishop endings the only winning chance arises when the inferior King is on the edge of the board or can be driven to that sector. In all cases the superior King must be in opposition to the other, or must be in position to take the opposition at an opportune moment.

White Wins

This position is a set up.

1	**R-R2ch**	**B-R5**
2	**R-R1**	**Resigns**

Black must abandon the Bishop.

A MORE PRACTICAL TEST

One of the standard winning positions follows. Here the Black King is in a mating net. No matter how the Bishop squirms, Black will lose.

White Wins

The general plan is to force the Bishop to a poor square, from which point it can be attacked with fatal results.

1 R-QB6   B-Q1

A poor square is Black's B5. Then 2 R-B4, B-K6; 3 R-R4ch, B-R3; 4 R *tempos* on the file, K-R1; 5 RxB mate.

2 R-Q6   B-B2

2 ... B-N4 will not do because of 3 R-Q3. Black then cannot defend against the threat of R-R3ch; for, after 3 ... K-R3, 4 R-R3ch wins, the Bishop serving as a block. Nor is 2 ... B-R4 good because of the reply, 3 R-Q5, attacking the Bishop, followed by 4 R-R5ch, winning. Nor is 2 ... B-R5 good because of 3 R-Q4, attacking the Bishop. If then 3 ... B-N4, 4 R-Q3, as previously, wins. Or, if 3 ... B-N6; 4 R-Q3, B-R5; 5 R-R6, and White wins.

3 R-Q7   B-N3

3 ... B-N1 is also possible. Black is putting up the greatest resistance.

4 R-N7!   B-K6

On *4 . . . B-Q1* or *4 . . . B-Q3*, White wins with 5 K-K8dis.ch
or 5 K-K6dis.ch, winning the Bishop.

5 R-N3   Resigns

For there is nothing to be done against the menacing
R-R3(ch).

AN ILLUSION POINTS A RULE

The following position appears to be a win. It is, however,
only a draw.

White Draws

Black threatens *1 . . .* B-B5ch, which will keep White from
maintaining the opposition. For if 2 K-B8, K-R2. Hence, White
checks.

1 R-R2ch   B-R2
Draw

There is no way, with correct play, of making progress.
A Rook *tempo* only produces a stalemate.

The rule is that the game is a draw if the inferior King is
cornered where the Bishop controls the double corner and the
Bishop is able to interpose, or drive the opposing King away.

THE REAL TEST

Where the Kings are in secure opposition, which cannot be disturbed by a Bishop check (as in the previous position), the result is almost always a win. Precision technique, however, is required.

White Wins

With Black to move, the game is a draw. *1* ... K-R4 or *1* ... K-R6 is good enough. But White is on the move.

1 **R-R1**   **B-N7**

If *1* ... B-R6; *2* R-R1, Black must abandon his Bishop.
At N7 the Bishop creates a situation on which White must capitalize.

2 **R-R5**   ....

An important move. This restrains the movement of the Black King. For if now *2* ... K-R6; *3* R-R5 is mate, the Bishop serving as a block.

Hence, the Bishop must move, and there is a way of exploiting each one of its moves.

2   ....   **B-B8**

The Bishop returns. On other tries, Black also loses: e.g., *2* ... B-R8; *3* R-R3 (preventing a King move), B-N7; *4* R-KN3,

and the Bishop must fall in a few moves. To continue: *4* ...
B-Q4; *5* R-N5, B-B3; *6* R-N6, B-K1; *7* R-R6ch, B-R4; *8* Rook
tempos on the file, King moves *9* RxB, etc.

White is able to trap the Bishop no matter where it goes.
For a good exercise, try the alternate possibilities until you
have full command of what is involved.

3 **R-KN5!** ....

This is a key play. It permits Black momentarily to break
the opposition.

3 .... **K-R6**

Again there are Bishop moves which create problems. There
are, however, solutions to them. For instance, *3* ... B-R6 is
met by *4* R-N8, and the check at R8 is fatal.

Or *3* ... B-Q6; *4* R-N3, B-B5; *5* R-QB3, B-N4 (Black tries
to keep off a poor square which will permit a lateral attack and
a later threat of mate); *6* R-N3, B-B5; *7* R-N4. The Bishop is
lost: *7* ... B-Q4 or *7* ... B-Q6; *8* K-K5dis.ch or *8* K-K3dis.ch,
respectively. Or *7* ... B-K7; *8* R-N2, followed by *9* R-R2ch,
etc. Or *7* ... B-B8; *8* R-N1, B-N7; *9* R-N8, K-R4; *10* R-R8ch,
K-N3; *11* R-N8ch and the Bishop falls.

It is to be noted that, with *7* ... B-B8, the position is nearly
the same one as in the diagram. The main difference is White's
Rook on the Knight file and able to play to N8; whereas, in
the diagrammed position, when Black's Bishop is forced to
Black's N7, White is unable to continue with R-R8, for that
square is controlled by the Bishop.

4 **R-N3ch** ....

This brings the Kings back into opposition or creates a position similar to our second diagram.

4 .... **K-R7**

If *4* ... K-R5, *5* R-N1, B-R6; *6* R-KR1, etc.

5 **K-B3** **B-K7ch**

A spite check, of no avail.

6 K-B2   Resigns

No matter where the wicked Bishop may flee, the White Rook pursueth.

EXCEPTION AGAIN!

There is no rule that will cover all positions. Here, for example, the Kings are not in opposition. If White takes the opposition with *1* K-N6, Black breaks it with *1* ... K-B1. Yet, because of the geometric limitations of the Bishop and the board, White wins.

1 R-Q4!   . . . .

Black is in *zugzwang*. If he did not have to move, he could draw. But he must move.

1 . . . .   B-B8

Clearly *1* ... K-B1 allows mate on the move. *1* ... K-R1 or *1* ... K-R2 allows 2 R-R4ch, winning the Bishop. Bishop to any other square allows an immediate capture of the Bishop or the gain of the Bishop in a move.

2 K-N6!   . . . .

Threatening mate, and there is no valid escape.

2 . . . .   Resigns

After *2* ... K-B1, 3 R-B4ch wins the Bishop. Since the Bishop cannot break the opposition by a check, Black resigns.

AND AGAIN!

The unhappy situation of the Black Bishop here, too, is enough for Black's downfall.

| 1 K-B5 | . . . . |

Threatening mate.

| 1 . . . . | K-R3 |

There is no Bishop check to break the opposition, and 1 . . . K-R5 loses to 2 R-B4ch.

| 2 K-B6 | . . . . |

Taking the opposition and threatening to win as in the first example.

| 2 . . . . | K-R4 |

Breaking the opposition.

| 3 R-B5ch | K-R3 |

Forced, for, after 3 . . . K-R5, 4 R-B4ch wins the Bishop.

| 4 R-B4 | Resigns |

The check at R4 is fatal.

FINAL TEST

Often in a Rook and Bishop ending the win is there. But, as Tarrasch has said, "You must see it." To see it, of course, presupposes that you have a fundamental idea of what is involved.

White Wins

1 **R-B3** . . . .

Threatening mate.

1 . . . . **B-Q2**
2 **R-KN3!** . . . .

The star move. Observe the various moves at Black's command. *1* . . . B-B1 loses the Bishop to a check. Other Bishop moves leave the Bishop subject to capture, except *2* . . . B-B4.

2 . . . . **K-R2**

If *2* . . . B-B4; *3* R-N8ch, K-R2; *4* R-N5, and White wins the Bishop.

3 **R-N5** . . . .

Threatening mate.

3 . . . .   **K-R3**

To break the opposition.

4 **K-B6**   **Resigns**

Taking the opposition and reaching the standard position. Black may not break the opposition by 4 ... K-R2 on account of 5 R-N7ch, winning the Bishop.

16

Know your endings! *How does White win here? Don't let preconceived notions influence you here. Solve the problem on your own merits. Can you? For answer, see last example.*

Rook and Pawn versus Rook

I<small>T IS NOT</small> so strange that many epic battles of the chessboard culminate in an ending with a Pawn plus for one of the players. It is, indeed, a likelihood that a game between more or less evenly matched adversaries in a contest of attrition will produce such an insignificant difference. When that extra Pawn is in a position which has simmered down to Rook and Pawn play, as is often the case, the result is problematical. There are times when the Pawn wins perforce, and there are times when the Pawn can be checked.

To distinguish between the resulting wins and draws demands a refined technique. In some cases, for example, the only drawing method is to bring the Rook behind the Pawn. In other cases, the only method is to bring the Rook to the side or in front of the Pawn. To know these ideas is the certain path to correct planning and projecting in Rook and Pawn endings.

A BASIC EXAMPLE

With a Pawn behind here, White can hold the game even.

White Draws

Because White is a Pawn behind, the onus of proving the draw rests with him. From the diagrammed position many moves, if correctly pursued, will draw. There is, however, one principle that embraces the correct technique. It involves the defense on the third rank. Black's King shall not cross onto White's third rank.

1 R-KN3 . . . .

For all intents and purposes, a stall. White bides his time until Black threatens to enter White's third rank.

1 . . . . R-R7ch

Black drives the enemy King to the first rank.

2 K-K1 . . . .

2 K-Q1 is just as good.

2 . . . . K-Q4

Black's plan is to play 3 ... K-B5, followed by ... P-Q6 and ... K-B6, when the concerted action of all his forces will smooth the path of the Pawn to the eighth.

> 3 **K-Q1** ....

White stalls again. His stand is on the third rank.

> 3 .... **K-B5**
>
> 4 **R-KR3** ....

Still biding his time, White holds the third rank.

> 4 .... **P-Q6**

Now Black threatens ... K-B6. The time has come for counter-action.

> 5 **R-R8!** ....

White dare not permit the Black King to reach B6 unmolested.

Why did White select this particular moment to go to R8? The reason is simple and clear. Heretofore, a Rook move to the eighth allowed the Black King to go to B6, after which a Rook check from behind would have driven the King to Q6, where it would have been sheltered. Black would then have been in a winning position. Since Black's Pawn moved to Q6, however, the Pawn no longer can afford shelter to the King. Hence, the timing of the Rook move.

Draw

No matter how Black plays, he is subject to flailing checks, which he cannot very well avoid. A Rook interposition, for example, permits the exchange of Rooks and a subsequent draw.

Before examining the next position, let us summarize the salient features of the drawing method.

(1) White maintains his Rook on the third rank, preventing the Black King from crossing onto that rank.

(2) When the Black King threatens to invade, White essays his Rook to the eighth, and Black cannot successfully ward off the ensuing checks.

Worthy of note is that this ending is basic. The same method applies if Black's Pawn is on some other file or rank. Then White takes his stand on another rank, never permitting the Black King shelter in front of the Pawn.

AN UNLIKE PAIR OF EXAMPLES

With the Pawn advanced to the sixth rank, as in the following position, and the superior King sheltered from molesting checks, the result is usually a win for the Pawn. Here it does not matter who moves first. White wins.

White Wins

1 **R-KR2** . . . .

White threatens mate. With Black on the move, the result is the same, since his Rook is tied to the first rank to prevent mate.

1	. . . .	**K-N1**
2	**R-N2ch**	**K-R2**

If *2* ... K-B1; *3* P-K7ch, followed by *4* R-N8ch, decides.

3	**K-B7**	**Resigns**

There is nought can be done about both the threat of R-R2 mate and that of the advance of the Pawn simultaneously.

In many respects the following position is similar to the previous one. There is, however, one vital difference—the Pawn is on the Knight file. Because of that factor, the position is a draw.

1	. . . .	**R-R7**
2	**R-QB1**	. . . .

Or any other move with the Rook on the first rank.

2	. . . .	**R-N7ch**
3	**K-R1**	. . . .

Not *3* K-B1, for then ... K-R7 wins.

3	**R-R7ch**
4 **K-N1**	. . . .
Draw	

Black can make no further progress. He must not advance
. . . P-N7 on account of 5 R-B3ch.

THE LUCENA POSITION

When, as in the following diagram, the inferior King is cut
off from the defense, the Pawn generally wins. The winning
technique, however, is a matter of knowledge.

White Wins

1	**R-Q8**

There is no valid defense for Black, but he can put up strong
resistance. The text move offers the best chances.

2 **K-B5**	. . . .

White makes way for the advance of the Pawn.

2	**R-B8ch**
3 **K-Q6**	. . . .

Thereby White leaves the square, Q5, vacant, so that the
Pawn can advance.

3	R-Q8
4 P-Q5	R-Q6

Black can do no better than stall.

5 K-B6	R-B6ch
6 K-Q7	....

Again White leaves Q6 vacant for the advance of the Pawn.

6	R-Q6
7 P-Q6	R-Q8
8 K-B7	R-B8ch
9 K-Q8	R-Q8

So far so good. White has made progress in getting the Pawn down. Following the next move, White's play will require a new plan.

10 P-Q7	R-QB8

Now, how does White extricate his King and succeed in queening his Pawn?

11 R-B2ch	....

The first of the important moves. The Black King must be driven away from guarding the exit.

11	K-N2
12 R-B5!	....

A star move. White can make no progress by exiting with his King to K7, thus: 12 K-K7, R-K8ch; 13 K-Q6, R-Q8ch; 14 K-B7, R-B8ch; 15 K-Q8, R-QB8.

After the text move, White does threaten to exit with his King. For, assuming it is White's move, 13 K-K7, R-K8ch; 14 K-Q6, R-Q8ch; 15 R-Q5, and it is over. The Rook, by going to the fifth rank, is preparing to interpose on one of the checks.

12	K-N3
13 R-B4	....

13 K-K7 works also by tricky play. It resolves the ending, however, into a Queen versus Rook ending. And it is not the thematic continuation.

Now White threatens to bring his King out, and, after exhausting Black's checks, interpose his Rook at either K4 or Q4 and so cut off Black's Rook from the action on the Pawn.

13	. . .	**K-N2**

If *13* ... K-N4; *14* R-B7 and the threat of *15* K-K8, followed by queening of the Pawn, cannot be met.

14	**K-K7**	**R-K8ch**
15	**K-Q6**	**R-Q8ch**
16	**K-K6**	**R-K8ch**

Otherwise *17* R-B5-Q5. If *16* ... K-N3, *17* R-B8 and the Pawn cannot be stopped.

17	**K-Q5**	**R-Q8ch**
18	**R-Q4**	**Resigns**

THE ROOK PAWN EXCEPTION

In almost every phase of the ending, the Rook Pawn plays its exceptional part. With Rooks on the board, the Rook Pawn, too, voids all preconceived principles.

Here is one of the important exceptions. The Black King is ahead of its Pawn and the White King is cut off from participation in the critical sector. Yet the result is a draw.

Draw

Despite the advantage in Black's favor, there is little he can do. For, on the edge of the board, the Black King is limited in scope. There is only one try. It is to bring the Black Rook to Black's KN6, N7, or N8. When the Rooks are opposed, the White Rook will be compelled to abandon the file. Then, maybe, the Black King will exit.

1	....	**R-QR2**	
2	**K-K2**	....	

White must anticipate Black's action. If he merely temporizes, he will lose. He must bring his King, at the first opportunity, to KB1 or KB2.

2	....	**R-R7ch**	
3	**K-B1**	**R-KN7**	

Now the Rooks are opposed, and White must abandon the Knight file.

4	**R-KB8**	....

There are many moves that are sufficient here. The text move is made with a view to preclude Black from checking on the Bishop file later on, and driving off the White King.

4	....	**K-N6**

The King is out. But not for long.

5	**R-N8ch**	**K-R7**

The King popped out but has nowhere to go. On other moves, such as ... K-B6 or K-R5, the Rook checks relentlessly until such time as the King abandons the Pawn. Then the Rook attacks the Rook Pawn, and Black is unable to make progress.

6 **R-KB8**   **Draw**

If Black continues with ... K-R8 and ... P-R7, he is unable to exit with his King.

THE EXCEPTION EXCEPTED

The following position has all the earmarks of the previous one with a vital difference. That difference, however, is enough to turn the usual draw into a win for White.

White Wins

The Black King is now limited to the Bishop file. This factor gives White ample time to describe the winning maneuver.

1 **R-KR1**   . . . .

The plan is to bring the Rook to QN8 as quickly as possible.

1 . . . .   **K-K2**

As before, Black hurries to post his King on ... QB1 or ... QB2.

2 **R-R8**   **K-Q2**
3 **R-QN8**   . . . .

Now Black must abandon the file, while White has an exit for his King.

3	. . . .	**R-QB7**
4	**K-N7**	. . . .

White threatens to queen.

4	. . . .	**R-N7ch**
5	**K-R6**	**R-R7ch**
6	**K-N6**	**R-N7ch**
7	**K-B5!**	. . . .

White queens perforce.

It is to be noted that, had Black played his King to Q3 to guard the exit at White's B5, White would still have won by playing his King to B8.

7	. . . .	**Resigns**

ROOK TO THE FORE!

Generally speaking, the Rook is most effective behind the Pawn. There are times, however, when the vantage point is in front of the Pawn. Here is an instance.

Draw

White has much in his favor here. He is not only a Pawn to the good but also the Black King is shut out of the defense.

Yet Black's King and Rook are sufficiently disposed to hold matters even.

1 **K-B4** . . . .

Or *1* K-R4, R-R1ch; *2* K-N5, R-N1ch; *3* K-B4, reaching the text position.

1 . . . . **R-KR1**

Now White is at a loss to make progress. If his Rook moves, then *2* . . . K-B3, after which Black's King joins the defense, and Black draws as in "A Basic Example." White dare not advance his Pawn on account of *2* . . . R-R5ch, after which White's Rook is vulnerable. Hence, White is reduced to temporizing or taking a stand on a slim prospect.

2 **K-N3** . . . .

White returns, hoping that Black may go wrong.

2 . . . . **R-QN1**

As good as any. But not, for example, . . . R-R8 with the idea of getting behind the Pawn, for then *3* R-B3 gives White the necessary setup to be able to advance his Pawn to N5.

3 **K-R4** **R-R1ch**
4 **R-R5** **R-R1**

Of course not the exchange of Rooks.

5 **K-N5** **R-N1ch**
6 **K-B4** **R-B1ch**
7 **R-B5** . . . .

White can make no headway.

7 . . . . **RxRch**
8 **PxRch** **K-B3**
Draw

ILLUSION!

According to all the rules and regulations, the following position ought to be an easy win for White. It isn't.

Everything is favorable for White here. He is a Pawn to the good; his King is in front of the Pawn; and the queening path is clear. Yet Black can hold the game.

1 ....   **R-N3!**

The star move. What is White to do? His King cannot move without giving up the Pawn, and on R-K7, Black temporizes.

2 **P-K7**   ....

The only attempt at progress. 2 R-KR8 avails nothing: *2* ... RxP; *3* R-R5ch, K-N4; *4* KxR, KxR.

2 ....   **R-B3ch**
3 **K-N7**   **R-N3ch**
4 **K-R7**   ....

If *4* K-R8, R-R3.

With White out of check at last it now appears that Black is doomed.

4 ....   **K-B3!**

Black must win the Pawn.

5 R-B8ch   . . . .

On most other Rook moves there follows ... R-N2ch, and the gain of the Pawn.

5 . . . .   KxP

Draw

Each Rook is *en prise*.

17

Know your endings! *Black on the move can draw in the above position. White on the move wins. There is a problem involved which is well worth knowing. The principle is easy; the practical discovery of the best move may not be.*

Queen versus Pawn

THE DIFFERENCE in value between a Queen and a Pawn is so ridiculously great that it seems a discussion on the subject hardly warrants the expenditure of good space, time, and effort. As for so many apparent contradictions, however, there is, indeed, room for elaboration.

When a Pawn reaches the eighth rank, it can be converted into equal force, an opposing Queen. This ever-menacing threat to equalize the game crops up so often in this type of ending that it is imperative to know the technical procedure in winning positions. And, as we have seen so often in study of the end game, the technical procedure involves both general rules, exceptions, and even exceptions to the exceptions. Hence, even this chapter has its special significance.

GENERAL RULE 1

A Pawn even as far as the sixth rank always loses to a Queen except when of course the Queen is subject to immediate capture or when the Pawn can immediately reach the seventh rank and achieve a special drawing position.

White Wins

The goal here is the capture of the Pawn. The procedure calls for concerted action by Queen and King.

1 Q-B3 . . . .

There are any number of ways of beginning this position. *1* Q-Q6ch, *1* Q-B5ch or even *1* K-B5, are sufficient for examples. White's aim is to compel Black's King to assume a post immediately in front of the Pawn. Then, when the Pawn cannot advance, White's King gains time to approach, eventually to pick off the Pawn or incidentally to checkmate.

1 . . . .   **K-Q7**

Black's choice is limited. If he abandons the Pawn, he loses at once. To defend it, he must play the text or 1 ... K-Q5. The latter will not do because, once the White Queen assumes a post in front of the Pawn, White's task is easy. He approaches with his King and drives the Black King away from the defense of the Pawn.

2 Q-B4!   . . . .

Here again White has a vast choice of moves. The text move, however, restricts the Black King more than any other.

2 . . . .   **K-Q6**

Black must abandon the Pawn, get in front of it, or play the text move. Each is equally futile. If 2 ... K-K7, the White King closes in with 3 K-B5.

3 K-B5!   . . . .

This play seems to be out of context, yet it is very strong. Observe that Black must return with his King. For 3 ... P-K7; 4 Q-QB1, followed by 5 Q-K1, leaves the White Queen in front of the Pawn, and the rest is merely a matter of closing in and mopping up.

3 . . . .   **K-Q7**
4 **K-Q4**   **Resigns**

The Pawn falls.

Observe, too, that the strongest move in the initial position is really 1 Q-B4. After that move, Black may not advance his Pawn because of 2 Q-QB1, and his King can only shuttle back and forth, around the Pawn, until it is forced to abandon it.

A RULE AND AN EXCEPTION

When a Pawn is on the seventh rank, opposing a Queen, the winning procedure is exactly the same as if it were on the sixth or any other rank. The plan is to force the inferior King in front of the Pawn and then to close in with the superior King.

There are, however, a number of exceptions to the general rule. The first exception is that of a Pawn on the seventh which is a Bishop Pawn.

White Draws

The Bishop Pawn makes all the difference. With Black to move, he can make no progress.

1	**Q-N3ch**
2 **K-R8!**	....

We immediately get to the crux of the situation. If the Pawn is a King or Queen Pawn, White cannot afford to abandon the Pawn. Here, however, the Pawn can be left *en prise*. For, on 2 ... QxP, the result is stalemate. Black can make no progress.

2	**Drawn**

EXCEPTION TO THE EXCEPTION

White Wins

With the superior King in bounds, in this case able to reach N3, White can yet win.

1 K-B4!   . . . .

Right into the adverse check!

1 . . . .   **K-R1**

If *1* . . . P-B8ch; 2 K-N3, Black cannot avoid being mated. The text move, however, is a trap, so to speak, Black's last gasp.

2 Q-Q2   . . . .

Of course not 2 QxP stalemate. But also, of course, not 2 K-N3 on account of *2* . . . P-B8(N)ch, forking King and Queen.

2 . . . .   **K-N7**

To hold the Pawn, to hold off White's King and to give White the opportunity to blunder.

3 K-N4   **K-N8**

4 K-N3   **Resigns**

For, on *4* . . . P-B8(Q), 5 Q-R2 mate. Or, on *4* . . . P-B8(N)ch; 5 K-R3, the Knight goes lost.

THE ROOK PAWN EXCEPTION

Whenever there are exceptions to a general rule, it is a sure thing that the Rook Pawn will play a role in them. Here is a case in point.

White Draws

The great disparity of material means nothing here, even with Black to move. The edge of the board favors White.

1	. . . .	Q-N3ch
2	K-R8	. . . .

Usually, when the King plays in front of the Pawn, the adverse King has an opportunity to inch in. Here, however, no such opportunity exists. For on 2 . . . K-K4 the result is stalemate. Black can make no progress.

Drawn

A PARADOX

It is not often that an extra Pawn is a liability. Here it is a distinct one.

White Wins

This position, in most respects, is similar to the previous one, except that Black has an extra Pawn. Curiously, this works to Black's disadvantage. It is truly an exception to the exception.

1 Q-N3ch	K-R8

Black cannot afford to abandon the Pawn.

2 Q-B2	. . . .

Because Black has a move, White can temporize.

2	P-R5
3 Q-B1 mate	

A MASQUED BATTERY

There is another case of the exception to the exception. With a Rook Pawn on the seventh rank, the Queen will win if its King can assist in setting up a mating net.

White Wins

1 **K-N6** ....

By masking the Queen, the King is able to approach the sector of the enemy King.

1	**K-N7**	
2 **K-B5dis.ch**	**K-B7**	

Or 2 ... K-R8; *3* K-N4, K-N7; *4* Q-R2ch, K-N8; *5* K-N3, etc.

3 **Q-K5**	**K-N8**
4 **Q-K1ch**	**K-N7**
5 **Q-Q2ch**	**K-N8**

Of course not 5 ... K-R6 or 5 ... K-N6. Then follows *6* Q-B1, and the Black Pawn falls in short order.

6 **K-N4**	**P-R8(Q)**
7 **K-N3**	**Resigns**

Black cannot avoid mate.

Except for the previous text position, where the White King is able to use the position of the Queen as a maneuvering point for approach to the Black King, the superior side will win when the King is within the bounds outlined on the following diagram.

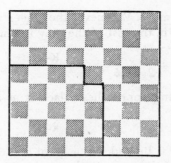

It is to be noted that each square is within two squares of striking distance of either KN3 or KB2. When the King is able to reach either of these two squares within two moves, a mating net can be set up.

RULE 1 AGAIN

When a Pawn is on the sixth rank, as previously stated, it loses to a Queen, unless the Pawn can move at once to the seventh and reach an exceptional position.

The following position, which is a prelude to the next one, is a case in point.

White Wins

1 **Q-N7** . . . .

The thematic move. Whenever the Queen is able to pin the Pawn on the sixth, the rest of the play is simple.

1	**K-N7**
2 **K-K6**	. . . .

The White King approaches. Black is at a loss for a continuation.

2	**K-N6**

Black's choice is limited. He may go to N6 or B7. In either case, he does not threaten to advance his Pawn. And, in each case, the White King closes in.

3 **K-Q5**	**P-B7**

Black takes his stand. Otherwise after *3* ... K-B7, White plays *4* K-B4, and it is over.

4 **Q-R1**	**Resigns**

It is only a question of a few moves before the Pawn falls.

QUEEN VERSUS BISHOP PAWN

A Pawn on the sixth rank generally loses, as noted above. Sometimes, however, the win is difficult, as in the following position.

White Wins

With Black to move, there is no problem. Black plays . . .
P-B7 and secures a draw. With White to move, however, there
is a problem. It stems from the fact that White is unable to
play his Queen onto the long diagonal on the first move
(Q-N7), because the White King is inopportunely posted. And
White is unable successfully to maneuver his Queen to the long
diagonal. Yet there is a way.

Because this position embraces all the ideas of Queen versus
Bishop Pawn, it belongs in the repertoire of all aspiring chess
players. The actual win is easy. To understand all the ideas
which this position embraces, however, is quite a task.

1 Q-R1ch?   . . . .

This is not the best move. In fact, from here on, with best
play, the position is a draw. It is, however, the most likely try.
It is essential for the student to understand why the try will
not work before he can understand fully the thoughts involved
in the position.

1 . . . .   K-N7!

1 . . . K-R7 loses quickly. White follows with 2 Q-Q5ch, and
no matter how Black plays, White will be able to pin the Black
Pawn on the diagonal.

2 Q-N7ch   . . . .

Otherwise, 2 . . . P-B7 draws.

2 . . . .   K-B8!

The first of a series of star moves. On any other move, White
is able to maneuver into a diagonal pin of the Pawn: e.g.,
2 . . K-R8; 3 Q-R6ch, K-N8; 4 Q-B1ch, K-N7; 5 Q-B6, pinning
the Pawn for an easy win.

The position still offers many hurdles for Black.

3 K-B6!   . . . .

Already having misplayed the position, White pursues his best chance. On other moves (except the repetition of checks) Black advances his Pawn. Then, because the Bishop Pawn reaches the seventh, and because the White King is out of bounds, Black draws. The text move is an attempt to bring the King within bounds.

| 3 .... | **P-B7** |
| 4 **K-K5** | .... |

Still approaching in an effort to bring the King within bounds.

| 4 .... | **K-Q7** |

Now Black threatens to Queen.

| 5 **Q-Q5ch!!** | .... |

Black has five different replies. Four of them lose, one draws.

| 5 .... | **K-K8!** |

The drawing move.

5 ... K-B6 loses to 6 Q-Q4ch, followed by 7 Q-R1 and 8 Q-QB1.

5 ... K-B1 loses after 6 Q-R2, K-Q7; 7 K-Q4, K-Q8; 8 K-B3! P-B8(Q)ch; 9 K-Q3 as Black cannot avoid mate.

5 ... K-K7 loses in the same fashion. 6 Q-R2, K-Q6; 7 Q-N2, K-Q7; 8 K-Q4, K-Q8; 9 K-Q3, P-B8(Q); 10 Q-K2 mate. In this line, if 6 ... K-Q7 (instead of 6 ... K-Q6); 7 K-Q4, K-Q8; 8 K-B3, P-B8(Q)ch; 9 K-Q3 and mate soon.

5 ... K-K6 loses to a sharp retort. 6 Q-N2! P-B8(Q); 7 Q-N5ch, followed by picking off the Queen. In this line, if 6 ... K-Q6, then 7 Q-N5, followed by Q-B1, suffices.

| 6 **Q-R5ch** | .... |

White has not yet given up hope. There is still room for blunder.

6	**K-Q8**

6 ... K-K7 loses to 7 Q-R2, as previously demonstrated.

7 **Q-R4**	**K-Q7**

7 ... K-B8 loses to 8 K-Q4, as previously demonstrated.

8 **Q-R2**	....

It appears now that White will win, for the position is similar to the winning ones of the previous variations. But there is a difference. Black's King is on Q7, instead of K7. Hence, there is a saving clause.

8	**K-B6!!**
Drawn	

White can make no progress. Thus, 9 Q-R3ch, K-Q7. Now 10 Q-R2, K-B6, repeats the position. And, if 10 Q-N2, K-Q8. White's Queen is on N2 instead of R2, and this slight distinction makes for the draw.

If all of the foregoing leads to a draw with best play, how does White win? That is the problem.

1 **Q-R6!!!**	**Resigns**

For Black dare not advance his Pawn to B7 on account of 2 Q-B1ch, capturing the Pawn on the following move. If Black fails to advance his Pawn, White is able to maneuver his Queen into a position where he pins the Pawn on the diagonal, and the rest is easy.

18

End Games—Max Euwe

F ROM time to time we have stressed the point that theoretical knowledge is of little value without practical application. The theorist usually wins the "post mortems," while the practical player wins the games.

The following section, contributed by former world champion, Dr. Max Euwe, is all on the practical side. It comprises a selection of end games culled mostly from practical play among the experts and masters. It will give the learner a small idea of the problems confronting the over-the-board player in converting theory into practice.

KINGS AND PAWNS

In the course of Dr. Euwe's main thesis, the difference between composed endings and end games from actual play, he demonstrates some particularly fine points about King and

Pawn end games and the related King and Queen versus King, Queen, and Pawn end games. The one special finesse involves a surprise sacrifice of a Pawn to prevent a winning liquidation (exchange of Queens, reducing to King versus King and Pawn).

On the whole, however, the main lesson may be in the value of probing apparently simple positions deeply enough to uncover the great number of hidden, winning, or drawing finesses which actually often do exist.

We start off with an end-game composition by the famous Pawn artist N. D. Grigoriev.

White to Play and Win

This end game shows once more what finesses lie concealed behind seemingly simple positions, and it demonstrates especially the great number of facets in an end game of such limited material.

1 P-N4! . . . .

First of all, it is evident that, after 1 . . . PxP; 2 P-R5, White wins as his Pawn queens with check. Black's passed Pawns, true enough, are as far advanced as the White one; but, even so, Black must lose an extra *tempo* to get one of his through: 2 . . . P-N6; 3 P-R6, P-N7; 4 K-B2, P-B6; 5 P-R7, P-B7; 6 P-R8(Q)ch, etc.

1	K-K2
2 P-N5	....

Clearly White's only move as, after 2 PxP, K-Q2, the Black King has entered within the Pawn's "square."

2	K-Q3

Seemingly the end of the fun. White has a protected, passed Pawn which ties up Black's King so his own King can go undisturbedly after Black's Bishop Pawn.

3 K-K2	K-K3
4 K-B3	K-K4

Black's King just barely guards the Bishop Pawn without quitting the square of White's passed Pawn. If it were now Black's move, his King would be committed to a choice of going after that Knight Pawn fruitlessly or leaving its square, to hold the Bishop Pawn, equally fruitlessly. From White's point of view, therefore, it obviously now becomes a matter of gaining a *tempo* (or losing one) by means of "triangulation." Not so; Black's King neatly copies all of White's King figures: e.g., *5* K-B2, K-K3; *6* K-K2, K-Q3; *7* K-Q3, K-Q4; *8* K-K2, K-Q3; *9* K-Q2, K-K3, etc.

So White has but one try left.

5 K-N4   K-K5

Now Black's King, it is true, has quit the "square," so White's Pawn can advance to queen. But then so can Black's.

6 P-N6   P-B6
7 K-N3   K-K6

The interpolation of these two King moves is of no importance whatever to the Pawn ending; but it is of decisive significance with regard to the coming Queen end game.

8 P-N7   P-B7
9 P-N8(Q)   P-B8(Q)

Believe it or not, White now wins by force!

10 Q-K5ch   K-Q7

Not *10* ... K-Q6?? *11* Q-N5ch.

11 QxPch   K-Q8

Other possibilities are: (1) *11* ... K-K6; *12* Q-K5ch, K-Q7; *13* Q-B4ch, etc. (2) *11* ... K-B7 (or K-B8); *12* Q-QB5ch, K-N6 (or 7 or 8); *13* Q-N5ch, etc.—or *12* ... K-Q7; *13* Q-KB2ch, etc.

—or *12* ... K-Q8; *13* Q-Q4ch, K-B7; *14* Q-B2ch or *13* ... K-B8; *14* Q-R1ch.

12 Q-Q5ch   K-K8

On *12* ... K-B8; *13* Q-B5ch, we arrive at the variations in the preceding note.

13 Q-K4ch   ....

And White wins after *13* ... K-Q8; *14* Q-N1ch or *13* ... K-Q7; *14* Q-N2ch.

Splendid work, but a composition remains a composition. We have a feeling that this and similar surprising developments would, in practice, occur only by high exception. So we can value the composed end game as an expression of art but must deny it any practical significance.

One who examines end games regularly, however, and who thus often makes surprising discoveries rather inclines to the conclusion that the beautiful windings actually do lie concealed in most practical end games but are usually missed because they are too deeply hidden.

For example, here is the position from a game played in the latest Marshall Chess Club championship in New York City. It makes a remarkable comparison with the Grigoriev composition.

Allen Kaufman

Frank Howard

It is Black's move. After some concentration on this position, the issues are seemingly rather simple. The Black King will proceed to capture the Queen Pawn—whether voluntarily or by compulsion—White takes the Knight Pawn, the two passed Pawns advance, both sides queen their Pawns, and a draw becomes the likely result.

Let us convert this idea into a variation.

(1) *1* ... K-K5; *2* KxP, KxP; *3* K-B4, K-Q6; *4* P-KN4, P-Q5; *5* P-N5, K-B7; *6* P-N6, P-Q6; *7* P-N7, P-Q7; *8* P-N8(Q), P-Q8(Q).

Halt! Here already is our first "point": with *9* Q-N3ch, White exchanges Queens and wins the Pawn ending (*9* ... K-B8; *10* QxQch, KxQ; *11* P-N3! P-N5; *12* K-K4, K-B7; *13* K-Q4, K-N7; *14* K-B4, etc.). This last phase must still be carefully managed, but it all proves to work out right.

Hence, Black's King seems to have moved to an unfortunate square. Black could have tried *5* ... K-K7, instead of *5* ... K-B7. But then, too, things go amiss with Black: *6* P-N6, P-Q6; *7* P-N7, P-Q7; *8* P-N8(Q), P-Q8(Q); *9* Q-N4ch, with the same consequences as before.

Rather nice, but commonplace even so. These developments present about the highest we can expect from actual practice: the side first to promote then forces the exchange of Queens and wins the resulting Pawn ending.

But we have not finished yet. These two pretty but somewhat trite checks are the forerunners of a series of finesses.

But first let us demonstrate that a number of other initial moves but lead to a loss for Black:

(2) *1* ... K-N6? *2* K-N5, KxP; *3* KxP, and White wins easily with no real problems whatsoever.

(3) *1* ... P-N5; *2* P-R4, PxP e.p.; *3* PxP, K-K5; *4* P-R4, KxP; *5* P-R5, K-B4; *6* KxP, K-N4 (or *6* ... P-Q5; *7* P-R6); *7* K-B4, and White captures the Queen Pawn and wins with his Knight Pawn.

(4) *1* ... P-N6; *2* K-R4, K-K5; *3* KxP, KxP; *4* K-B4 leads to

our first variation, whereas 2 ... P-N5; 3 P-R4, PxP e.p.; 4 PxP comes to about the same as our last.

As yet there is still no special finesse in sight. We do observe one if we continue incorrectly for White:

(5) 1 ... P-N5; 2 K-R4? K-K5; 3 KxP, KxP; 4 K-B4 (let us observe, in passing, that, after 4 K-B5, K-K6, Black queens first and, after 4 K-B3? K-Q6, Black subsequently queens with check), K-Q6; 5 P-N4, P-Q5; 6 P-N5, K-B7; 7 P-N6 (so far, all quite ordinary, but now comes the finesse), P-N6!!

Now, after 8 PxP, P-Q6; 9 P-N7, P-Q7; 10 P-N8(Q), P-Q8-(Q), White has lost his chance to check (11 Q-N3ch, comparable to 9 Q-N3ch in our first variation, is impossible here), and Black achieves a draw without too much difficulty.

So now let us start over, and make use of the development just shown, without White's making an error.

(Start from diagram labeled Howard—Kaufman)

| 1 .... | K-K5 |
| 2 KxP | P-N5! |

Black's last is a venomous move. If White now plays 3 K-N3, Black attains the draw in the manner indicated above: 3 ... KxP; 4 K-B4 (or 4 K-B2), K-Q6; 5 P-N4, P-Q5; 6 P-N5, P-N6!

| 3 P-R4! | PxP e.p. |
| 4 PxP | KxP |

5 P-R4   . . . .

Again a difficult situation has come up. It is typical of this sort of end game in which both sides are threatening to queen.

If Black's King now disposes of the Rook Pawn, he loses his own passed Pawn, whereby Black's fate is settled, of course: e.g., 5 ... K-B4; 6 P-R5, K-N4; 7 K-B4, etc.

Consequently, Black must let it come down to a race and move his King in such manner as not to hinder the advance of his Pawn. 5 ... K-K6 is obvious, but the sequel leads to a disappointing outcome: 6 P-R5, P-Q5; 7 P-R6, P-Q6; 8 P-R7, P-Q7; 9 P-R8(Q), P-Q8(Q)ch; 10 Q-B3ch! The same cross check by White is conclusive after 5 ... K-B6; 6 P-R5, P-Q5; 7 P-R6, P-Q6; 8 P-R7, P-Q7; 9 P-R8(Q), P-Q8(Q)ch; 10 Q-B3ch!

At his wit's end, Black has a try with the correct move.

5 . . . .   K-B5!

One is inclined at first to reject this move also, as White's King can now return—but this is an illusion: 6 K-B3, K-B6! For now Black is exempt from that murderous cross-check on White's KB3, and he is safe enough with either 7 P-R5, P-Q5; 8 P-R6, P-Q6 after which he queens with no difficulties or

7 K-K2, K-B7; 8 K-K3, K-B6 which presents no new viewpoints. Hence, White's King cannot return. The race is unavoidable.

6 P-R5	P-Q5	9 P-R8(Q)	P-Q8(Q)ch
7 P-R6	P-Q6	10 Q-B3	. . . .
8 P-R7	P-Q7		

Although it is true that this interposition does not take place with check, it is nevertheless very useful. The White Queen guards its King against perpetual check, and so White's Pawn plus begins to matter.

Also, now with Black's King much less favorably posted, there is constant danger of an exchange of Queens, and one may suppose that this Queen ending is, in the long run, won for White: e.g., 10 ... Q-Q2ch; 11 Q-B5, Q-N2ch; 12 Q-N5, Q-Q2ch; 13 K-R4, Q-R2ch; 14 Q-R5, Q-K2ch; 15 K-R3, Q-K6ch; 16 P-N3, Q-N8; 17 Q-K5, Q-R8ch; 18 K-N4, Q-Q8ch; 19 K-R4, Q-R8ch; 20 K-N5, and White always progresses, slowly, very slowly, but steadily.

The last variation may not rank as proof that White has a forced win; but there is, nevertheless, occasion for Black to try to find a continuation which may perhaps offer better drawing chances. And such a continuation, indeed, proves to be present. Let us start over again.

(Start from diagram labeled Howard—Kaufman)

1 . . . .   K-B4!

Now White can choose between the following, vainly:

(1) 2 P-R3, K-K5! 3 KxP, KxP; 4 K-B4, K-Q6; 5 P-KN4, P-Q5; 6 P-N5, K-B7; 7 P-N6, P-Q6; 8 P-N7, P-Q7; 9 P-N8(Q), P-Q8(Q), and here White lacks that winning check, with Q-QN3;

(2) 2 P-QN3 (or P-QN4) yields even less: 2 ... K-K5; 3 KxP, KxP; 4 K-B4, and Black has the important *tempo*, 4 ... K-B6! following which he is in no danger of losing;

(3) 2 K-R4, K-B5, and White gets no further, since the moves, 3 P-R3, 3 P-QN3, and 3 P-QN4, lead into the above variations, while 3 P-N3ch, K-K5 transposes into the following variation.

White, therefore, has only the following text.

2 P-KN3   ....

This move forces Black's King to give ground, and we again arrive on familiar terrain.

2 ....   K-K5

After 2 ... P-N5; 3 P-R4, PxP e.p.; 4 PxP, K-K5; 5 P-R4, White wins easily as previously demonstrated.

3 KxP   P-N5!

Now this finesse again. As we know from previous discussion, Black manages nicely on 4 K-N5, KxP; 5 K-B4, K-Q6; 6 P-N4, P-Q5; 7 P-N5, P-N6! 8 PxP, K-B7, etc.

4 P-R4   PxP e.p.
5 PxP   KxP
6 P-R4   ....

After 6 K-B3, K-B6, White can only force a draw by repetition of moves: 7 K-K2, K-B7; 8 K-K3, K-B6 (9 P-R5 permits

Black's Pawn to go through, queening first by gain of *tempo* from 9 ... P-Q5ch).

Now we have the same situation as diagrammed earlier, except that White's King Knight Pawn stands on N3 instead of N2, an important difference!

6	K-K6!	9 P-R7	P-Q7
7 P-R5	P-Q5	10 P-R8(Q)	P-Q8(Q)ch
8 P-R6	P-Q6		

Thus here (without the Pawn on N2) White lacks the cross-check at KB3. Also, in other respects this Queen ending is significantly better for Black than the one in the previous diagram.

The following variations tend to demonstrate that Black obtains a draw:

(1) 11 K-N5, Q-Q3! 12 P-N4, Q-K4ch; 13 K-R6, Q-K3ch; 14 K-R5, Q-B2ch; 15 K-R4, Q-B7ch; 16 K-R3, Q-B8ch; 17 Q-N2, QxQch; 18 KxQ, K-B5;

(2) 11 K-R4, Q-Q5ch; 12 P-N4, Q-B3ch; 13 P-N5, Q-B5ch; 14 K-R5, Q-R7ch; 15 K-N6, Q-Q3ch; 16 K-N7 (16 K-B7, Q-B5ch), K-B5; 17 P-N6, Q-Q2ch; 18 K-N8, K-N4; 19 P-N7, Q-K3ch, etc.

The comparison of these two end games demonstrates the difference between composition and practice. The composed end game is a finished product in all variations, the practical end game still raises doubts at some points. Is the next to the last diagram indeed a win? Is the last indeed a draw?

Therein lies the difference between composition and practice, not in the presence of surprise turns, because those are to be found in the practical game as well, if one only probes deeply enough.

A PAWN END GAME

We are inclined to undervalue Pawn endings. They contain fewer possibilities: we know the various little *tempo* tricks, we are familiar with the rules of the "protected passed Pawn" and the "outside passed Pawn"—what is there left? Only the exact counting to see who queens first?

Just the same, it is precisely in the Pawn endings that radical errors of judgment are often committed—all the more serious as the difference between winning and losing may be a single *tempo*.

The present position is from a game between G. Van Keulen and G. R. D. Van Doesburgh, Laren, Holland.

White is a Pawn down, but his King takes up a mighty position and can unimpeded capture Black's King Knight Pawn and so establish a passed Pawn. One is consequently inclined to judge White's chances as the better.

Our investigation will reveal otherwise. The chances for

either side turn on small things. If White were allowed two moves, P-QN4 and P-KN4, he'd not only be beyond danger of losing but also able with good chances to play for a win. Two Black moves, however, ... P-QR4 and ... P-KR5, are sufficient to secure the win for Black.

Thus we have already given away the critical moves. Their significance is easily explained:

(1) ... P-KR5 holds down White's King side;

(2) P-KN4 forestalls this intention;

(3) P-QN4 delays the emergence of a Black passed Pawn as, for ... P-B4 and ... P-Q5, preparation by ... P-N3 is then required;

(4) ... P-QR4 hampers this last plan.

Note, too, that *zugzwang* can arise only for White's King! Black's shuttles at will between QB1 and Q1 as White's K-K7 is worth no more than K-K6 which will always be possible.

Now we shall take up successively the different systems, beginning with the simplest and most obvious.

A. The Primitive Method

1 K-K6, an immediate "pass" at the Black King Knight Pawn, is met by *1* ... K-B2; *2* K-B6, P-B4! Already White cannot make the capture as Black's Queen Pawn simply goes through. On *3* K-K5, K-B3, moreover, Black's extra Pawn insures a clear win.

B. First Compromise

1 P-QN4   P-R5

Both sides have made one of the "desirable" moves. Having delayed the emergence of the hostile passed Pawn, White may retry the primitive method.

2 K-K6   K-B2

Note that 2 ... P-N3 is not yet possible; 3 K-Q6 wins the key Bishop Pawn.

3 K-B6   P-N3

4 KxP   . . . .

Here White has regained his Pawn and will get the King Rook Pawn. It seems he is on the way to win. Black contrives, however, just in time to guard the latter indirectly—and, by that, he wins.

4	P-B4	7 PxP	PxP
5 PxP	PxP	8 K-B4	K-Q3
6 K-N5	P-Q5	9 K-K4	K-B4
		10 K-Q3	K-Q4

In the outcome White's King will be forced into a stalemate position on Q1, he must eventually move his King Knight Pawn, and mate in three follows, with ... P-N8(Q) mate.

From the last diagram, if White sets out for Black's King Rook Pawn, counting on returning just in time, he is met by a well-known but treacherous twist: 4 K-N5, P-B4; 5 PxP, PxP; 6 KxRP, P-Q5; 7 PxP, P-B5! and Black's Pawn goes through.

C. A Sharp Continuation

(Resume from first diagram)

1 P-QN4   P-R5   *2* P-N5   . . . .

This sharp move threatens completely to upset Black's win-ning methods as seen in the previous variations.

2 . . . .   PxP   *3* KxP   . . . .

Now things look much better for White as Black's doubled Pawn is not worth much and White's King continues to have attacking chances on both wings.

3 . . . .   K-K2!

Black rightly disregards the vulnerability of his Queen Knight Pawn. Getting a passed Pawn, he wins the race: e.g., *4* K-B5, K-K3! *5* KxP, K-K4; *6* K-B5, K-B5; *7* K-Q6, K-N6; *8* K-B7, KxP; *9* KxP, KxP; *10* P-B4, K-N6; *11* P-B5, P-R6; *12* P-B6, P-R7; *13* P-B7, P-Q8(Q) *with check*.

4 K-K5   . . . .

White's only move: he cannot permit Black's King to pass.

4 . . . .   P-R4!

Not solely a "waiting" move.

Now the play can follow 5 courses.

1) 5 K-Q5, K-B3; 6 K-B5, P-N5! 7 PxP, PxP; 8 KxP, K-B4; 9 K-N5, K-B5; 10 K-N6, K-N6; 11 KxP, KxP; 12 P-R4, KxP; 13 P-R5, K-N6; 14 P-R6, P-R6; 15 P-R7, P-R7; 16 P-R8(Q), P-Q8(Q) and again *with check*. Black has just made it.

2) 5 K-Q5, K-B3; 6 P-R3 (preventing the preceding, but the *tempo* gained is lost on the move itself), K-B4; 7 K-B5, K-B5; 8 KxP, K-N6; 9 K-N6, KxP; 10 KxNP, KxP; 11 P-B4, K-N6; 12 P-B5, P-R6; 13 P-B6, P-R7; 14 P-B7, P-Q8(Q) again with check!

3) 5 P-R3, P-N3; 6 K-Q5, K-Q2 (now White's King cannot keep its ground); 7 K-K5, K-B3; 8 K-B6 (8 K-Q4, K-Q3 and Black must get in ... K-B4 and ... P-N5 to decide the issue), K-B4; 9 KxP, K-B5; 10 K-N5, KxP; 11 KxP, P-N5 and Black will win.

4) 5 K-B4, K-B3; 6 K-N4, P-N4; 7 K-B3 (on 7 K-R5, K-B4; 8 K-R6, Black wins by 8 ... P-KN5), K-B4; 8 K-K3, P-KN5; 9 PxPch, KxP; 10 K-B2, K-B5; 11 K-K2, K-K5; 12 K-Q2, K-Q4; 13 K-Q3, P-N3; 14 P-R3, K-B4 and Black can break through.

5) 5 K-K4, K-K3 leads into the variations already discussed.

D. White's Best

(Resume from first diagram)

We have seen that White's P-QN4-5 sets Black knotty problems. Now we try this push only after proper preparation. Black's task becomes even more difficult; and, though the chances remain on his side, White succeeds, by problem moves, in bringing about a draw.

1 P-QN4   P-R5   *2* P-R4   ....

This way P-N5 gains in force. White regains his Pawn without more ado.

         2 ....   K-B1

Or 2 .. P-R3; 3 P-R5, paralyzing the Black Pawn majority whereafter White's King can proceed King sideward safely.

3 P-N5	PxP	4 PxP	K-Q1
		5 KxP	....

Materially, the game is now even, and White's King still stands more favorably. Yet White's chances are not correspondingly better. His chances at the King side are forfeited: as soon as his King moves far enough from the center, ... P-QR4 gives Black the outside passed Pawn.

5 ... P-R4 too soon loses: 6 PxP e.p., PxP; 7 K-B6! And, too late: e.g., 5 ... K-Q2; 6 K-B5, K-B2; 7 P-B4, P-R4, success is far from assured: 8 PxP e.p., PxP; 9 K-Q5! P-R4; 10 K-B5, and White wins the Rook Pawn—or 9 ... K-N3; 10 K-Q6, and White promotes his passed Pawn.

Therefore Black dare play ... P-R4 only when White's Bishop Pawn has advanced to B5 or Black's King is on that square. Hence, Black aims for ... K-QN3.

5	K-Q2	7 P-B4	P-N4
6 K-B5	K-B2	8 K-Q5!	....

8 K-N4, K-N3 grants Black his objective of either 9 P-B5ch or 10 ... K-QB4, as in the last note.

8	K-N3	9 K-Q6	K-R4

After 9 ... P-R3; 10 PxP, KxP (forced); 11 K-B7! K-R4 (11 ... P-N3; 12 K-B6, K-R4; 13 K-Q5 and 14 P-B5); 12 KxP,

K-N5; *13* K-B6, KxP; *14* K-Q6, White easily arrives in time: *14* ... K-Q5; *15* K-K6, K-K5; *16* K-B6, K-B5; *17* K-N6, P-N5 Drawn.

10 K-B5 ....

10 K-B7 is a loss for White: *10* ... K-N5; *11* KxP, KxP; *12* KxP, KxP, and Black arrives one *tempo* earlier.

10 .... K-R5

10 ... P-N3ch is also possible with about the same consequences as shall soon appear.

11 K-Q4! ....

11 K-Q5 loses: *11* ... K-N5; *12* K-Q4, P-N3! and either *13* K-Q5, K-B6; *14* P-B5, PxP; *15* KxP, K-N6; *16* K-B6, K-B5; *17* P-N6, PxP; *18* KxP, K-Q6—or *13* K-Q3, K-N6; *14* K-Q4, K-B7! *15* P-B5, PxPch; *16* KxP, K-N6; *17* K-B6, K-B5 as Black wins the race for the King-side.

11 .... P-N3

After *11* ... K-N6; *12* P-B5, White's Bishop Pawn marches on; and, after *11* ... K-N5; *12* K-Q5, P-N3; *13* K-Q4, Black makes no further headway as White retains the opposition.

After the text move the situation appears critical for White. On *12* K-Q5 or K-Q3, K-N6 or *12* K-B3, K-R6, White is in trouble.

12 K-K4!!   . . . .

By assuming the distant opposition, White forces a draw: *12* ... K-N5; *13* K-Q4 or *12* ... K-N6; *13* K-Q3 or *12* ... K-R6; *13* K-K3 or, in this latter case, *13* K-B5.

If we now, incidentally, have another look at the diagram after *10* K-B5, we see that *10* ... P-N3ch likewise produces a draw after *11* K-Q5, K-R5; *12* K-K4!

This Variation D, consequently, leads to a draw and, in fact, in a surprising manner. In viewing the first position, who would ever have given a thought to a possible distant opposition!

Still our investigation has not covered all. About every Pawn end game, of which the outcome has not been determined beforehand, volumes could be written. In order not to stretch out too much, we present the rest in condensed form.

(Resume from first diagram)

E. *1* P-QN4, P-R5; *2* P-R4, K-B1; *3* P-R5 is sharper, to be sure, but not so strong as D: *3* ... K-Q1; *4* P-R6, K-B1! *5* PxPch, KxP (e.g., *6* K-K6, K-B2; *7* K-B6, P-B4! *8* PxP, P-R4).

F. *1* P-KN4, PxP; *2* PxP, P-R4! (White would win if permitted *3* P-N4—analogous to Variation D); *3* P-N5, K-B1; *4* K-K6, K-B2 (*4* ... P-N3; *5* K-Q6, K-N2; *6* P-R4 is in White's favor); *5* K-B6, P-B4; *6* KxP, P-Q5; *7* PxP, PxP, and Black has only slight winning chances: e.g., *8* K-B5, P-Q6; *9* P-N6, P-Q7; *10* P-N7, P-Q8(Q); *11* P-N8(Q).

G. *1* P-KN4, PxP; *2* PxP, P-R4! *3* P-N5, K-B1; *4* P-N3 (to enforce P-N4 anyway: *4* P-R3 fails against *4* ... P-R5), K-N1! *5* P-R3, K-R2; *6* P-N4, PxP; *7* RPxP, K-N3; *8* K-K6, K-N4, and again Black has only small winning chances: e.g., *9* K-B6, K-B5; *10* KxP, KxP; *11* K-B5, P-Q5; *12* P-N6, P-Q6; *13* P-N7, P-Q7; *14* P-N8(Q), P-Q8(Q); *15* Q-N7ch.

Our conclusion, therefore, reads first, that White achieves a draw by a narrow margin, by means of *1* P-QN4, followed by *2* P-QR4 and *3* P-N5.

And, second, that we're dealing here with a difficult Pawn end game in which one can very easily make mistakes.

A TRIO OF SNAPSHOTS

Herewith are three positions from the Clare Benedict Tournament. Each represents a different type of end game. The first is one of pure technique. The second is technical with a combinational angle. And the last is a purely combinational one. But all of them feature unexpected turns and a surprise point.

QUEEN'S GAMBIT DECLINED

	H. JOHNER		R. G. WADE	
	White		*Black*	
1	P-Q4	P-Q4	*11* BxP	N-N5
2	P-QB4	P-K3	*12* Q-N3	QN-B3
3	N-QB3	N-KB3	*13* B-K2	NxB
4	B-N5	P-B4	*14* QxN	Q-N5ch
5	N-B3	PxQP	*15* Q-Q2	B-B4
6	KNxP	P-K4	*16* QxQ	NxQ
7	N-B3	P-Q5	*17* O-O	P-B3
8	N-Q5	B-K2	*18* P-QR3	B-Q6
9	NxB	QxN	*19* KR-K1	BxB
10	P-K3	PxP	*20* RxB	N-Q6

21	N-Q4	N-B5
22	R-K3	O-O-O
23	N-N5	R-Q7
24	P-QN4	P-QR3
25	N-B3	KR-Q1
26	P-B5	R/1-Q5
27	K-B1	N-Q4
28	NxN	RxN
29	K-K1	K-B2
30	R-K2	R/7-Q6
31	R-B2	K-B3
32	P-QR4	R-QN6
33	R-B4	R-Q5
34	RxR	PxR
35	P-N5ch	PxP
36	PxPch	RxP
37	R-R8	RxP
38	K-Q2	R-Q4
39	R-B8ch	K-N3
40	K-Q3	R-Q2
41	R-B1	K-R2
42	R-R1ch	K-N1
43	R-QN1	R-Q3
44	R-K1	K-B2
45	R-B1ch	K-Q2
46	R-QN1	P-QN3
47	P-B4	K-B2
48	R-B1ch	K-N2
49	R-K1	R-Q2
50	R-QN1	P-B4
51	P-N3	P-N3
52	R-N2	R-Q4
53	R-N1	P-QN4
54	P-R4	K-N3
55	P-R5	R-Q3
56	P-R6	R-Q2
57	R-N2	R-K2
58	KxP	R-K8
59	R-QB2	R-Q8ch
60	K-B3	R-KN8
61	R-K2	K-B4
62	R-K5ch	K-Q3
63	RxNP	RxPch
64	K-Q4	R-KR6
65	R-R5	K-B3
66	R-R7	RxP
67	K-K5	R-R5
68	R-KN7	K-B4
69	R-B7ch	K-N5
70	K-B6	RxP
71	RxP	R-N5
72	R-QB7	P-B5
73	K-K5	P-N4
74	K-K4	R-N6
75	R-B8	K-N6
76	R-B5	K-N7
77	R-B8	P-B6
78	K-K3	P-N5
79	K-K-B2	R-N7ch
80	K-B1	R-QB7
81	R-KN8	R-B5
82	K-B2	K-B7
83	R-Q8	R-K5
84	R-B8ch	K-Q6
85	R-Q8ch	R-Q5
86	R-KN8	R-R5
87	R-Q8ch	K-K5
88	R-K8ch	K-B4
89	R-B8ch	K-K5

About the last 60 moves of this end game all sorts of observations could be made, of course; but we confine ourselves to the final phase.

Black has two connected passed Pawns. At first glance, therefore, a simple job; but, when looking more closely, one keeps encountering difficulties and is even inclined to conclude that Black cannot win. For that matter, a number of analogous positions do end in a draw. The truth lies in the middle: Black wins, but by a highly problematic method: in order to win on the King side, Black's King moves to the Queen side.

Even so, the whole process works in a strictly logical manner. The main point of the solution lies concealed in this, that Black wins when his Rook arrives on the seventh rank with check while his King stands no further removed from the board's edge than Black's QB8.

✧   ✧   ✧

Consequently, let us consider the second position.

> 1 .... R-B7ch

Now there are three possibilities. The least favorable is 2 K-N3? (or the analogous 2 K-K3?) after which there follows simply 2 ... R-N7ch; 3 K-R4, P-B7; 4 R-KB8, P-N6 and 5 ... R-N8.

Variant 1

> 2 K-B1 ....

We shall take up 2 K-N1 presently.

> 2 .... R-KN7

Now White's Rook can stand watch on the King Knight file or check or cut off Black's King.

Sub-variant A

> 3 R-N7 P-N6 4 R-B7ch ....

4 R-KB7, R-B7ch; 5 K-N1 (not 5 K-K1? R-K7ch; 6 K-B1, P-N7ch), K-Q8 comes to practically the same thing.

> 4 .... K-Q8 5 R-KN7 ....

After 5 R-Q7ch, R-Q7, it is even easier: 6 R-KN7, P-N7ch; 7 K-N1, K-K8, etc., or 6 R-KB7, R-B7ch; 7 K-N1, K-K8, etc. And the same holds for 5 R-KB7, R-B7ch; 6 K-N1, K-K8.

> 5 .... R-B7ch 6 K-N1 K-K8

It cannot be done without sacrificing a Pawn.

> 7 RxP R-B8ch 8 K-R2 ....

8 ....   K-B7

Not 8 ... P-B7? 9 R-K3ch, K-Q7; *10* K-N2! But now Black wins with 9 R-N8, R-K8; *10* R-QR8, K-B8, etc., or *10* R-KB8, K-K7, etc.

Sub-variant B

3 R-B8ch   K-Q7

4 R-K8   ...

Under no circumstances must White pursue Black's King further as it escapes to KN6: e.g., *4* R-Q8ch, K-K6; *5* R-KN8, R-QR7 (with threat of mate); *6* R-K8ch, K-B5 (and threat now of 7 ... R-R8ch; 8 K-B2, P-N6 mate); 7 R-B8ch, K-N6. And 4 R-KN8, K-K6 comes to the same thing.

4 ....   P-N6   5 R-Q8ch   ....

Now there is not so much harm in the checks as Black's King no longer has a place to hide. But White is compelled to give check, anyway: e.g., 5 R-K8, R-K7; 6 R-Q8ch, K-B6; 7 R-B8ch, K-N5 and Black's Rook can now handle the situation single-handed: 8 R-KN8, P-N7ch; 9 K-N1, R-K8ch; 10 K-B2, R-B8ch, etc.

5 ....   K-B8

And here we are at a position in the winning Sub-variant A.

Sub-variant C

3 R-Q8   P-N6

This continuation also leads at once to the winning Sub-variant A.

Variant II

(1 ....   R-B7ch)   2 K-N1   R-N7ch

Now it appears by 3 K-B1, P-N6, we can lead automatically into Variant I; but White can play differently.

3 K-R1!   ....

The point is that White's King is now "stalemated" so that Black cannot have his King march to KB5 because of the well-known "cling check"—e.g., *3 ... K-Q8; 4 R-Q8ch, K-K8; 5 R-Q1ch! K-B7; 6 R-B1ch! K-N6; 7 RxPch!* etc.

	3	P-N6

With the threat of *4 ... R-R7ch; 5 K-N1, P-B7ch,* etc.

4 R-B8ch	R-B7	5 R-KR8	....

Otherwise, *5 ... R-R7ch* decides.

	5	K-N7

And now Black wins as again his Rook can handle the queening alone. On checks, Black's King comes back down the Rook and Knight files.

With the experience now gained we can probably manage Position No. 1. There followed from that position this play in the actual game.

90 R-K8ch	K-Q6

91 R-Q8ch	....

It is clear that White cannot play a "waiting game"—*91 R-K7?* R-R7ch, etc. But why doesn't he play here *91 K-N3?* The answer is *91 ... R-R7!* (threatening *92 ... R-N7ch*); *92 KxP* (checks merely drive Black's King to KB8, the main objection to *91 K-N3*), P-B7; *93 R-KB8, K-K7; 94 R-K8ch,*

K-Q8 (also *94* . . . K-B8 is good); *95* R-KB8, K-K8; *96* R-K8ch,
R-K7, and Black wins.

> *91* . . . .   R-Q5   *92* R-QR8   . . . .

White's Rook could also "bide" on the King Knight file.

> *92* R-QB5

With the threat of *93* . . . R-B7ch, which wins.

> *93* R-Q8ch   . . . .

Not *93* R-R6ch because of *93* . . . R-B6 and *94* R-B7ch next.
Nor *93* K-N3 because of *93* . . . R-B7!

> *93* . . . .   K-B7   *94* K-N3   . . . .

Or *94* R-Q7, K-B8 after which *95* K-N3 becomes compulsory,
anyway, because of the threat of *95* . . . R-B7ch.

> *94* . . . .   K-B8!

Note the resemblance to our second diagram.

Perhaps the question may be asked if all this could not just
as well have been brought off on the Queen file. The answer
is "No." For in that case White's Rook would have been able
to defend from the flank, operating from QR1 and QR2 (which
requires the White King to be posted at KB2).

95 R-Q7   . . . .

Two other possibilities call for our attention here.

1) 95 R-KB8, so as to make it a draw on 95 . . . R-B7? with 96 KxP, P-B7; 97 K-N3, etc. Black continues, however, with 95 . K-Q8! 96 R-Q8ch, K-K8; 97 R-K8ch, K-B8; 98 R-QR8, R-B8; 99 KxP, P-B7; 100 K-N3, K-N8, etc. Or 99 R-KR2, K-N8 and 100 . . P-B7! Nor in this variation is a "waiting line" possible: 95 R-KB8, K-Q8! 96 R-B7, R-B7; 97 KxP, P-B7; 98 K-N3, K-K8 or, likewise, 96 R-QR8, R-B7; 97 R-R1ch, K-K7.

2) 95 R-QR8, K-Q8 (95 . . . R-B7? leads to a draw after 96 KxP, P-B7; 97 K-N3, K-Q8; 98 R-R1ch, K-K7; 99 K-N2); 96 R-R1ch, R-B8; 97 R-R4, K-K7, and again it just works (98 R-R2ch, K-B8 or 98 KxP, P-B7).

95 . . . .   R-B7!

The key to the solution.

96 KxP	P-B7	98 K-N3	K-K8
97 R-KB7	K-Q8	99 R-K7ch	R-K7
		100 R-QR7	. . . .

The last point now comes up.

100 . . . .   R-K6ch   Resigns

Because Black now queens, but at least White did reach the 100th move.

RUY LOPEZ

C. B. VAN DEN BERG

White

W. NIEPHAUS

Black

1	P-K4	P-K4
2	N-KB3	N-QB3
3	B-N5	P-QR3
4	B-R4	N-B3
5	O-O	B-K2
6	R-K1	P-QN4
7	B-N3	P-Q3
8	P-B3	O-O
9	P-KR3	QN-R4
10	B-B2	P-B4
11	P-Q4	Q-B2
12	QN-Q2	B-N2

13	N-B1	BPxP
14	PxP	QR-B1
15	B-N1	P-Q4
16	KPxP	P-K5
17	N-N5	BxP
18	NxP	NxN
19	BxN	BxB
20	RxB	B-B3
21	N-N3	KR-K1
22	B-B4	Q-Q2
23	B-K5	BxB
24	PxB	QxQch
25	RxQ	....

White has a Pawn plus. He cannot, however, protect his Queen-side Pawns by direct methods. Hence he resorts to indirect, combinative methods.

25 ....   R-B7

Not 25 ... N-B5; 26 P-N3, NxP; 27 QR-K1, P-B3; 28 P-B4, and White wins.

26 R-Q6   R-R1?

It is due to this last move that White is enabled to reap the fruits of his tactics. Black's only chance of salvation consists in *26* ... RxNP; *27* RxP, RxRP; *28* R-QN4, R-R8ch; *29* K-R2, N-N6; *30* RxR, NxR; *31* RxP, N-B7. Then, with the remaining Pawns all on one side of the board, Black has excellent drawing chances, though a similar end game, Taimanov—Stahlberg, Challengers Tournament, 1953, was won by White.

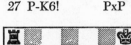

27 P-K6!   PxP

28 R/4xP   . . . .

White bases his counter-action principally on the seventh rank. Thus, *28* ... RxNP is refuted by *29* R-Q7, RxRP (*29* ... R-KB1; *30* N-K4 as in the game); *30* R/6-K7; e.g., *30* ... N-B5; *31* RxPch, K-B1; *32* R/Q-B7ch, K-K1; *33* R-N7, K-B1; *34* RxRP, K-N1; *35* R/N-N7ch, K-B1; *36* N-R5, and *37* R-R8 mate.

28 . . . .   R-KB1   *29* N-K4   . . . .

Naturally, White does not permit his opponent to crash in on his KB2.

·   *29* N-N2

Here, too, *29* ... RxNP is pernicious: *30* R-Q7, R-B2 (does not help); *31* R-K8ch, R-B1; *32* R/8-K7, etc.

30 RxP   ....

Simpler is 30 R-Q7 as 30 ... N-B4 gives no relief: 31 NxN,
R/1xP? 32 R-K8ch, etc. Contrast the game continuation.

30 ....   N-B4!

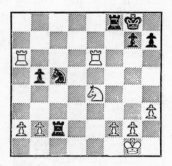

A particularly pretty riposte, which brings to mind the
proverb: "Dig a pit, and get caught in it yourself." After
31 NxN? R/1xP, it is White who faces the miseries of the
"seventh rank" and so has to resort to draw by perpetual check.

31 R/R-B6!

The saving move.[1]

31	R-B8ch	32 K-R2	NxR
		33 RxR	....

White won easily with his material plus.

[1] We beg to differ. Surmounting the fear of a near-perpetual is
31 NxN, R/1xP 32 R-R8ch, K-B2 33 R-R7ch, K-B1 (or K-N1
34 R-K8ch, R-B1 35 RxRch, etc.) 34 R-Q6! and White wins.—I.A.H.

BENONI COUNTER-GAMBIT DEFERRED

	J. H. DONNER			H. JOHNER	
	White			*Black*	
1	P-Q4	N-KB3	21	B-R3	PxP
2	P-QB4	P-B4	22	BxQ	PxQ
3	P-Q5	P-Q3	23	B-B6	R-R4
4	N-QB3	P-KN3	24	RxQP	P-B5
5	P-KN3	B-N2	25	R-Q1	BxN
6	B-N2	O-O	26	PxB	N/2xP
7	N-B3	P-QR3	27	B-R3	R-KB4
8	P-QR4	Q-B2	28	BxQP	NxP
9	O-O	P-K4	29	R-K1	N/6-Q4
10	PxP e.p.	BxP	30	R-K8ch	K-B2
11	N-Q5	BxN	31	R-K4	R-B3
12	PxB	QN-Q2	32	B-K8ch	K-N1
13	P-R5	P-QN4	33	B-R3	R-R1
14	PxP e.p.	QNxP	34	B-N5	R-QB1
15	N-Q2	P-QR4	35	R-QB1	P-B6
16	N-N1	Q-Q2	36	BxP	NxB
17	N-B3	P-R5	37	RxN/4	P-B7
18	P-K4	N-K1	38	R-R7	R-N3
19	Q-Q3	N-B2	39	K-B1	R-N8
20	R-Q1	P-B4	40	K-K2	N-B6ch

After heavy time pressure, the players reached this position.
It is, therefore, not exactly of great importance to remark that

Black could have won quickly by *40* ... N-N5 (*41* K-Q2, R-Q1ch and *42* ... R/1-Q8). In a certain sense, it is fortunate that Black overlooked this continuation as we would otherwise have been deprived of witnessing the combinational phase of the game which follows.

41 K-Q2   ....

41 K-Q3 loses to *41* ... N-N4; *42* R-R5, R-B6ch, and *43* ... RxB.

41 ....   N-K5ch

Here *41* ... N-N4; *42* R-R5 produces nothing. Following the text move, however, the struggle grows particularly complicated because White's King can move three different ways:

1) *42* K-K3, see the game;
2) *42* K-K2, R-B6! and White has no parry to the threat of *43* ... RxB: e.g., *43* P-B3, RxB; *44* R/7xR, RxR; *45* PxN, R-KR8 —or *43* R-R8ch, K-B2; *44* R-R7ch, K-B3; *45* B-K7ch, K-K3, etc.
3) *42* K-Q3, NxPch; *43* K-K3, R-B6ch; *44* KxN, RxB, *45* R/7xR, RxR; *46* R-QB3, R-KR8!—or *43* K-K2, R-B6; *44* R-R8ch (*44* B-N2, RxB; *45* KxN, R-QN8; *46* R-QR1, RxR/R8!), K-N2; *45* R-R7ch, K-B3; *46* R-R6ch, K-K4; *47* R-R5ch, K-K3; *48* R-R6ch, K-Q2; *49* R-Q6ch, K-B2; *50* KxN, RxB, etc.—or *43* K-Q2, N-K5ch; *44* K-Q3, N-Q3; *45* RxBP, R-N6ch; *46* K-Q2, N-B5ch; *47* K-K2 (*47* K-B1 loses to *47* ... R-KB6), RxB! *48* RxR, R-K1ch and *49* ... NxR.

42 K-K3   N-Q3

Now Black threatens *43* ... N-B5ch as well as *43* ... N-N4, and the finish is forced.

43 RxBP	RxR	*45* KxK4	R-K7ch
44 BxN	R-N6ch	*46* K-Q4	RxBP
		47 P-R4	R-Q7ch

With the full Exchange ahead, this end game is now won for Black. Unfortunately the Nestor of the Swiss team (and

of the Benedict Tournament as a whole) blundered after
48 K-B4, R-K6; 49 R-R8ch, K-B2; 50 R-R7ch with 50 ... K-K3?
(instead of 50 ... K-K1) and, after 51 R-K7ch, had to content
himself with a draw.

THE EXCHANGE—PLUS AND MINUS

A fine study in the use of the advantage of the Exchange
under very adverse factors: a Pawn minus and also a deficit in
most of the positional considerations.

In Dr. Euwe's theories of chess play, the value of the Exchange is somewhat less highly regarded than in the past, even
the recent past. In the middle game, indeed, he has suggested
that a minor piece may give battle to a Rook on equal or very
nearly equal terms. So this exposition of the winning power
of the Exchange is highly significant, the more so that the
lesser side has so many other factors in its favor. The summary
of the positional factors is in itself a worth-while lesson. And
the whole, with a generous coverage of both tactical and strategical features, is a valuable demonstration of what is vaguely
called "technique"—and what may here be termed "the higher
technique."

In all this both players, as well as the commentator, exhibit
some remarkably impressive chess.

Yugoslav Championship

December, 1953

KING'S INDIAN DEFENSE

by transposition

VASYA PIRC		SVETOZAR GLIGORICH	
White		*Black*	
1 N-KB3	N-KB3	5 O-O	PxP
2 P-KN3	P-Q3	6 NxP	P-KN3
3 P-Q4	QN-Q2	7 P-N3	B-N2
4 B-N2	P-K4	8 B-N2	O-O

9	N-QB3	R-K1	26	N-Q3	N-R1
10	P-K4	N-B4	27	NxN	PxN
11	R-K1	P-B3	28	P-B4	PxP
12	Q-Q2	Q-N3	29	PxP	N-N3
13	P-KR3	B-Q2	30	N-B5	B-QB1
14	QR-Q1	QR-Q1	31	B-KB1	B-B1
15	K-R2	QB-B1	32	N-K4	NxRP
16	P-B3	Q-B2	33	N-B6ch	K-B2
17	Q-B2	Q-N3	34	NxR	RxN
18	N/4-K2	N/4-Q2	35	B-R1	B-N5
19	QxQ	NxQ	36	R-K3	K-K2
20	P-B4	P-Q4	37	P-R4	B-Q2
21	P-K5	N/3-Q2	38	P-R5	R-QR1
22	N-Q4	N-B1	39	PxP	PxP
23	P-QR4	P-QR4	40	P-N4	R-R1ch
24	N/3-K2	B-Q2	41	R-R3	RxRch
25	N-B1	N-K3	42	KxR	N-B4

White has the Exchange for a Pawn. From the purely materialistic point of view, White therefore stands better. For the Exchange equals 1½ Pawns. That is, according to the old-fashioned way of assessing positions of this type. Only in special cases, must it be added, do positional factors compensate for a plus in material.

Yet nowadays opinions differ in regard to the Exchange, in this sense, that the emphasis is placed less on the factor of material than on that of position. As positional factors in the contest between Rook and minor piece there are considered, among others: (1) the presence of passed Pawns; (2) the presence of other minor pieces; (3) the presence of strongholds (or outposts); (4) the Pawn configuration; and (5) the position of the King.

(1) The passed Pawns are important to the side with the minor piece especially because these can occupy the attention of the Rook to such extent as to eliminate the differential in values between the Rook and the minor piece.

(2) The presence of other minor pieces also has a neutralizing tendency. Conversely, in the contest between Rook and a single minor piece, the superiority of the Rook is so paramount that it cannot be offset sometimes even by two Pawns.

(3) The presence of strongholds is indispensable to a proper development of the power of the minor piece. For a Knight that can be continually driven off by the Rook does not come into its own.

(4) The Pawn configuration may give the Rook occasion for going off on a foray. Pawns difficult to protect signify a serious handicap to the side with the minor piece.

(5) The position of the King is likewise especially important to the weaker side. For the Rook, particularly in combination with other pieces (including a King), is a dangerous offensive weapon.

Examining the current position on the score of these positional factors, we must come to the conclusion that the majority of the factors are in Black's favor. He has a passed Pawn and threatens even to acquire still another. There are minor pieces on the board. And Black possesses strongholds for his minor pieces (QN5 and QB4 among others). In contrast, however, the position of Black's King is definitely insecure: shut in on the first and second ranks. Therefore, if White is to win, it is this factor which must decide. In fact, we shall observe the attack motif weaving throughout this entire end game.

43 B-Q4 ....

White's first step emphasizes the attack motif, for which he conveys his Bishop to the other wing.

His move, moreover, prevents the advance of Black's Rook Pawn. Consider: 43 ... P-R5? 44 R-R1 and

(1) 44 ... P-QN4; 45 PxP, PxP; 46 R-N1, N-R3; 47 RxB! etc.
(2) 44 ... P-R6; 45 R-N1, N-R3; 46 RxB!

43 .... N-N6   44 B-B2 ....

Here White's Bishop stands very well for attacking purposes. 45 B-R4ch, K-K1; 46 B-Q3 is threatened, winning a Pawn. Consequently, Black still has no time for advancing his passed Pawn.

44 .... N-B4

Black protects his Queen Bishop and also observes White's Q3.

45 R-N1 ....

Again White prevents ... P-R5 and also threatens RxB!

45 .... N-K5   46 B-R4ch   K-B2

46 ... P-KN4 leads to a quick loss after 47 B-Q3! by which White gains a Pawn and establishes the needed passed Pawn.

47 B-Q3   N-B6

Black must remain active. After 47 ... N-B4; 48 B-QB2, he would be halted on the Queen side, whereupon White would gain a free hand on the other wing.

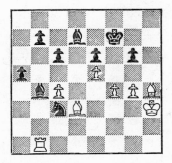

White's strategy now could be to set up a mating attack by R-KR1, B-B6 and K-N3, except that Black, thanks to his last moves, holds just sufficient counter-measures in reserve. Note: 48 R-KR1, P-B4! 49 B-B6, B-B3! 50 R-R2, N-K5, and White gets no further.

In the original position given, if White's King stood on KN3, instead of KR3, this variation would have brought about a speedy decision.

48 R-QR1   P-B4

Black aims to follow up with ... B-B3 and thus guard against a later execution of the attack just mentioned. A drawback of his last move, however, is that now the possibility of establishing connected passed Pawns is out of the picture.

49 B-K1   ....

For the time being White limits himself to the defense. He must first bring his King to the other wing, to lessen somewhat the power of Black's passed Rook Pawn.

49 ....　　　　　B-B3　　　　　50 K-N3　　　....

It is instructive to investigate what effect the exchange of one or more of the minor pieces might have at this juncture.

Thus Black might try: 50 ... B-K5; 51 BxB, NxBch; 52 K-B3, but he stands to lose after 52 ... N-B6; 53 K-K3 because of the threat of losing a piece on 54 K-Q3. (53 ... P-QN4 is no help in view of 54 BxN, BxB; 55 PxP!) And, on 52 ... N-Q7ch, White wins a Pawn by 53 BxN, BxB; 54 R-Q1 and 55 R-Q7ch. Or, finally, 52 ... BxB only loses a Pawn by either 53 KxN, B-N5; 54 R-R1, K-N2; 55 R-Q1—or 53 ... B-B6; 54 R-R1, K-N2; 55 R-Q1, B-Q5; 56 R-QN1.

And on 50 ... N-K5ch White can seize the occasion to exchange; for, after 51 BxN, BxKB; 52 BxB, RPxB; 53 R-R5, he stands to accumulate Pawns by 53 ... P-N6; 54 R-N5, B-B7; 55 RxPch or 53 ... P-N3; 54 R-N5, B-Q6; 55 RxP/6, BxP; 56 R-B6 (also very strong is 56 R-N7ch, K-K1; 57 K-R4, followed by the advance of White's King), P-N6; 57 RxBP (for, on 57 ... P-N7, White has 58 R-B7ch and 59 R-QN7).

A number of these variations wind up in an end game of Rook versus Bishop, with Pawns equal. Such present no special technical problem for White, for he can always, by bringing his King in closer, effect an exchange of Rook for Bishop and Pawn and then win the resulting end game.

As a side issue, it should be noted that *50* ... P-R5 costs a Pawn: *51* K-B2, P-R6 (or this advance may be forced by *52* B-B2); *52* BxN, BxB; *53* RxP.

| *50* .... | N-R5 | *51* K-B2 | .... |

White does not exchange Bishops as that results only in advancing and strengthening the passed Pawn.

| *51* .... | N-N7 |

Black stays on the offensive. He must; for, after *51* ... N-N3, White continues the same way as in the game (K-K3 and B-Q2) and Black cannot make a single counter-blow count because of the inactive position of his Knight.

| *52* K-K3 | .... |

| *52* .... | P-R5! |

Forward at last! And, indeed, what else? Exchanging Knight for Bishop here gains nothing at all. For, after *52* ... NxB; *53* KxN, White actually threatens *54* BxB, RPxB; *55* R-R5, and there is no adequate reply: e.g., *53* ... BxB; *54* RxB, P-R5; *55* K-B3, B-B6; *56* P-N5, B-B3; *57* R-K2, B-B6; *58* R-QR2, B-B3; *59* R-R2, K-N2; *60* R-Q2, K-B2; *61* R-Q8, K-N2; *62* R-QR8, K-B2; *63* R-R5, and White wins a Pawn.

Or, on *61* ... K-K2, Black lands in *zugzwang* after *62* R-KR8, K-B2; *63* R-R7ch, K-B1 (*63* K-N1; *64* R-K7); *64* K-N2.

Or if Black tries *53* P-R5 (instead of *53* ... BxB), he can be maneuvered out of position by *54* B-Q2, K-K2 (not *54* ... P-R6? *55* B-B1); *55* R-QN1, B-R6; *56* B-R5, K-B2; *57* K-B3 and *58* R-QR1.

53 B-Q2! ....

To bring the Bishop to QB1.

53 .... P-R6 *54* B-QB1 N-Q8ch

A new resource again for Black.

55 K-K2 N-N7

After *55* ... N-B6ch, Black's Rook Pawn soon goes: *56* K-B1, P-R7; *57* B-N2.

56 P-N5 ....

White aims to reserve a *tempo* in case Black should ever try ... B-KB6 later. It is remarkable that the text move detracts nothing from White's King-side Pawn majority. That is a fact since the move, P-KB5, will, under proper conditions, create a passed Pawn.

56 .... K-N2

Not best. Properly *56* ... NxB; *57* KxN, P-N4 transposes back into the actual game.

57 R-R2 ....

But White returns the favor. He can win more quickly with *57* BxN, PxB; *58* R-R8, P-N4 (else *59* R-QB8); *59* R-R7ch,

K-N1; *60* BxP by virtue of his own passed Pawn. Apparently, fault begets fault!

57 . . . .   NxB

On *57* . . . N-R5 there follows *58* K-B1, N-B6; *59* R-R1, after which Black must lose his Rook Pawn.

58 KxN   P-N4!

Passed Pawns!

59 BxP   PxPch   *60* K-K3   . . . .

Not *60* KxP?? B-Q4ch.

60 . . . .   B-Q4

An entirely different situation has now arisen in which both the Rook's capacity for the offensive and the compensating power of Black's passed Pawn have been heightened. The Pawn, moreover, is guarded by Bishops stationed at secure strongholds.

61 B-B1   . . . .

Of course not *61* BxB, PxB. With two passed connected Pawns for the Exchange, Black has no danger of losing.

61 . . . .   K-B1   *62* R-R7!   . . . .

For the Rook, the promised land: the seventh rank.

62 ....   B-QB6   63 B-R3   B-N5

The Black Bishop returns because, after the plausible 63 ...
B-Q5ch; 64 K-K2, P-B6, White wins a Pawn by 65 R-QB7.

64 B-N2   K-N1

Perhaps here one might expect 64 ... P-B6. Black rightly
omits this advance since his King Bishop then loses its mobility.
It cannot then, among other things—as happens in the game
—come to the rescue via B6 to counteract White's King-side
operations.

65 R-Q7   ....

White prepares the decisive breakthrough, P-B5.

65 ....   B-B3   66 R-Q6   ....

Here he forces the Bishop back.

66 ....   B-Q4   67 R-Q8ch   K-B2
                            68 R-Q7ch   K-N1

With an eye toward things to come, Black's King prefers to
avoid the black squares. Note also 68 ... K-K1 fails against
69 R-KN7.

69 B-B1   ....

A last preparatory measure. On 69 P-B5 at once there follows
69 ... NPxP; 70 K-B4, B-Q7ch.

69 ....   B-QB6

On 69 ... B-B3; 70 R-Q6, White gains a *tempo* by the same
method as with moves 66-68. With the text move, Black's King
Bishop can at least come to the support of the defense.

70 P-B5!   ....

A clear demonstration of the power of White's Pawn majority on the right wing. Upon 70 ... NPxP; 71 K-B4, to be followed by 72 P-N6, White's King marches in.

| 70 .... | BxP | 71 P-B6 | .... |

Now White has a tremendous passed Pawn. It will sooner
or later assert itself.

| 71 .... | B-Q5ch! | 72 K-K2 | B-K5 |
| | | 73 B-R3! | .... |

A subtle threat: 74 P-B7ch, K-N2; 75 P-B8(Q)ch, KxQ;
76 RxB!

| 73 .... | B-Q6ch | 74 K-Q2 | P-K4 |

By this extra protection of his King's Bishop, Black parries
the threat mentioned (which would begin now with 75
P-B7ch).

| 75 R-N7ch | K-R1 | 76 R-Q7 | .... |

A little measure to gain time on the clock.

| 76 .... | K-N1 | 77 R-N7ch | K-R1 |
| | | 78 R-QB7 | P-K5 |

Again an extremely critical situation has come up. The Black passed Pawns may march on on all sides. A single *tempo* can decide the issue.

Just how much the initiative counts is clearly revealed here. Had White not made timely provision for a passed Pawn which carries attendant mating threats, his advantage of the Exchange would have become quite worthless. And he'd be faced now with a grim task of holding back Black's passed Pawns.

79 BxP	....

White has no choice, but there is no need for one.

79	P-K6ch	80 K-B1!	....

80 K-K1? B-B6ch! etc.

80	P-K7	81 B-N4	...

Again, the only move.

81	B-K6ch

On *81* ... P-B6, *82* R-K7, and thereafter *83* P-B7 decides the issue.

82 K-N2   BxP   *83* P-B7   B-B3ch

Now Black's move is forced (*83* ... B-R3? *84* B-B3ch, and White queens *with check*).

84 K-R3   B-N2   *85* B-B3!   . . . .

Anyway!

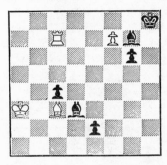

85 . . . .   Resigns

An end game rich in combinations, but one in which the strategical outlines are clearly defined, too.

BUGABOOS OF "BISHOPS OF OPPOSITES"

The major theme of this remarkably thorough end-game study is White's winning chances against that drawing bugaboo, Bishops of opposite colors. As for the themes subsidiary to this one, Dr. Euwe's own summations, particularly those after the first, second, and fifth diagrams, are so apt and develop so logically with the progress of the game that we feel we do best to refer the reader to them.

Championship of the Netherlands
Amsterdam, 1954
FOUR KNIGHTS' GAME

	N. CORTLEVER			J. BARENDREGT	
	White			*Black*	
1	P-K4	P-K4	12	PxP	PxP
2	N-KB3	N-KB3	13	Q-K2	P-N3
3	N-B3	N-B3	14	QxP	QxQ
4	P-Q4	PxP	15	RxQch	K-Q1
5	NxP	NxP	16	B-B4	B-QB4
6	QNxN	Q-K2	17	R-Q1	R-K1
7	P-KB3	P-Q4	18	RxRch	KxR
8	B-QN5	B-Q2	19	BxP	B-K3
9	BxN	PxB	20	P-QN3	R-B1
10	O-O	PxN	21	B-Q6	BxNch
11	R-K1	P-KB4	22	RxB	P-B4

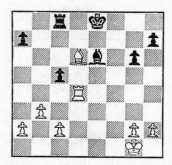

Bishops of opposite color, but at least the Rooks are still on the board, and so the winning chances for the stronger side are considerably enhanced. Expressed in numbers, the winning-drawing proportion is 3 to 7; but with the Rooks, the ratio is exactly reversed.

Other characteristics that favor the stronger side are:

(1) Freedom of movement for the attacking King, possi-

bilities for invading the hostile position, which applies to the
end game in general;

(2) Complications on both wings, especially applicable if
not essential when the Bishops of opposite color only are
present;

(3) Vulnerability of one or more of the enemy Pawns, which
especially is the case in the present end game.

In view of the last point, it is clear that White must prevent
the further advance of Black's Bishop Pawn. After 23 R-Q1,
P-B5, for instance, a draw soon becomes an accomplished fact.
White must therefore force through P-B4 himself. Yet he cannot do this simply by 23 R-KR4, P-KR4; 24 P-B4 because of
the surprising 24 ... B-N5! (threatening 25 ... P-N4); 25
B-B4, R-Q1; 26 P-KR3, R-Q8ch; 27 K-R2, B-B4 with all sorts
of chances for Black.

Hence there is nothing left but the continuation in the game.

23 R-QR4!   ....

White gains time for blocking Black's Bishop Pawn by the
threat on his Queen Rook Pawn.

23 ....   R-B3

Thanks to this *tempo*, Black can save that Rook Pawn.

24 B-B4   P-QR3   25 P-B4   ....

White has realized his first objective. The remarkable thing about his process, however, is that he has done so by incurring what seems to be a most serious handicap: the shut-in condition of his Rook. True, Black can make no serious attempt to capture that Rook. But White, on the other hand, can free it only by the expedient of eliminating Black's Bishop Pawn.

That is the problem which White now faces, and it does not look as though he can solve it in a satisfactory manner. For P-QN4, at one time or another, must cost White his Bishop Pawn, and even the isolation of that Pawn in itself scuttles White's chances of winning. Hence, the only possibility lies in the capture of Black's Bishop Pawn.

To capture that Pawn, White must attack it more often than it can be defended. He can bring about the following setups: White: R on QR5, B on K3; Black: K on Q3, R on QB3; or White: R on QR5, B on KB8; Black: K on QN3, R on QB3. But, in either case, the Black defense is adequate. So White's King must somehow play a role. But how?

Let us, therefore, permit the players first to have their say.

25	K-Q2	27 B-K3	K-Q3
26 R-R5	B-B4	28 K-B2	P-R4

Since in some variations to arise later the unguarded state of Black's KN3 becomes a pertinent factor, it is important to note here that (28) ... P-R4 is unavoidable, in the long run. As soon, in fact, as White's King arrives at KN5, the capture of Black's King Rook Pawn (at R2) is threatened, by K-KR6 in conjunction with B-N5. For Black's King and Rook, both committed to the defense of his Bishop and Queen Rook Pawns, will be unable to aid the defense of the King Rook Pawn. (A vivid demonstration of the import of Characteristic 3 listed after the first diagram.)

29 P-N3	B-N8	30 K-K2	B-B4
		31 K-Q2	B-N5

For the time being both engage in a rather pointless bit of wood shifting: probing the terrain. But possibly also diversional maneuvering.

32 K-B3   B-K3

But this Black move thoroughly deters White from any future intent of forcing his Queen Knight Pawn through: his Bishop Pawn falls after 33 P-QN4? PxPch.

33 K-Q3	B-B4ch	35 K-B2	B-B4
34 K-K2	B-N5ch	36 B-B4ch	K-Q2
		37 B-K5?	....

White lifts the pressure on QB5 and by so doing enables Black to undertake a counter-attack which causes his chances for drawing to rise significantly.

37	K-B1	38 B-B4	....

White's Bishop hurriedly resumes its former post but is already too late.

38	K-N2	39 B-K3	K-N3

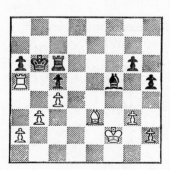

Now *40* RxBP, RxR; *41* P-QN4 does not work because of *41* ... B-K3. Black then wins the Bishop Pawn and secures a matter-of-fact draw. *40* P-QN4, moreover, is impractical in view of *40* ... B-Q6, likewise compensating Bishop Pawn for Bishop Pawn. So the White Rook is forced to retreat.

40 R-R3   K-B2?

Time pressure! It is clear, true enough, that *40* ... P-R4? fails against *41* B-Q2. But Black's text move definitely is not necessary.

He probably feared (*41*) P-QN4, but he can, for the present, prevent that advance with *40* ... B-Q6. If White thereupon prepares to approach with his King, Black's Rook goes into action: *41* K-K1, R-K3; *42* K-Q2, B-B8, and soon there remains nothing for White but P-QN4, again swapping Pawn for Pawn and bringing the draw much closer.

The text move soon reinstates the former situation: Black's King tied down at Q3; White's free as a bird.

41 P-R4   ....

Better is *41* K-K2, to forestall ... B-Q6, plus ... K-QN3.

41 ....   B-K5   *42* K-K2   ....

Now ... B-Q6 is ruled out, and so, too, ... K-QN3 (as then White has the resource of P-QN4).

42 ....   B-B4   *43* R-R5   K-Q3

43 ... K-N3 fails against *44* P-QN4, as *44* ... B-K3 is met by *45* K-Q3.

44 K-B3   ....

White could also have reached this position by his thirty-sixth move. So it is evident that the Queen-side intermezzo was entirely superfluous. Meanwhile it is not at all clear as yet just what White aims at with the King's march which follows.

| 44 .... | B-B7 | 45 K-B4 | B-N8 |

Black must stall. He can play the Bishop only.

| 46 P-KN4! | .... |

Ultimately the exchange thus initiated serves to extend the KN-3-Q6 diagonal, whereby White's Bishop can deliver checks at more than one square.

| 46 .... | PxP |

Upon *46* ... B-Q6 there follows *47* K-N5, and Black virtually must submit to *47* ... B-K7; *48* KxP, BxNP (not *48* ... PxP; *49* P-R5! etc.); *49* K-B6 after which the position is much like that after move 51 in the actual game. The sole differences are in the positions of the Bishops, and the reader can readily verify that White can also win in this position after seeing our subsequent comments.

| 47 KxP | B-B4ch | 48 K-N5 | B-N8 |

The crucial position. White's plans assume more substantial patterns: to gain K5 for his King, whereby Black's King will no longer be able to protect its Bishop Pawn.

In its simplest form White's plan is K-B6, B-B4ch, K-K5 and B-K3, winning the Bishop Pawn. For the moment, however, a tactical rejoinder exists: *49* K-B6, K-Q2dis.ch; *50* K-K5, R-K3ch; *51* K-B4, R-K5ch.

From this it is seen that White's Bishop is not posted to advantage as of now. Also, we now sense the reason for White's forty-sixth move—as well as for his next one.

49 B-B2   B-Q6

Now the effectuation of White's plans meets with other objections: *50* K-B6, K-B2dis.ch; *51* K-K5, and White's Bishop Pawn falls if *52* P-N4.

50 B-N1!   . . . .

Nothing more than a *tempo* move. Black's Bishop stands at a crossing: on the one hand, it is important to keep White's Bishop Pawn under attack as just indicated; on the other, the Bishop must guard its Knight Pawn (compare the comments to Black's twenty-eighth move).

50 . . . .   B-N8

Black suffers from a species of *zugzwang*. He cannot give up the Knight Pawn. So he foregoes the attack on White's Bishop Pawn.

51 K-B6!   . . . .

It is all over. Black now has his choice between two losing variations:

(1) *51* . . . K-B2dis.ch; *52* K-K5, K-N3; *53* P-N4! B-Q6; *54* BxPch and *55* K-Q4;

(2) *51* . . . B-Q6 as in the game.

51 . . . .   B-Q6   *52* B-R2ch   . . . .

Here at last the original plan.

52 . . . .   K-Q2dis.ch   *53* K-K5   K-B2

Black realizes that to allow *54* B-N1 plus *55* BxP is altogether hopeless.

54 K-Q5dis.ch   . . . .

A series of discovered checks with the Kings. At this point *54* B-N1, K-N3; *55* P-N4 fails as before since White's Bishop Pawn falls. On the other hand, the continuation chosen would also have been fruitless if Black's Bishop now stood at N8.

54 . . . .   K-N3   *55* RxRPch!   . . . .

The final finesse.

55	KxR	57 KxP	BxP
56 KxR	B-N8	58 P-N4	....

White has won and preserved a two-Pawn lead and secures the game with ease.

58	K-N2	62 P-B6ch	K-R1
59 P-N5	B-N8	63 K-B5	B-N7
60 K-N4	B-K5	64 P-N6	BxP
61 P-B5	B-B6	65 KxB	P-N4
		66 P-N7ch	Resigns